Also by Helen Thomas
Dateline: White House

FRONT ROW

AT THE

WHITE HOUSE

My Life and Times

HELEN THOMAS

A TOUCHSTONE BOOK
PUBLISHED BY SIMON & SCHUSTER
NEW YORK LONDON TORONTO SYDNEY SINGAPORE

TOUCHSTONE
Rockefeller Center
1230 Avenue of the Americas
New York, NY 10020

DESIGNED BY COLIN JOH

Set in Minion

Manufactured in the United States of America

3 5 7 9 10 8 6 4

The Library of Congress has cataloged the Scribner edition as follows:
Thomas, Helen, [date]
Front row at the White House: my life and times/Helen Thomas.
p. cm.
"A Lisa Drew book."
Includes index.
1. Thomas, Helen [date]. 2. Women journalists—United States—Biography.
3. Presidents—United States—Biography.
4.United States—Politics and government—1945–1989.
5. United States—Politics and government—1989–
I. Title.
PN4874.T424A3 1999
070'.92—dc21
[b]
99-13787
CIP

ISBN 0-684-84911-9
0-684-86809-1 (Pbk)

I dedicate this book to all my family—
brothers, sisters, nieces, nephews and so many relatives—
and to all Unipressers past, present and future.

ACKNOWLEDGMENTS

A project like this is by no means a one-woman enterprise. All along the way I've had encouragement from all and help from many who graciously and generously gave of their time and memories when I was putting this together.

Diane Nine finally convinced me, after much prodding, that it "was time" to take on another book, and it was she who navigated the business of getting it off the ground.

I also owe a debt of gratitude to her father, Paul Nine, our legal mentor, and to her mother, Susan Nine, who helped me to catalog the photographs and did so many other things. Diane's grandmother Lily Seigert helped me recall my early childhood.

My editor at Scribner, Lisa Drew, demonstrated the wit of Wilde, the eye of an eagle and the patience of Job, which I tried continually. I am grateful for her constant good humor and her understanding when the daily deadlines at work interfered with the "other deadlines" she would remind me of, periodically but gently. Her suggestions and hard work on this manuscript helped in countless ways and make it what it is.

My thanks to my very talented Washington editor and friend Kathleen Silvassy, for her help through this entire project.

My sisters Jo and Barbara, the self-appointed librarians of "all things Helen," helped me pack, unpack and organize more papers than I ever thought possible for one person to accumulate—and when I would call for yet another piece of paper, always seemed to have it handy. My brother Matry and my sisters Anne and Isabelle also were there for me when I needed them. I cannot forget all the kindnesses of my brother Sabe and his family.

My nieces Terri DeLeon and Judy Jenkins, daughters of my beloved sister Genevieve, got caught up in the "Helen paper trail" as well and were of immense aid when it came time to do battle with my computer. Their husbands, Yuri DeLeon and Tim Jenkins, were always there for me in good times and bad. Their children have been a great joy to me always.

It fell to my nephews Robert Geha, Steven Geha and Edward Geha to reassemble the volumes of data and pack it all up again and to make cassettes for me of some of the programs I have appeared on.

Former UPI colleagues John Vogt, Al Spivak, Grant Dillman, Maggie Kilgore, Cheryl Arvidson and Leon Daniel took the time to write their memories of some events that occurred when we were somewhere in the world on some trip, and they provided some fascinating details; Grant Dillman collected many anecdotes gleaned from the "UPI chatwire" e-mail system, put together by former Unipresser Dick Harnett, and passed them along to me. Two papers by Professor Martha Joynt Kumar of Towson State University pointed me in the right direction for a historic perspective of the presidency, and I thank her for sharing them.

I thank former UPI White House colleague Tom Ferraro for his good humor in our years together in the booth, and most of all, for a telephone call in the spring of 1998 when I was trying to think of a proper title. Tom nailed most of it down in a few well-chosen words and Muriel Dobbin suggested that "Front Row" needed to be in there.

My UPI colleagues at the White House at the time—Lori Santos, Ken Bazinet and Paul Basken—shared many experiences and observations, and like all good UPI reporters pitched in and went the extra mile so every now and then I could cadge the time I needed to work on this.

Via fax, Lesley Stahl of CBS and Tom Brokaw of NBC weighed in with a few priceless recollections, as did Sheila Tate, press secretary to Nancy Reagan. Former Master Sgt. Howard Franklin and I talked long and fondly of days traveling aboard Air Force One. Joe Laitin was always just a phone call away to lend his memory to some events in his inimitably humorous way. Even a couple of my "competitors," Larry Knutson and Rita Beamish of AP, lent a hand with some details. Abigail Van Buren was a real "Dear Abby" from time to time, and notes from Barbara Bush and Nancy Reagan helped to keep my encouragement levels up.

Whenever I needed help, I knew I could call on the wonderful family of the late Diane Auger—Harriet and the late John Maroules, and their children, Margaret and the late Andrew Tscherferis. Diane was my longtime mentor.

When it came time to unpack the boxes and volumes of notes and clippings collected over the years, Marge Coffey and her two daughters, Maggie Morris and Colleen Copland, came to the rescue.

Then there are "the ladies of the club"—Dorothy and Gloria Ohliger, Dorothy Newman and Fran Lewine. We've been sitting down to dinner once a week for more years than any of us can recall, and our conversations of our "earlier days" in Washington helped considerably.

I am grateful to the impeccable guidance of Harry Middleton and the staff of the LBJ Library and Museum in Austin, Texas, who helped me find my way through that labyrinth of materials; an unforgettable lunch with Liz Carpenter and George Christian was also a memory-inducing event. In Austin, my hostess and beloved friend of thirty-four years, Jean Baldwin, and I sat for hours reminiscing—all in the name of research, of course. I'm also grateful for the Texas-style hospitality of my longtime friends Gene and Betty Spence.

For all the unsung heroes—the many, many brilliant men and women reporters and editors of UPI who have passed through its portals in the fifty-five great news years I have spent here and who loved the business as I do—I can only marvel at their grit, determination, professionalism and steadfastness through late nights and long hours, bankruptcies and bounced paychecks. I'm proud to be part of this special group.

Merriman Smith, the man in charge of UPI's White House coverage when I started over there, wrote: "One never knows in this business, but at this moment, I am a correspondent for United Press." I salute the hardworking, dedicated professionals who have labored to keep "this moment" alive. Those are my sentiments.

And above all, to the greatest reporter and writer I've ever known, AP's Doug Cornell, my late husband.

CONTENTS

FOREWORD

There are two things in life you should keep to yourself until the last minute: (1) that you're going on a trip and (2) that you're writing a book.

With the first you get peppered with questions like "When are you leaving?" "What's your itinerary?" "Have you packed yet?"

With the second it's "How is it going?" "What are you writing about?" "When will you be done?" How's it going?

How did it go? It went rough, easy, tough, tumultuous, happy, sad, joyful, tearful, bitter and sweet. Or, as I told that great former UPI editor Lucien Carr on the phone one night, "It's like being on a psychiatrist's couch."

Trying to decipher old notes taken on the run and stopping to read stories written so long ago took a lot of time.

But like a trip that brings you back to a favorite spot on the globe where you learn more about it on the second or third visit, this project also has been a great journey. I've had a chance to take a new look at my career as a White House reporter and at each of its inhabitants over the past thirty-eight years, and even though I've said it before, it still holds true: The presidency may awe me, but not the president.

Yes, my career has been a big part of my life, but as my friend Abigail Van Buren said once, "There are three things that matter most to Helen Thomas: her job, her family and her friends." She also used to tell me and all of her readers, "This is not a dress rehearsal," always making me aware that we only pass this way once.

Much has been written about the presidents I've covered. So I chose to take the personal route and make this an impressionist view of what I saw, what I heard and what I felt through eight administrations. I have left it to others to tell the story of the policies and actions and legacies they left for history to judge. I've offered some opinions, a luxury I'm not allowed as a wire-service reporter, but one I decided to indulge in for once.

On the personal side, I have heard every president I've covered say that the White House belongs to the American people. I revere that statement and do feel that in many ways it is hallowed ground. So I have been immensely privileged—lucky—to go to the White House each day, every day, and to keep an eye on presidents at such close range, to see their human side—sometimes.

I submit that to live in that house is the greatest honor that can come to anyone, since it symbolizes the public trust that presidents hold.

As for reporters, we also hold a trust: to seek the truth and to keep faith with the people's right to know. In so doing, we must let the chips fall where they may.

I have witnessed presidents in situations of great triumph and adulation, when they are riding the crest of personal fulfillment, and I have seen them fall off their pedestals through an abuse of power or what President Clinton called "a lapse of critical judgment." I have seen presidents in times of great crises who are forced to make awesome decisions that affect us all. And I have seen them give way to personal arrogance that has shamed us all. For all that, one cannot help but feel great sympathy and sadness. We all suffer when we lose faith in our leaders.

Only in a democracy are reporters allowed to interrogate their leaders. Since we do not have a British-style parliamentary system, it falls to the reporter to hold government officials accountable and to explain their actions and policies.

It's been said that the questions I ask of presidents are the kind that are on the mind of a "housewife from Des Moines," and I hope that is true. To me, she personifies what the nation wants to know, and too many times these presidents have forgotten they are responsible and accountable to her and the country.

Too often we are seen as prosecutors, judge and jury. But I believe we serve the people best when we refrain from those roles for which we have not been chosen and instead present the facts as objectively as possible. That is the best way we can serve the public good.

ONE

Beginnings

A reporter's work involves observing, listening and writing about people, places and events. I've been fortunate in that I've spent most of my time as a reporter writing about people in high places.

But it's difficult for me to write about myself. I am always astonished when I'm out speaking to one group or another about the leaders and prominent figures of our country, the movers and shakers who make it all happen, and someone will inevitably raise a hand and ask the question: "What about you?"

I believe such a query stems from a sincere curiosity about what makes someone want to be a reporter and to make journalism a life's work. The answer is that the excitement associated with the field, the daily rush in one's search for the whys and wherefores and all the other clichés attached to the profession through the years are real.

Glamour has been another word I've heard bandied about to describe my profession, and sometimes it may apply, but believe me, glamour is the last thing I'd think of when I've been standing in a cold, pouring rain from 6:30 A.M. on, held captive with my White House colleagues behind a rope, getting pushed and jostled as we all wait for someone to come out and give us the details of what just went on in the Oval Office.

How many times have I heard, "You meet such interesting people." That's true enough, as is "You lead such an interesting life." But as for anyone else who chooses this kind of work, the real magnet that draws one to such a demanding way to make a living is the irresistible desire to "be there" when the major historic events of our time occur. The driving force is and will ever be an insatiable curiosity about life, people and the world around us.

Let me be quick to point out that I've always felt it's not my life as a White House watchdog that may be interesting, but the lives of those I've been privileged to catalog at the seat of power. And that privilege has carried a huge responsibility. Little did I know when I was growing up that I would choose a profession that was an education every day.

In addition to observing, listening and writing, a reporter learns how to ask the important—though sometimes unpopular—questions.

I suppose I displayed signs of wanting to know everything early in my childhood. I remember when a young woman friend came to visit my older sisters and I started asking her about herself, her clothes, where she lived and on and on.

In exasperation, she chided me, "You're so inquisitive."

Well, what could I do but ask my sisters, "What does 'inquisitive' mean?"

"Helen, you ask too many questions," they responded.

I guess some habits are hard to break, but that is one I'm glad I've hung on to over the years. I'm sure any number of presidents will disagree with me on that point.

Strangers still approach me on the street, or in airports, and ask me, "Aren't you a reporter, the one in the front row?" Or they will say to me, "You ask tough questions." And many will add an encouraging, "Keep asking those questions. You're asking them for us."

Perhaps the most colorful comment of that type came in 1988. I was on my way home from work one night and the woman cabdriver turned around and said, "I've been trying to figure out who you are. Aren't you the woman the presidents love to hate?"

General Colin Powell, the former chairman of the Joint Chiefs of Staff, once offered another solution to my penchant for questions. It was Christmas 1992, and he and I were guests at a party given by my friend and fellow enfant terrible Sam Donaldson.

The *Washington Post* had reported that President-elect Clinton was going to tap Powell as his secretary of state. I spotted Powell at the party and naturally I had to get the story from the subject.

I walked up to Powell and asked, "Is it true that Clinton has asked you to be secretary of state?"

Powell kind of sighed, looked at the person standing on the other side of him, pointed to me and said, "Isn't there a war somewhere we can send her to?"

One of my family's dearest friends, Lily Siegert, who was my sister Isabelle's roommate in nursing school at Deaconess Hospital in Detroit, once reminded me that I told her when I was twelve years old that I intended to become a newspaperwoman. It was the Christmas season and Lily was spending the holidays with us, and as was our custom, we were gathered around the black upright piano in our parlor.

They say there is a little bit of ham in every reporter, and even though I had been shy as a child—believe it or not—I wanted to be a star in my close family of nine children. So when it came time for me to perform, I tried to imitate the Broadway singer-actress Fanny Brice and belted out a rendition of "My Man," complete with a catch in my throat and a tear in my voice.

Lily remembers asking me: "Helen, do you intend to become a torch singer when you graduate from school?"

"Oh, no," I replied. "I want to be a newspaper reporter," and added I wanted to be a great one. It's a goal I still aspire to.

Three years later, my choice of career was sealed. I was a sophomore at Eastern High School in Detroit and my English teacher liked a story I'd written and had it published in the school newspaper, *The Indian*.

Seeing my byline for the first time was an ego-swelling event, and soon afterward I joined the staff of the paper. I loved the ambience, the collegiality and the just plain fun of putting out the weekly. Printer's ink was in my veins, I decided, and I became dedicated to the proposition that this was the life for me. In my last year of high school I was presented with a book of poems, *Wine from These Grapes* by Edna St. Vincent Millay. It was inscribed: "To Helen Thomas: In appreciation of the long hours spent with the staff, January 26, 1938."

I'm sure many other reporters of my generation and those succeeding got their start this way as well, and the same was true later on when I attended the local city college, Wayne University (now Wayne State University), and worked on the college paper, *The Daily Collegian*. In fact, I can safely say that working on that paper was my vocation while attending classes and getting a degree became an avocation.

The experiences on those school papers gave me a sense of direction and dedication that have stood me in great stead throughout my life. Little did I dream, however, that I would someday become a White House correspondent covering presidents, oftentimes at eyeball range, with the audacity and insouciance to interrogate them and put them on the spot. Then again, asking questions was never a problem for me.

I am often asked whether I had any role models when I was growing up. Without a moment's hesitation I always reply, "My parents." My teachers inspired me, but my parents were my foundation and my guiding lights.

My father, George, immigrated to the United States in 1892 from Tripoli, Syria, which later became part of Lebanon. He was seventeen at the time and traveled in steerage. His possessions consisted of a few cents in his pocket and a small pouch he wore around his neck that contained a prayer in Arabic for voyagers. To this day, in my family, we say we're glad our father did not miss the boat.

At Ellis Island, the immigration officer Anglicized his surname, Antonious, to Thomas and sent him on his way to Winchester, Kentucky, where he had relatives. He bought a wagon, loaded it up with fruit, vegetables, linens, candy and tobacco and sold them around the countryside.

In 1901 he returned home and married my mother, Mary, who was seventeen. My sister Kate was born in Syria in 1902, and when she was six months old the family returned to Kentucky.

I will always marvel at the courage, determination and independence of my parents. Their story is the story of every immigrant of every era. They had great hopes and worked hard for the fulfillment of the promise of a better life, especially for their children. I know my parents never thought it would be easy. They knew what was expected of them as new citizens of a remarkable new, young, vibrant nation.

I was born in Winchester on August 4, 1920, the seventh of nine surviving children—Katharine, Anne, Matry, Sabe, Isabelle, Josephine, myself, Barbara and Genevieve. My older brother Tommy was killed when he was twelve in a terrible accident when he and my brother Matry had gone to the theater. A wall that had been left standing in the empty lot next door collapsed on the roof of the theater during a blizzard, killing 115 people inside. Many times, as a young girl, I remember coming home from school and seeing my mother, holding my baby sister Genevieve in her arms, crying over him.

My family has been blessed with a makeup that has given most of us long life and good health, but in 1988, my sister Genevieve, the baby of the family, was the first to pass away. Like my mother, to this day I cannot think or speak of my beloved sister without choking up. Later on, I lost my dear brother Sabe and my sister Kate.

We moved to Detroit in July 1924, urged on by my parents' relatives, who preceded them to the auto boomtown, and we settled in at 3670 Heidelberg Street on the East Side, a five-bedroom home on a lovely, tree-shaded street. My father paid $7,000 for the house, and we lived there until we sold it in 1946—for $7,000. The house developed its own history after we left. After passing through several owners, one decided to turn it into some kind of monument to abstract art: It was painted in a variety of colors and certain household plumbing items were attached to various parts of the roof, the front and the sides. The house drew so many gawkers who came to look and comment that complaints from the neighbors finally forced the owner to tear it down in the 1990s.

My parents adapted to their new midwestern home and we children did our best to Americanize them, but my father still traveled every year back to Kentucky to visit family and friends. We would eagerly await his return because we knew his suitcases would be crammed with hot Kentucky sausage, blackberry preserves and other goodies pressed on him by family and friends.

In Detroit, my parents set about raising our large family, and that meant long hours, hard work and services at the Greek Orthodox church every Sunday. My parents were deeply religious. My mother instructed us that if we dropped a piece of bread—the sustenance of life—on the floor we should pick it up and kiss it. One of my father's favorite expressions was *inshalla,* or "God willing." From my mother we always heard—when things turned out and we were safe—the phrase *nichke Allah,* or "we thank God."

For my father, the American dream meant owning property and seeing his children get college educations. He bought a grocery store and a few pieces of real estate consisting of several rental houses and a building that housed six stores. He paid $20,000 for that building and lost it in the stock market crash of 1929, but he managed to hang on to the other properties.

My father couldn't read or write, but he understood numbers and he had a quick mind for figures. Sometimes I think he had a computer in his head to figure out the bills that had to be paid. He kept his daily "business papers" in a bag, and at the end of the day, one of us children would read them out to him and he would do his daily accounts. And even though he couldn't understand our report cards, he was thrilled when we'd tell him what our grades were.

My father looked like Theodore Roosevelt. He was a tall and imposing figure but full of humility, a very sociable man who loved people. My parents loved company and their social life revolved around parties at home and visits with their Arab-speaking friends, who would regale them with stories of the old country.

George Thomas also had a sense of social responsibility. He kept his store all through the Great Depression, and several times a week he would bring home the unsold produce in a burlap bag, which my mother would distribute to our neighbors on the block.

A botched cataract operation left him blind in one eye and a few years later, when I was eight, he developed the same condition in the other eye. Fortunately, this time the operation was successful.

But while his vision was impaired, before the second operation, I remember walking with him and guiding him as he would make a round of visits with his friends.

In those days poverty was all around us and everyone knew hardship. Our neighborhood was a real mix of German and Italian families—we were the only Arab family on the block—but everyone helped everyone else in time of need. At school, I was one of three students designated to go from homeroom to homeroom, picking up pairs of shoes that needed new soles or heels. The shoes went into a paper bag with each student's name written across it, and the local shoemaker would repair them and return them to the school.

Next door to us lived Eva Kay and her six children. She had arrived from Germany to work as a housekeeper and was perhaps the best baker I have ever known. I have always marveled at how she kept herself and her children alive during the Depression, especially since many weeks the only income was a $13-a-week stipend from the city.

When I look at the old newsreels from that era—rich men selling apples on street corners, autoworkers lined up in the bitter cold outside the Ford Motor Company praying to get called in to work that day—I'm struck by the immense deprivation that went on, and yet, the sense of community prevailed.

Many years later, when I was working at United Press, a highly skilled Teletype operator, Gregory Eaton, told me of the despair all around him in those days in Washington and recalled the comforting words of Franklin D. Roosevelt in his inaugural address on March 4, 1933: "The only thing we have to fear is fear itself." These words raised his hopes and inspired him and millions of other Americans.

We did not think of ourselves as hyphenates, which seems to be the standard description when one talks of ethnic background. The term *melting pot* has fallen into disrepute these days, but that is how we saw ourselves on Heidelberg Street. There was a wealth of diversity of heritage and culture in our neighborhood that instilled in us a tremendous sense of tolerance. It was the epitome of the American dream that so many presidents speak about.

There were about sixty children on our block and everyone looked out for everyone else's kids. We played on the sidewalks and in each other's backyards. We stayed out late. Growing up in those years, I'm still astounded at how we felt no fear. It was, in retrospect, a fairly tranquil life for a youngster. We had no petty crime, no assaults. I can look back and be really thankful I grew up in such an environment.

That is not to say we were immune from discrimination. My parents and we children have been the victims of slights and insults along the way, but we grew up in a household that gave us the strength to overcome such treatment. Although I will admit, to this day, it still rankles me that, before we moved to Detroit, my father wanted to buy a lovely old home on top of a hill in Winchester, Kentucky, but the owner refused to sell him the property because we were "Syrian." That kind of bigotry was commonplace in those days, and sadly it still exists, especially in matters of race.

We struggled financially, but again, we didn't think we were deprived. After church each Sunday we gathered around the dining room table to eat the delicious Arab food my mother had prepared. During the week, with eight children coming and going at all hours in a rather lively household—my sister Kate was married and with a family of her own by then—my mother was always home when we came home from school. I would immediately call out to be sure. I remember often when she would fry potatoes—or try to—and as she put the golden-brown potatoes on a platter, we would grab them as we walked by.

But Sundays were another matter. Chicken and rice were always served, as well as *kibbe,* the national Lebanese dish, along with my personal favorite, meat pies. Around the table it was quite the scene: big, dramatic and loud, since everyone always had something to say, some opinion to offer, and we usually all did so at the same time.

Afterward, we would pester our parents for a dime apiece so we could go to the movies. Invariably they acquiesced, probably to give themselves some peace and quiet for a few hours.

While vacations were few, we did go on our share of family outings. I can recall many picnics at Belle Isle, a park near the city, and concerts there as well. Belle Isle was one of my favorite places back then because it meant a hot fudge sundae at the local Sanders Ice Cream parlor. Bob-Lo Island, an amusement park across the river, was another favorite trip.

I had fun growing up in that busy household, but I also was taught early that education was the Holy Grail. The house was filled with books and newspapers, and my parents instilled in all of us a love of learning and the value of an education. Also to their credit, my parents instilled in each of us, for lack of a better term, a sense of self—we were taught early on that great things were expected of us, and we all did our best to live up to the high standards they set. My brothers and sisters gave me an education beyond the classroom in my younger days, always bringing home books and records. When I was in junior high school, one of my sisters held us in rapt attention reading Shakespeare's plays aloud.

Squabbles between siblings are to be expected in large families, and mine was no different. But we managed to get along most of the time, and each of my brothers and sisters has had some influence on me. Gen, the youngest, was our jewel: gentle, sensitive and courageous. Barbara, who discovered the poetry and romantic music we loved to listen to, is an inspiration even today. Josephine was voted the prettiest girl in high school, with brains to match. She became a teacher and still teaches science courses. Isabelle became a nurse and is still the guardian angel who comes to our rescue when called.

We think of my second-oldest sister, Anne, as our second mother. Still going strong in her nineties, she keeps tabs on each of us and watches over us, as she did when we were children.

My brother Sabe, who passed away, was kind and caring and was always giving me his extra change when I was in school.

Matry became a lawyer and has functioned as the family mentor for many years.

My oldest sister, Kate, was married when I was very young, but not so young that I cannot remember her gorgeous trousseau—especially the pink satin and wine-colored cut-velvet gowns—when she was married. The mother of fourteen children, she died at ninety in 1993.

Living through the Great Depression also created a tremendous awareness in each of us of the political system—something that has obviously served me well. Even though my father could not read, he kept abreast of the issues of the day by having one of us read the newspaper to him, and he let us know that we were responsible for keeping up as well. We were thrilled when he voted for the first time in 1932, marking an "X" after the name of Franklin Delano Roosevelt—I think we were thrilled, too, that he'd voted for the right man, in our estimation—since all hopes were pinned on Roosevelt in those days to pull the nation through its economic crisis.

I enrolled at Wayne in 1938 and since there was no full-time journalism program, I pursued a course of study as a liberal arts major in English. I wasn't exactly the best student—I was freewheeling, iconoclastic and undisciplined, truth be told—but I did enjoy my history and sociology classes. One history professor by the name of Butterfield brought the subject alive for me. His lectures were dramatic, thought-provoking and inspiring. I also took a few psychology courses. In retrospect, those subjects have come in handy in my line of work; sometimes I think the classes in abnormal psychology have served me almost too well, if you think of the presidents I have covered.

One story I wrote for the *Collegian* in 1940 stood the test of time. It was a profile about Dr. David Dodds Henry, the third president of the university, who served from 1945 to 1952. When he passed away in 1995, *Wayne State Magazine* reran part of my profile of him. The article began: "Advisor, mediator, coordinator and chief trouble-shooter is only a cursory description of Dr. David Dodds Henry. As Wayne's 'man in the know' there is perhaps no administrator on the campus better acquainted with the university or more aware of its needs."

My best friend in college was Jane Stedman and we were a most unlikely pair. She was Methodist, straitlaced, proper, never without her hat and gloves. I was lucky if I remembered to run a comb through my hair. She was brilliant, a poet, and knew all the scores of the Gilbert and Sullivan operettas, and would play them from her vast record collection when I visited her family home on the West Side.

She ended up teaching literature at Roosevelt College in Chicago, but her devotion to music stayed with her all her life. She wrote for a well-regarded publication, *The Opera News,* and married English professor George McElroy. I was a bridesmaid at her wedding.

I had a few jobs along the way to pay my college expenses. I worked in the college library cataloging books and reshelving them. And I'm sure my brother Matry's heart was in the right place when he hired me to keep the books at his gas station, but they probably were never in worse shape than when I held that job. Those who know me today and my complete lack of driving skills find it more than amusing that I was anywhere near a gas station, much less working at one, but it was a nice way to make a few bucks. Matry sold the station to my brother Sabe later on, and fortunately by that time I didn't need a job as a bookkeeper.

But college is also a time for "hanging out," and I did my share with my friends. Across from Old Main, one of the now-landmark buildings on campus, was a drugstore, and my friends and I would meet there regularly to eat sandwiches, drink Coca-Cola and talk, talk, talk. We would shop at J. L. Hudson's—still, to my mind, one of the finest department stores ever—where the service and the merchandise were first class, gift-wrapping was free and items could be returned anytime.

Virginia Nicoll, another of my college friends, sent me a letter in October 1996 that reminded me of those days of "hanging out," but also of why many of my friends were working hard to get a college education:

Dear Helen,

Years ago, when we used to meet in the drugstore across from Old Main, with Iris Olin and Doris Watters, I would look at you with wonder and disbelief. Though you seldom said much about it, we all knew you were planning to become a journalist. You had a "dream."

As a child of the Depression with an intimate knowledge of hunger and cold, I was seeking a rock, a shelter forever from those twin scourges. That rock, that shelter, was to be a teaching certificate and a job with the Detroit Board of Education. . . .[1]

In 1940, as the storm clouds of World War II gathered over the United States and the debates raged on between the interventionists and the isolationists, my father passed away. At sixty-five, after so many years of hard work, his heart gave out.

Dad, ever the one to prepare for any contingency, had purchased cemetery plots at Forest Lawn and he was buried there. He'd also purchased life insurance policies to cover the funeral costs and had even bought $500 policies for each of us from the Maccabees Insurance Co. I decided to cash in the policy in 1997 and got a check for $480, but not before getting a letter from the insurance company asking me why I wanted to cash it in.

After the war was over, my mother moved to another house on the East Side, 3910 Buckingham, where she lived with my sisters Anne and Isabelle.

On Sunday morning, December 7, 1941, my family received a telephone call that told us that the son of a friend had been wounded in the Japanese bombing of Pearl Harbor. For the rest of the day, we stayed glued to our Atwater Kent radio and the following day, December 8, listened to President Roosevelt on Capitol Hill asking for a declaration of war, calling the day of the attack "a date which will live in infamy."

The treachery apparently was compounded by the fact that two Japanese peace emissaries, Ambassadors Kichisaburo Nomura and Sabiro Kurusu, were sitting outside the Oval Office at the time of the attack. But as we read history today, we can only think of so many mistakes that cost so many lives because of miscalculations, lack of communication and bad judgment.

My brothers enlisted almost immediately, the same as thousands of other American men. Sabe served in the Army and was wounded. He recuperated in a hospital in Chicago and eventually was sent home.

Matry also enlisted in the Army, but he was sent to Officer Candidate School and was transferred to the Army Air Corps. He saw action in North Africa and Italy and came home a major. He remained in the Air Force reserves after the war and eventually retired with the rank of colonel.

With the United States fully engaged in the war, I decided Washington was the only place I wanted to be. I was a journalist-in-waiting, but I didn't want to be chasing fires and monitoring police calls. I graduated in the summer of 1942 with a bachelor's degree in English, and with my sights set on a job at a newspaper, told my mother I was going to "visit" my cousin Julia Rowady, who was working for the Social Security Administration.

To my mother's credit, I don't remember her ever asking any of her daughters, "When are you getting married?" But she did ask me, "When are you coming home?" I don't remember how I answered her, but we both knew the real answer. As my Washington "visit" grew from weeks into months, she would raise the question again from time to time, to the point where it became a kind of private joke. She knew what it meant to me to be in Washington, to be a reporter and to be on my own.

She suffered a series of small strokes and a massive one killed her in 1954. I often think of how brave and tolerant my mother was, as well as independent, a woman who had a passionate sense of justice. She was always "there" for us.

I was lucky to be born into a big family, with the enduring love of my brothers and sisters that continues to sustain us. Those of us who are left remain close to one another—and to the many children who have followed.

My parents had come to America to pursue a better life for themselves and their children. They worked hard and sacrificed to give us every possible advantage. Save for their wanting us to further our education beyond high school, they never told us what we "should" or "should not" do. They gave us a great gift: the kind of independence we needed to make our own way in the world.

On July 30, 1986, Democratic congresswoman Mary Rose Oakar of Ohio stood in the House of Representatives to have some text entered into the *Congressional Record*. It was taken from a news interview done with me about my father, and Oakar cited the piece in its entirety. The reason she gave for entering the text into the official proceedings was, as she said:

> The story of George Thomas typifies the story of so many Lebanese and Syrian immigrants who have become role-model Americans. Recently, people of Middle East ancestry have undergone tremendous bias in this country. This is the story of a man who is indicative of the positive elements of this fine culture. It is a tribute to all immigrants who become model Americans. I hope by repeating this story that we not only pay tribute to the wonderful Thomas family.

Oakar read the article into the *Record* and the final paragraph makes me proud all over again of my parents, my upbringing and my career:

> I feel that my ethical standards for life came from my father. He gave me a strong sense of right and wrong—and all the guilt that comes with defying it. He gave me a sense of morality almost by osmosis. Every time I make a stand for integrity, I feel my father. My desire to become a better person comes from him. That's why I'm always fighting about discrimination and civil rights and the people's right to know. My father saw injustice around but I never heard him complain. He was not a man to upset the status quo. His children did that.[2]

I will always be in my parents' debt, and yes, I've done what I could to upset the status quo when it needed upsetting, and yes, they will always be my role models.

TWO

Washington: The Early Years

Washington has been described many times as a "sleepy southern town," and despite the hordes of people working there for the war effort and the soldiers guarding the White House, I had to agree with that assessment when I first arrived. It was white collar, compared to my blue-collar Detroit roots.

It had beautiful monuments, parks and green trees everywhere. But it also reeked of strong racial and gender prejudices designed to keep blacks and women in their place, despite the efforts of the first lady, Eleanor Roosevelt.

I have always loved the story about Harold Ickes, who was secretary of the Interior Department in the Roosevelt administration. It seems that two young black government workers at Interior decided to have lunch in the department's cafeteria, which had been off-limits to them because of their color. Two white women in the cafeteria were so upset they reported the incident to Secretary Ickes and demanded to know what he was going to do about it. "Not a damn thing," he told the women.

When I first started with United Press, working the early morning radio slot, the bureau was in the old National Press Building on E Street. I remember a restaurant nearby where a few colleagues and I would gather for coffee or breakfast before beginning work. The restaurant allowed blacks to place takeout orders but they were not allowed to sit inside. I was flabbergasted at such treatment in the nation's capital; it ran counter to every value I'd been brought up with. I'd attended integrated schools in Detroit, and segregation seemed so unreal to me. It was only the first of many revelations I would experience in my new environment. It's still difficult for me to accept that

Washington could have remained in such a primitive state well into the 1960s, when Lyndon B. Johnson blew the walls down with the far-reaching Civil Rights Act and Voting Rights Act, heralding the Great Society.

I settled in with my cousin Julia and her sister, also named Helen, my sights set on getting a job at a newspaper. It never occurred to me that I might be trespassing into a man's world. It never occurred to me that I might not get a job in journalism right away. But I was and I didn't.

I knocked on a lot of doors and got turned down in a lot of places. But I was determined to stay. I knew my family was there if I needed them, but I was determined and very proud that not once did I call or write home asking for money.

My first job was as a hostess at a downtown seafood restaurant, the Neptune Room. I didn't like it and I wasn't very good at it. The waitresses were a tough bunch to deal with; I'm sure they wondered who the hell was this new girl in the black dress seating customers. I remember them carrying on loud and long whenever a customer stiffed them on a tip. Maybe that's why I tend to be a sympathetic tipper these days.

In any case, I didn't last long. The owners complained that I "didn't smile enough," and luckily, I found a newspaper job the day I was about to be let go.

The *Washington Daily News* was owned by the Scripps-Howard chain and it was there, at twenty-two, I got my foot in journalism's door as a copy girl for $17.50 a week. My duties included fetching coffee for the editors in the morning; sometimes I even made the coffee. But I guess I would have swept the floors if they told me to. As far as I was concerned, I was working in journalism.

Teletype machines clattered and cranked out the wire copy coming in with news of the war from correspondents all over the world, and when five bells rang, signifying a bulletin, I ran to cut the copy from the Teletype and race it over to the desk. The bells rang several times a day, with stories detailing the battles in the Pacific and the armies on the move in North Africa.

The famous war correspondent Ernie Pyle worked for Scripps-Howard and I would read his eloquent dispatches from the front. I remember most of the office being in tears one day after he filed a story about an Army captain who died fighting with his men trying to reach a hilltop. No one brought the war home more vividly or more tragically.

Women reporters, who more often than not were relegated to the society pages, were beginning to be moved into news beats as more men were drafted. After a few months I too was "promoted" to cub reporter, assigned to cover local news.

I was having a fine time running around town and writing stories. The Linotype men and the pressmen became my friends, as did the Teletype operators when I went to work for United Press. They were newsmen at heart and caught our mistakes more often than I care to remember.

Being in a newsroom was like having my every dream as a student come true. Watching great newsmen and newswomen perform under deadline pressure with the presses rolling was a heady experience. Listening to the headline writers argue over the right word was bracing.

One day, the sports headline writers were carrying on a lively debate, trying to think of the right word that would fit in the allotted space. I happened to be walking by during this discussion and said "clout." It was the word they'd been trying to think of, and they all turned to me, their faces filled with shock and disbelief. That, however, was the beginning and the end of any voluntary involvement I've ever had with sports copy—or sports, for that matter. I've had to endure presidents who played golf, skied, jogged, sailed, threw horseshoes, hunted and drove speedboats. Athletic I'm not.

One of the more unpleasant jobs I had as a cub reporter was when the wire machines would print out the war casualty lists. They seemed endless at times, and it was painful just to watch as the copy paper filled up with name after name. We had to look for those casualties who were from the Washington area and contact the families. How I dreaded that, and the task was made even more painful if the military had not notified them by the time the list was published. I wince even now, thinking about it.

I moved out of Julia's apartment and into one rooming house, then another, both of them run by southern women who seemed to be doing Blanche DuBois impersonations. No matter, my career seemed set and I was on my way. My satisfaction was short-lived.

When I became a reporter, I of course joined the Washington Newspaper Guild. After all, I was from a union town and joining a union was second nature. When a strike was called at the *Daily News*, I walked out with my colleagues. In short order we were all fired.

I had struck up a friendship with Betty Lersch. Another midwesterner, she had worked for the newspaper in Lorain, Ohio, before her arrival in Washington to work at the *Daily News*. We decided to become roommates and in the bargain became lifelong friends.

For women of that era, having a career was considered something to do until marriage came along, or so their parents thought. Unlike my parents, Betty's mother continually wanted to know when she would stop this nonsense about a career, get married, settle down and raise a family. I didn't know what to make of such a situation, but it was clear it pained Betty. Here she was a reporter working a job she loved in a fascinating city, and the only reaction she got from home was "When are you getting married?"

Betty ended up writing her mother a rather long letter, which her daughter Siran passed along to me. Her eloquent words bear repeating if only because they reflect some of the things that perhaps many women were feeling at the time but couldn't express, and likely many more women since, before the idea of an independent life took hold.

> In college I also found out how the other half lives. I hadn't thought much about that before. My personal ideals stretched into broader ideals for all humanity. I love life. I love people. I love trees and rivers and hills and lakes and fields and good books and music and fires under great trees and in fireplaces. I love good conversation and heated debate and politics and newspapermen and politicians. I love good, kindly, mellow, well-balanced people. I love green grass and blue skies and F Street when it rains. . . .
>
> Nothing you or anyone else can say, can make me fall in love. If I do not fall in love, I may not get married. Don't you see that, while my life is not your life, I am happy living my life. . . . I am happily and courageously living my life in the way that seems best to me. . . .[1]

On the job front by this time, since every young man with a pulse was being drafted, Betty and I quickly found jobs in the National Press Building. She went to work for TransRadio; United Press, also owned by Scripps-Howard, coincidentally, hired me.

Aubrey Graves, the managing editor of the *Daily News,* gave UP the green light, saying I had not been given a chance.

I went to work for Arch Eddy, who had created and ran UP's City News Service, called WCNS, an abbreviated news wire for clients that included government agencies and the Washington news bureaus of out-of-town newspapers. I also wrote local radio news. My day started at 5:30 A.M. and I even saw my wages increase to the princely sum of $24 a week.

Betty and I shared a fourth-floor walk-up at 1914 G Street, a few blocks from the White House. It was two small rooms, a kitchen and a bath. It also turned into a virtual salon for friends and reporters who dropped by for conversation and cheap wine several times a week. It was so small, Liz Carpenter once reminded me, that at one party we threw, we were so short of serving space that guests who wanted salad got it from a bowl kept chilled in the bathtub.

So many nights of so much conversation. We talked about everything, we debated ideas endlessly. One night we dissected the word *money.* One friend, George Blanksten, who later headed the political science department at Northwestern University, came up with one of the night's best answers: "It's a promise."

When I think of those many, many nights, I think of how my education extended beyond the classroom, not unlike the scenes at home in Detroit with my brothers and sisters.

Betty was covering the Senate for TransRadio and one of our buddies who showed up at the "salon" was Allen Drury, then a United Press reporter who also covered the Senate. He later wrote the Pulitzer Prize–winning novel *Advise and Consent*.

I also met my longtime friends Dorothy and Gloria Ohliger. Dorothy worked as the secretary to Lyle Wilson, UP's Washington bureau chief—a conservative Republican. He was also a fair boss and one who backed up his staff.

In those early days—literally—on the WCNS desk, I worked with two magnificent newsmen who taught me a lot. My pal Lee Hannify wrote a farm column for UP Radio, which was quite popular over the airwaves. Lee had been stricken with polio when he was seven and endured leg braces and crutches, but he never let his handicap get in the way of pursuing his calling as a journalist. He was a smiling Irishman who told wonderful stories of his childhood in Montana and his early days as a newspaperman in the West. And, like most newsmen of his day, he liked to imbibe a bit—but he never missed a deadline.

Then there was George Marder, a pioneer in radio writing, whose column "Under the Capitol Dome" reflected the depth of his knowledge of politics and the Washington scene.

The Ohligers introduced me to Mexican food and, in doing so, did me quite a favor about twenty years down the road. Those hot jalapeño peppers and tongue-singeing chilies didn't bother me a bit when it came to sampling Tex-Mex cuisine at Lyndon Johnson's ranch in Texas.

Also on hand was our upstairs neighbor, Dr. Anne Caldwell, who had fled Vienna at the start of the Nazi occupation. She worked in the Army medical library and cherished the freedom she found in this country. I always admired her strength and courage; listening to her tell how she refused to submit or sign a loyalty oath taught me that there are some things you don't have to do in this world. She raised a wonderful daughter, Gisela, a lawyer and a fighter for human rights.

One of the most patriotic expressions I remembered from my childhood was "My country right or wrong," and I remember asking Betty if Germany believed that sentiment applied as well. Later I learned that the complete expression by Admiral Stephen Decatur was a bit more equivocal. "Our country, may she always be in the right; but our country, right or wrong."

It was my friend Dr. Pauline Stitt, an outstanding pediatrician, who enlightened me on that. She also had been afflicted with polio as a child, but like Lee, she did not let anything stop her as long as she lived. She also used to remind me again and again when I would quip "Ignorance is bliss" that I had to recite the full line, "Where ignorance is bliss, / 'Tis be folly to be wise."

My life in wartime Washington was a dream come true: I was a reporter, I had great friends, I lived in a fascinating city. We'd go out to eat at reasonable—read cheap—restaurants, we would walk to the Potomac River, and we would sit on steps and listen to concerts at the Watergate, which back then was just a point of reference in the city. The hotel/condo complex under the same name was built much later. We would stay out late and scout the town. We knew all the good restaurants—all two of them—the Place Vendome and Le Salle DuBois, but we saved those for when visitors showed up and took us out to dinner.

My brothers and sisters would visit and a few times I acted as the official tour guide. As any Washingtonian knows, that gets very old very quickly, and on future visits I prepared as best I could for their arrival by stocking up on maps of the city. One time, however, Genevieve came to visit after her studies at the University of Michigan and she turned into a walking civics lesson as we strolled around the city. She knew the background and history of most of the historic sites and buildings better than I did.

For me, June 6, 1944, started out the same as any other workday—the 5:30 A.M. shift. We knew from the dispatches that had been coming in for days that the Allies were preparing to invade Europe—that was no secret. Where and when, though, were kept under wraps. Still, we knew it was imminent.

The night of the invasion, Betty and I and some friends gathered around a small radio on our dining room table and listened intently, with prayers on our lips. We stayed up all night as the hair-raising reports came in, recounting the landings in Normandy. At first the details were sketchy. We knew the long-planned invasion was under way, but reporters who were landing with the troops on Omaha Beach were at first unable to transmit. The first audio report came through in the early morning of June 7.

George Hicks of ABC, who was aboard the warship *Ancon,* could be heard describing the ships, and in the background was the sound of the exchange of batteries between the Allied ships and German batteries on shore.[2]

As the days and months wore on we routinely watched the wires all day at work, and when we arrived home, the radio became our link to the devastating carnage being wrought overseas.

I was filled with nostalgia for our nightly routine when, many years later, I traveled to France on assignment and saw the beaches of Normandy.

I first went to Normandy with President Reagan to commemorate the fortieth anniversary of D-Day, and returned with President Clinton ten years later to celebrate the fiftieth anniversary of the climactic invasion of Europe by the Allied Expeditionary Forces—marking the beginning of the end of the war.

Reagan made a memorable speech to a teary-eyed audience, including many of the American Rangers who had scaled Pointe du Hoc, a one-hundred-foot sheer cliff, to face the Germans. We then went on to Omaha Beach, which became a bloodbath during the invasion until a foothold was secured against the enemy.

In the mid-1950s, years after the invasion, General Charles DeGaulle took France out of the military arm of the North Atlantic Treaty Organization (NATO) and kicked U.S. troops out of the small French village where they had been posted. As President Eisenhower watched the Stars and Stripes being ceremonially lowered, he asked, "Do they want to send the bodies back, too?"

I was in the newsroom when the end of the war in Europe, V-E Day, was announced. Like thousands of others, I took to the streets, joining the joyous, hysterically happy throngs celebrating. I don't remember going back to work that day. It was pretty much the same on V-J Day shortly after President Harry Truman made the electrifying announcement that he had dropped an atomic bomb on Hiroshima and then another one on Nagasaki.

Years later I learned how my future husband, Douglas Cornell, an Associated Press reporter, spent the day the war ended. While I was out celebrating, he was standing in the AP newsroom, dispatches from all the major European capitals—Paris, London, Berlin—and copy from the White House, the State Department and the War Department spread before him. He quickly scanned each dispatch and, standing over the Teletype operator, dictated for ninety minutes straight the unfolding drama of the end of the war. His editor took one look at the lead and said to the Teletype operator, "Let it roll."

I have a framed copy of Doug's story as it appeared on page one of the *Charlotte Observer*, dated August 15, 1945. The headline is in four-inch-high bold type: "PEACE: IT'S OVER." The significance of the story and the elegance of his style still give me goose bumps. Anyone who has ever worked for a wire service knows what it is like to compose a story under the gun. The first three paragraphs of his story read:

The Second World War, history's greatest flood of death and destruction, ended tonight, with Japan's unconditional surrender.

Formalities still remain, the signing of surrender terms and a proclamation of V-J Day.

But from the moment that President Truman announced at 7 p.m. Eastern War Time, that the enemy of the Pacific had agreed to Allied terms, the world put aside for a time woeful thoughts of the cost in dead and dollars and celebrated in wild frenzy. Formalities meant nothing to people freed of war at last.

It is difficult to believe that in my lifetime I have seen America's worst enemies become friends. Well, allies—that is certainly true of Japan and Germany. But for me, forgiving once-mortal enemies took some time. I remember telling the Japanese ambassador on one occasion, much to the chagrin of my journalist colleagues, "I remember Pearl Harbor."

Another time we were in Bonn for a summit between President Reagan and German chancellor Helmut Kohl. Kohl made some remark I found irritating and I shot back, "Who won the war?"

Brash? Perhaps. But forgiveness is one thing, forgetting is quite another. For me, the memories of thousands of casualties at Pearl Harbor and four years of a world war are not easy to erase.

A lot of women reporters who got their break into journalism during the war got their pink slips immediately afterward to make room for the men returning home. Many publishers, however, were laboring under the false impression that the same young reporters they once knew would be coming back. They came back all right, but most of them did not want their old jobs. Still, about eight women were let go at UP; I guess working the dawn patrol and being low on the totem pole saved me. I survived, along with Ruth Gmeiner, who eventually married the Washington news editor Julius Frandsen, and Liz Wharton, who covered the Hill and eventually became one of the best—and most feared—copy editors on the Washington desk.

One of my colleagues, John Vogt, did return and turned the City News Service into a very profitable operation, where I continued to work until 1955.

But enough was enough. I was thirty-five and it was time for me to speak up, spread my wings and try my hand at reporting again. My friends, especially Sid and Eleni Epstein, the fashion editor at the *Washington Star,* had been urging me to tell my bosses that I'd paid enough dues on the dawn patrol.

UP was busy with a few changes of its own in those years as well. During World War II, the UP logo was a familiar sight on the front pages of the nation's newspapers. AP, UP and INS (International News Service, owned by William Randolph Hearst) competed fiercely to be the first with the news, and the war years intensified the competition to fever pitch. But after the war, the American newspaper market started to shrink—and it's been doing so ever since. Television, that new kid on the media block, could deliver breaking news stories faster, and newspapers began to fold or merge in competitive markets.

AP, a nonprofit cooperative that could cover any shortfall by raising its membership rates, had the edge thanks to a 1945 Supreme Court ruling that left intact its exclusive right to transmit news generated by its member papers.

In 1954, UP and INS began talking about a merger, and those talks went on and off for several years. On May 16, 1958, in a suite at New York's Drake Hotel, UP president Frank Bartholomew and INS president Richard Berlin signed a merger agreement. The UP I worked for became UPI three years after I began working as a beat reporter.

At work, my boss at the time was Bob Serling, the brother of Rod Serling, a pioneer in the early days of television drama and the creator of the series "The Twilight Zone." Bob went on to write the best-selling novel *The President's Plane Is Missing*.

With Bob's approval, I approached the Washington bureau manager, Lyle Wilson, and made my pitch. I got a beat much to the consternation of Julius Frandsen, who wasn't particularly thrilled having women reporters around—something I couldn't understand. After all, he and Ruth did get married and she covered the Supreme Court.

That same year, I traded in my old digs with Betty for an apartment of my own at 1711 Massachusetts Avenue, which was home until Doug and I were married in 1971.

With my nonstop work schedule and my propensity for burning the candle at both ends, living in an apartment was one thing, keeping it in order was quite another. In the early 1960s I found a wonderful housekeeper, Nellie Wigginton, who not only kept my house in order but me as well. I can only describe her as I describe my sister Isabelle, a guardian angel, as she was always there when I needed her. She was always up on current events and had saved the yellowed newspapers of historical significance back to the Roosevelt and Truman eras because she loved both presidents. She kept up with the news—and her favorite soap operas.

Nellie followed us to Doug's apartment on Q Street, where we stayed until 1973. When we bought our place on Calvert Street she kept order there as well, and continued to do so well into her eighties. She loved to play the numbers and often told us that if she ever hit it big, she would buy a Rolls-Royce and hire a full-time chauffeur—and ride to work in style every day.

Ask Washington reporters today what their beat is and you will usually hear "I cover the Justice Department," or "I'm at State." I called my beat the kitchen sink: I covered Justice, the Post Office, the Federal Communications

Commission, the Interstate Commerce Commission and the Department of Health, Education and Welfare. Every day I would run up and down Pennsylvania Avenue, picking up releases from each department or agency, which were issued at set times each day. A release could contain something as mundane as fifty feet of railroad track being moved somewhere in Minnesota to a stunning announcement of an FBI crackdown on organized crime.

The best stories came from the Justice Department. I remember covering the news when the FBI arrested a group of organized crime figures who had been meeting secretly in upstate New York. I was there when Attorney General Herbert Brownell sent federal troops in to protect nine black students entering Central High School in Little Rock, Arkansas, in compliance with a federal court order.

I also remember a rumor that used to circulate around the FBI: J. Edgar Hoover would add the name of a criminal suspect to the bureau's Ten Most Wanted list and then—surprise—announce the suspect's capture the next day.

I covered HEW in 1956 when Surgeon General Luther Terry announced there is a link between smoking and lung cancer. It took many years for that message to sink in.

One of the worst periods in post–World War II history was the McCarthy era, often compared with the Salem witch-hunts. It was a tormented, painful time for the victims and the observers. Senator Joseph McCarthy, a Republican from Wisconsin, tore a few pages out of the House Un-American Activities Committee's book (I think it was the ethics part he threw away) and, in doing so, made a name for himself—an infamous one. He cited State Department officials as Communists and "pinkos." His two investigators, Roy Cohn and David Schine, toured U.S. embassies abroad and targeted homosexuals.

Fear pervaded Washington. Friends turned on friends and informers named names to save themselves. Several took the Fifth Amendment against self-incrimination and still lost their jobs, their homes and their families. No one was exempt; even General George Marshall, the supreme commander of the Allied forces in World War II, was called a "traitor."

Finally, some memorable, courageous people decided to take a stand. Among them was Republican senator Margaret Chase Smith of Maine, who delivered a "Declaration of Conscience." And during the Army-McCarthy hearings, after a line of questioning that can only be described as brutal, Joseph Welch, a defense lawyer from Boston, cried out to McCarthy, "Sir, have you no decency?"

I will never forget that televised scene of the gentle, white-haired Republican senator Ralph Flanders of Vermont slowly walking down the center aisle of the chamber to hand McCarthy a notice that there would be a vote to censure him.

After that, nothing could save the junior senator from Wisconsin. His notorious tactics had done him in, along with the insightful, provoking, warts-and-all profile of him by the incomparable Edward R. Murrow on CBS. The Senate, as it rarely has done, rose to censure one of its own. After wreaking much damage, havoc and incredible pain on the lives of so many people, McCarthy was finished. He died a few years later.

While covering the Justice Department in 1954, I was sent over to be part of the team covering the Supreme Court, to await its momentous *Brown v. Board of Education* decision, which stated that segregation in America's schools must end "with all deliberate speed."

It was an electrifying decision, and UP had a top-notch correspondent up for the task, the late Louis Cassels, who eventually became the service's religion editor. When decisions came down, reporters in the courtroom would grab the "paper" and send it via pneumatic tube to the office in the court's pressroom.

When *Brown* came down, Cassels grabbed it out of the tube, turned to the last page and dictated a "flash"—which would make the bells ring fifteen times on wire copy machines in newsrooms all over the country—by telephone to the news bureau in the National Press Building.

None of us could predict at the time the effect that decision would have on our society, and the way it led to future legislation banning segregation in public facilities, hotels and restaurants.

The Supreme Court decision brought to mind those early mornings in that snack bar near the National Press Building where blacks were not permitted to sit inside. I thought it might be the beginning of better racial relations, but that was not to come for at least another ten years, when Lyndon Johnson, in his first presidential term, building on John F. Kennedy's early inroads to break down the barriers, drove a few more nails into racism's coffin with the Civil Rights Act and the Voting Rights Act.

In his Senate days, LBJ was essentially considered a southerner, but on the liberal side. When he assumed the presidency and began proposing his far-reaching legislation that comprised the "Great Society," a group of southern senators came to him and demanded to know what he was doing, reminding him that in his populist days in the Senate he did not espouse such radical social change.

Johnson told them simply: "I'm president now—president of all the people."

THREE

A Little Rebellion
Now and Then

Q: When you first started out, did you face obstacles as a woman that you
might not have faced if you were a man?

A: Where did you come from, Mars?

—Helen Thomas, interview with the *San Francisco Chronicle,* January 29, 1995

The ranks of women journalists in Washington thinned a bit after the
war, but membership was healthy in the two professional organizations
open to them. I joined both: the Women's National Press Club and the
American Newspaper Women's Club, which later became the American
News Women's Club. And boy, did I get another taste of "a woman's place" in
journalism.

The National Press Club was organized in 1908 mainly as a men's social
club, a convivial hangout where they could drink and smoke and gossip—
and presumably pass on news tips. As time went on, the club became recognized as an elite press forum in Washington, where government officials and
foreign dignitaries would make major news announcements. Women
reporters were left out in the cold and could not cover these events.

In 1919, twenty-eight women journalists formed the Women's National
Press Club and, as the years went on, began to give their counterpart a run
for the money as they competed for the top-ranking personalities of the
time to be their speakers.

The Women's Press Club took in an honorary member in the early 1930s
who was a legitimate journalist—Eleanor Roosevelt, who wrote a daily syndicated column, "My Day."

Learning of the plight of the women reporters who were shut out of the all-male club and access to their speakers, Mrs. Roosevelt held regular news conferences in the White House exclusively for women reporters. And she made news, since most of her information came from none other than her husband; so women reporters got a few "scoops" in the bargain, shutting out the men.

On April 3, 1933, Mrs. Roosevelt announced to the assembled women that "beer would be served at the White House as soon as it was legal to do so," indicating that the Volstead Act—Prohibition—was on its way out. Mrs. Roosevelt's little "announcement" gave the women who covered her not only a heads-up about Prohibition but a one-up on the men covering her husband.

On the twenty-fifth anniversary of the admission of women to the National Press Club, I gave a luncheon speech and recounted how, in 1949, the club had renovated its bar and showed it off at a rare social event in which members could bring women as guests. The event coincided with the stunning news that Florence Chadwick had succeeded in swimming the English Channel in both directions.

At the bar stood Homer Dodge, a curmudgeonly but sometimes courtly gentleman who usually wore pearly gray spats.

As Ida Mae W. Ade, a journalist of the time, recalled years later, Dodge, who was always being quoted by his colleagues who considered him quite the wit, was moodily staring into his half-finished beer when he announced in stentorian tones, "A woman's place is in the English Channel."[1]

So much for courtly demeanor. But one day, a well-dressed woman showed up at the club, briefcase in hand, and demanded to see the bar. The club president informed her it was for men only. She then informed the president that she was from the Alcohol Beverage Control board and could refuse to renew the club's liquor license. He quickly reversed himself and escorted her into the bar. But membership was quite another matter, and the mentality of the male reporters who kept us out was sometimes something to behold.

William Lawrence, who worked for the *New York Times* and ABC-TV, complained during his tenure as club president that there were only a few refuges where "men could retire from the shrill argumentative voices of the lady reporters."

In 1955, the feisty and outspoken Sarah McClendon, a correspondent for a string of Texas newspapers, made her move. Sponsored by two brave members, she filed an application to join the National Press Club. I think they're still looking for that particular application, but she did get in—sixteen years later.

In 1956, Liz Carpenter, a newspaperwoman from Texas who went on to become Lady Bird Johnson's press secretary, was president of the Women's National Press Club and managed to make a deal: Women reporters could sit in the balcony during NPC press luncheons. But it was stipulated they had to be escorted up the fire exit steps, out of sight, and be escorted out of the club immediately afterward. At the same time, a subcommittee was appointed to study the admission of women as members. Sometimes I think that "study" must have qualified for government funding, considering how long it took them to make up their minds.

I remember columnist Mary McGrory used to bring her lunch in a brown bag and eat it as she sat in the balcony with the rest of us. In later years, when there was another breakthrough and we were allowed to sit in the dining room and have lunch, Mary was asked how she liked it. The food, she said, was better in the balcony.

By the mid-1960s, the Women's National Press Club had hit its stride, commanding newsmakers as speakers who were equal to, if not better than, some of those who appeared at the "other place." In 1964, Senator Margaret Chase Smith announced from the club's podium that she would seek the presidency of the United States.

But the National Press Club was still a favorite spot for government officials. When Lyndon Johnson asked an aide why his people went there instead of the Sans Souci—a very popular Washington restaurant—he was told that "it's the only place they can go without being overheard by a journalist."

I became president of the Women's National Press Club for the 1959–60 term. Attending my "inauguration" were Attorney General William A. Rogers and FBI Director Hoover. Hoover was a real coup for me, as he rarely attended social functions. The FBI also contributed to the decor that day, pasting "mug shots" of me around the staid Shoreham Hotel.

Competition for speakers continued at a furious pace. Through the fifties and sixties, a number of women journalists—Alice Frein Johnson of the *Seattle Times,* Gladys Montgomery of McGraw-Hill, Lee Walsh of the *Washington Evening Star,* Fran Lewine of Associated Press, Bonnie Angelo of *Newsday,* Patty Cavin of NBC, Elsie Carper of the *Washington Post,* and I—continued to press the issue not only with the National Press Club but with the State Department and foreign embassies, which regularly scheduled heads of state and other dignitaries to speak at the all-male club, and members of Congress who would also speak there. We also pushed the issue with the newly formed Commission on the Status of Women, trying to get the message across that we were being denied access to legitimate news events.

Strangely enough, it was President Eisenhower's invitation to Soviet leader Nikita Khrushchev to Washington that gave the women's club an ally to access.

The Women's National Press Club, the National Press Club and the Overseas Writers Club all sent cables inviting him to appear at a luncheon they would sponsor. When the NPC sent its invitation, Khrushchev sent word that he would not participate unless women were admitted.

The State Department insisted the press luncheon should be held at the National Press Club, and women reporters were determined they would not be shunted aside for this major historic event.

We stirred up a storm of publicity, demanding our rights. We went to White House press secretary James Hagerty and insisted he intervene. After much back and forth, women reporters were allowed 33 of the 220 seats—or, as stated in the decree of club president William Lawrence, 10 men to every 1.4 women—and they had to fill out forms explaining the need to cover the event.

Because I was president of the women's club, I got a seat at the head table.

It was September 16, 1959, and that was the speech in which Khrushchev told the audience: "We will bury you." After that, the Cold War continued—and so did the ban on women becoming members of the National Press Club.

We did, however, get a chance to get our licks in. Today, there are several club events in Washington that feature "roasts" of honored guests. But back then, the Women's National Press Club used to stage a "roast" of the national leadership every year. We sang, danced and lampooned the VIPs of the time.

In my year as president of the Women's National Press Club, our performance was held over the weekend of May 14–15, 1960. Betty Beale, a staff writer for the *Evening Star*, began her story that appeared the following Monday:

> Washington can now return to normal. The Women's National Press Club has finished its annual hysterical flight into histrionics, having roasted the powers that be both Saturday night at dinner and yesterday afternoon at a reception.
>
> As always, we normally mild, sweet-natured feminine scribes applied the needle with such gusto we don't mind sheathing it for another year and returning to our hot typewriters for the benefit of world enlightenment.[2]

We were missing some of the more important guests that year, though. President Eisenhower was out of town for a summit, and as I explained in my remarks at the evening's festivities, "Vice President Nixon is at Hot

Springs, Virginia, hobnobbing with millionaires on the theory that you have to know one to beat one." I also, in keeping with the theme of the night, "Politics Is Poppin'," went on to note that "Hubert Humphrey has proved that a non-Catholic can't win.... The Democratic Party has switched its campaign slogan from 'Me, too' to 'U-2'.... Former President Truman is trying to negotiate a new Missouri Compromise ... and the initials LBJ now stand for 'Let's Beat Jack.'"

One might think these government officials would have been lobbying the National Press Club to admit women just so they wouldn't have to listen to or read about us eviscerating them—nicely, of course.

Finally, in March 1971, twenty-four women were admitted to the National Press Club. Even then, the president, Vernon Louviere, who had initially opposed admitting women, was hardly the soul of gallantry.

In his welcome he noted, "I have the privilege of being the president on this auspicious and historic occasion.... In a sense you ladies have carved out a piece of history for yourselves. Look what women have accomplished over the years and centuries. Perhaps your names will be added to the list.... Joan of Arc, Amelia Earhart, Carrie Nation, Pocahontas and Lizzie Borden...."

His list went on to include Jeanette Rankin, Mata Hari and Daisy Mae Yokum.

And the job front wasn't such a picnic either. While we were fighting for press club access we also came up against some strange goings-on while covering the president. I ran across this entry in H. R. Haldeman's book, dated August 16, 1971, when Nixon decided to go golfing at the all-male Burning Tree Country Club:

> We had a really ridiculous motorcade going out there with a huge police escort, which was really horrible, and they drove right onto the club grounds and up in front of the caddie house, which was very embarrassing, and then it was topped off by (UPI correspondent) Helen Thomas getting out of the car and standing there watching him while the press car wasn't even supposed to come in and no women are allowed at Burning Tree.[3]

Since those battles, the National Press Club has had five women presidents—I was elected financial secretary in December 1971—and speakers ranging from Indira Gandhi to Golda Meir to Gloria Steinem to Julia Child.

Steinem's appearance as the first luncheon speaker of 1972 prompted the club's new president, Warren Rogers, to comment on the recently won battle for admission, and he noted that he was a "principal leader in the opposition ... but that was in the early dark days of my middle age. The scales have been lifted from my eyes. You know that, in the recent election, our entire slate won—including the biggest vote-getter on the slate, Helen Thomas of UPI."

Warren's remarks were nice, but I should point out that at the end of her speech, he presented Gloria with the traditional thank-you gift given to speakers: a National Press Club necktie.

Even today we search for the answers to blind prejudice that so long has ruled in our society—and is so damning to our profession that holds the public trust.

But the door of the National Press Club had finally been opened—kicked in?—and in later years, women gained entry into other male-only strong-holds. In a few of them, I was the first to walk through the door. I can honestly say I don't know why I ended up the standard-bearer, but when the opportunity presented itself, I wasn't about to say no.

In my early days covering the White House, there was one off-campus event that women reporters were not allowed to attend, and again, we made some noise about it. We were fully accredited White House reporters and joined the White House Correspondents Association by dutifully paying our $2 annual dues. However, women were banned from attending the annual dinner in honor of the president.

Once again, we stood together and told President Kennedy he should not attend the dinner if we couldn't. Kennedy agreed with us and that year women were allowed to attend, marking the first time in fifty years that females graced that banquet.

These days, the yearly dues are $25, the dinner is held in the cavernous ballroom of the Washington Hilton, draws an estimated 2,500 or so guests at $125 per person, is broadcast on C-Span and is considered one of the "hot tickets" when it comes to glitzy Washington events. It also has become a big game of one-upmanship among media outlets as they try to attract Hollywood celebrities to sit at their tables.

That scene couldn't have been more improbable when I was inducted as the association's president in 1975—the first female to hold that post. The executive board thought it would be a good idea—maybe a good gimmick—to ask Danny Thomas to be the entertainment at the annual dinner: at the head table would be two Thomases with the same ethnic background.

Accompanying Danny to the dinner was his daughter Marlo, well known for her stance on feminist issues. Maybe if Marlo had explained some of those issues to her father before the dinner it would have alleviated a few tense moments during the evening.

Thomas began his comedy routine and at first it all went well. Then he launched into a string of battle-of-the-sexes jokes, talking about "women in the kitchen" and other incidents of domestic humor. Some women reporters in the audience were taken aback by his lines and the hissing was noticeable.

After Thomas finished and the hissing subsided, it was my turn to speak. What to say?

I stood, took a breath and said, "Thank you, Danny Thomas, for advancing the cause of women."

At a reception afterward, Thomas said he heard the hissing, and that was what prompted him to quickly add another line to his routine: "If you want to run for president, I'll vote for you, honey, but don't drop your pedestal, honey," was how it went.

Marlo assured her father afterward that he had been a big hit and also tried to assure some of the women reporters that he had meant no harm. But some of the guests weren't having any of it, and after making a few more comments at the reception, Marlo finally told her father, "Daddy, get out of here. If we make it out of here in one piece, we'll be lucky."

In 1975, I also was inducted as the first woman member of the Gridiron Club, which broke a ninety-year-old men-only tradition. This stronghold also had been the target of pickets, protests and a counteroffensive.

Every year the club, which exists primarily for this purpose, holds an annual dinner at which the members—reporters and editors—perform political skits and songs lampooning many in the audience, most notably the president and members of Congress.

For six years, an ad hoc group of men and women reporters called Journalists for Professional Equality had been picketing and protesting this white-tie affair and urging government officials not to attend.

In 1974, they staged a counter-Gridiron party to raise money for the Reporters Committee for Freedom of the Press, a group that helps journalists in First Amendment cases and other matters. They went ahead with plans to hold another party in 1975, the year I was elected as the first woman member. The journalists' group released a statement praising the Gridiron Club's action and hoping that my admission would be more than a "token" gesture.

Unlike the battle for equality with the National Press Club, which had to do with access to the speeches of important officials, I wasn't all that interested in the machinations of the Gridiron and I didn't seek membership. When I was voted in, some of my female colleagues were quick to attach that "token" tag on me. But as I told the *Washington Star*, "I'm for any barrier crumbling against any discrimination. We shouldn't have to fight for it, but when it finally becomes accessible, I won't thumb my nose, I'll just walk right in." The vote to admit me, it was later disclosed, was 41–0, and one of the most important ones belonged to my boss Grant Dillman, who had done a lot of lobbying, cajoling and maybe some arm-twisting on my behalf. Grant's action benefited not only me but all the women members who have followed, and he deserves credit for being the forward-thinker he was back in 1975.

The symbol for the Gridiron is a huge griddle; its slogan is "to singe but never to burn" the people who are being lampooned, but I do admit that there are times it's been a close call.

Every president since Grover Cleveland has attended. Franklin D. Roosevelt attended eleven during his presidency. It's the kind of evening where Washington's reporters and the high-powered people they cover drop the adversarial relationship for one night—well, maybe not completely—and have enough freedom to laugh at one another. It helps to have a sense of humor and the hide of an armadillo.

Sometimes even presidents get into the act. Ronald Reagan appeared one year to sing adjusted lyrics to "Mañana." George Bush and his press secretary Marlin Fitzwater brought the house down with Fitzwater playing Ed McMahon to Bush's version of Johnny Carson's "Karnak the Great" routine, with Bush appearing as "Tarmac the Magnificent." Rosalynn and Jimmy Carter did a mean jitterbug and Bill Clinton entertained with a saxophone solo. Even Richard Nixon gave a piano recital.

My first year of membership, I got to strike a blow—more specifically, toss a pie—for equality in a song I sang with Newbold Noyes, the former editor of the *Washington Star*. We spoofed the lyrics to "Stout-Hearted Men," declaiming the victory of "news hens" over "news hounds":

> *Give me a hen who's a stout-hearted hen, who will fight for her right in the sun*
> *Add in some frails disenchanted with males and before long the war has begun . . .*

On the last verse, which ended "When stout-hearted hens can stick together chick to chick" I smashed a pie into Noyes's face. Let me point out it wasn't my idea.

The Gridiron has admitted a number of women members since those early days, and I must say, I wonder how the men got along without us. Just like our shows from our Women's National Press Club days, we have given our all in our performances.

Over the many "roles" assigned to me through the years, I've had a few favorites: In 1997, decked out in full western regalia, I got to portray Secretary of State Madeleine Albright as a "Pistol Packin' Mama" who let everyone know she was the "new gun in town," and in 1985—the one hundredth anniversary of the Gridiron and when the show was taped for its only time in history and aired on PBS—I went out onstage in full Italian opera diva garb and sang "I like my pasta / not 'cause I hasta" to vice presidential candidate Geraldine Ferraro; in 1995, as Connie Chung, I told Newt Gingrich's mother "you can whisper in my ear."

I served as Gridiron president in 1993 and it was quite an evening, as it was President Clinton's first dinner and we all had plenty of fodder for remarks: the health care plan; the number of young, inexperienced people at the White House; and the president's jogging, among others.

The festivities began with the traditional "speech in the dark," and I made reference to that milieu "as Mrs. Clinton's health care meetings."

The White House press office had already begun to close itself off from the press by this time, so I also got a chance to lob a few on that score: "You may have wondered why we're gathered here tonight. It is to explain the new ethics rule. And after tonight we understand we should not talk to any government official for five years."

I did compliment Clinton on choosing so many women for high-ranking posts in his administration:

> Mr. President, you came into the White House with a mandate for change. It's different all right and you have really lived up to your word to appoint women to the cabinet and other high places. But you really broke the glass ceiling when you named Dee Dee Myers as your press secretary.
>
> So how come you gave George Stephanopoulos Marlin Fitzwater's office?
>
> Incidentally, we know that first cat Socks has been put on a leash so he won't roam around the White House. That puts him in the same category as the reporters covering the place.

Senator Bob Dole, who gave the Republican speech of the evening, got a few singe-but-never-burn remarks of his own in. "Helen Thomas—who talked me into this—you look elegant," he said. "The lovely dress Helen is wearing is from the new 'J. Edgar Hoover collection.'"

Dole also took a few shots at the new Clinton presidency and his mandate:

> When the White House found out that tonight was closed to outsiders, they decided to hold a health care meeting. . . . Anyway, we

Republicans lost, and now we have a former Democratic governor in the White House. But there's a big difference between running a small state and a nation. The main difference being that when the chickens come home to roost in Arkansas, they're real chickens.... This week, of course, we considered the president's plan to raise taxes, increase spending and gut defense. I've been asked what numbers to look for in analyzing the Clinton plan. The number that comes to my mind is "1996."

When it was the president's turn to speak, he gave as good as he got that night.

Preeminent among you is my great dinner companion, the first lady of White House journalism, and the club's first woman president, Helen Thomas.... She's spent more time in the White House than anybody here tonight. Still, it hurt my feelings when she demanded a security deposit when we moved in. Helen's been in Washington so long, she remembers when the Electoral College was a high school. What brings us together—public servants and public nuisances alike—is our common love of politics. According to my language expert, George Stephanopoulos, politics comes from the word "poli," which is Greek for "many," and "tics," which means bloodsucking leeches.

He did remind us all—and some days I think we need some reminding—that this is the kind of country that allows us to poke fun, lampoon and get in a few shots now and then at the person who runs the country. As he characterized the night, "It is a reminder of how fortunate we are to live in America, where every man and woman has the right to question, to criticize, and, just as important, to laugh at our leaders. This evening is not just a celebration of laughter but a celebration of liberty...."

I wonder what he thought in 1998, when, decked out in a Hillary Rodham Clinton–type pantsuit, I belted out new lyrics to the tune "Ball and the Jack":

> *First you call your pollsters ev'ry night*
> *They say ratings are high and the folks have seen the light*
> *Ask poor Mike McCurry not to be forthright*
> *Watch him spin around and spin around with all his might*
> *Go before the Congress with style and grace*
> *Tell them that you're sending John Glenn out in space*
> *When you're through you leave them all agog—*
> *And that's what I call "waggin' " the dog.*

Like the Women's National Press Club, the American News Women's Club was organized to give women reporters access to political figures, personalities and other VIPs who came to town. It maintains a permanent clubhouse at 1607 Twenty-second Street NW, thanks to the efforts of Sarah McClendon, who took on the massive project of finding a residence and won approval for the purchase. Every year the club sponsors a "roast" of a media figure and raises money for its scholarship fund.

On May 6, 1993, I was the "roastee" and my "critics" on the dais included Abigail Van Buren, Sam Donaldson, Andrea Mitchell, Sarah McClendon, the former Democratic congresswoman from Louisiana Lindy Boggs, President Carter's press secretary Jody Powell, President Clinton's press secretary Dee Dee Myers and syndicated columnist Carl Rowan.

Andrea got things off to a rousing start by remarking on how President Clinton had picked up his jogging pace since he entered the White House, "which is easy to do when you're trying to get away from Helen."

Sam paid tribute to me by saying, "She taught me everything I ever knew about questioning presidents, an act," he said, pointing to me, "that St. Peter will someday punish you for." Let me point out I take no credit for teaching Sam about asking questions; he is his own unique creation.

My favorite recollection is the story Sam told, one that he has told over and over and seems to have incorporated into his repertoire over the years. He remarked that "There was a day on the South Lawn when reporters were *allowed* on the South Lawn."

It was during the Carter administration, and on that day, a cedar of Lebanon had been planted—an event that had me rather emotional. The president had shoveled in a few mounds of dirt and after he left, my colleagues urged me to pick up the shovel as well. So I picked up the shovel and began covering the roots. And, Sam recounted, "All I could hear were the ghosts of presidents past, present and future, saying 'Shove her in, shove her in.'"

My dear friend Abigail Van Buren spoke of how the two of us met in 1973 on Dinah Shore's talk show and proceeded to bring down the house by rereading a "Dear Abby" letter she read on Dinah's show that cracked me up:

Dear Abby: Two women recently moved in to the apartment across the hall from me. One is a middle-aged librarian . . . the other is a gym teacher . . . they keep to themselves and I never see any men going in or out of their apartment. Do you think they could be Lebanese?

Looking over these "firsts" that fell to me gives me pause: They all made their point and they all advanced noble and justifiable goals. But being "first" wasn't the point or the goal for me. I was in a certain place at a certain time and did my best to contribute to those causes. I remarked to a friend awhile back that "if you're around long enough, they get around to noticing you." I don't think that was the reason behind my being named the first woman recipient of the National Press Club's Fourth Estate Award, but of all the honors bestowed on me these many years, this one is special. I was the first woman and first wire service correspondent to receive the prestigious award, which put me in very heady company; other recipients included Walter Cronkite, James Reston, Theodore White, Herbert Block and Eric Sevareid.

The award ceremony was a black-tie dinner on December 5, 1984, and about four hundred guests attended, including President Reagan's deputy press secretary Larry Speakes; Nancy Reagan's press secretary Sheila Tate; NBC's Andrea Mitchell; UPI's managing editor Ron Cohen and my White House colleagues at the time, Norm Sandler and Ira Allen; and my former White House cohort from the Kennedy days, Al Spivak. I was especially touched that Jim and Sarah Brady made the time to attend as well as my dear friends Abigail Van Buren and Sam Donaldson.

As Larry Speakes pointed out, he had been "waiting four years to roast Helen Thomas" but decided to backpedal a bit, "because I still have to face her at the briefing tomorrow." But he did engage in some good-natured ribbing about my reporter habits: "She's the only reporter who writes what the president means to say before he says it."

Then he read a nice letter from President Reagan, who wrote: "Congratulations on a well-deserved tribute to your professionalism as a journalist. You have become an important part of the American presidency."

Abby, in her inimitable way, let everyone know in no uncertain terms the path of my politics. As she recounted, she was at the Gridiron dinner the year before and someone asked her where Fran Lewine was and Abby pointed over to where I was standing.

"There's Fran," Abby said, "just to the left of Helen Thomas. Now, I don't remember who it was I was talking to but the person looked at me and said, 'No one is to the left of Helen Thomas.'"

Sam, who had made quite the grand entrance as only Sam can—his plane had been delayed and it was uncertain whether he would even show up—told a story of the Carter administration, when the door to the press office was closed because the staffers were having a going-away party for a colleague. Someone spotted Sam and asked him in; later on, Ed Bradley of CBS got the same invitation, and eventually, I got invited. Then, lo and behold, President Carter showed up.

"Of course, Helen started out polite," said Sam. "Hello, Mr. President, now about your energy program . . . well, of course, Carter ran away. So if you want to have a president at your party, don't invite Helen or keep the door closed. But she taught me a valuable lesson: Never stop working."

My former bureau manager Grant Dillman decided to weigh in with a warts-and-all portrait of me, telling the crowd "she always ignores her bosses. I can't tell you how many times she's been told to cut down on those sixteen- and eighteen-hour days."

The festivities ended about 11:00 P.M., only to be followed by a UPI party at which my colleagues made more toasts and presented me with an inscribed vase with a lovely floral arrangement. We partied on till the wee hours of the morning.

When UPI's Washington day editor Pat Killen called the White House at 7:30 A.M., he was a little astonished to hear my voice on the other end.

FOUR

New Frontiers

It was a serendipitous trip to the Soviet Union that oddly enough put me on the path to becoming a White House correspondent.

While I was president of the Women's National Press Club, I invited Madame Nina Popova, head of the Soviet Society for Foreign Friendship and Culture, to speak at a luncheon. Several members were up in arms that I had invited a Communist to our club. But I stood firm on my choice and we ended up having a good turnout.

Her appearance in May 1960 coincided with a time of international stress. She had arrived in the United States just after the U-2 incident in which a U.S. spy plane piloted by Francis Gary Powers had been shot down over Soviet territory, and the Paris Peace Conference had collapsed.

Popova wore what seemed to be the regulation black serge suit and delivered a speech that conformed to her ideology. Afterward, she opened the floor to questions.

A member got up and asked her, "Why don't your women wear makeup?"

"If they need it, they will" was Popova's withering reply.

The mood was getting just a little hostile when another member got up and asked Popova if a member of the Women's Press Club would be given "a platform" in Popova's country similar to the one she was being given here.

"How many people would you like to address, Helen?" she said, looking at me. "Three thousand?"

I assured her I wasn't looking for a platform but I wouldn't turn down a chance for an interview with Madame Khrushchev.

Popova promptly invited me to be a guest of the Friendship Society and to tour the Soviet Union, so off I went in October 1960 for a three-week visit to Moscow, Leningrad—now St. Petersburg—and Tashkent.

My treatment by the Russians could not have been more friendly and hospitable. Flowers seemed to appear out of nowhere upon my arrival in

ent cities, and a tea party followed every visit I made to a factory, a
ool or a farm.

My interpreter was a very nice, intelligent woman and a good companion,
nd when we got to Tashkent, I found myself doing a little "translating" for
her as well. The cuisine was reminiscent of the wonderful food my mother
used to prepare, and I would explain to her its origin and ingredients.

It was an exciting and exhausting three weeks, but even though my hosts
were gracious, I found myself becoming more and more defensive and
patriotically American as the days went on. It was an exhausting dialogue all
the way, especially when the Russians would come up and say to me, "Why
do you want war?"

I carried the flag on both shoulders. The people I met were kind and
friendly enough, but I began to feel that peaceful coexistence would not be
seen in my lifetime. I am glad I was eventually proved wrong, even though it
took a few decades to get there.

I didn't get my interview with Nina Petrovna Khrushchev, but I carried
with me thirty questions prepared by Herbert R. Mayes, the editor of
McCall's magazine, in the hope that she would answer them. Mayes had said
that if she did, the answers would be printed exactly as she had written
them. I left the list with Nina Popova.

Of the thirty questions, *McCall's* printed the answers to ten in its May
issue.

They were in the form of a letter to me from Mrs. Khrushchev, which was
relayed from Moscow to the Russian embassy in Washington. The embassy
forwarded the letter along with its own translation.

In her letter to "Mrs. Thomas," she stressed some of the questions were
"personal and should not be the subject of an interview." She sidestepped
the political questions that were submitted, diplomatically avoided giving
any answers to questions about the Cold War, insisting that Soviet statesmen
spoke for all the Soviet people. She chose instead to dwell on "the Soviet
woman who wants her children to have a happy, joyous childhood
unclouded by grief."

She went on to say that Soviet women are not worried about their children's
future "to whom all paths are open for the accomplishment of their brightest
hopes and ambitions," but she added that "one thing that can disturb their
young lives—the deadly searing breath of war. That is why we hate war so thor-
oughly and we shall do our best for its hardships never to strike our children
and the children of all other nations. . . . We Soviet women have experienced
the terrible ordeals of war and the undying grief of the losses."

That is the refrain I heard over and over again in my travels around the

Soviet Union: no more war. But I also heard Khrushchev say the Soviets would no longer be Communist "when the shrimps begin to whistle." And whistle they did—eventually.

En route home, I spent a few days in Paris, and it took me awhile to unwind and not feel that everything we were enjoying in the West was decadent and superficial. In short order I was walking down the rue de Rivoli, looking into shop windows displaying the latest haute couture, feeling like I had finally come home.

While I was in the Soviet Union, the presidential campaign was under way at home. In the pressroom at the American embassy in Moscow, I watched a debate between John F. Kennedy and Richard Nixon. Even watching him on a black-and-white TV set half a world away, I was struck by Kennedy's magnetism.

Funny how I didn't associate that word with the future president the first time I met him. In the early 1950s, I'd attended a party at the Pakistan embassy, and the young senator from Massachusetts offered me a ride home. He was pleasant and charming and friendly enough, and we made small talk. He dropped me off at my apartment, and the next day, my friend Eleni Epstein called and asked for my assessment.

"He's kind of dull," I told her. What *was* I thinking?

After the Kennedy victory, the White House was where I wanted to be. When I think of the battles endured at the press club, getting to cover the White House was easy. I just started showing up every day, and to their credit and my gratitude, UPI's White House bureau chief Merriman Smith and his colleague Al Spivak never turned me away.

I was forty years old and beginning what has become my life's work: covering the presidency.

I think Merriman Smith—"Smitty" to all—and Al knew, as did the UPI brass, that covering the Kennedys would be a seven-days-a-week, twenty-four-hours-a-day proposition. It seemed that the nation and the world were captivated by this group of young firebrands who were going to change the world.

After the Kennedy victory, I was assigned to cover the family at their Georgetown home on N Street, and my tenure began with a case of cold feet—literally.

I stood outside on those frigid November days watching people come and go. At least once a day, the president-elect would come out on the doorstep and announce to the press the appointment of a new member of his cabinet. It was the closest I got to "hard news" for a while.

In those days, a woman reporter at the White House was generally assumed to be little more than a specialized society columnist, and I did my share of "Jackie watching," keeping tabs on daughter Caroline and reporting what the first lady wore to lunch on a given day.

On Thanksgiving Day, Jacqueline Kennedy stood in the doorway with Caroline. She was entering her last month of pregnancy and saying good-bye to her husband, who was leaving for Palm Beach, Florida, the winter home of the Kennedy clan, to rest up from a fatiguing campaign and its aftermath.

After he departed his N Street house, I went to dinner and then went home, only to get a telephone call just before midnight with the news that Jackie had been rushed to Georgetown Hospital for the delivery of John F. Kennedy Jr., dubbed "John-John" in those early years. The baby was about two weeks premature.

Kennedy was alerted en route and a short time after he landed at Palm Beach he headed back to Washington on the press plane, which was faster than his campaign plane, the *Caroline*. By the time he arrived at the hospital, a mob of reporters and photographers had already gathered and their numbers increased when the press corps traveling with Kennedy joined the "baby watch."

For several days we clocked Kennedy in and out of the hospital, twice a day when he visited his wife and new baby. I remember buttonholing him on one of his departures and asking if he wanted his boy to grow up to be president. He paused and said, "I just want him to be all right."

In an article in *Editor and Publisher* magazine, Merriman Smith recalled that when John Jr. was born, I spent so much time at Georgetown Hospital that even Kennedy considered me a permanent fixture.

On the morning he was scheduled to have his preinaugural consultation with President Eisenhower, I was sent over to the N Street house to check him out as he left for the White House and call UPI.

"Helen was standing there having chilblains with the rest of us," Smitty said, and when the president-elect came out, "he looked taken aback when he saw Helen standing there and said, 'You've deserted my baby!'"[1]

The hospital assignment was tough. I spent long hours standing in the corridors approaching members of the Kennedy family as they came in— and remember, their faces weren't quite so familiar back then.

But it must have been a productive assignment. As Smitty recounted, "I told her her figure improved tremendously with all that activity and with no food half the time."[2]

Kennedy's administration was challenging "The New Frontier," and to conquer it, he brought with him from Boston what we in the press corps called "the Irish Mafia," bright, politically savvy men, many of whom went to Harvard and were dedicated to serving the new charismatic president.

The first big break for the White House newswomen came when press secretary Pierre Salinger announced that he would be handling Mrs. Kennedy's press as well as the president's, because, he said, "news is news."

My male colleagues greeted this with audible groans, visualizing their high-level political sessions invaded by the girls on the "diaper detail," but it gave those of us in the first lady's press corps a perfectly legitimate—and heaven-sent, it seemed—reason for being at the White House to cover those twice-daily briefings.

When the Kennedys flew to Palm Beach for the Christmas holidays and the final days of the transition period, I went along with Smitty as the backup reporter, my first trip as a White House correspondent.

For me it was an exciting time: I got to cover some of the daily briefings by Salinger at the Towers Hotel, where the press corps stayed. "Lucky Pierre," as he was nicknamed, gave his briefings dressed in Bermuda shorts until the day the cameramen photographed him from his ample backside. After that he wore slacks.

In addition to the "Jackie watch," I got to do some "JFK watching" as well. I tracked Kennedy to an exclusive men-only golf club and hid in the bushes. Afterward, when I regaled Smitty with my exploits, he knocked out a piece under my byline, headlined, "I Was a Girl Golf Spy."

I got a lot of play with that story, matched only in later years with the feature I wrote: "I Danced with the President." At a press reception, Lyndon Johnson was determined to have one dance with every woman in attendance. He said we could write home about the experience and thrill our families. I decided to go for a bigger audience.

I got my turn with Lyndon but it was more like a hundred-yard dash than a dance. What had happened was every time he went past the bandleader he would whisper, "Faster."

So the conductor adjusted the tempo. The next couple of times, Johnson again said, "Faster, faster." Finally, it seemed like the president was running wind sprints.

The next day, a White House aide called Colonel John Bourgeois, the director of the U. S. Marine Band, and asked him what had happened the night before to put the president in such high dudgeon. No one knew. The aide called back an hour later and told the director that when the president says "faster" he means "shorter."

I also had my share of "diaper detail" stories, especially down in Palm Beach. As Smitty said when I was down there, I "went around destroying businesses right and left." I interviewed the people in the shop where Mrs. Kennedy bought her children's clothes, and not only she, but Ethel Kennedy as well, eventually closed their accounts there.

I interviewed Jackie's hairdresser, her caterer and the pianist she would hire for parties. I even made good on the term *diaper detail* by interviewing the owner of the diaper service the family used. Fortunately, they couldn't fire him since he was the only one available in the area.

Jackie was more elusive, due I think to her shyness, and as time went on her antipathy to the press grew in proportion to her fear of a loss of privacy. Throughout her White House years she never came to terms with the reality of living in a goldfish bowl or the intense interest she and her family created by virtue of living in the White House.

The world of the Kennedy and later the Johnson White House parties made for great copy for the women—and it was usually women—who covered them. Invariably, after a long night of observing, note-taking and dictating our stories to our respective desks, we would retire to Nino's, one of our favorite restaurants, order spaghetti and veal and discuss and dish about what we'd seen and heard.

To be fair, we were an insatiable lot, and so were our editors. Fran Lewine, my counterpart at AP, and I often teamed up on the "Jackie watch," and the first lady eventually pegged us "the harpies." One Sunday, Fran and I were standing on the steps of the church Jackie attended, and she retaliated by alerting her Secret Service agents that "two strange-looking Spanish women" were stalking her.

I was told that at one point Jackie approached her husband and asked whether there was any way he could get me out of her way, out of her hair and off the White House beat—preferably an assignment somewhere overseas.

I did manage to get a written interview with her, and she told me, "People must be as sick of hearing about us and Macaroni [Caroline's pony] as I am." But her fierce desire for privacy was understandable. She was a devoted mother and wanted to shield her children from the glare of publicity. In our interview she told me that she had the "most affinity" for Bess Truman because "she brought a daughter to the White House at a most difficult age and managed to keep her from being spoiled."

When I asked her what was the best thing about living in the White House she responded, "Seeing my husband be a great president," but politics, to her, took a backseat to being a mother to her children.

"The official side of my life takes me away from my children a great deal," she said. "If I were to add political duties, I would have practically no time with my children and they are my first responsibility. My husband agrees with me."

Years later, Hillary Rodham Clinton sought her advice on maintaining privacy for her daughter, Chelsea.

The Kennedys set the bar higher in presidential news coverage, and ironically, Jackie did a great service to the women reporters who dogged her every move. Her elevated profile meant we were covering front-page news every day.

It wasn't exactly "hard news," but it was the territory parceled out to us and we made the most of it. Fran, myself and the other women covering the White House also paid our dues covering the many social events that marked the Kennedy style—even though I think Jackie would have preferred to put us in the kitchen or maybe have us stand outside in whatever weather befell us.

Two parties remain etched in my memory: the first was a Sunday reception for new presidential appointees nine days after Kennedy's inauguration. It was held in the State Dining Room where open bars had been set up. In addition, butlers circulated through the room with trays of champagne and mixed drinks.

The stories that appeared about the open bar unleashed a furor as certain parts of the country and one group in particular, the Women's Christian Temperance Union, weighed in with their outrage. The first couple abandoned the practice, but later on it was quietly resumed, and during such functions, one could walk up to a strategically placed bar for a drink. It's hard to believe in this day and age that something like an open bar would prompt such a backlash—and the practice became White House routine over time.

The other was the White House dinner on April 29, 1962, which brought together forty-nine Nobel Prize laureates. It was the event where Kennedy delivered that now-famous quip: "I think this is the most extraordinary collection of talent, of human knowledge, that has ever been gathered together at the White House, with the possible exception of when Thomas Jefferson dined alone." What I found even more remarkable about that evening was that Nobel prize–winning scientist Linus Pauling had spent the day outside the White House in a ban-the-bomb rally. After his picketing duty was done, he went back to his hotel, changed into his tuxedo and attended the dinner. On seeing him, Kennedy said, "I'm glad you decided to come inside."

I can recall going home to Detroit on summer vacations in those days and during family gatherings I would talk about the Kennedys, their children and the clan. They all had a star quality and were instant celebrities when they set foot in the White House on January 20, 1961, and they exuded a vibrancy and "vigah" as we teasingly noted in all the days they lived in the Executive Mansion.

One of my nieces, Suzanne Geha Merpi, who works in television news in Grand Rapids, Michigan, recounted those days of my "holding forth" in an introduction she gave when I received an honorary doctorate in May 1996 from Michigan State University:

> As one of her thirty nieces and nephews, I would comb our daily papers, the *Detroit News* and the *Detroit Free Press,* to find her bylines above a news article and we would alert the rest of our family by telephone. We could remember the thrill as we ran home from school to watch the presidential news conference with Aunt Helen asking the first or second question of President John F. Kennedy. We all sat around the one television set we had in our home with pad and pencil to take notes.
>
> We heard our presidents call her by her first name and we would see her name in print. Many times, we would receive large manila envelopes and we knew they contained pens the presidents used to sign legislation, press credentials, and photographs. . . .
>
> Her visits home were so exciting for all of us. Since she spent time with different families in our clan, we would pile into the family car and go wherever she happened to be. All of us cousins would sit on the floor and listen to the stories she told about her experiences in Washington. We loved to hear these stories from someone who covers the person occupying the most important office in our country.

FIVE

Where Everybody Knows My Name

Nino's was a favorite of mine, but when it comes to a restaurant that feels like home, there is only one in Washington for me: the Calvert Café, owned by a woman who was a constant presence and an enduring friend in my life, Ayesha Abraham.

I first met Ayesha in 1950 when she was working as a cook at the Syrian embassy. After attending a dinner there, I was taken back to the kitchen and introduced to her. As I gushed with compliments about the food she stood there quietly and then uttered a simple response: "But of course."

She was born Ayesha Howar in Palestine, on the Mount of Olives, and by the time she was twenty-one, she was married and running twenty-four farms. The cattle, pigs and produce raised supplied food for a large area of Jordan, and she also provided supplies to British officials and soldiers who controlled Palestine under the League of Nations mandate.

She was also quite fearless and had no trouble speaking her mind. She cussed out King Abdullah of Jordan when Jordan controlled the Old City of Jerusalem and, as a result, was charged with profaning the king.

She was summoned to a trial court in Amman and she did show up a couple of times. Her properties were confiscated and her life was threatened. So, with the help of influential friends, generals in the Arab Legion, she fled to Damascus where friends took her in and arranged for her to escape to America. Before she left, she and her husband divorced each other according to Arab dictates by saying "I divorce thee" three times.

She arrived in Washington and was hired by the Syrian ambassador Faiz El Khouri. A proud woman, she did not ask for help from her cousin, Washington builder Joseph Howar, a multimillionaire.

She toiled at the embassy and later went to work at several restaurants around town—wherever she cooked, I followed—including the Desert Inn and the Caravan, was married and widowed, and worked as a housekeeper.

She scrimped and saved her money for ten years, and in 1960, I stood with her when she turned the key and entered her own restaurant at 1967 Calvert Street, where, in the beginning, she was the cook, the bartender, the waitress and the dishwasher. It was known as the Calvert Café, but you won't find that in a phone directory today. In her memory the name was changed formally in 1994 to Mama Ayesha's. Even back then, though, people "went to Ayesha's."

It was one long rather dark room with a very long bar on the right as you entered and Formica-topped booths on the left. The booths had those small individual jukeboxes so you could listen to anyone from The Temptations to Elvis to Perry Como while you enjoyed your stuffed grape leaves, roast lamb kebabs, hummus and baklava. There were also a few Arabic tunes on the jukebox that the great *Washington Post* reporter Myra MacPherson dubbed "short-hand music" in a piece she did on the restaurant.

Ayesha later added a second room on the other side of the wall behind the bar.

As you proceeded to the back of the main room, the last booth in the corner belonged to Ayesha, complete with comfortable pillows and a small TV. It was here she would hold court, conversing with guests and passing the time—but always with an eye on the night's receipts. She did it every day from 10:00 A.M. to 2:00 A.M., seven days a week, every week of the year.

For some who drank the strong Arabic coffee after dinner—recommended only if you didn't want to sleep that night—she would empty the grounds and read the fortune contained therein. There was only one catch: While she had no problem telling you about your impending fame, fortune, travel or romance, I don't think she could bear to break any bad news to anyone. When she read my grounds, I always suspected she was really reading my eyes and could intuit whether they reflected joy or anxiety. But my future always looked bright to her. Is it any wonder I always went to her for reassurance?

I don't know whether she considered it breaking her rule—maybe she considered it good news—but one night I told her I was leaving the next day on a trip with Lady Bird Johnson. Ayesha told me I'd be staying home. I insisted that we were leaving and my bags were packed. The next day, Mrs. Johnson came down with laryngitis and canceled the trip. "See, I told you," she said triumphantly.

It wasn't the future in coffee grounds but a phone call in 1973—there was a round of tension in the Middle East—that showed me her incredible instinct for survival. Ayesha took the call and immediately stood up, bustled about gathering her things and demanded to be taken home. Everyone asked her what had happened; it was only 9:00 P.M., and very unusual for her to leave the restaurant before closing time. But she only repeated that she had to be taken home.

So one of the young men who worked there took her home while the rest of us continued with our meals, still wondering about her consternation. A little while later, the phone rang again.

It was Ayesha asking, "Did the bomb go off?"

When reporter Sally Quinn wrote about the restaurant in the *Washington Post*'s Style section, Ayesha told her, "Business is all I care about. All my life I work hard for the business. I don't have time for men. I don't go anywhere. In 20 years I never go anywhere but New York one time. This is my life. I love it." And she used to tell me, "I only like music and money."[1]

Well, she may have said that, and I do believe that, to her, making a profit was important. But many times I saw her tear up a bill when someone came up a little short, and she was willing to help someone out in a crisis, be it a late rent payment or an overdue electric bill.

The place attracted people from every social stratum in the city: college students, soldiers, hippies, they all stopped by. Barbara Howar, the high-powered hostess during the Johnson administration, who at the time was married to Edmund Howar, the son of Ayesha's cousin Joseph, brought Henry Kissinger in. My guests included Liz Carpenter and Martha Mitchell.

"I like everybody," Ayesha told Quinn. "I have more Jews for customers than Arabs. This is my home and this is their home."[2]

In the days of the Vietnam War, many young soldiers came in to have a meal and let off some steam before they shipped out. The steam venting usually took the form of dancing on tables and other rowdiness, and when one of them broke a table, I never saw her demanding payment for it. "They are young, they are going off to war, let them have some fun," she used to say to me.

She became a U.S. citizen in 1968 and we threw a celebration to mark what she always referred to as getting her "pomegration papers." Liz Carpenter made a speech and brought her a small American flag that had flown over the Capitol.

She was always there for me and her restaurant became my home away from home. Somewhere along the line, I can't recall when, a table—my table—got set up in the back near her booth. The staff still refers to it as "Helen's table" and it's always kept available for my guests and me.

Also somewhere along the line "Helen's salad" began appearing on the menu, a mix of tomatoes and onions in a snappy oil-and-lemon dressing.

As her business expanded, Ayesha made it possible for many of her relatives to come to America and enjoy the life she herself did. I've lost track of the many family members who worked their way through the restaurant and on to other lives, but her nephews Abdullah and Samir have kept up her traditions of good food and a convivial atmosphere.

I had urged her over the years to make a will and she would retort half-apprehensively, half-defiantly, "Why, do you think I'm going to die?" But she did finally give in and left Abdullah the restaurant when she passed away in 1993. She was in her nineties, but exactly how old we're still not sure.

Several years before that, she and I had gotten into the issue over her having a will. Ayesha had been admitted to Sibley Hospital for a gallbladder operation. Our friend Dorothy Newman and some of Ayesha's relatives gathered in her hospital room the night before the surgery and we persuaded her that it would be good for her to have a will. I had long attributed her stubbornness to the superstition that if you made out a will it was a guarantee you were going to die.

But we finally got her to consent and someone found a yellow legal pad and proceeded to write down her wishes, one of which was to finance a hospital wing for Palestinian children in her hometown.

Her surgery went well and everyone was much relieved. We were waiting for her in her room when they brought her back from the recovery room. She opened her eyes and saw me standing there. "Give me back the will," she said. "I didn't die."

In 1994, Abdullah embarked on a massive renovation of the restaurant. Out came the booths with the Formica tops, the tiny jukeboxes, the long bar. In came higher ceilings, two large airy rooms that can be divided for private parties, new carpeting and walls in pale yellow paint. The booths were replaced with tables sporting linen tablecloths and napkins. The smaller, marble-surfaced bar is in the back of the main dining room and the tiny rest rooms, which we all used to joke about with their outmoded plumbing and dark lighting, were expanded and now sparkle in white tile trimmed with blue. In warmer months, outside tables are available for dining.

But my table is still there inside at the back of the room, "Helen's salad" is still on the menu and the clientele is still an eclectic mix of students, tourists, government and embassy personnel and folks who live in the neighborhood. One of my dinner guests in 1996 was National Security Council chief Tony Lake. He liked the place so much he threw a preinaugural party there after President Clinton's reelection.

Ayesha may be gone, but sometimes I think Mama Ayesha's—and all that it embodied about her, her spirit and her generosity—will go on forever. I know I'll never forget her. I can't. On the right-hand wall above my table is a picture of the two of us, both dressed in bright red outfits. There are times I glance up at that picture and it's 1960 all over again.

While Ayesha's was the friendly place I'd gravitate to off-campus in my early years at the White House, inside the compound were my UPI colleagues Merriman Smith and Al Spivak.

I've often been quoted as saying "I assigned myself" to the White House after the Kennedy election, and as I've said, Smitty and Al welcomed the extra body. As Al told Amanda Spake in a 1990 profile in the *Washington Post Magazine*, "I was desperate for help," since Smitty would hit the road for various speaking engagements and appearances.

Even though I had worked a beat for UPI for four years, this job was going to be a little different, and any new job, as anyone knows, has a learning curve. Fortunately, I had two excellent teachers.

Al Spivak, who remains a dear friend, taught me a lot. UP "inherited" Al when the merger with International News Service went through, and the White House got the best part of that deal when Al came aboard. He was a great reporter in the best wire service tradition: fair, objective and in all respects a pro.

He left UPI and worked for Hubert Humphrey's presidential campaign and later went to what we sometimes call "the other side of the information flow," as chief public relations officer at General Dynamics.

He was helpful to me when I found myself on the business end of Lyndon Johnson's wrath with a story I wrote in October 1965. LBJ was at his Texas ranch recuperating from gallbladder surgery and read my bulletin story that his eighteen-year-old daughter Luci was on her way to the ranch with Patrick Nugent of Waukegan, Illinois, in tow and they planned to ask her father's approval to become engaged.

They were supposed to land at Bergstrom Air Force Base in Austin, but as word spread about the engagement, reporters descended on Bergstrom and their plane was diverted. LBJ was steaming—at me, at Luci, at having to read about Luci's news in my story rather than hearing it from his own daughter.

All the while, there was no word out of the Johnson ranch—no confirmation, no denial and a lot of anxiety for me. Johnson's press secretary, Bill Moyers, was out of town and his brother Jim shouldered the duty of the first press briefing after my story broke. When someone asked the question, he had his answer prepared: "Luci is a nice girl. Someday, when she is twenty-one or twenty-two she may marry."

I was about to stand up and defend myself and my story but Al gestured to me to stay still and whispered, "You're looking golden."

But it was still touch and go; for nearly two more months my story was hanging out there. Finally, on Christmas Eve, back in Austin on the LBJ "body watch": I was at an Italian restaurant with some colleagues and White House press officer Joe Laitin. A call came in for Joe, who thought it might be best to take it beyond the earshot of a bunch of reporters, and asked if there was a private place where he could talk. It turned out he could—the restaurant had a telephone in the freezer.

So in he went to take the call from Liz Carpenter and out he came, shivering slightly, and announcing that we had to get back to the hotel for a briefing. I pressed him for details. As Joe remembers it, he told me "it's going to make you look awfully good." I do remember bolting for a telephone, racing with AP's correspondent Frank Cormier.

When we got back for the briefing, President and Mrs. Johnson announced Luci's engagement.

How do I even begin about Merriman Smith? He was a reporter's reporter. He was fractious, flamboyant, glib, irascible, complicated, aggressive. He was also respectful of the presidency and mindful of the responsibilities involved in covering the leader of the free world. And his stories played the front page nearly every day.

I never heard him bark into a telephone, "I've got a story that will break this town wide open," but he often did bark at the poor soul on the other end of the line who couldn't keep up with his dictation—and he did break the kind of stories that blew a few lids in town.

Smitty and my husband, Doug, covered the Roosevelt White House together. They were buddies, but they were also furious competitors who would go to any lengths to score a beat on a story. It was a small cadre of reporters who covered FDR's twice-a-week news conferences in the Oval Office—believe it or not—and after such gatherings, the race to be the first with the news was something to behold.

The pressroom back then, in the lobby of the West Wing, was one large room with direct proximity to the Oval Office, and it contained three telephone booths reserved for the wire services. A reporter picked up the telephone in his designated booth and was immediately connected to his copy desk at company headquarters.

In his book *Thank You, Mr. President,* Smitty related the details and consequences of one such race to the booths. Roosevelt had ordered the doors to the Oval Office locked when he announced he would seek a fourth term; inside the room with all the reporters was a public relations man from the Civil Aeronautics Board.

Smitty noticed that the man was standing "in a direct line between the wire service reporters and the door" and as the news conference went on, he suggested to the man that he might want to get out of the way or he might be hurt.

The news conference finished with Roosevelt barking, "You've got your news, now get out," so Smitty shouted, "Thank you, Mr. President," the doors were opened and the race was on:

> Since I was first in line, I lowered my head and drove, fullback style, until I reached the door. I passed the C.A.B. man all right, but heard a commotion back of me as Doug Cornell of the AP and Bob Nixon of INS followed through the crowd. . . .
>
> I finally rammed my way to the door, threw it open and started running. The sprint from the president's office entails a wide swing in the lobby around a huge, circular Philippine mahogany table. . . .
>
> As I swung around the table . . . I was praying that I would not slip as I turned into the press room. I made it, however, with an inch to spare and hit my telephone booth squarely in the middle. . . .
>
> When we finished our dictation, the men stood around in front of their booths and joked about the scrimmage in getting out of the president's office.
>
> While we were talking, Bill Simmons, the towering receptionist for the president's office, stalked into the press room to inform us that the centrifugal force of our departure from the president's room had spun the poor C.A.B. man like a celluloid windmill in a strong wind. . . .
>
> Mr. Roosevelt was pop-eyed with amazement when the crowd cleared. Flat on the floor in front of the gadget-littered presidential desk was a figure looking for all the world like a corpse. Staff members quickly helped the public relations man to his feet. We never saw him around a conference after that.[3]

On another occasion, Smitty broke out of the pack early but wasn't so lucky. He slid across that table and suffered a shoulder separation. But getting to a telephone was everything to him.

It was Smitty who coined the phrase "Thank you, Mr. President" to conclude the news conferences with FDR, a tradition that was passed on to me.

I know he would have loved all the tools we use these days: laptop computers, cellular telephones, satellite telephones, pagers, electronic calculators/address books/datebooks. He loved gadgets and was always fascinated by any newfangled device that came along.

But all the high-tech "toys" that are now part and parcel of a reporter's job still can't replace what Smitty and Doug had: the ability to witness an event or scan a release, mentally organize it in a matter of seconds—lead, second paragraph, et cetera—pick up a phone and dictate a coherent story at the speed of light, complete with details and proper punctuation. It was a skill demanded by the nature of wire service work but one they consistently demonstrated with near-genius. And their stories usually hit the wire with very little, if any, rewrite.

Smitty's journalistic talent was never more apparent than on that horrible day of November 22, 1963, a day that started out for me like any other at the White House. I had drawn "check-out duty," where reporters not traveling with the president and his family stand outside watching him board the presidential helicopter, waiting until it takes off and is out of sight, and then notify the desk that the president is in the air and on his way to Andrews Air Force Base.

In fact, that day I was getting ready to go home to Detroit and spend a few days with my family. I wound up my duties at the White House and went to lunch with Fran Lewine and Pierette Spiegler, one of Mrs. Kennedy's press staff.

In the restaurant, we heard the news that Kennedy had been shot. Fran and I jumped from the table and raced out, heading for our offices, which were in different directions.

The story of how Smitty won the Pulitzer Prize for his coverage of the Kennedy assassination has been written and rewritten over the years. Two of my former colleagues, Ron Cohen and Greg Gordon, give a stirring version in their book *Down to the Wire*:

> At the sound of gunfire Merriman Smith lunged for the mobile radio telephone in the press limousine.
>
> As the black auto lurched forward, Smith crouched in the front seat, knuckles white on the phone, and barked the news to his colleague in UPI's Dallas bureau. . . .
>
> "Bulletin—three shots were fired at President Kennedy's motorcade in downtown Dallas," said Smith. . . .
>
> The reverberations of rifle fire in Dallas's Dealey Plaza had barely stilled when the bulletin arrived in newsrooms around the world.
>
> Calmly, professionally, rapidly Smith dictated, telling himself to ignore the sirens, the flashing lights, the horror of the moment.
>
> When he had finished dictating, Smith told [Jack] Fallon, "Read that back, will you, Jack?"
>
> Even in the confusion, Fallon sensed Smith was stalling to keep the phone line open. Slowly, very slowly, Fallon began reading back Smith's words. [AP's] Jack Bell had been angry enough that Smith had beaten him to the phone, but he was furious at this stunt. His frustration boiling over, he aimed a wild, roundhouse right at his competitor. Smith ducked, and the punch grazed the driver. Still grasping the

phone in a death grip as Bell tried to wrestle it away, Smith kept talking slowly, evenly, to Fallon. . . .

Nine minutes after the shooting, UPI flashed the news around the world: "Kennedy seriously wounded, perhaps fatally, by an assassin's bullet."[4]

Back in Washington, with the early reports indicating Kennedy was still alive, I was told to get to Andrews where a press plane had been arranged to fly reporters to Dallas. On the way to the airfield, I heard the news of Kennedy's death on the radio.

Smitty was aboard Air Force One when it returned to Washington bearing the body of the slain president. On the trip back, he witnessed the swearing-in of Lyndon Johnson.

He had dictated nonstop to Jack Fallon in Dallas and while flying home took his first opportunity to compose a complete story, which he pounded out on a borrowed typewriter.

At Andrews, as the Boeing 707, tail number 26000, touched down, I watched with members of the Kennedy family, government officials, members of Congress and other grieving Americans.

The Kennedy assassination had shocked the world and America had lost its vibrant young leader. I believe America lost a lot of hope, certainly inspiration, that day, and I can still recall Mary McGrory's words: "We'll never smile again."

We watched a grief-stricken Jackie, still wearing her bloodstained pink wool suit, as she stepped down from the plane and was met by her brother-in-law Bobby Kennedy.

Standing with the pack of reporters in the roped-off area, I spotted Smitty coming down the back exit of the plane and shouted to him. He ran over to where we were all standing and thrust into my hands a roll of copy he had written during the flight back. While he headed back to the White House, I grabbed a phone at the airfield, called the office and began dictating. It was hard to hold back the tears as I read his simple but compelling and beautifully written story.

My colleague Al Spivak, who had also arrived at Andrews, also ended up dictating copy Smitty had tossed to him.

Other apocryphal stories surround that incredible day: how Smitty punched out Jack Bell when he tried to reach for the telephone, that they got into a fistfight, that Smitty somehow "disabled" the phone before Bell could get to it. None has been confirmed as true, but my former managing editor Ron Cohen did run across one that has more than a basis in fact:

Ron had met with Pat Sloyan, who now works for *Newsday*. Ron was working UPI's night desk when Kennedy was assassinated, and after the copy had been filed for the night, Smitty suggested to him and another staffer that they head over to the National Press Club for a few drinks.

Smitty was finally unwinding from the incredible pressure of that day and began complaining about a sore back. He pulled his shirt up and showed his exposed back to Sloyan and asked if there was anything wrong.

Sloyan said the welts where Jack Bell had been pounding him were huge and red. To think that Smitty filed all that breaking copy, made his way to the airport, wrote a story aboard the plane, raced back to the White House and wrote a few more leads and endured what he did—before he realized the kind of shellacking that Bell had given him—was nothing short of miraculous.

Smitty was a hands-down star and he made the most of it with his appearances on a number of talk shows, including Mike Douglas and Jack Paar, and he was a particular favorite of Merv Griffin's.

But he was also a troubled man and battled a drinking problem for years. In 1966, he went through a divorce. In 1967, his oldest son and namesake, who was an Army captain, a helicopter pilot serving in Vietnam, was killed. Lyndon Johnson attended his son's funeral at Arlington National Cemetery.

In 1970, his depression escalated. He had been in and out of various rehab programs, was involved in a difficult second marriage and I think he saw no way out from the demons that beset him. He called me the night of April 12, and while in the past nine years I had seen and heard him in his "down" moments, I never heard him sound so low as in that telephone call.

The next day, he put a gun to his head and committed suicide.

I have received very few personal telephone calls from presidents, but Richard Nixon did take the time to contact me and express his sympathy at Smitty's death. In an almost unheard-of move, given his attitude toward the press, Nixon also ordered the White House flag to be flown at half-mast.

A wonderful, brilliant journalist was gone and it was journalism's loss. They don't make them like Smitty anymore, but he taught me well about being aggressive, being first and being right with a story.

In 1970, the duo Simon and Garfunkel recorded a hit song and I remember Smitty remarking on more than one occasion that it was his favorite. It was "Bridge Over Troubled Waters."

There is one last anecdote about Smitty. In 1998, the Freedom Forum's Newseum held an exhibition marking the 150th anniversary of Associated Press. Somehow, the *Washington Post* reporter covering the event managed to reassign Smitty to the AP. It must have caused a bit of confusion, since Smitty's picture is prominently displayed in the permanent exhibition, along with an old UPI wire machine and a copy of his "Kennedy shot . . ." flash.

The correction that appeared on page sixty-four of the *Post*'s Weekend Section, for anyone who might have missed it, said:

> Comeuppance comes swift and sure to a careless critic. I managed to misidentify not one, but two outstanding journalists in last week's review of Newseum's celebration of the 150th anniversary of the Associated Press.
>
> Merriman Smith, the great White House correspondent for United Press International, no doubt spun in his grave when I reassigned him to the AP. . . .

SIX

Access Denied

Is it entirely unreasonable to ask men and women of our government, whatever the level—people who literally control our lives—to speak to us on occasion—not always, because that, indeed, would be too much to ask—but on occasion, speak to us in antiseptic, nonpartisan, even cruelly accurate verity?

It is only logical that a government conducted by humans would, of natural inclination, attempt to accentuate the positive, putting the best foot forward. This being so, it is our business in journalism to accentuate the actual and this is where the trouble starts; when we refuse to accept as gospel some of the rubbish a government spews out in the name of news.

—Merriman Smith, address at the Editor and Publisher Color Awards, September 26, 1969, New York

I was working at home late one night, collecting my thoughts and once again doing battle with this computer, when my eyes wandered about the walls of my office. On two walls are floor-to-ceiling bookshelves, and each of the six shelves on one side is about nine feet long. The six shelves on the other side are about seven feet long.

So I started counting: Right wall, top shelf 54 books; second shelf, 68 books; third shelf, 71 books . . . Left wall, top shelf 65 books; second shelf, 117 books; third shelf, 101 books . . . I stopped counting after 500, got up, walked into the living room—and saw more books.

I'm sure this constitutes a marginal library by some estimations and a well-stocked one by others. But the titles and the authors were books by and about everything from Abraham Lincoln (no, I didn't cover his presidency) to Zbigniew Brzezinski, from front-runners to also-rans, from Afghanistan to Vietnam, from the fall of Saigon to the collapse of communism, from

Camelot to campaign financing, from the Great Society to "voodoo economics," from *The Best and the Brightest* to *The Boys on the Bus*, from the New Frontier to *The Final Days*.

In one way or another—and another and another—the presidency has been examined from a number of vantage points: the politics, the policies, the worldview, the place and time in history, the personality.

In covering eight administrations, what I've learned is that without credibility, a president cannot persuade, convince or govern. I saw two presidents go down the drain—LBJ with Vietnam and Richard Nixon in the Watergate scandal—because they were no longer believed. Later on, Bill Clinton paid the price for misleading the public and becoming embroiled in his own scandal.

But after listening to and observing eight presidents over the past thirty-eight years, I can also offer a few views, a few snapshots, if you will, and in doing so, illustrate the changing relationship between the press and the presidency, its effect on presidents' credibility, and how I think that has affected the people's right to know.

I can say that after all these years of president-watching, I'm still in awe of the presidency and what it means to Americans, but not necessarily in awe of the man who was sitting there at any given time.

I should point out that it has become increasingly more difficult over the years to get a fix on the person occupying the Oval Office, and that is unfortunate. Lincoln once said, "I am a firm believer in the people. If given the truth, they can be depended on to meet any national crisis. The great point is to bring them the real facts." He also said, "Let the people know the facts and the country will be safe."

I've always believed people can handle the truth—and they deserve no less.

The relationship between the press and the president? For example, I went through a number of entries in the White House logs during the Johnson administration and found a few that gave me pause:

Feb. 23, 1965: South grounds walk with Frank Cormier, Chuck Roberts, Hugh Sidey, Helen Thomas

Oct. 4, 1966: Rode with LBJ to St Matthews Cathedral with Doug Cornell

Nov. 11, 1966: Toured ranches with LBJ, Cassie Mackin, Helen Thomas, Fran Lewine, Muriel Dobbin

Nov. 17, 1967: Oval Office, off-record with Helen Thomas, Fran Lewine

April 1, 1968: Chicago, address to National Association of Broadcasters

12:05 p.m. CST: The president and Air Force One remained on the ground for 30 minutes for the press to catch up. They had stayed behind to file but were delayed by an accident, which put the bus out of commission. LBJ invited the following to lunch aboard Air Force One: Helen Thomas, Doug Cornell, Jack Sutherland, U.S. News & World Report; Dan Rather, CBS; Dave Martin, Reuters; George Packard, Philadelphia Bulletin; Max Frankel, New York Times.[1]

LBJ was a lot of things—mercurial and complex come to mind—but he was accessible. In those days, if I had a question for the president, I took it to the press secretary, and likely as not, I'd get an answer. And likely as not, if we asked questions during a "photo op" in the Oval Office, we got answers.

A couple of times Johnson invited me and AP's Karl Bauman to ride with him in the presidential limousine. One time I was standing with Peggy Stanton, then of ABC, outside Blair House waiting for Johnson to arrive and drop off a visitor at the guest house. He spotted the two of us, waved us over and told us to get in. "Wave to crowds, as if you're Luci and Lynda," he instructed. So we did.

However, if he didn't like what I or any other reporter wrote, he froze us out for a while; eventually, he got over it.

When I broke the story about Luci's engagement, the Johnsons barely spoke to me at a reception that occurred a few days later. When Doug wrote a story about Johnson pulling the ears of one of his pet beagles, it was Doug who ended up in the doghouse.

On April 28, 1964, Johnson was tangling with a number of issues, including delays in passing his government pay raise bill, the transportation bill, complaints from House Speaker John McCormack about the possible closing of the Boston Navy Yard. With all that, he still found time to get rankled about Doug's story.

The day before, Johnson had greeted a businessmen's group in the Rose Garden and had pulled the beagle upright by the ears, saying, "If you ever follow dogs, you like to hear them yelp. . . . It does them good to let them bark."

After Doug's story and the accompanying picture went out, dog lovers across America denounced the president and the head of the Chicago Humane Society was quoted as saying, "How painful it is to any living creature to be picked up by the ears."

In a conversation with his press secretary George Reedy, LBJ inveighed against the brouhaha:

> LBJ: Hell, the pictures . . . show that the dog is standing on his hind heels and there's not anything that hurts him doing that. He barks all the time. He's been here barking a dozen times today. Who was it? Doug Cornell?
>
> Reedy: Yes sir.
>
> LBJ: Well I want to know what that son of a bitch looks like, and I want to give him the silent treatment for a while. Did he carry on interviews with everybody over the nation too? Did he carry on interviews with all the pet experts?
>
> Reedy: No sir. That came in from their bureaus.
>
> LBJ: So he's got a great feeling for hurting a dog, huh?[2]

To add fuel to LBJ's irritation, this occurred around the same time his landmark civil rights bill was being hashed out in the Senate. The majority leader Mike Mansfield of Montana and Republican senator Everett Dirksen of Illinois had come to terms about shutting off the filibuster, but Dirksen, who didn't want it to appear that he was caving in, went on record to reporters complaining about LBJ's cruelty to his pet.

The very next day, Johnson and Mansfield had a conversation about the bill's fate—and LBJ, never one to forget headlines, put the dispute in the context of dog-handling:

> LBJ: Mike, what should I tell Dirksen when he starts trying to put me on the spot down here on this civil rights thing today? Just work it out with the leaders?
>
> Mansfield: That's right. Tell him that . . . it would be your suggestion that he and I just keep working together and it is our responsibility now.
>
> LBJ: I'm going to tell him that I support a strong civil rights bill. He gave out a long interview of what he's going to tell me today before he comes, which is not like him. I don't know what is happening to him here lately. He's acting like a shit-ass.
>
> Mansfield: Yeah.
>
> LBJ: First thing—he said he wouldn't treat his dog like I treated mine. . . . It's none of his damned business how I treat my dog. And I'm a hell of a lot better to dogs—and humans too—than he is.[3]

For Johnson, the unpardonable sin was that he was out of the loop, and he expected his aides to keep him informed of everything because he wanted to know everything—his penchant for gossip was legendary. And woe to the reporter who wrote a story about something he didn't know about. As he told me once, "You announced Luci's engagement, you announced Luci's marriage, you announced when she was going to have a baby—and I resent it." Resent it he did, but he still talked to me off the record, on the record and in-between.

LBJ used to joke that "I go to bed every night and read my FBI reports," and it wouldn't surprise me if he considered this a perk of the job. Through the years, many books have been written about his obsessive need to know exactly anyone's location, feelings or political persuasion at any given time. In his latest book on Johnson, *Flawed Giant,* Robert Dallek disclosed that LBJ went so far as to bug Hubert Humphrey's telephone, so distrustful was he that Humphrey would deviate from the administration line on Vietnam in his race for the presidency.

No one was immune. Smitty once recounted one of his own experiences:

At other times, the depth of his personal knowledge about some relatively unimportant person's background could be very surprising. I once asked him privately in an interview on his 58th birthday how he could enjoy such a day when he had such a painful accumulation of crises—Vietnam, inflation, racial violence.

"You've got to remember," he said, "that a president can concentrate on his official problems with almost no thought of daily personal detail. Hell, I don't have anything like the troubles you have—you lost your boy in Vietnam when you were going through a divorce from your first wife, behind in your taxes, poor-mouthing me on the Merv Griffin show to make money for big tuition bills—I've got it a lot better than you have."

I was more than a little startled and taken aback. I don't know to this day whether he had deliberately run a check on me or whether he had just been asking around.[4]

I got my own version of "the Johnson treatment" on the morning of July 23, 1967, when reports were barreling in over the wire that race riots and looting had overtaken my hometown.

Detroit was burning. I had called home to see if everyone was safe, and much to my relief, they were.

But I also learned that the riot had begun on the West Side in a part of town where my brother-in-law Edward Geha owned a party store. A small fire was started in the store and shortly afterward the rioters stormed in, grabbing everything off the shelves.

Some of the regular customers, who liked my brother-in-law and his sons who worked there, tried to form a circle around the place to protect it but to no avail. When Eddie got there, it was a shambles of broken glass and melting ice cream. He began to clean up the place and when customers came in, told them to just take what they wanted.

My brother Matry was at his farm in Mt. Clemens and he got a call about what was happening, but he never thought the rioting would spread to the East Side, where he owned a building that housed his law office, four stores and four apartments. It burned to the ground, but fortunately no one was hurt.

Matry called some of his friends at the nearby fire station and they told him to stay away because there were still shootings going on. But he decided to go and inspect the ruins with a friend who was in the construction business. When he arrived, he saw only rubble and debris.

A wall remained standing and he told me it brought back the frightening and tragic memory of the blizzard in Winchester, Kentucky, when he and my brother Tommy had gone to the theater and Tommy had been killed. Matry called immediately for a bulldozer to tear down the remaining wall of the burned-out building.

I was in the White House pressroom alone, reading every word I could, when LBJ walked in. He was enraged at what was happening and he blamed Governor George Romney for not sending in the National Guard sooner.

Everybody talks about how our current president has been able to "compartmentalize" all the issues he faces and the personal travails he endures, how he takes certain things and "puts them in a box" in his mind. But Johnson could really shock you with how capable he was of doing just that.

He stood over the three news tickers in the corridor and noticed the glass was smudged and motioned a secretary to come over.

"Now," he said, "if you use a little Bon Ami . . ." Detroit was in flames and here was the president of the United States telling a secretary what kind of cleanser to use to get the glass clean.

Then he saw me. I don't know if he knew where I came from—most likely he did—or picked up on the concern I was feeling for my family, but he greeted me and said, "Have you had your lunch?" and invited me to join him in the family quarters. So up I went with his deputy press secretary Tom Johnson and Mrs. Johnson's secretary, Ashton Gonella. It was quite a gesture on his part, for whatever reason. Johnson kept complaining about Romney and his reluctance to appeal to the White House for help because of the potential humiliation.

Afterward, we stopped in to see LBJ's grandson Lyn and I remember

Johnson telling his aides, "If Lady Bird calls, tell her I'm in the bedroom with you-know-who."

I thanked him for his generosity and kindness on what was a rough day for me. He smiled and graciously reminded me that everything we talked about was off the record.

Contrast that with a day I spent at the White House in December 1997. President Clinton met with House Speaker Newt Gingrich, Chinese dissident Wei Jing Sheng, other members of Congress and a businessmen's group. The word from the White House press office to the press corps: "No questions."

The sad equation is that there are more media outlets devoted to covering the president and more demand for coverage that have left us with less access than ever. Presidents don't talk in today's media circus as freely as they used to. But then again, things are a little different. Twenty-six years ago, Bob Woodward and Carl Bernstein were double-checking their facts with their sources—and then checking again. In 1998, there were about fifteen Web sites about Monica Lewinsky—and it seemed no one wanted to let the facts get in the way of a story.

Separating "spin" from reality is not easy. It's become the incredible shrinking presidency in terms of access, and in my opinion, we are all being shortchanged. It is astounding to realize how far some administrations will go to confuse and distort when all they have to say is they are sorry.

The term *news management* was coined in the Kennedy administration and, as Pierre Salinger once said, the Reagan administration turned it into a state-of-the-art concept.

There has always been news management, and every president likes to see his image projected in a favorable light. But what gets me is the corollary that news must be "managed" because the American citizen—and voter—is viewed as some kind of "problem": presenting controlled information in a controlled environment presumes that the audience has no ability to make a connection or draw an intelligent conclusion.

My first real measure of Ronald Reagan, his style and his wit, was in the hour after the many exhausting hours of his inauguration day. After the parade, he went into the Oval Office and, for the first time as president, sat down at the desk that was to be his for many years.

His top aides, including chief of staff James Baker, Edwin Meese, who served in the capacity of presidential adviser before he became attorney general, and Michael Deaver, deputy chief of staff, formed a semicircle behind the desk. With a big smile, Reagan signed his first executive order, freezing the federal payroll.

He looked up with an even bigger smile and said, "Can I go home now?"

It foretold of things to come in many ways. In several of his early speeches, Reagan insisted that the only role of the federal government was national security. I always felt that in his opinion, the only government building that was important was the Pentagon.

In his first few months in office, Reagan was freewheeling, refreshing, a delight to quiz, and he spoke as the moment moved him, sometimes shooting from the hip. Early in his presidency, Sam Donaldson, an equally adept hip-shooter, asked him, "Do you believe the Soviet Union is interested in detente," and questioned whether the Cold War tensions would continue.

Reagan, in a preview of what was to be referred to as the "Evil Empire," intimated to reporters that the Communist leaders in Moscow lie, cheat and cannot be trusted. It was not a surprising statement from a well-known hard-liner. As the years went on, however, at his wife's urging, he softened his view, which paved the way for friendlier summits with Soviet leader Mikhail Gorbachev. Eventually, relations between them would add two more words to diplomatic parlance: *perestroika* and *glasnost*.

His aides, however, would become apoplectic when Reagan wandered away from the script, because they believed it was their job to write the scenario and control the information flow. And most of the time, Reagan went along and seemed to prefer it that way.

When we asked substantive questions at picture-taking sessions, his aides told him to say, "This is not a press conference." On one occasion, Sam Donaldson and I refused to accept that answer and we pressed the question at hand. Reagan looked at his top aides on the sidelines—the "troika" of Deaver, Baker and Meese—and explained, "I can't answer that because they won't let me."

At that point both Sam and I protested, "But you're the president!"

With the kind of access we used to have there was a real chance to have a real conversation with the chief executive—and not necessarily to break a story—and real conversations were possible with White House aides and with the officials in the press office.

My colleagues still seem surprised when they hear me talk about the press access—and the fun—I had riding around with Lyndon Johnson at his ranch in Stonewall, Texas, or taking a quiet walk down the streets of Plains, Georgia, with Jimmy Carter.

In Santa Barbara, California, a scenic paradise overlooking the Pacific Ocean, the White House press corps would be ensconced in a hotel that had seen better days. President Reagan, meanwhile, had flown to his mountaintop ranch twenty miles north of the city and there he would stay, out of sight for several weeks. Oh, the public had plenty of stories about him chopping wood and riding horses. The best we reporters could do was attend daily briefings with a press officer and ask a lot of questions that didn't get answered.

With Jimmy Carter at home in Plains, it became a ritual for me and other reporters to walk down Main Street on Saturday mornings, side by side with the president, and just chat with him as he dropped in at various stores owned by longtime friends. We always saw hugs and kisses and listened to them reminisce. It was always "Jimmy," and only rarely "Mr. President."

Also around and accessible was his irrepressible mother, Miss Lillian, who captivated the press corps with her irreverence for the whole scene in Washington.

I recall Carter's inauguration day, which he recounted in November 1997 at the dedication of the Bush Presidential Library in College Station, Texas. The family had walked the parade route to the White House and was strolling up the driveway when a reporter ran up to Miss Lillian.

"Aren't you proud of your son?" the reporter asked.

"Which one?" she said.

Miss Lillian was truly something else. In an interview I once had with her, she remarked, "Sometimes when I look at my children, I wish I'd remained a virgin." And she had no time or truck with the self-important. In 1976, I had an interview with her and she was still fuming over one that she had done a few days earlier with a French journalist. The journalist was hectoring her just a little too much, and asked Miss Lillian, "Would you ever tell a lie?"

"Well, I might tell a little white lie," said Miss Lillian. The reporter asked her what she meant. "Well, you remember when you came in the door and I told you how beautiful you looked? Well, that's a little white lie."

On her eightieth birthday, she breezed through the White House pressroom and I asked her, "Miss Lillian, what great wisdom can you impart to us after all your eighty years of experience?"

"I learned never to open my mouth around Helen Thomas," she answered with a gleam in her eye.

The president's brother Billy, the target of barbed press reports, was nonetheless a favorite of mine down there because of his openness and honesty. He ran the corner gas station on Main Street, a hangout for many of the locals, who were most likely amused and curious when the Washington press corps invaded their town.

President Carter had made no secret that he had become a born-again Christian, and on a trip to Plains I asked Billy if he too had been born again like his brother.

"Once is enough," he replied.

In any event, as reporters we felt we got to know the members of the first family—and their extended family—in a close and unique way, far from the rarefied and super-controlled surroundings of the White House.

I remember Carter playing softball with the reporters and photographers—my contribution was as spectator, watching the game and getting eaten by gnats—and more likely than not, we would be guests at a catfish and hush puppy dinner he threw for the press. He and Rosalynn were genial hosts, though we always had the feeling they did not suffer us gladly. Still, they made an effort to suffer us, period.

In those settings we got a better fix on how a president thought, what he felt—those intangibles that helped us understand the man when it did come time to write a story.

I admit, I miss those times. You got a picture of the person, his roots and how his earlier life shaped his views. You understood better why a president did what he did. You didn't necessarily like what he did, but you understood it better.

Even a quiet moment in the Oval Office could speak volumes about what a president was about. I was part of the small "pool" of reporters and photographers who poured into the Oval Office the day after President Bush was inaugurated.

Bush sat in the elegant presidential armchair in front of the fireplace, and seated next to him, in the chair usually reserved for visiting heads of state and other dignitaries, was his lovely, beaming, white-haired mother, Dorothy, who had such a tremendous influence on his life.

Seeing the two of them sitting quietly, I remembered that when President Reagan wanted then–Vice President Bush to break a tie in the Senate on a bill permitting research on gas warfare, Bush told Reagan he would do it only if he got his mother's approval.

He called Dorothy and undoubtedly expressed the need for national security. She reluctantly agreed and Bush broke the tie.

When the Kennedys moved into the White House, the press corps was still a tight little island, not the mammoth media entourage it is today. But as I've said, they changed the rules with respect to presidential coverage just by who they were—a young, vibrant couple who sparked an insatiable curiosity. The public wanted to know all about them, and we in the press corps did our best to comply.

For the men and women who covered the more sedate, staid Eisenhower administration, this was a switch.

In retrospect, we had more access to Kennedy than I realized and we saw him often in his elite ambience, but remember, this is around the time the term *news management* got coined.

I can't say it was access that bred familiarity with the Kennedys; it was the job, and a tough job it was. I never walked down the street with Jackie in Newport and just asked how she was doing. I never ran into JFK on the White House grounds and talked to him about his children. I'm sure it stemmed from their fear of reading all about it the next day—which they usually did.

One time the president and I did share some "quality time" shortly after his election. He was on his way to church and I was riding behind in the "pool" car when, suddenly, Kennedy got out and decided to walk the rest of the way. I likewise hopped out of the car and trailed him. Later that afternoon he stopped by the pressroom to visit and we had a pleasant conversation that included that always-safe topic, the weather.

With the Kennedys, there was access, though sometimes it all turned into a game of hide-and-seek. The press corps quickly understood the first couple wanted it both ways: They wanted to be viewed as public servants of the highest order and they wanted their privacy—and plenty of it—when they were having fun or letting off steam.

So we dogged them everywhere: at their weekend hideaway in Middleburg, Virginia, on vacation in Hyannis Port, Massachusetts, and Palm Beach, Florida.

Smitty was not about to let them out of his sight—on land, at sea or in the air, and especially when they went boating.

Al Spivak reminded me that as a measure of defiance against the Secret Service and the Coast Guard and also of pride, Smitty arranged to have a "White House Press" banner made that was flown on the press boat while Kennedy-watching. Spivak has a photo at home of himself and a couple of photographers saluting the wind-waved flag as they got under way.

He recalled that Smitty was on the press boat at Narragansett Bay when the Kennedys were at Newport. A Coast Guard escort boat came close to the press boat and executed a maneuver that, in Smitty's view, put him and his fellow passengers in mortal danger. He wrote about the Coast Guard/Secret Service boat almost "swamping" him and his fellow newsmen, and his story appeared on the front page of the *New York World-Telegram*, and many other papers across the country.

Kennedy's sailboat, the *Victura*, once ran aground when he was at the helm. It happened on a Sunday, and while Spivak and the rest of the press pool were flying back to Washington with the president on Monday morning, JFK saw a front-page UPI story with Al's byline in the *Washington Post*. Kennedy—a man who cared about symbols, a former PT boat commander, and a man who didn't want to be known as a less than expert skipper at the helm—flew into a rage. At least that's what Pierre Salinger told Spivak after being summoned to the presidential cabin on Air Force One almost immediately after takeoff.

Al was sitting in the press compartment when Salinger stormed down the aisle to tell him he'd never seen the president so angry before and stated that the president flatly denied the story and wanted UPI to run a retraction.

Salinger began by asking, "Spivak, are you trying to cost me my job?"

Al told him the story was accurate, that UPI would not run a retraction, and he had a solution to his problem. Salinger, his face still gray with fear and anger, responded that there could be no solution but to run a retraction.

Al dipped into his bag and said, "Here, Pierre, show this to the president."

Salinger didn't know whether to smile or quake as he accepted an 8 x 10 photo of the *Victura* aground on a sandbar some distance from its pier, with JFK and companions hip- and shoulder-deep in the water trying to push it off. Salinger took the photo back to JFK, who returned it to Al with no comment and no further discussion of a retraction from the PT boat hero of World War II.

At Palm Beach, the press dubbed their charter boat the *Honey Chile,* a play on the *Honey Fitz,* and their skipper was a very savvy captain who knew the Atlantic and the best fishing waters.

Once, following the *Honey Fitz,* reporters aboard the *Honey Chile* spotted Jack and Jackie swimming in shark-infested waters, which the locals thought was insane.

Once again, Al ran afoul of an indignant White House that accused him and the other reporters of trying to spoil the first family's fun, along with other offenses stopping just short of high treason. But from that point on, when the Kennedys swam in those waters (and they continued to do so) one or more Secret Service agents in one or more of those water jet speedboats hovered nearby with one or more high-powered rifles in case a shark fin appeared. None did, to the best of our collective memory.

Back at the White House, Jackie resented anything written about her children but loved seeing pictures of them. She had tall rhododendron bushes planted to prevent the press corps from seeing the youngsters at play. Her husband supported the desire for privacy, especially when he gathered with his friends for private parties at the White House.

On the public side, though, Kennedy understood the importance of getting the right message out. Whenever we bounced into the Oval Office for a picture-taking session, he would quip, "Here comes the thundering herd."

But one thing I've noticed after all these years with all presidents is that photographers are always welcome while reporters are grudgingly accepted. After all, photographers don't ask questions.

By any stretch of the imagination, despite his on-again, off-again, love-hate affair with the White House press corps, Lyndon Johnson, I think, liked having us around for the most part, if only because he could keep tabs on us and what we were writing.

He also seemed to know so much about us—our professional and private lives, where we had dinner, what we ate—at times it was a little unsettling. But we knew he ordered FBI and security checks every year on his White House aides, so checking up on the press was part of his game, I suppose.

If it was a game of hide-and-seek with the Kennedys, it was a contest of wills with LBJ. He would rail against a reporter who wrote a story he didn't like, but he couldn't stay out of the pressroom. He invited Smitty and Doug a number of times to lunch in the family quarters and would launch into a long off-the-record briefing or work the "trial balloon" trick, where he would want the information to leak out. Other times he'd purposely plant a story on the record and if it met with adverse public reaction, he would deny it.

And a number of times Smitty and Doug were summoned by LBJ to the family's private quarters—sometimes to his bedroom where he was settling in for his regular afternoon nap—just to listen to what he had on his mind. For all his quirks, LBJ was a people person, and reporters were people to him—sometimes.

On the many trips to Texas, one regular feature was a walk over to his cousin Oriole Bailey, an elderly woman who gave as good as she got when it came to badinage with her cousin Lyndon.

I first met her when Johnson was vice president. Perle Mesta and I and two other reporters were down at the ranch and we walked over one morning and woke her up. She came to the door in her bare feet. Later I wrote a story about her and referred to those bare feet and to her house as ramshackle. Furious, she called LBJ and asked him, "Does Helen Thomas sleep with her shoes on?"

I wrote him a note to thank him for the weekend at the ranch and got the following response:

Dear Helen:

I was down at Cousin Oriole's recently and you have no idea how much your story is in circulation along the Pedernales. Visitors just pass the ranch by now to stop at the most famous landmark of all, Oriole's house. You girls have an elevating influence, however. She sleeps with her shoes on, so no one will catch her otherwise. And after you referred to her house as "ramshackle," she's hit me up for a paint job.

Anyway, it was fun having you and we thank you for the kind words which you had to say and which keep cropping up in your wake.

Affectionately,
Lyndon B. Johnson[5]

Reporters—those on his good side—covering him down at the ranch also got invited to barbecues featuring mariachi bands and lots of margaritas. As a host, LBJ reigned supreme, circulating among his guests, standing still for any camera pointed his way, and introducing special guests over a microphone.

For a reporter, those were generous but telling times. We saw how he lived, how he related to his family and longtime friends, and how much he loved the hardscrabble land of his childhood.

He would regale us with stories, stem-winders we called them, as we walked around the ranch or, more often, went with the ritual: a ride in his Lincoln Continental. He especially liked to go out at sundown and watch as the deer came out of the woods.

He would tell us of his hopes and dreams, but he'd also use us as a sounding board to berate whoever was standing in his way at the time, politically speaking.

We listened to his complaints and saw his frustrations firsthand. In that respect, no other president has been as open or as vulnerable. He was the "can-do" arm-twisting master of persuasion who still at times seemed to be appealing for support, especially during the darkest days of the Vietnam War.

LBJ also liked to know what we were up to, not just the stories we were writing. While the press corps all kept an eye on each other at the Driskill Hotel, Johnson would call Joe Laitin for any gossip he might have heard about us. That went both ways. Now and then, Johnson's many friends in Austin would give us some little-known information about the man.

With President Nixon and his palace guard, headed by chief of staff H. R. Haldeman and domestic adviser John Erlichman, news management was relentless, and all that "management" eventually became "cover-up" and we all know where that ended.

Nixon, try as he might, had arrived with a built-in animosity toward the press dating back to his days in Congress, and his antipathy never wavered. Long before the break-in at Democratic National Headquarters in 1972, the machinery to control the press corps was up and running, as a memo from the National Archives shows:

June 1, 1970
Confidential:
Memorandum For: Mr. Ziegler

There is to be no one from Associated Press on any social list for the next three months. That means until after Labor Day. There is also to be no one from Time, Newsweek, the Washington Post or the New York Times.

Also, you are to talk to Connie Stuart and try to work out with her ways and means of clamping down on the above four publications, plus AP, in any way she can without lousing up her basic operation on the social side.

It is essential that this be carried out. Don't let it get tangled up in someone's decision to ignore it.

H.R. Haldeman
CC: Miss Woods

During his vacations at San Clemente, Nixon would climb into a car with his pal Bebe Rebozo and roar off down the San Diego Freeway. Reporters and photographers would chase them, much to the chagrin of Nixon's press officers.

When we finally caught up with Nixon—usually at the beach or the golf course—we were well aware of his wrath and would give him a wide berth.

Strangely enough, Nixon did create something on behalf of the press corps that is still around today: He built a new press center.

What prompted the generous move to a new pressroom was a visit to the old one. A few days after he assumed the presidency in January 1969, he stopped by on Sunday evening when I happened to be working alone.

The old pressroom in the West Lobby—one large room crammed with desks topped with telephones, tables for card-playing, newspapers scattered everywhere, the three telephone booths for the wire services, camera equipment and, reportedly, a few whiskey bottles stashed in desk drawers—didn't exactly appeal to Nixon's sense of propriety or the regal grandeur that he hoped to bring to the White House. We also had the sneaking suspicion that he wanted the large reception room that resembled a men's club—with comfortable overstuffed sofas and chairs where we used to loll, nap and sometimes buttonhole special visitors—as his own private reception quarters, where visitors and guests could enter and exit far from the eyes of the prying press.

It had become even more crowded over the years as the ranks of the press corps swelled. But it was a great location, as visitors had to come through the official entrance and we could pounce on them at will.

Nixon walked in, took a look around and asked me, "Is this where you have to work?"

"You should see it when the others are here," I told him.

"This is a disgrace," he said, and set in motion a plan to build a new pressroom above the indoor pool in the West Wing.

The pool had been built for Franklin Roosevelt to use for his polio therapy and I remembered when schoolchildren all over the nation had collected pennies to help pay for it. I was one of those schoolchildren.

The new pressroom also eliminated the "dog room," where the White House pets had been fed, and an adjacent room called the Florist Room.

Nixon's press secretary Ron Ziegler, in an interview, called the pool "dead space" and noted that the renovation did not destroy it. "It will be there if some future president wants to use it," he added. We've always had our suspicions about that remark, considering what could happen if the floor ever showed signs of weakening.

About a year later, we moved into our new digs, which included a lounge and a formal briefing room—not quite the setup you see today on television when the president or his press secretary has an announcement to make. That renovation came later.

In March 1970, President and Lady Bird Johnson came to see the new facilities and Nixon himself conducted the tour.

As he looked around the new area, Johnson said, "You've really come up in the world here." As the tour continued, he said to Nixon, "This is a wonderful improvement in the physical facilities. Have you seen any improvement in the quality of the stories?"

Nixon shrugged and responded, "Not in the pictures, anyway."

The Nixon renovation was described variously as in the style of an English pub or high-class funeral parlor. Visitors would clasp their hands and ask if we knew the deceased. For a long time, signs were posted that said drinks and food are not allowed in the briefing lounge. Lounge?

The pressroom had coffee tables, the walls were freshly painted and prints were hung on them, there were sofas and high-backed chairs. On the coffee tables were vases of yellow and white chrysanthemums.

At one end of the room, which measures about twenty feet by fifty feet, was a heavy curtain. When press secretary Ron Ziegler prepared to begin his briefing, the curtain was drawn aside, revealing a podium recessed into the wall. The podium was then lowered, a lectern was put on it and someone would come in and slap a presidential seal on the lectern. Instant news briefing.

But tradition among reporters is a force to be reckoned with. Gone were our familiar clutter, our battered desks, our stacks of newspapers, our wadded-up stories that missed the wastebasket. There was work to be done. We ignored the signs. Someone brought in a television set. Newspapers, soda cans, coffee cups and notebooks littered the coffee tables. To cope with the chronic shortage of seats, some folding chairs and other odd chairs from somewhere in the White House appeared.

It got to be too much trouble to keep raising and lowering the platform, so it got left out, along with the lectern and the slapped-on presidential seal. In other words, we made ourselves at home all over again.

There was another renovation of the pressroom in 1981. To cope with the chronic shortage of chairs, movie theater–style seats were installed, and with those, a seating chart. The forty-eight news organizations that regularly covered the White House each had a little brass nameplate affixed to a seat. President Reagan's staff decided who sat where. The wire services and the three television networks at the time got the front row. The rest were divvied up among the newspapers that cover the president on a daily basis, newspaper chains, the newsmagazines, and one was reserved for a true Washington institution, Sarah McClendon. Other seats went to a then-budding Cable News Network and several radio networks.

At President Reagan's formal press conferences in the East Room, a rule had been imposed that reporters were to remain seated and raise their hands to be recognized. It seemed that Larry Speakes and David Gergen were about to insist on the same decorum at the daily briefings. They lost that battle.

As far as housekeeping was concerned, the place took on its familiar frat house tone with empty coffee cups all over the place, newspapers everywhere and TV cables snaking up and down the floor. Uncomfortable as they were and are, every now and then someone will be catching forty winks in one of those movie theater–style seats.

Another mini-"renovation," or maybe I should say revolution, came courtesy of Sam Donaldson. He conducted a one-man crusade to turn the entire press center into a smoke-free environment, and he was successful in the late 1980s. Up to that time, along with the empty soda cans, fast-food packaging and other detritus, ashtrays had overflowed in the pressroom.

In the summer of 1997, when President Clinton was vacationing on Martha's Vineyard, there was another major fix-up. In the intervening years even more reporters, technicians, cameras, ladders, cables and other equipment had come to roost.

At one of our briefings in 1997, shortly after the room was finished—new paint, new carpeting, reupholstered chairs and at least one window replaced because of a bullet hole—press secretary Mike McCurry remarked that somewhere in Washington, a saloon was probably missing its drapes, used as the fabric on our new chairs.

Nixon's effort to enlarge our press quarters seemed magnanimous enough, but Smitty, ever suspicious of Nixon and his staff, remarked, "Some day they're going to wall us in."

By the way, Nixon converted our old pressroom into Henry Kissinger's office.

Redecoration in the Nixon White House extended to an idea he had to outfit the White House police in tunics and helmets—they looked like a cross between a community theater production of *The Student Prince* and the Vatican's Swiss Guards.

Needless to say, reporters had a jolly time with that one, and reaction was swift and satirical. The White House had already purchased the uniforms, which were quickly sold to a costume house and eventually found their way to a high school marching band.

Most White House reporters have had their run-ins with the uniformed guards at one time or another. But when Nixon tried to outfit them in those ridiculous costumes, it was probably the only time in history they appreciated us for the stories we wrote about their new apparel.

There was another attempt at a White House "renovation" that didn't get very far. While we always try to be well-groomed and properly attired, the White House press corps has affected a rather utilitarian mode of dress. During the Reagan administration, we heard a rumor that they were thinking of imposing a dress code. As far as what happened to that, my former White House press colleague James Deakin of the *St. Louis Post-Dispatch* put it rather well: "When a rumor ran through the White House pressroom that the Reagan administration might impose one, the journalists reacted with a fury of a creationist reading a book. If Helen Thomas is ever compelled to give up her raincoat, it would be the end of American journalism as we know it."[6]

President Ford didn't try any renovations, redecorations or revamping. Maybe we were all still a little too raw from Watergate. He was a much friendlier, down-to-earth guy. As a member of Congress for some thirty years before he became vice president and president, Ford knew most of the national reporters by their first names and so did his wife, Betty.

In the aftermath of the traumatic Watergate scandal, the Fords were a breath of fresh air. We wrote stories about Ford making his own breakfast and other folksy details about the man who never aspired to be or expected to be president. They remained friendly to the press in their brief time in the

White House, although their press staffs went to great lengths to shield them from what they considered potentially embarrassing moments.

On those so-called embarrassments, it was no secret that Ford had a tendency to stumble, bump his head on the door as he entered or exited the presidential helicopter, fall down steps and fall victim to other slight accidents—which were always publicized.

When we once asked Betty Ford, "Do you know your husband always seems to be stumbling?" she responded, "So what else is new?"

Press secretary Ron Nessen's protective solution was to put the press behind bushes when Ford was boarding a helicopter, thinking we would not be able to witness any more mishaps. But they were hard to miss, especially with the able, Chaplinesque spin the comedian Chevy Chase gave to them on the NBC-TV program "Saturday Night Live."

Despite it all, Ford was good-natured and a good sport about the ribbing he got from us.

He's the only president who permitted me and an AP reporter to interview him at the presidential retreat, the sacrosanct Camp David that was always no-man's-land for members of the press. We met him in the relaxed surroundings of Aspen Lodge, all of us in casual attire and sitting on comfortable sofas before a roaring fire.

I understood then why presidents and their families found solace and privacy at the western Maryland mountaintop retreat. Called Shangri-La when it was built in 1943 by FDR, it was later renamed Camp David after Dwight Eisenhower's grandson.

That was the first—and last—time for me inside the living quarters at that heavily guarded compound surrounded by barbed wire.

For a number of years, when the first family decided to spend time at the presidential retreat in the Catoctin Mountains, wire service reporters assigned to the "body watch" were escorted to a duck blind. It was a three-sided, wooden affair that had two telephones, and we spent many hours in all kinds of weather just watching and waiting for helicopters from Washington to land.

Will someone please remind me how glamorous my job is?

Later on, orders came down and pine trees were planted in front of the duck blind, obscuring our vision completely.

Ford had no pretensions. The highest office he had aspired to was Speaker of the House, but there is no question that when he became president he found that he was not only up to the job but enjoyed it, and clearly it was a great regret when he did not win on his own in 1976.

President Reagan was friendly, as anyone dubbed "the great communicator" would be, but still there was a distant, scripted atmosphere permeating his White House and its relationship with the press.

Reagan, who took over the Oval Office as any chairman of the board would take over a blue-chip firm, relied on a savvy staff who had made the long march with him from California to call the shots.

Their philosophy was that appearances should be limited and the press shouldn't be encumbered with too many stories. They aimed for the audience of the nightly news and manipulated coverage so we reporters would focus on only one issue a day.

After a long career in radio, the movies and television, Reagan knew, perhaps better than any other president since Kennedy, how to handle the spotlight—hit the mark, say your lines, smile and leave—and he was a master at it.

Like all presidents, he had a stable of speechwriters, but like all good broadcasters, he knew enough to rewrite some of his speeches in a warmer, conversational tone. That was very effective. He was less sure of himself at news conferences when some of the questions veered away from the many briefing books he studied before the event.

Reagan was able to joke about his age, the attempt on his life and the illnesses he endured while in office. At the annual Gridiron dinner after his prostate surgery in 1988, he quipped, "I've been shot at, had skin cancer, colon cancer and prostate surgery—those were the good old days."

President Bush, like Ford and Kennedy, had been on the Washington scene for years and was friendly with many members of the press corps. He was particularly fond of the photographers, calling them "photo dogs"—no hostility intended—and every summer he would give a barbecue on the White House grounds for the still photographers who covered him daily.

On his vacations, Bush was friendly and entertained us at his home on the rocky coast of Kennebunkport, Maine, where he always seemed much more relaxed with his family around him. I think I saw more of the New England Yankee than the son of Texas, but I always saw a personable host.

It was much later that his wife, Barbara, somewhat bitter over her husband's defeat and partially blaming the press for his political demise, came up with a different assessment of us.

In the White House tradition, in November 1992, Mrs. Bush invited Hillary Rodham Clinton to visit her future home. When she arrived at the White House and was welcomed by Mrs. Bush at the diplomatic entrance, the South Lawn was jammed with reporters and photographers witnessing the moment. With a smile, Mrs. Bush gestured to the media horde, looked at Hillary and said, "Avoid this crowd like the plague. And if they quote you, make damn sure they heard you." Hillary nodded and said, "That's right. I know that feeling already."

I hadn't heard such an evaluation since the Carters occupied the White House. Much was being made of their decision to send Amy to public school. The photographers and reporters thronged either side of the door to watch Rosalynn, with Amy by the hand, leave the White House to escort her to her first day of school. Amy took one look at all of us standing there, notebooks and cameras at the ready, looked up at her mother and said, "Mom, do we still have to be nice to them?"

Bush remained friendly to the press until the presidential campaign in 1992, when he seemed to feel he was not getting a fair shake. He had been riding high in the aftermath of the Gulf War with popularity polls as high as 90 percent, and he appeared unbeatable.

At least so thought the heavy hitters of the Democratic Party, who decided to sit out that campaign, leaving a clear field for Arkansas governor Bill Clinton, who sensed a time for a change in the political climate.

I was in Texas with Bush on Election Day 1992, and we did our share of sitting around, waiting for results to update our stories and for the president or one of his aides to stop by. Bush did appear, talked for a bit and then decided to go shopping, and the press pool tagged along.

There was a certain air of resignation about him, although I do not believe he thought he would be defeated. The shopping trip, however, intimated a little more to me. When I saw what he was buying—fishing tackle and CDs by some of his favorite country singers—I thought he looked like a man who was getting ready for retirement.

We stayed with him all day, and by early afternoon, we could see that the exit polls were not looking good. I believe it was excruciating for him and Barbara to go before supporters in Houston that night, because he was and is a very proud man who thought of public service as a duty and an honor. But in political defeat, I always recall Adlai Stevenson's memorable line: "I'm too old to cry and it hurts too much to laugh."

In 1993, jokes were floating around about this new young baby-boomer president and his equally young staff—like people asking me how I was going to paper-train this crew as to the ways of the Washington press corps, and some asked if I was going to get on their good side by bringing them milk and cookies at the daily briefings.

But Bill Clinton and his team had arrived at the White House with a notable, but different, goal: make whatever end runs necessary to avoid the White House press corps.

On his first official day as president he gathered with his newly appointed top staff in what he thought was a private session and told them that he was going to hold televised town meetings, appear on "Larry King Live," and generally do what had to be done to avoid regular contact with those of us who cover the presidency on a daily basis.

What he and his team didn't notice was that a television technician was in the room with them, setting up the electronic paraphernalia in advance of a visit by the press to have a brief question-and-answer about the start of his administration.

The technician was kind enough to relate the contents of the meeting to his colleagues in the pressroom. Well, we knew we were off to a good start.

But let it be said that the White House press corps—"the lions," as Marlin Fitzwater used to call us, or "the beasts," as Dee Dee Myers tagged us—is not without a heart at the beginning of any presidency.

There is what's known as the "honeymoon" period as reporters get to know the chief executive and his team before the policies are announced, the programs are presented. It's a get-acquainted time for both sides and every-one tends to be a little easy on everyone else.

But Clinton and his aides brought with them the same kind of secrecy they had been able to exert in Arkansas in terms of keeping the press at bay and the doors of the campaign headquarters locked. They also brought a group of young staffers completely unschooled in the ways of Washington who couldn't quite leave the campaign trail, and what resulted was utter confusion.

From the first few days he was in office, the corridor we had trodden so often from the pressroom to the press secretary's office was ruled "off-limits" to reporters. The door dividing the briefing room from the office was ordered closed.

In other words, we could not go to the press secretary's office with our private inquiries.

George Stephanopoulos, however, then the communications director, made one slight miscalculation: He permitted the daily briefings to be tele-vised live.

As far as I was concerned, it was news when reporters were being denied access to the press secretary's office, and I made a point of it loud and clear at the start of several briefings—on television. My colleagues backed me up with the complaints. So the door to the press secretary's office got opened again, and along with it access to the corridor leading to the Oval Office.

But another problem cropped up. Rumors began to fly fast and furious that Hillary Rodham Clinton had decided that the pressroom would be handed over to her personal staff and that she was thinking seriously of moving the press corps out of the White House or to another location.

None of that came to pass, and with all due respect, the first lady was not the first to think of removing the press corps from the White House, nor will she likely be the last.

We always have the feeling that they want us at their beck and call—especially when there is good news to transmit—but at the same time often wish we were far, far away.

Clinton himself has run hot and cold toward the press. He takes substantive questions at photo opportunities, and his aides, trying to protect him, often try to cut him off by shouting "thank you" or "lights" to the photographers. After these kinds of sessions, I usually would tell the aide in no uncertain terms, "If the president wants to talk who are you to stop him?"

One of the ironies in this current situation is that, as Dean Rusk once said, "When we're asleep, half the world is making trouble," and sometimes it's been the press that's informed the president about that trouble. I have standing orders with the Washington copy desk at UPI that I am to be called at any time, awakened at any time, interrupted at any time should something happen that warrants my presence at the White House.

Bush had maintained he would have a "wake 'em and shake 'em" presidency, that he would be kept informed of events at all times. When the Ayatollah Khomeini died, Bush was on vacation at his home in Kennebunkport. I was on the early-morning "body watch" as he went jogging, and when he jogged on by, I shouted, "What about Khomeini?"

Bush gave me a quizzical look so I did a follow-up shout: "Dead!"

It seemed his staff hadn't bothered to wake him to deliver the news.

When Leon Panetta joined the Clinton White House as chief of staff in 1993 to bring some order to the chaos, he appeared at a Sperling Breakfast—a Washington event for movers and shakers—and the *Washington Post* reported he used the words "very gloomy, very dire" to describe the mood inside the Executive Mansion.

The morning that story appeared, I was in the press van following Clinton on his morning jog and shouted, "Is it all going down the drain?" Seems his staff hadn't alerted him to the story before he left to go running. Radio personality Rush Limbaugh picked up on that "going down the drain" question and used it for months to harp on Clinton's performance as president.

In the Reagan administration, an Air Force pilot was being detained in Syria, and my office tracked me down to give me the news. I called Larry Speakes and as it turned out, I was giving *him* the news.

And as Jody Powell once said about the painful relationship between the White House press office and the press, "There was some period in my life when I thought you could reason with these people," but he learned otherwise.

It was Easter Sunday and we were in Plains, Georgia, and word reached me that some Soviet trawlers had been spotted off Long Island. The press office had asked us to lay off the hard questions when Carter came out of the church. It was Easter, a holy day, and the president had just spent time in church. I was waiting for Carter to emerge.

"Beautiful weather for this Easter Sunday, Mr. President."
Carter agreed.
"A wonderful service, Mr. Carter?"
Carter agreed.
"Happy Easter, Mr. President."
Carter nodded.
"And what about those Soviet trawlers, Mr. President?"

However, there was one time in recent memory when I wasn't around to give or get the news and when the news did reach me, it was a heart-stopping moment.

I was at the vice president's residence, attending a Halloween party given by Vice President and Mrs. Gore. With me were my nieces Terri DeLeon and Judy Jenkins and their children. Everyone was having a fine time, especially the Gores: the vice president had dressed up as Frankenstein's monster, complete with green makeup and a bolt in his neck, and Tipper was decked out as the pale and mile-high-haired bride of Frankenstein.

As we were leaving, White House aide Mark Gearan came in and mentioned to me that "someone had shot up the White House." Terri and Judy remember the color draining from my face and me fighting to get my composure.

"Oh, my God," I said to Gearan, "is this some kind of joke?"

He assured me it wasn't and I raced for the telephone.

The desk told me that yes, a man had fired a semiautomatic rifle through the White House gates and put a few holes in some windows of the pressroom, but the Secret Service and police had subdued him.

I ran into Gearan a few days later and we were discussing the incident when I commented on the terror I had felt, thinking that the president might have been shot.

"You know," said Gearan, "all I could think about was Al Gore being sworn in as president dressed up like Frankenstein."

I will say that Clinton did become a little more comfortable with us "beasts" in the pressroom compared with his early days in office, and with the able Mike McCurry in charge of the spin every day, it became a less hostile place.

President Kennedy teasing me about playing Jackie in the Women's National Press Club spoof on Washington. *(Kennedy Library)*

Photo op in the Oval Office with President Kennedy in his favorite rocking chair. *(Kennedy Library)*

To Helen Thomas
The girl without a hat
Lyndon B Johnson

Tiptoeing through the tulips with LBJ. *(Johnson Library)*

1971: Pat Nixon "scoops" me and announces my engagement to Doug Cornell at a retirement party for Doug at the White House. We didn't know whether to laugh or cry. *(Nixon Library)*

One of Gary Trudeau's "Doonesbury" comic strips during Watergate.

You don't mean it, President Ford!
(Ford Library)

Florence Lowe, Fran Lewine and I covering a state dinner at
the White House. *(Ford Library)*

To Helen Thomas

Jimmy Carter

On vacation with President Carter in Idaho. *(Carter Center)*

The Carter family attends my sixtieth birthday party in the White House briefing room, which looked a lot classier back then. *(Carter Center)*

My sixtieth birthday gift, a caricature of a reporter's life in the White House. *(Carter Center)*

Partying with the president. *(Carter Center)*

Aboard Air Force One with President Carter and my colleagues Sam Donaldson and Diane Sawyer. *(Carter Center)*

An interview with President Reagan in the Oval Office. *(Reagan Library)*

An interview with Nancy Reagan in the family quarters; we would have an "annual" discussion every year at Christmastime. *(Reagan Library)*

1982: Nancy Reagan brings down the house at the annual Gridiron Dinner with her rendition of "Second Hand Rose." Also pictured is Gridiron president Charlie McDowell. *(Reagan Library)*

Aboard Air Force One with President and Mrs. Bush in the conference room, with reporters Larry McQuillan of Reuters, Jim Miklaszewski of NBC, UPI photographer Joe Marquette and AP's Tom Raum. *(Bush Library)*

President Bush greets Soviet leader Mikhail Gorbachev at the West Wing's diplomatic entrance. *(Bush Library)*

To Helen —

c'mon. This is serious business !!

Warm Regards, Gg Bush

Even a president likes to joke around, and Bush was no exception. *(Bush Library)*

Mrs. Bush at a White House dinner; I'm standing with Donnie Radcliffe of the *Washington Post.* (*Bush Library*)

Lunch with President Bush in the president's private dining room. (*Bush Library*)

My surprise seventy-fifth birthday party in the White House briefing room.
(White House Photo Office)

Vice President Gore interrupts my
birthday gift from President Clinton in
1995: a fifteen-minute one-on-one
interview. Little did I imagine how I
was being set up.
(*White House Photo Office*)

The cake at my seventy-fifth birthday
party. Before we both blew out the
candles, the president asked me,
"Who has more hot air?" Notice he is
still holding my tape recorder that
I left in the Oval Office.
(*White House Photo Office*)

For my friend Helen Thomas with many thanks, Al Gore

A surprise party for Vice President Gore. I couldn't resist asking him a couple of questions, like, "Why are you always praising Clinton?"
(*White House Photo Office*)

For Helen—You're always working! Love, Tipper and Al Gore

A Halloween party at the vice presidential residence. Al Gore as Frankenstein's monster with Tipper as the bride of Frankenstein. That same day, a gunman fired a semiautomatic rifle at the White House. (*White House Photo Office*)

Even the bad days are good! *(White House Photo Office)*

Every president eventually gets used to the "body watch"—in light of the events of 1998, let me say I don't feel comfortable calling it that anymore—the demand for coverage, the reality of living in the public arena where privacy is at a premium and there's news to be written every day.

I've seen President Clinton in moments when he felt free enough to let his personal feelings be known, but moments strung over six years don't add up to a full picture. I remember the genuine grief at the death of his mother—the warm, witty and charming Virginia Kelley. She passed away just as Clinton was readying for a trip to Moscow and several European nations. Clinton went home to Arkansas for the funeral and then came back to Washington to leave for his trip. He was interviewed by Ted Koppel on "Nightline" shortly before he left and Koppel asked him why he didn't speak at Virginia's funeral. "I just thought it was time to be a son," he said.

Then too I recall the flashes of anger.

At a Rose Garden ceremony awhile back, ABC's Brit Hume asked Clinton a question that talked about the "zigzags" on certain issues in his presidency and Clinton snapped, "I have long since given up the thought that I could disabuse some of you of turning any substantive decision into anything but a political process."

The White House has become a much different place, and I suppose presidents, whoever they are, have adjusted to the fact that their public and private lives intertwine whether they like it or not. The hide-and-seek that began with the Kennedys will be the modus operandi from here on out, and presidents undoubtedly feel hide-and-seek turns into search-and-destroy, justifiably or not.

The cycle has turned back to press-bashing for picking on the president the last few years on the issue of privacy. I was a little astounded at all the hoopla that erupted when photos appeared of Clinton and the first lady dancing together on a beach while they were on vacation. I was even more than a little astounded when reporters and photographers asked Mike McCurry if he thought the press had gone too far.

When the official response came down that yes, the Clintons felt their privacy had been invaded—but they liked the pictures—I snapped to McCurry, "If he wants his privacy then he shouldn't be president."

I seemed to be a majority of one on that score. I received a letter from former NBC correspondent Richard Valeriani chastising me for my remark:

Dear Helen:
    Here's a suggestion: Stay away from television.
    You came across as really stupid and arrogant when interviewed by ABC on the Clinton vacation pictures.

When people hear remarks like yours, it's no wonder they hold the media in such low esteem.

Regards,
Dick Valeriani

Well, given the events that began in January 1998 with Monica Lewinsky, the entire issue of privacy and the presidency has gone far beyond a picture taken of two people dancing on a beach. And as far as the media being held in such low esteem, well, it's not like *that* hasn't happened before.

I also recall when Jimmy Carter was first elected and the press pool followed him down to Georgia for the Christmas holidays. There we all were, standing outside the house, with lights, cameras, notebooks and tape recorders at the ready. Carter's son Jeff came out to talk to us and a photographer asked him, "Don't you feel sorry for your dad? The press is always watching, the cameras and lights are everywhere."

"No," said Jeff. "He asked for it."

And despite all the physical changes that have been made for our convenience and comfort, I'll still say there is something to be said for walking the acreage on a Texas ranch at twilight, standing with a president and watching for the deer to come out, and listening to him talk about his hopes and dreams for the country.

SEVEN

". . . And I'd Like a Follow-up"

Every one of the eight presidents I have covered has always looked for a "first" to accomplish in his administration for citation in the history books: first with major legislation, first to put a man on the moon, first with a balanced budget in far too many years, first to open relations with a foreign power. Each one has done so either admirably or ignobly. Richard Nixon was the first to reestablish relations with China; he was also the first president in history to resign.

I've had my share of professional "firsts," and over in the White House pressroom, I can lay claim to another: I have covered the White House on a day-to-day basis longer than any other reporter and I've been there considerably longer than any president. And every president I've covered has been on the business end of a ritual that began with Franklin D. Roosevelt and persists to this day.

The ritual has been modified, expanded, tweaked, tightened and bent every which way depending on the occupant of the Oval Office, but it has been inescapable: the presidential news conference.

They have been brief, they have been interminable, they have been friendly or hostile, amiable or adversarial.

If one credo of journalism holds that you're only as good as your last story, then it might be said of chief executives that they are only as good as their last appearance before the press in a news conference.

Presidents and their staffs may flood the airwaves with speeches, stage hundreds of photo opportunities, make any number of personal appearances, but for me, it is the news conference that takes an important measure of the man in office.

Of the fifty-five years I've spent as a reporter in Washington, thirty-eight of them have been at the White House. I've witnessed some of the great events in history and some of the tragic ones, and I have cherished all those moments as a reporter on the scene.

When it comes to the news conference, I have never lost my sense of awe that I am able to quiz a president of the United States—politely I hope, but if necessary to hold his feet to the fire. The media is the linchpin of our representative democracy and the presidential news conference is the most visible evidence of it.

Columnist Walter Lippmann once said that the presidential news conference, no matter how imperfect, was not a privilege but an organic necessity in a democracy.

Every president probably knows that. But I've yet to encounter one who would admit it. There is no designated time at which the president is held accountable, except when he is facing the press. There is no other forum where the president can be questioned on the issues of the day. His annual State of the Union address, delivered at the beginning of the year, usually outlines his agenda for the coming months, but he doesn't always report back to the nation on the misfires of the previous year—and there are no questions and answers afterward.

And there is no other forum but the news conference where the press can let the president know what the public is thinking.

As reporters, we find ourselves acting as surrogates for all Americans who want to know what's going on—and there is no question that this is also a two-way street. While we're asking the questions for the nation, we're also letting the president know what is on the minds of Americans.

Harry Truman had a singular attitude toward the press. Speaking at the White House Correspondents Association dinner, he told the assembled reporters, "For eight years, you and I have been helping each other. I have been trying to keep you informed of the news from the point of view of the presidency. You, more than you realize, have been giving me a great deal of what the people of this country are thinking about."

If only every president since then would keep that observation in mind. Instead, too many administrations have come into power over the last few decades thinking of the press as an irritant at best, an enemy at worst, and not as representatives who ask the questions on the minds of most Americans.

Today, because of the immediacy of the live TV appearance with the direct quote, the presidency seems hamstrung with governing by polls and turning the chief executive into an actor. And the world is his stage.

Franklin Roosevelt was the first president in modern history to hold regular news conferences. Smitty and Doug would tell me of those sessions, with reporters gathered around FDR's desk in the Oval Office.

While friendly, Roosevelt made it clear he was in command and brooked no challenges from reporters. He was wont to tell a reporter to put on a dunce cap and go stand in the corner if a question riled him, and once, during World War II, he got really annoyed at a columnist for the *New York Daily News* and handed him a Nazi Iron Cross.

And when the questioning got a little too persistent on an issue, FDR would simply say, "There is no news on that today."

One caveat was that despite their close proximity to the president inside his office, reporters were not allowed to quote him directly. His remarks were not for attribution but the "source" quoted in the newspapers was not exactly a mystery.

We in the press have a special role since there is no other institution in our society, short of impeachment by Congress, that can hold the president accountable for his policies and his actions. Presidents can fire up their spin machines and set them on warp drive when disclosures and press reports are less than flattering to their administrations, but the forum of the presidential press conference insists on the people's right to know. It is not prescribed in the Constitution, but the media is sometimes the only check on the power of the presidency.

The presidential news conference can become a courtroom—think of President Nixon and Watergate; President Carter and the Iran hostage crisis; President Reagan on Iran-Contra; President Clinton on the Whitewater land deal, campaign fund-raising practices and his Oval Office affair with former White House intern Monica Lewinsky—one witness being bombarded with questions from about sixty hostile prosecutors. The questions can become more penetrating, the atmosphere can become intense, extreme and bitter. So can the answers.

While the presidential news conference gives the media that rare chance to go on the offensive and question the president as if he were in the dock, the press has some points against it going in: If the president is enjoying a wave of popularity, the public weighs in with antimedia telephone calls, cards and letters expressing its displeasure. They like the president and they don't like watching reporters intimidating him or asking him those tough questions—that shows a lack of respect.

I heard remarks to that effect when I was on the road with Johnson as Vietnam got uglier, the nation was being torn apart and it seemed as if no answer was in sight or was ever going to be. Emotion ran high on both sides.

People would ask me why I didn't do more to persuade the president to end the war and one man came up to me one day and snarled, "Why don't you write the truth?"

After the Watergate scandal unraveled and Nixon resigned, the media star was on the ascendant for a while. In the days of independent counsel Kenneth Starr, it took a few dips and a couple of nosedives.

But I've always believed that the people can handle the truth, no matter how unpalatable it may sometimes be.

In recent times, presidential news conferences have become the bitter medicine chief executives have to take now and then, so presidents and their staffs have taken great pains to make them as useful to their administrations as possible. Sometimes that works. Sometimes it doesn't.

In our modern era of news management, I've always been amused to hear presidential candidates on the campaign trail promise an "open administration." It seems that promise gets packed away with the victory banners and the inauguration party favors. Once they have the key to the front door at 1600 Pennsylvania Avenue, the "open administration" gets put under lock and key—like the documents, papers, tapes and other important information pertaining to their presidencies.

It sometimes seems a work order to paint a particular room a particular color would be stamped "top secret."

Because of all of this, the need for the presidential news conference in this day and age is more vital than ever before.

All presidents hope to put their stamps on the pages of history, and their personas come through best in news conferences. They can prepare, they can rehearse, and they can come in with a seating chart in order to recognize who is sitting where. They can and do decide on whom to call.

But when it's time to stand behind that podium in the East Room, a president is on his own. Sometimes, all the preparation, all the homework, all the rehearsals fly out the window when a question comes whistling in that nobody—president or staff—prepared for. At those times, the public gains a better picture of the man they voted for—or didn't. Many presidents have attested to their devotion to freedom of the press, but sometimes their actions have proved otherwise.

Following the invasion of Grenada, President Reagan visited the island, and at a reception for the reporters and photographers accompanying him, he spoke of Thomas Jefferson's ideals regarding the need for a free press. But when reminded that he had conducted the invasion in secrecy and that reporters and photographers were barred from the island for about ten days until the operation was completed, Reagan said Jefferson was "wrong."

With rare exception, I don't think any president has ever really liked the press. As I once remarked to Jody Powell that I thought President Carter didn't like us very much, he responded, "Helen, what rational human being in his right mind *would* like reporters?"

But most have tolerated us doing our jobs on the round-the-clock "body watch," and some over the years have had their own take on what we do:

Franklin Roosevelt once signed a photograph for reporters and photographers who covered him "from your devoted victim."

Harry Truman once said, "When the press stops abusing me, I'll know I'm in the wrong pew."

John Kennedy said of the coverage, "I'm reading more and enjoying it less."

What Lyndon Johnson said was colorful but unprintable.

Richard Nixon, who kept the now-famous "enemies list" that included names of reporters, once looked up when reporters and photographers bounded into the Cabinet Room and remarked, "It's only coincidental that we're talking about pollution when the press walks in."

Jimmy Carter always seemed to be implying if not saying outright, "Lord forgive them for they know not what they do."

And when the Sandinistas fired on a press helicopter at the Honduran border, Ronald Reagan remarked, "There's some good in everyone."

After he left office, George Bush remarked, "When I was in the White House, I believed in freedom of the press. Now I believe in freedom from the press."

When President Clinton was asked by a friend why the press always followed in the motorcade when he went jogging, he laughed and said, "They just want to see if I drop dead." (That's true.)

The relationship between the president and the press at news conferences began changing into what we see on television today during the Truman administration, largely because of the advent of television itself.

Before television, the dozen or so reporters would meet with the president in his office, take notes and after the news conference was over, race for the available telephones to call their copy desks and dictate their stories. If the president made an especially newsworthy announcement, the competition to be the first one with the story turned the scramble for telephones into a combination footrace and wrestling match, with reporters in the lead fighting off reporters behind them.

Once, the competition between Doug and Smitty turned almost comical: The White House had released copies of a statement from the president and the two of them ran to the bin and started grabbing. Unfortunately, when they grabbed all the statements at the same time, they ended up tearing them in two. No matter: They bolted for the telephones and began dictating from their respective torn pieces of paper and looking over their respective shoulders to try to see what the other half of the announcement said.

The immediacy of television precludes such rough-and-tumble angling. These days, the copy desks of various media outlets will sit and write what is known as the "running story" directly off the television while we White House reporters are in the briefing room asking the questions. When the news conference is over, we can return to our desks and take a few extra minutes writing a new version of the "running story" that wraps all the details and gives more perspective on what occurred.

With the advent of television, the Truman administration began restructuring the press conference to give the president more control: Truman began meeting with his advisers beforehand to prepare for any question that might be asked; he began each session with a prepared statement; and he would refer reporters back to a point in his opening statement if the questioning got touchy.

As the number of members of the press corps grew, the site of the press conferences moved from the Oval Office to a 230-seat room in the Indian Treaty Room of the Old Executive Office Building. The change of location gave the sessions a more formal air.

Truman also began the practice of having reporters identify themselves before asking a question and the entire session was captured on film. In recent history, presidents have called on reporters by name. The net effect: The press conference turned into a public event and, in turn, created the need for a president to exercise more control over that event, to come to the press conference more prepared and to answer reporters' questions more carefully.

And they usually have a good idea of what kinds of questions are going to be asked. The wire services and the networks will go for the hard news questions on the pressing issues of the day, but as the session wears on, the questions will become more esoteric.

President Eisenhower didn't like having news conferences but, like Roosevelt, he held them an average of twice a week. He also allowed his news conferences to be filmed and, with that, instituted two new practices: He allowed the media to quote him directly in news stories and for the filmed news conferences to be used afterward on network broadcasts.

These two new privileges, however, were not without a price. All material had to be cleared first by his press secretary James Hagerty—a former newspaperman who was respected by the press corps and whom many acknowledge as the best press secretary ever—who reviewed them more to clean up his boss's syntax than to do any wholesale editing. Eisenhower often thought faster than he talked and as a result would leave out parts of sentences.

Kennedy, the first president I covered on a daily basis—and the first to permit his news conferences to be televised live—was witty and disarming. Those sessions were held then in the huge State Department auditorium, several blocks from the White House. Kennedy clearly understood the power of television but he also clearly enjoyed the give-and-take and the sometime sparring that went on with the newsmen and -women who covered him.

In July 1963 a reporter asked him, "The Republican National Committee recently adopted a resolution saying you are pretty much a failure. How do you feel about that?"

"I assume it passed unanimously," Kennedy responded.

I remember when it first fell to me to close one of his news conferences—becoming the first woman to do so—when Smitty was out of town. It marked my national television debut as well and I was anxious about the timing.

After what I thought was an appropriate time, I stood up and said, "Thank you, Mr. President," only to be drowned out by the rest of the press corps seeking recognition. Terror overcame me: I was about to lose my moment—and how would I explain this to Smitty?

So I waited a few minutes more, and as luck would have it, Kennedy was struggling with a complicated question. I shouted, "Mr. President!" and when Kennedy looked my way, I said emphatically, "Thank you." With a large smile of relief he replied, "Thank you, Helen."

Pierre Salinger said that when Kennedy prepared for a news conference, his aides could predict 90 percent of the questions. But the questions from women reporters sometimes stumped him.

When the venerable May Craig, then a fixture on NBC-TV's "Meet the Press," asked Kennedy what he had done for women lately, he grinned and said, "Well, obviously, Miss Craig, not enough."

Lyndon Johnson was never comfortable with televised news conferences. He preferred to gather privately, and with only a few moments' notice, for on- or off-the-record sessions with reporters in the Oval Office, the family quarters, aboard Air Force One or bring them down to his Texas ranch—places where he was in charge and could ramble on.

He also liked to stroll the South Lawn at the White House, and those of us in the press corps who covered him will never forget those grueling walks in the hot sun, which we dubbed the "walkie-talkies," or the "Bataan death marches," especially we women who wore the pointy-toed high-heeled shoes in fashion at the time. We had a few casualties on those "death marches." Peter Lisagor of the *Chicago Daily News* was following along and taking notes and didn't notice the cast-iron lamp pole directly in his path until it was too late. LBJ gave him a campaign button as a Purple Heart.

Johnson's first press secretary, George Reedy, suffered from a condition known as hammertoes and wouldn't walk with us, but that didn't stop him from standing outside at the diplomatic entrance and watching us as we made our daily series of fifteen or more laps around the White House. He did not look unhappy to be missing the stroll.

In those sessions we were at Johnson's mercy. He could speak to whom he liked, ignore whom he didn't or cut off whoever had earned his ire that particular day for writing something he considered uncomplimentary. No matter the setting, Johnson read his press coverage daily and granted the favor of an answer as he saw fit.

He finally abandoned the death marches in early 1965, complaining there were too many "leaks" of his remarks and too many complaints from reporters who weren't able to hear him in the first place.

Like FDR, when he did hold a press conference, Johnson preferred to do so in the Oval Office and often on the spur of the moment. Most of all, he loved the element of surprise, and televised news conferences didn't fit that equation.

"When I have something to say, I'll announce it," he used to say.

While Kennedy used the prearranged televised news conference to solidify his appeal to the American people, perhaps the best example of the disdain that Johnson had for the format was a story he told some members of the White House press corps about a televised news conference that had been arranged for him.

There must have been some miscommunication somewhere along the chain of command because the event was to be a full-blown, live televised news conference, but Johnson was under the impression he only had to go over to tape three statements that would air later.

"Someone ran in all out of breath, and said 'Mr. President, Mr. President, you're late,' " he told us. "And I said 'Late for what, I'm not on any time schedule.' And he said, 'But it's on live TV and they're having a fit.' And I said, 'Well let them. Goddamn it, I'm the president of the United States and who the hell told them to put it on live television anyway?' So I finished what I was doing, and I went over there and I guess I was a half-hour late but I walked a little fast and I was even a little out of breath when I got there."

President Nixon disdained the podium most presidents use at news conferences, preferring a stand-up microphone. When he did hold a news conference, like many of his predecessors and successors, he did his homework. He would study briefing papers and have his staff quiz him on potential questions and answers.

I still wonder, though, whether he practiced for his first news conference as president in 1969. I got the first question and asked him to elaborate on his peace plan to bring the Vietnam War to an end, which had been one of his major campaign agendas. He said his strategy was to leave Vietnam "in an honorable way" but none of the details were forthcoming. I would ask that question every which way I could but it took me a long time to get a straight answer. It was Vietnamization: turn the war over to the South Vietnamese and steal away.

Nixon did tell me once, "You always ask tough questions, tough questions not in the sense of being unfair, but hard to generalize the answers."

Maybe that's why it took so long to get an answer from him about Vietnam.

I did get one answer to one question about Vietnam that, in retrospect, probably lasted a good five minutes. On Thursday, April 29, 1971, this was my question:

> In view of the antiwar demonstrations or the growing congressional demand for withdrawal from Vietnam, and the latest statements in Paris, will this influence in any way your Indochina policy?

I took out a ruler and measured the newspaper column inch my question took up—one inch.

Nixon's answer began:

> Miss Thomas, as I stated my Indochina policy at considerable length on April 7, as you will recall, and I have considered all of the demonstrations and I have considered also the arguments made by others after that statement, I believe that the position I took then is the correct one.
>
> I would not want to leave the impression that those who came to demonstrate were not listened to. It is rather hard not to hear them, as a matter of fact. I would say that demonstrators have come to Washington previously about the war. They came now. I was glad to note that in this case most of the demonstrators were peaceful. They indicated they wanted to end the war now, that they wanted peace. That, of course, is what I want. It is what everybody in this room wants and it is what everybody in this nation wants....[1]

That part of Nixon's answer measured about three and a half inches. The rest of it went on for another ten.

I will say that Nixon was more than a match for reporters at news conferences—prepared and always wanting to prevail as the coolest guy in the room. He managed to pull it off until the Watergate scandal began to unravel. After that, his news conferences began to take on an even more heated courtroom atmosphere, with reporters relentlessly cross-examining him. During one, he became so agitated he walked off in a huff before the formal "thank you" was delivered.

For me, the most excruciating news conference, and the lowest point ever between the president and the press in such a venue, occurred on October 26, 1973. It was televised from the East Room, and came on the heels of the "Saturday Night Massacre," when Nixon fired Watergate special prosecutor Archibald Cox, who had filed suit to get the Watergate tapes. The firing led to the resignations of Attorney General Elliott Richardson and Deputy Attorney General William Ruckelshaus. The action had created a firestorm of public anger and talk of impeachment filled the air.

At his news conference, Nixon opened with a statement about peacemaking efforts in the Middle East, but the barrage of questions all had to do with Watergate.

Dan Rather of CBS News asked, "Mr. President, I wonder if you could share with us your thoughts, tell us what goes through your mind when you hear people who love this country and people who believe in you say reluctantly that perhaps you should resign or be impeached."

"Well," Nixon responded with a tight smile, "I'm glad we don't take the vote of this room, let me say."

He later went on to a lengthy diatribe about biased reporting, especially by the electronic media, when Robert Pierpont of CBS stood to be recognized.

Nixon ignored him at first, answered several other questions and then called on Pierpont:

> Pierpont: Mr. President, you have lambasted the television networks pretty well. What is it about television coverage of you in these past weeks and months that has so aroused your anger?
> Nixon: Don't get the impression that you arouse my anger.
> Pierpont: I'm afraid, sir, that I have that impression.
> Nixon: You see, one can only be angry with those he respects.

In 1974, as Watergate kept raining down on Nixon, he began a news conference by congratulating me on being named UPI's White House bureau chief. He noted that "This is tremendous, the first time in history a woman has been singled out for that post."

I think I thanked him; I hope I did. But I had come to the news conference armed with a tough question and I thought, "How is this going to look to the public asking this very tough, very rude question? They're going to think 'what an awful person.'" Then I thought of my peers saying, "flattery will get you everywhere."

So after he had been so gracious, he pointed to me for the first question.

"Mr. President," I said, "Mr. Haldeman, your former top aide in the White House, has been charged with perjury because he testified you said it would be wrong to pay hush money to silence the Watergate defendants...."

But it's like I say to young people who ask me about going into journalism: If you want to be loved, don't go into this business.

There was one time with Nixon, though, that not asking a question sufficed. We were in San Clemente in the final dark days of his presidency and his staff decided to cheer him up with a birthday cake. I was the designated pool reporter in Nixon's office when they rolled the cake in.

Nixon stood up and leaned over to read the inscription on the cake; when he stood back I noticed that icing had smeared all over his maroon blazer. I came back out to describe the scene to the pool reporters and as Tom Brokaw wrote to me in a note years later, "I will never forget you describing for us, through tears of laughter, the utterly Nixon moment ... [when] his faithful Irish setter, King Timahoe, approached and as cameras rolled, proceeded to lick away at his master's jacket as Nixon stood there with that frozen grin on his face.... I believe it was the first time you were in a president's office without asking a question. There was nothing more to be said."[2]

Following Nixon's resignation, Gerald Ford was like a living armistice when it came to dealing with the press. He was more at ease with reporters and seemed to actually enjoy himself at news conferences.

Ford even believed in the personal touch. In March 1975, I asked him the opening question at a news conference and he congratulated me for becoming the first woman member to be inducted into the Gridiron Club.

After a momentary digression, I said, "Thank you, Mr. President. Now in response to my question ..."

The questions I ask have come to be known as the "multiparter." For example, at a Bush news conference in 1992, I asked, "Mr. President, are you going to go for a middle income tax cut and are you going to cut the Pentagon budget by $80 billion and are you going to break the budget agreement—and I'd like a follow-up ..."

Bush's eyes got a little wide but he was quick: "Helen, you have six days to wait for the answers to all those questions."

News conference protocol calls for the first question to be asked by either UPI or AP on a rotating basis. Over the years, I've noticed that when I stand up first, the body language has told me a lot: there was the "Carter wince," the "Reagan crouch" and the Bush "Oh no! Not Helen!"

Ford's first news conference after Nixon's resignation was held twenty days after he'd taken the oath of office. He held a dress rehearsal before the official event, and spent about ten hours in study and preparation. His staff decided that rather than have him appear before the presidential drapes as Nixon had done, he should speak to the press corps before an open door in the East Room, giving the impression of an easier, less-hostile atmosphere than the one that had permeated the place during Watergate.

As Ford and his staff anticipated, the press conference began with my question about what might be in store for Nixon.

"Mr. President," I asked, "do you agree with Governor Rockefeller that former President Nixon should have immunity from prosecution? And specifically, would you use your pardon authority if necessary?"

He said he would not act until the judicial process had been followed. Eleven days later, he granted a "a full, free and absolute pardon unto Richard Nixon for all offenses against the United States which he has . . . or may have committed."

At a news conference on September 26, I asked him, "Throughout your vice presidency you said that you didn't believe that President Nixon had committed an impeachable offense. Is that still your belief or do you believe that his acceptance of a pardon implies his guilt or is an admission of guilt?"

Ford replied, "The fact that thirty-eight members of the House Committee on the Judiciary, Democrats and Republicans, have unanimously agreed on the report that was filed that the former president was guilty of an impeachable offense, I think is very persuasive evidence."

So I repeated: "Was the acceptance of the pardon by the former president an admission of guilt?"

"Acceptance of a pardon, I think, can be construed by many if not all as an admission of guilt," Ford replied.

President Carter was always well prepared before he faced the press and came to the podium with facts and figures at his fingertips. What got left outside, sadly, was his sense of humor, and the seriousness of his demeanor made for lackluster sessions.

One of the more painful sessions I witnessed with Carter ran for more than an hour as he defended his brother Billy, who had been accused of questionable ties to the Libyan government.

Billy had accepted an invitation to go to Tripoli with a group of Georgia businessmen as the guest of Libyan leader Muammar al-Qaddafi and he later acted as host when a Libyan trade delegation arrived in Atlanta.

Thomas Jordan, an Atlanta real estate developer, said he had set up the trip because Qaddafi was seeking to invest in U.S. businesses. "I was told that the wealth of the Libyan state would be at my fingertips if I would deliver the younger brother of the president of the United States to Tripoli, so I delivered him," Jordan said.

The Justice Department later asked Billy to register as a foreign agent and at his brother's urging, he did, but he always maintained his connection with Libya was personal.

At the news conference, Carter stood his ground but, as with Nixon at the end of his administration, the sight of a president on the defensive is a painful one.

When the economy began faltering in 1977, Carter asked Congress for an income tax cut, which it approved, reducing income taxes by about $35 billion over a three-year period, mostly for low-income families. But the economy continued to spiral downward and Carter asked for another tax cut of about $25 billion. The bill got bogged down but Congress eventually passed an $18.7 billion tax-reduction measure. However, with double-digit inflation and a recession in the making, things were not looking good for Carter.

At a news conference I asked, "Was it worth it to you to cause some destabilization of the dollar and demoralization of the federal government, spreading doubt through much of the land in order to repudiate your cabinet?"

Years later, Sam Donaldson still remembered that question, and at a dinner he remarked, "You know, if he'd just hung his head and answered 'yes,' he probably would have been reelected."

In the Reagan administration, news conferences took on an even more formal and controlled ambience. They were full-dress affairs and televised during prime time. Reagan prepared for them as if he were getting ready to defend his Ph.D. dissertation, reading briefing books the size of the Yellow Pages that contained probable questions and proposed answers.

Reagan's team also made it clear to us that the news conference was the only allowed venue in which to ask questions and spared no effort to shut us down at photo opportunities in the Oval Office.

In August 1981 there was a "photo op" at 10:45 A.M. in the Oval Office with Reagan and Egyptian president Anwar Sadat. The meeting was important but so was a certain incident going on in the country: The nation's air traffic controllers had gone on strike and Reagan had imposed an 11:00 A.M. deadline for them to go back to work or be fired. With fifteen minutes to go, we all wanted to know what he was going to do. So I popped the question about the deadline and Reagan murmured, "Just you wait."

His staff had a fit. A written notice later went up warning reporters not to ask any questions during "photo ops" with heads of state and it went on to discourage asking questions at any photo opportunity. The word also was passed that reporters would be barred from photo opportunities if we ever tried it again. The notice later came down after, I suppose, they thought about the stories that would be written about that.

He also rehearsed in the White House theater. Members of the staff stood in for reporters, playing their parts as well. I always had the impression that when Reagan got an uncomfortable look on his face, the question had veered away from the briefing book.

But leave it to reporters with a taste for irreverence to spoof the formality Reagan's staff tried so mightily to maintain.

The president once remarked that he also liked the color red—his wife's favorite—and added that reporters stood a better chance of getting called on if they wore that color. At the next news conference, television cameras showed rows and rows of reporters sitting in chairs sporting red dresses, red ties, red sweaters, red vests, red jackets—one woman even donned a red mitten when she raised her hand to ask a question.

Reagan went along with the gag and even complimented a few on their attire, but he did protest later that there were many other colors he liked as well. To this day, when I make a speaking appearance, someone will ask me, "Where is that red dress?"

During prime-time news conferences I would wear two wristwatches to time them to thirty minutes, the allotted news conference time limit under an agreement between the White House and the television networks. I created a few temporary enemies under this setup when I would rise to say, "Thank you, Mr. President," leaving some reporters out in the cold, their questions unasked.

I vividly remember one news conference in Reagan's second term when all the questions save one dealt with the U.S. naval buildup in the Caribbean and all speculation was on a possible invasion of Nicaragua.

Reagan was bobbing, weaving and feinting right and left to avoid directly answering most of the questions—to paraphrase that old saying, if it wasn't for the honor of the thing he probably would have preferred to be in Philadelphia.

Twenty-five minutes into the news conference, a perspiring Reagan glanced my way and the look in his eyes seemed to say, "Can't we cut this off?"

I checked my watches, looked up and shook my head. When the half-hour was over I gave the traditional closing, but it struck me: For five minutes I'd had power over the president. I don't think he ever held it against me.

At another news conference, Reagan had spoken at length on the importance of tithing part of one's income to church and giving to charity. I stood up to signal the end and was about to give the traditional "thank you" when columnist Mary McGrory stood up as well. Reagan said he would take her question before wrapping up the session.

McGrory then asked him how much he tithed to his church. Reagan looked at me and quipped, "I should have taken your advice."

While the Iran-Contra story raged, Reagan's news conferences bordered on the surreal. At one of them, *Washington Times* reporter Jerry O'Leary, a former Marine colonel, found himself not asking a question but explaining to Reagan the finer points of military ordnance—that is, exactly how the TOW missiles that had been secretly shipped to Iran were fired.

Other times, Reagan's aides would scurry around the pressroom after a news conference telling reporters, "What he meant to say was ..."

A couple of news conferences, though, put even "the great communicator" on the defensive. President Reagan had enjoyed a high quotient of credibility through most of his administration, but it almost came crashing down in 1986. On October 5, a military cargo plane was shot down by the Sandinistas in Nicaragua. The plane had been carrying arms for the Contra rebels. Documents found in the plane and a statement from Eugene Hasenfus, a mercenary from Wisconsin who was captured, unleashed a storm of headlines detailing a secret supply network that had been set up to circumvent Congress at a time when supplying military aid to the Contras was against U.S. law.

The White House denied any connection but later news reports told how the Reagan administration had been secretly selling arms to Iran in exchange for hostages and how those profits were funneled to the Contras.

Months later it was disclosed that Reagan had conducted a meeting on November 10 and told everyone assembled "don't talk specifics" about the arms shipments. The president and his aides tried to repair the damage but the public was outraged. Polls showed that the people no longer believed Reagan was telling the truth, and on November 19, he tried to defend his decision. It was, to my estimation, one of the toughest, most critical crossexaminations of his years in office.

Reporters at every turn accused Reagan of duplicity, challenged his credibility and shattered his composure. I began by bluntly asking Reagan to "assess the credibility of your administration, in light of the prolonged deception of Congress and the public, in terms of your secret dealings with Iran, the disinformation (Libya), the trading of [Soviet spy Gennady] Zakharov for [*U.S. News & World Report* correspondent Nicholas] Daniloff..."

Reagan denied any loss of credibility, but Sam Donaldson then asked Reagan if he could "justify this duplicity."

"Sir, if I may," Donaldson began, "polls show that Americans don't believe you. Your credibility has been severely damaged. That the one thing you've had going for you more than anything else—your credibility—has been severely damaged. Can you repair it? What does this mean for the rest of your presidency?"

"Well," Reagan responded, "I imagine I'm the only one here who wants to repair it and I didn't have anything to do with damaging it."

Six days later, Attorney General Edwin Meese came into the pressroom to announce that profits from the arms sales had been diverted to the Contras.

A special prosecutor was appointed, select investigating committees in the House and Senate began joint hearings on May 25, 1987, and for a while, press and public attention refocused on that familiar question from Watergate: What did the president know and when did he know it? People later began to make jokes about that phrase, turning it into "What did the president forget and when did he forget it?"

On March 19, 1987, there was an ominous but electric atmosphere in the East Room as we gathered for another news conference. The weekend before, Reagan had huddled with his team at Camp David, going over a few volumes of talking points. After that he held an intensive rehearsal with his staff in the White House theater.

I began the questioning with, "Mr. President, there have been reports that you were told, directly or indirectly, at least twice, that the Contras were benefiting from the Iran arms sales. Is that true or were you deceived and lied to by Admiral [John] Poindexter and Colonel [Oliver] North? And I'd like a follow-up."

Reagan answered that as soon as he discovered the diversion of arms sales profits to the Contras, he'd told the American people and the Congress.

"Mr. President," I said, "is it possible that two military officers who are trained to obey orders grabbed power, made major foreign policy moves, didn't tell you when you were briefed every day on intelligence? Or did they think they were doing your bidding?"

"Helen," he began, "I don't know. I only know that that's why I have said repeatedly that I want to find out, I want to get to the bottom of this and find out all that has happened. And so far, I've told you all that I know and, you know, the truth of the matter is, for quite some time, all that you know was what I'd told you."

Later on Sam Donaldson weighed in: "Sir, Robert McFarlane, who was then your national security adviser, says that in August of 1985, he called you on the telephone and asked if you wanted to give the green light to Israel to send arms to Iran and have them replenished from U.S. stocks, and then you said you did. And he said that he reminded you in that conversation that your secretaries of state and defense were against it and you said you understood it, but you explained to him the reasons why you wanted to authorize it. Do you have no memory of that, whatsoever?"

Reagan said he could recall the authorization but he just didn't remember when.

I said, "Thank you," but then I moved toward the podium and said, "Mr. President, you didn't answer my question."

Reagan began heading toward the double doors and beat a retreat. But I should not have been surprised. Not getting answers was par for the course.

After "Black Monday," October 19, 1987, with the trade deficit soaring and the United States turning into the world's largest debtor nation, I asked him, "How high does unemployment have to go and how much of the economy has to deteriorate before you are willing to accept cuts in the defense budget?"

I must say, Reagan breezed through it all. The public debt skyrocketed, the savings rate plummeted and "Reaganomics" left the country in hock up to its eyeballs, but most of the letters I got around that time accused me of unfairly "picking on the president."

President Bush's syntax at news conferences could best be described as freewheeling. He spoke in fractured sentences, convoluted images and sometimes a language without verbs. Even he used to joke now and then that "some say English is my only foreign language." That pattern seemed to be set at his first news conference as president-elect in 1988, when he announced that Marlin Fitzwater, who had served as acting press secretary in the Reagan administration, had agreed to serve as press secretary in the Bush administration.

In the briefing room, Bush was asked why he didn't name someone new since Fitzwater "represents the Reagan administration."

"He represents the old and the new," Bush responded. "He represents the Reagan administration, he also represents the Bush administration. He's one of the two who bridged that very important breach, you might say.

"He's done . . . he'll do well. See, he worked for me and we'll have lots of changes, as I've said. So this is continuity in the best sense."

It turned out that Fitzwater, as spokesman for both administrations, was of the highest order.

Sometimes the short quick jab works better than the steady counterpunch. I have asked simple questions from time to time. The Berlin Wall had fallen, the Soviet Union had collapsed and communism was disappearing in Europe. Bush came into the pressroom to announce his defense budget, which ran close to $290 billion, the same figure as the year before.

"Who's the enemy?" I asked Bush.

"What?" he said, a little taken aback.

"Who's the enemy?"

"Insecurity and instability."

I was a little befuddled at a news conference with Bush on February 5, 1991, during the Gulf War and what he considered a complicated versus simple question—and a simple answer:

> HT: Mr. President, I think you showed today that you are little disturbed that people might think the goals have changed. But you don't deny, do you, that in addition to driving the Iraqis out of Kuwait there is a sort of systematic destruction of the infrastructure, the essentials of daily living in Iraq? I mean, and that maybe—
>
> GB: No that's not what we're doing. No, we are not trying to systematically destroy the functions of daily living in Iraq. That's not what we're trying to do—or are we doing it.
>
> HT: No water, no electricity, no fuel.
>
> GB: Well, I would say that our effort, our main goal, is to get this man to comply with the resolutions. But we are not trying to systematically destroy the infrastructure or to destroy Iraq. For example, I can tell you about—on targeting petroleum resources, we're not trying to wipe out all their ability to produce oil. We're not trying to wipe out all their ability to refine oil. We are trying to wipe out and keep them from resupplying their military machine.
>
> HT: May I follow up?
>
> GB: Yes.
>
> HT: You say everything is on schedule, on course. What is your schedule for ending this war?
>
> GB: Well, we'll just have to wait and see, Helen. That's a very complicated question.

I will say that Bush could start out succinct and to the point when he wanted. On November 6, 1991, after he had canceled a trip to Asia, I asked him:

> HT: Mr. President, there is a feeling that it's panic time at the White House and that you can't—that you have canceled your Asian tour because you are afraid of the voters, the people getting more and more resentful of your foreign travels and having no real solutions to the problems of joblessness and so forth. What is your response?
>
> GB: My response is, that's crazy. I'll be honest with you, I had thought that when this trip was scheduled for the end of November that definitely the Congress would be out of session. The Congress had

a target date; I think it was for November 4 or November 2. We've passed that date. It's not surprising. But, nevertheless, that was the date that was announced at the time this trip was set. But I think it is prudent, to use an overworked word, to be around here when the Congress is still in session and especially when you get down to that year-end crunch where a lot of crazy things can happen.

When the "Monica situation" broke in January 1998, it touched off one of the most incredible series of leaks, lying, stonewalling and obfuscation I've ever seen. In any case, I did get a chance to ask Clinton one question on February 6:

> HT: Mr. President, despite the ongoing investigation, you've felt no constraint in saying what your relationship with Monica Lewinsky is not, was not. So it seems by logic that you ought to be able to say here and now, what was your relationship? Her lawyer says—call it "colleagues"— is that an apt description?
>
> BC: Well, let me first of all say, once again, I never asked anybody to do anything but tell the truth. I know about the stories today. I was pleased that Ms. Currie's [White House secretary Betty Currie] lawyers stated unambiguously this morning—unambiguously—that she's not aware of any unethical conduct.
>
> But this investigation is going on, and you know what the rules for it are. And I just think as long as it is going on, I should not comment on a specific question, because there's one, then there's another, then there's another. It's better to let the investigation go on and have me do my job and focus on my public responsibilities, and let this thing play out its course. That's what I think I should do, and that's what I intend to do.

Well, the mail that week was plentiful, and most of the letters read like these:

> Miss Thomas: . . . Instead of asking about world affairs your first question to the president was about his sex life. Shame on you. . . .

> Dear Helen Thomas: I watched the press conference with Tony Blair and President Clinton and could not believe it when you asked the president about the Lewinski [sic] girl! Here we are in a serious situation with Iran and you lead off with a question about Lewinski. Absolutely amazing. It certainly is proof that you and all the other media have one thing on your minds and that is to humiliate and

embarrass the president in every way you can. . . . There are plenty more important things going on in the world today which need coverage by the media so why don't you all take a deep breath and back off from the situation with Clinton? I truly feel the media have acted in a disgraceful, unprofessional and unethical manner ever since this started. I hope President Clinton keeps quiet. . . .

I believed then—and I still do—that I asked a valid question, especially when subsequent events led to an impeachment inquiry, and eventually, the first impeachment of a president since 1868.

In another case of simple questions might be best, I remember a December 1970 end-of-year news conference with Nixon. On November 21, a joint task force had landed twenty miles from Hanoi to find and rescue American POWs, and as a cover for the raid, Nixon had ordered a two-day bombing offensive, with some of the bombers ranging more than two hundred miles north of the Demilitarized Zone. It signaled that U.S. policy of not bombing North Vietnam might be changing, so I asked Nixon, "What is our policy?" Simple, yes, but it netted quite an answer—an explicit threat to Hanoi:

> At a time when we are withdrawing from South Vietnam, it is vitally important that the president . . . take the action that is necessary to protect our remaining forces. . . . If the North Vietnamese, by their infiltration, threaten our remaining forces . . . then I will order the bombing of military sites in North Vietnam, the passes that lead from North Vietnam into South Vietnam, the military complexes, the military supply lines. That will be the reaction that I shall take.

I suppose, after all that time, that was my answer to my often-asked question about his peace plan to end the Vietnam War.

The tradition of giving the wire services the first question sometimes even extends to trips overseas or for visits from heads of state to America. I'm sure Boris Yeltsin once wished that the tradition had not been so honored.

We were in Moscow in 1993, and perhaps in hopes of emulating the give and take of presidential news conferences—and to show his openness with the press—Yeltsin gave me the first question at his joint news conference with President Clinton.

I was a little surprised, but quickly went into my familiar routine.

"Thank you, President Yeltsin," I began. "When are you going to get out of the Baltics?"

He was being gracious; I was being a reporter. And he did say there would be a pullout. But I wondered whether he thought I was rude.

And I'll admit my diplomatic skills could use some polishing. But when a reporter has a chance to ask a question, I think he or she should ask it, no matter where, no matter when. British prime minister Margaret Thatcher thought otherwise—twice.

At the Tokyo Economic Summit in 1986, I tried to ask a question when President Reagan and Thatcher were at an official reception. I asked Reagan about some small bombs thrown at the embassy at the start of the visit to Japan. Protective of the president, Thatcher brushed me off with a wave of her hand and said, "I'll take the question."

"My, but we're feeling our oats today, aren't we?" I said to her.

She blinked. "Oats? Oats?" she said, then turned to her aide and asked him what the American colloquialism meant.

A few years later, President Bush met with the prime minister in London and, as usual, I was staking out the meeting with the rest of the press pool. When Thatcher and Bush came outside, Britain's "Iron Lady" saw me standing there. I think I saw a bit of that steely resolve quiver, just a bit.

"Oh, no," said Thatcher, ducking her head, "it's *that woman* again."

I remember one other matchup with Thatcher, and that one could best be termed a draw. She and Bush were in Paris, having lunch at the U.S. embassy, and on their way in, I of course tried to get in a question. Thatcher looked at me and said, "We don't take questions at lunch."

After their lunch, Bush and Thatcher took a walk through the garden; again the press pool was cordoned off and, again, she saw me. As they came toward us, I waved her off, saying, "No questions," the same way she'd done to me.

Some reporters from the British press who were in the pool with me when that happened called me a few months after that incident. They just wanted me to know they dined out on that story for weeks.

Yeltsin got a chance to turn the tables on the press and give it a taste of its own medicine in one of the funniest of news conferences. It was October 23, 1995, in Hyde Park, New York.

Clinton and Yeltsin agreed to talk to reporters after their mini-summit, a meeting that the media had been harping about for days, predicting failure upon failure in headline after headline. "Dear ladies and gentlemen, dear journalists," Yeltsin began, warming up the crowd.

> I want to say first of all that when I came here to the United States, at the invitation of Bill Clinton, I did not at that time have the degree of optimism which I have now on departing.
>
> And this is all due to you because coming from my statement yesterday at the United Nations and if you looked at the press reports, one

could see that what you were writing was that today's meeting with Bill Clinton was going to be a disaster.

Well, now for the first time, I can tell you that you are a disaster.

Clinton got hysterical, the reporters broke up and Yeltsin smiled broadly. Touché.

So while their irritation level with the press may ebb and flow, I think presidents understand the importance of having the press around and have learned to live with the periodic trial by fire known as the presidential news conference.

But with all the formality in covering the White House that has been layered on over the years, there's something missing, especially when we are roped off, cordoned off and kept away, treated as intruders.

I think we've lost something on both sides—the press and the presidency. We've lost our ability to size up the man in front of the TV cameras because the performance aspect has become paramount. We've lost, for lack of a better phrase, that human touch, the intimacy, we felt for many years. It lessens our ability to know the man in the Oval Office.

That informality between a president and the press in a news conference setting did resurface once, on August 4, 1995, but this time the tables were turned and I found myself standing behind the presidential podium in the White House briefing room, facing a most able interrogator.

It was my seventy-fifth birthday, and as a "gift," Clinton was going to give me a fifteen-minute interview. So at the appointed time I went in to the Oval Office, set my tape recorder down on the president's desk and started firing questions at him about Bosnia.

A little while later I noticed Vice President Al Gore standing in the doorway and was unhappy to hear him say, "It's time, sir," and the president stood up and began escorting me to the door. I was ready to start arguing I didn't get my promised fifteen minutes but the president and the vice president began walking back to the pressroom with me in-between them. I figured something was up.

Something was. The White House staff had arranged a surprise party in the briefing room and I walked in to a loud round of "For She's a Jolly Good Fellow" sung by staffers and colleagues. Then I saw Clinton with my tape recorder in his hand—in all the confusion I'd left it on his desk.

As if on cue, Clinton turned on the tape recorder and shoved it in my face: "Miss Thomas," he began, "all these years, listening to all these presidents, listening to all the double-talk, all the confusion, catching people in lies, the deceit ... how have you stood it for so long?"

"My sentiments, exactly," I said.

But it was a nice surprise and a nice party, even though when it came time to blow out the candles on the cake, Clinton looked at me first and said, "Who has more hot air?" Thanks anyway, Mr. President.

By the way, the formal "Thank you, Mr. President," to close a news conference ended in the Bush administration. He liked to hold his news conferences in the afternoon, and to his credit, they would go on as long as we asked questions, since the prime-time network rule of a designated half-hour didn't apply.

Did I complain? No way. Even though it was my privilege to give the designated closing all those years, I felt it was much better for more reporters to have a crack at the president and for those sessions to go on for as long as there were questions out there that only a president could answer. In our era of managed news, I say the more questions, the better.

One inevitable offshoot for me after all these years of asking questions, once LBJ gave the television networks a home in the White House pressroom, is that the more I was up there and out there asking a question, the more my face became known—the antithesis of the usually nameless and faceless wire service reporter.

I was there, the cameras were there and I've ended up a bit player on the national stage. Very often I get stopped on the street and it's gratifying to hear, "I saw you on television, keep asking those questions."

I explain that I'm not a television correspondent but I am covering the same story with the TV networks, scores of affiliates and, like everyone, am wired and on camera. And while I don't consider myself a celebrity, it sure beats anonymity.

Then again, I'll get phone calls or letters from friends who say things like, "I saw you on television—why didn't you get your hair done?" Or, "Why were you wearing that dress?"

Thank heaven for my friends who keep me grounded—I think.

A few words, though, about those people who, when they see me on television, think that because I or any of my colleagues are standing eye-to-eye with the president, we have easy access to him. I have always felt a sense of helplessness at certain times, in certain cases.

Cabdrivers, people who stop me on the street and those who send me voluminous documents of court cases and those with the heartbreaking stories—families in crisis, sick children, loss of jobs—some believe I can walk up to the president to explain their problems to him. If it were only that easy. But it's not and I can't. Sometimes in a great while I can pass on a letter to an agency, a bureau or an office that may be able to help, in hopes that something can be done to address a particular problem.

I cannot put myself in the role of advocate, but I haven't dropped out of the human race—though I'm sure a few presidents might have had that thought from time to time.

This kind of contact usually happens after a news conference. An Eritrean cabdriver one night asked me, "Why don't you ask questions about what's going on in my country?" On another night I heard, "Why don't you write about the killings in Nigeria?" Why don't you ask the president about our country? Why don't you ask about our war?

In any of those circumstances, if I could have waved a magic wand and alleviated a lot of troubles, I would have tried to deal with those pleas and those complaints.

But that was not and has never been possible. I know I let a lot of people down, disappointed many who thought I was close enough to a president to ask his help on someone's personal problem.

But look at it this way: If such petitions for help come to me personally on a daily basis, one can imagine how swamped the White House must be with hundreds of like-minded letters pouring in each day.

Sometimes a letter may arouse interest or strike an aide that this is something the president may want to pursue. It's all selective, since there is no way a president can read all the mail addressed to him. But believe it or not, sometimes a letter, plucked from that huge pile, does draw the president's personal attention.

At the same time, we should all bear in mind that beyond the White House there are people struggling, as President Clinton said in 1993, "people who do the work, pay the taxes, raise the kids and play by the rules, people who find themselves facing any number of problems, who try to live decent lives and, in one fateful moment, find themselves in any number of situations ranging from a bureaucratic tangle to a devastating catastrophe. It's an easy thing to lose sight of in federal Washington. But as Lyndon Johnson once put it, when his advisers and aides said he shouldn't put his presidency on the line with the civil rights issue: 'Well, what's the presidency for if you can't put it on the line?'—to make people's lives better, to improve their station and to provide opportunity."

And those are my sentiments, exactly.

EIGHT

Not Exactly Nine to Five

She cares about things. She has a real soul. She cares about the stories that she writes about and cares about the people that she covers as human beings. But she always has that sixth sense when something is up. I will no sooner put down the phone, when I've just been told something is about to happen and I look up and she comes walking through the door.

—Mike McCurry on Helen Thomas; interview for the PBS documentary "Ageless Heroes"

I'm often asked, "Do you get any exercise?" If you're talking about golf, tennis, swimming, skiing or jogging, let me say "hell, no." If you're talking about running, the answer is yes. I do it every day and I'm usually running toward someone who wants to run away from me—the president of the United States.

But I don't run all the time. When President Bush was on vacation, he sometimes invited younger reporters to accompany him on his morning jogs. I, on the other hand, got invited to the opening of the horseshoe pit when he installed it at the White House.

But it can be an exhausting business, and when people ask me what it takes to cover a president, the answer to that is stamina, determination, energy and enthusiasm. I got my early grounding in the Kennedy days and not much has changed: It's a nonstop round-the-clock job and sometimes it's in a time zone twenty-two hours ahead of my body clock.

Perhaps it was my early training at UPI on the radio desk that got me in the habit of being up at dawn, but getting to work early is standard operating procedure with me. I'm usually in the pressroom by 6:00 A.M., cup of coffee in hand, reading the papers, the wire stories that moved overnight and preparing for the morning ritual of "the gaggle" with the White House press secretary. Another belief that hasn't changed is that it's crucial to have a reporter on the scene as an impartial observer.

A little history here: If it weren't for a reporter named William "Fatty" Price, I wouldn't have a place to put my coffee or sit and read the newspapers in the early morning hours.

Long before Richard Nixon built the new pressroom in 1970 that took us out of the West Lobby, there was no place for a White House reporter to hang his hat because there were no full-time White House reporters.

The White House was the president's home, period. In 1896, Price quit his job as the editor of a weekly newspaper in South Carolina and applied for a job at the *Washington Star*. The newspaper's editor, George Juergens, wanted to get rid of him so he gave him an assignment he knew Price would never accomplish: go to the White House and dig up a story. Juergens knew President Grover Cleveland hated reporters—a not uncommon feeling that still exists, I'd like to point out.

Price did not get an interview with Cleveland, but he would plant himself outside the White House and grill every person that came in or out who had talked to the president. He scored one big story after another and landed the job with the *Star*. Soon enough, editors from around town began sending their reporters to stand outside the gates and do the same.

By 1900, there were so many reporters hanging around the White House gates and on the street that President William McKinley ordered an aide to hold daily briefings with them outside. When McKinley was assassinated, Theodore Roosevelt moved into the White House.

We have him to thank for establishing a few press/presidency traditions that have continued to this day. Roosevelt, who had used the media to make a name for himself when he was New York's police commissioner and later governor, knew how to play the press. He began holding daily briefings himself, but he played favorites. He talked to those who wrote favorable stories and ignored those who didn't. Presidents would like to have that choice today but they rarely do.

Wait a minute. Who said "news management" started with the Kennedy administration? And maybe that's where Lyndon Johnson got his "playing favorites" idea. . . .

Reporters didn't like this kind of manipulation, but they managed to overlook it because Roosevelt gave them a permanent workplace inside the White House. As the story goes, on a cold, rainy day in 1902, he saw the drenched reporters huddled beneath the trees on the North Lawn and invited them in. They never left.

He ordered an anteroom next to his study be set aside for the press and Congress later appropriated $540,000 to build office space in the West Wing.

In 1913, President Woodrow Wilson, just eleven days after taking office, convened the first White House news conference. Wilson didn't like to kibitz with reporters the way Roosevelt did but he understood the value of good press. He later began holding twice-weekly press conferences. But about a year later, he got annoyed by some of the questions and gave up the practice.

In 1914, reporters organized the White House Correspondents Association to try and resolve some of the problems between the press and the White House. The group's first chairman was William "Fatty" Price.

For more than sixty years, reporters worked out of the West Wing office in the space assigned by Teddy Roosevelt. Up through the Korean War, only a few dozen reporters were assigned to cover the White House on a daily basis.

But that number began to soar—myself among them—in the 1960s with the Kennedy administration. The power of TV also was increasing and, with it, gave both presidents and reporters more exposure.

In 1964, Lyndon Johnson allowed CBS, NBC and ABC to build a TV studio sixty feet from the Oval Office in what was known as the Fish Room, so named because it's where Franklin Roosevelt kept his tropical fish. Johnson also had AP and UPI wire machines installed in the Oval Office so he could read immediately what we were writing about him. He also had three televisions installed and kept them tuned to CBS, NBC and ABC. After all, if he gave them the space to build a studio, he might as well check up on what they were reporting.

So, I suppose I have Mr. Price to thank for giving me the roof over my head that Richard Nixon, Ronald Reagan and Bill Clinton all saw fit to modernize from time to time. But since my colleagues and I were banished from the West Lobby in 1970, we still have to go stand outside if we want to talk to anyone who's been in a meeting with the president. And if it's raining, we'll get drenched, just like those reporters huddled under the trees ninety-seven years ago. What goes around . . .

There are no "typical" days at the White House, but sometimes there are routine days. The major order of business is gathering news. Sometimes that news is of major importance; sometimes it's minor. And sometimes what may seem minor turns into something major.

When I arrive at work, I head for the UPI booth, an enclosed cubicle about seven feet wide and nine feet long. An old Olivetti standard typewriter serves to keep the door propped open. On the other side is the AP booth. It's a tight squeeze for the reporters assigned to work there, with computer terminals, a television, telephones, bookshelves and about three miles of computer, telephone and cable TV cords all vying for space. But it's prime real estate compared with some of the other cubicles where reporters have just enough room for a computer, a telephone and maybe an elbow.

Before any of that, though, there is the little matter of getting onto the White House compound. Reporters are issued press credentials that have to be renewed periodically by filing the proper paperwork with the Secret Service. The security checkpoint at the northwest gate used to be a simple enough affair: you showed your credential to the uniformed guard sitting nearest the window of the booth, the door would buzz and in you would go through the metal detector, handing your briefcase, purse and whatever packages you had over the counter so they could be hand-searched and sometimes placed inside a device similar to an X-ray machine. The more complicated the items, sometimes the more complicated the inspection.

For guests and others who have been given prior clearance to enter the compound, it's a matter of the uniformed guards inspecting a photo ID, checking certain personal statistics and then granting you access.

While it may sound like an awful lot of steps to go through to get to work, it's become more necessary and more bureaucratic over the years because of the mounting concern for the president's security. Let's not forget that in the first few years of the Clinton administration, a man shot at the White House with a semiautomatic rifle, another one scaled the wall and almost made it to the South Lawn and yet another slammed a light plane he was piloting into a wall on the south grounds. In 1995 the part of Pennsylvania Avenue directly in front of the White House was closed to vehicle traffic entirely.

And even when your face was once a familiar one, there is still the procedure. In March 1993, Betty Ford called on Hillary Rodham Clinton at the White House to urge that treatment for substance abuse be included in the health care overhaul plan that was being formulated.

In the "how soon they forget" tradition, Mrs. Ford had to be checked in at the gate. She had been cleared to enter but she still had to dutifully supply her Social Security number and date of birth for the guards to verify. She laughed about it afterward.

And then, even if your face is a famous one, something you may have said or done long ago or some manner in which you treated someone can come back to haunt you. In the spring of 1998, my colleague Paul Basken was walking through the entry one afternoon and saw a man standing at the guard's desk, looking through his pockets, bringing up one item after another while the guard kept shaking his head no. It seems the visitor had forgotten to bring a photo ID and his credit cards weren't proof enough of his identity.

Paul leaned over to the guard and said quietly, "Hey, that's Henry Kissinger."

The guard leaned over to Paul and said, equally quietly, "I know."

My White House credential? I never leave home without it.

In the morning, before I settle in with my coffee and the newspapers, I check the bins. They are in a narrow hallway between the press quarters and the briefing room. There's also a bulletin board on which the press secretary's staff posts announcements, sign-up sheets for trips, schedules and other information. In the bins are additional copies of this material, or copies of a statement or an announcement. Through the day, you can hear on the PA system that connects the press secretary's office to the pressroom, "A copy of the president's statement on [whatever subject] is now available in bin five."

About mid-morning, the press corps heads into its first briefing in the press secretary's office. Dee Dee Myers began calling it the morning "gaggle" and the name seems to have stuck. To get there, I walk out of the booth, down the short hallway, through the briefing room—the one with the movie theater style–seats—up two steps and into the press office. We gather around the press secretary's desk, ask our questions and then head back to our offices to write our stories.

Since coffee is one of a reporter's four basic food groups, there's another cup waiting for me outside the press secretary's door before the morning gaggle. When she was deputy press secretary for operations, Evelyn Lieberman kindly had one delivered every day from the White House mess after I described to her the quality of the beverage in the pressroom's machine. When she went over to become the new chief of the Voice of America, she left orders that the daily cup of coffee for me stay on someone's "to do" list. Who says this White House has no heart?

Another briefing is usually held later in the afternoon in the briefing room, and sometimes, in the event of breaking news, they are televised.

The rest of the day can be spent either traveling with the president to cover a speech he's making in town, covering a ceremony either in the Rose Garden or the East Room, which can run the gamut from an appointment being announced to a visit by this year's winner of the World Series, to an official response to the latest economic figures—you name it. There are busy times and slack times and there's "the lid," when a disembodied voice over the PA system tells us, in effect, "there will be no news" for a given period of time, be it lunch or the end of the day. Regular reporters learn not to take a "lid" seriously. Too many times there has been a newsworthy announcement after a lid.

And then again, there have been announcements after a "lid," but most reporters who have been around awhile learn never to trust the lid. That often works to their benefit and sometimes makes for an interesting exchange:

Thursday, December 31, 1970:

The P [president] spent most of the afternoon over at the EOB. He told Ziegler not to let the press leave because as long as he was working they might as well too. So Ron didn't put a lid on and some of the press had to stay around. At 6:00 the P called Ron and told him to bring whatever press was left, there were only about six, over to the EOB for a drink. This apparently worked out pretty well. The P gave them a 40-minute Q&A session standing up. It was kind of funny when they walked in—Frank Cormier, Helen Thomas, and Herb Kaplow were the only reporters—plus a couple of photographers and a radio technician. Helen Thomas, while the P was mixing the martinis in his little bar, said, "Now I know why you spend so much time at the EOB office."[1]

Still, we were there because, plain and simple, the president makes the news. His agenda dominates, from his annual State of the Union address to his budget, from his state visits overseas to his policies, from his reelection to his inauguration to his martini mixing. From the New Deal to the Great Society, from Vietnam to Watergate to Iran-Contra to Whitewater to White House interns.

Twice-daily briefings began in the Eisenhower administration with Jim Hagerty and have pretty much continued to this day. What has changed is the size—of the White House press office, the media office and the first lady's press office—all of which have grown and proliferated with each succeeding administration.

Hagerty worked with one assistant. Pierre Salinger likewise had one assistant and then increased his staff to two. Lyndon Johnson's press staff looked small—on paper—but there were a few "press assistants" here and there who weren't listed in any directory. Joe Laitin, for example, was not mentioned but he functioned as an assistant press secretary, and to some minds, much more. George Christian, Johnson's last press secretary, had an assistant press secretary, Lloyd Hackler, and Tom Johnson, now chairman of CNN, was designated as a "press assistant."

Richard Nixon overhauled the communications structure by redesigning the traditional venues—the existing press office—and adding new ones, like the Office of Communications. The Office of Communications focused on three types of presidential publicity: the out-of-town newspapers, the specialty press and coordination of public information officers in the executive branch—all designed to get the message out of Washington and beyond the Beltway.

In the press office was press secretary Ron Ziegler and eventually three deputy press secretaries, a director and deputy director of communications.

Under Ford, it began its leviathanlike expansion: press secretary, two deputies, seven assistants, an assistant to the president for public liaison and a deputy director of public liaison.

The spread continued in the Carter administration: press secretary Jody Powell and thirteen others associated with White House communications.

Then there are others in the White House also concerned with communications and publicity about the president's programs: the chief of staff with his phalanx of deputies, all of whom manage the president's time; the people who schedule the president's appointments and do the advance work for presidential appearances; those responsible for managing presidential relations with Congress, interest groups and political constituencies.

And let's not forget the president's speechwriters, the White House photographers, the White House travel office, the travel office's advance staff, and on and on and on . . .

It's been metastasizing ever since.

I've seen administrations come and go and with each one, the "presidency" grows. New offices associated with White House operations have sprung up with each administration, not to mention entire new departments. In FDR's time, the National Security Council didn't exist.

These days, there are twenty-five different offices all associated with the White House, from the National Security Council to the office of National Drug Control Policy, from the office of Scheduling and Advance to the Council on Environmental Quality. Economics? Choose one from column A, the Domestic Policy Council, or from column B, the National Economic Council, or go for the combination plate, the Council of Economic Advisers. There's Cabinet Affairs, Legislative Affairs, Intergovernmental Affairs and Political Affairs. The White House has an office of Strategic Planning and Communications; the NSC has an office of Strategic Planning and Speechwriting. And all of them have press officers with their staffs.

I tried to do a quick count of all the names listed in one directory under the title "The White House." My eyes started glazing over at the 450th name.

And that's just the staff listed with a title. There are assistants, deputies, associates, associates to the deputies and assistants to the associates. In times of crisis, more personnel are borrowed from other departments.

There are scores of people tucked into tiny cubicles in the West Wing or down in the basement—clerical workers, stenographers, other service personnel—who also labor to keep the publicity machine well-oiled. I have wondered now and then how it all holds together without collapsing under its own weight. Sometimes I've thought there's some obscure, low-level functionary who's been down in a subbasement since the Roosevelt administration, some "Wizard of Oz" type who knows every detail, every move, every facet of the operation and late at night, when all these high-level types are looking for answers, they seek out this person who tells them what to do.

But despite all the growth on both sides, there is one enduring principle at work that has defined the relationship between the White House press office and the White House press corps: the press office wants to release information that makes the president look good, which the press corps considers marginal news. The press corps wants answers to questions about information, usually ferreted out by reporters or released by political opponents, that has raised a question or two about the presidency or the president, and therein lies the rub of the relationship between reporters and officials.

After the morning "gaggle," where we've received a rundown of what the president's day holds, and after we've spent time on the phone and after we've written more stories and compiled more questions about statements that were made earlier in the day, the press secretary holds a more formal afternoon briefing in the pressroom.

When the news is good, the press secretary may produce the president to make the announcement. When it is bad, the curtain comes down and we rarely see the president.

Many people, including the many editors I've had over the years, have insisted from time to time that the public is not interested in the problems the press may have when the White House decides to choke off the flow of information. I beg to differ. Stories about a news blackout or battles with White House press secretaries who are not giving us the full story often get play.

Secrecy is endemic in the White House, of course, and therein lies the friction that is inherent in the adversarial relationship between the press and the administration. I have always felt it did not have to be so fractious. But even with the best intentions, most administrations—Democratic and Republican—have had their troubles with the media.

And most have decided that more spin is needed for damage control when their credibility is on the line. Instead of spin, stonewalling or silence, maybe it's best to remember what George Aiken, the late Republican senator from Vermont, once said: "If you tell the truth, you don't have to remember what you said the last time."

It's been my experience that most so-called leaks are self-promoted and generated inside the White House—Smitty's and Doug's experiences with LBJ bear remembering—to serve their own purposes.

But what president has not complained loudly and cynically about leaks? In the White House, they go with the turf. And there are times when White

House aides are at each other's throats and have slipped a piece of information or two to a reporter to make his or her colleague look bad.

In the annals of political history stands "Deep Throat" from the Watergate scandal, perhaps more highly motivated because he could not stand what was going on in the Nixon White House.

President Reagan, who usually kept his temper in check, once complained about "leaks up to my keister," when stories surfaced about his forthcoming budget decisions or a summit with Gorbachev—but he also joked about "bugs" in the chandeliers. At one point, Reagan mentioned that he longed for the days, as in Franklin Roosevelt's time, when you had to have a president's permission to quote him. And Reagan's press secretary Larry Speakes once ranted so much about the problem, a reporter gave him a can of leak sealer.

Many, many times, White House press aides and others have done their share of leaking, and the stories written afterward usually begin "a top-ranking official said today. . . ." But I have to say, I have never in all my years of watching presidents seen more enthusiastic zeal unleashed than in the story that engulfed the Clinton White House in 1998. I have to add I would have been happy to have a story "leaked" that would have held up.

There is no question that the White House's feelings toward the media quickly become evident. One of the most blatant "take no prisoners" attitudes, of course, was in the Nixon administration. In 1969, with the help of his aides, Vice President Spiro Agnew led the administration's full-court press against the media, especially television's instant analysts. The enemies were those "nattering nabobs of negativism," and the antipress campaign was quite effective. It put fear in the minds of TV executives, who began to curb the commentaries broadcast on their networks. But in the end, Nixon must have come to rue the day his paranoia against the press led to the creation of an "enemies list"—and to quote Judge John Sirica, let me set the record straight: I did *not* make the list. The attempts of "the plumbers" to discredit the opposition would have been funny had it not been so tragic.

Pierre, George, Marlin, Mike—and All the Rest

I like to tell people my office, you know, is perfectly situated as geographic metaphor here in the White House. Fifty feet in one direction is the Oval Office and fifty feet away is here, where we are dealing with you. And that's the role of the press secretary, to be equidistant between two combatants in this adversarial relationship. . . . You know, the press secretary of the president, we come and go, but we didn't get elected to be anything. . . . We have but one requirement, which is to report truthfully and accurately on the work the president has done, and it—you know, our guess and always our assumption is that if we get good, accurate, truthful reporting on the work of the president—since we think we are doing the right thing—that will engender support in the American people.

—White House press secretary Mike McCurry on his last day on the job, October 1, 1998

At a presidential news conference, the White House press corps can put the nation's leader on the spot, but the opportunities for that happening have been rare, occasional or sporadic, depending on whatever administration I was covering. In the line of fire every day, twice a day, is the person who has what I consider the second-toughest job in the White House: the press secretary. He or she is always in the eye of whatever presidential hurricane is blowing through the nation's headlines. And he or she gets it from both sides: from the person they work for, who's trying to keep the message positive, to the press corps that keeps trying to ferret out the other side.

Great press secretaries wear two hats: The first is that of the voice of the White House, the president, the administration, the federal government and the United States. Those responsibilities are laden with pitfalls, so it can only be with fear and trepidation that one would choose to speak.

The other hat is more elusive but just as important. I believe the press secretary is responsible to keep the American people informed with truthful information on a day-to-day basis and to battle from within for a credible flow of that information against those who want to suppress, conceal or deprive the nation of an explanation of the government's goals.

In the heat of the battle, I have often told press secretaries that they are public servants paid by the taxpayers, and if a president wants a public relations spokesman, he can go out and hire one and pay that person's salary out of his own pocket.

Harsh? Yes, but it might help a press secretary to understand that he or she serves two constituencies: the people who run the government and the people who pay taxes so the government can run.

I have to admit that most of them have not seen it that way. It is difficult enough, undoubtedly, to try to appease or comfort a president and give him only the good news, along with answering a daily barrage of questions. Much has been written about the phenomenon of "yes men" around the president with no one to tell him the unvarnished truth—and it's that truth that inevitably gets him in hot water with the press and the people. Many former officials of many former administrations have been temporarily exiled for laying it on the line to a president.

When a press secretary gives the impression that he or she does not know what the president is doing or his position on an issue, or when a press secretary seems to hedge when a reporter asks a question, the White House press corps can more than live up to that image of lions in the arena—a label that was bestowed upon us by Marlin Fitzwater. Mike McCurry once described dealing with the White House press corps in the daily briefings as "running the day-care center at a MENSA convention." When the press corps' radar picks up that a press secretary may be covering up or suppressing information, the questioning becomes relentless. But when a press secretary answers questions straightforwardly, the press corps feels confident that the information being conveyed is "the right stuff." A press secretary's greatest assets are that confidence and the perception that he is speaking for the president. It gets respect. To have the knowledge they need, they must have access to the Oval Office. While I've tangled with nearly all of them, I have respected them, or at least sympathized with all of them, considering their dilemma. Having two masters is difficult.

The first White House press secretary I dealt with was Pierre Salinger, and like any "first" professional encounter in my early days at the White House, he remains one of my favorites.

He was thirty-five when he was appointed Kennedy's press secretary. He had been a reporter and editor for the *San Francisco Chronicle,* and then he worked for *Collier's* magazine as an investigative reporter where he wrote a story involving corruption in the Teamsters union. This story got the attention of Robert F. Kennedy, who was the chief counsel of a Senate committee investigating labor racketeering. Salinger joined the committee's staff, and when JFK decided to run for president, he asked Salinger to be his press secretary.

I believed he would steer a reporter in the right direction even if he could not divulge the details of what was going on in the Oval Office, and when it came to "managed news," he played it straight when he could.

It is ironic that the Kennedy administration, supposedly the most open administration of the postwar era, came up with formalizing that concept of managed news that has raised concerns ever since about press-government relations.

Under Salinger, the system of news dissemination was streamlined, codified and expedited. He instituted a "coordinating committee" comprised of the chief information officers of government departments and they met every Tuesday afternoon. Together they would review a range of issues: (1) tracking the latest executive policies and news developments within each department, (2) discussing the form and procedure for releasing information, (3) getting a handle on questions that may come up from reporters covering the departments.[1]

The arrangement served a variety of purposes but it was still "news management." Yet it was pretty tame considering what has happened since. Salinger was convivial, warm and witty, and I think what I liked best about him was that while he took his job seriously, he never did the same with himself.

He was popular with the press corps and often asked to handle sticky family matters when they hit the headlines involving Jackie or the children. He was up to the task and the infinite variety of responsibilities of his assignment.

I still hang my head in embarrassment when he reminds me of my telephone call in the wee hours of the morning to check on a report that Caroline's pet hamster had drowned in JFK's bathtub—it was true and I did have to write a story about it.

And he helped me through a thorny patch about a story I'd written on Anthony Matarrese, the pianist for the Marine Band combo that played at a number of White House functions. During our interview, Matarrese mentioned that at a party, the actor Peter Lawford, who was then married to Kennedy's sister Pat, descended the grand staircase snapping his fingers—a minor but colorful detail I put in my story. The Kennedys thought otherwise and threatened to fire Matarrese. I went to Salinger and asked that he intercede and perhaps try to smooth things over. He did and the young pianist kept his job. I learned painfully that I could have ended a twenty-year Marine Corps career by provoking presidential pique. And you know, back then, that story was considered a "leak." How times have changed. . . .

Salinger served briefly during the transition period as Johnson's press secretary and resigned in March 1964. The leadoff press secretary for Lyndon Johnson—there were four official ones, five unofficial ones and six if you count Joe Laitin, and many did—was George Reedy. He had covered Johnson as a reporter for UP and went to work for him in 1951, serving as staff director of the Senate Democratic Policy Committee and then working on Johnson's vice presidential staff. He was forty-six when he began working at the White House, and at one point weighed over 250 pounds—a big man with a big job for a big boss with a big ego.

When George left UP to go to work for LBJ on Capitol Hill, he told me and many of my colleagues that Johnson would be president someday. As I recall, we all laughed at such a preposterous idea.

Reedy did his best in that impossible job because he worked for a man who was going to put an LBJ monogram on every spot in the nation if he could. And let's face it, LBJ never had a problem speaking on his own behalf, handling his own press relations and finding out what we were writing about him. I don't think he could stand anyone speaking for him.

At the morning "gaggle"—it was called "the briefing" back then—we reporters would gather around George's curved desk and get a rundown of the president's activities of the day, ask our questions and just generally kibitz with him.

The briefing, however, was regularly interrupted because the telephone would start ringing. George would answer it and, invariably, his face would go white, his teeth would clamp down even tighter on his pipe and his voice would go down an octave or two. It was usually LBJ calling to correct or clarify some remark George had just made. Much was made later of how Richard Nixon wired the White House, but this was a first for us: LBJ listening to the morning news briefings? Who else could it have been? The switchboard would block all calls to George's office except those "from POTUS"—the button on his phone designating "president of the United States" —during our morning sessions.

Reedy was cautious. He spoke very slowly, his deep baritone rumbling carefully through his answers to our questions. But he was well-informed on national issues and when a reporter needed help on that subject, he was willing to lend a hand.

When it came time to alert us to travel plans—one area where Johnson was always ultrasecretive—Reedy would try to keep us as informed as possible without the boss getting wise. He might not be able to tell us where Johnson was headed, but he would pass the word that "a prudent reporter would pack a bag."

For all the guff Reedy might have suffered under LBJ, his first defender was the president himself if Johnson thought we reporters were being too hard on him.

"You're always pick, pick, picking on George Reedy," he once told us, and went on to point out what a great press secretary Reedy was. "He calls me four or five times a day to get answers to your questions and he goes from office to office and stands and looks over people's shoulders to find out what's going on. And then he makes himself available to you two times a day—and he has to listen to these insulting questions.

"If I were press secretary and people insulted me the way they do him at those briefings, I'd say 'fuck you!' And I wouldn't answer their questions. I'm not going to kiss the ass of any reporter."

Reedy and Johnson parted company (some say Reedy made a break for freedom) in July 1965. Johnson used to say, "Poor George, we had to let him go because of his hammertoes."

Reedy later wrote *Twilight of the Presidency,* an incisive, penetrating book about the insulation and isolation of the White House. Johnson never forgave him and did not invite him to the dedication of the LBJ Presidential Library in Austin, Texas.

Reedy must have forgiven me somewhere along the line after he left the White House even though I was part of the press pack that probed for details and insisted on clarity and was not sympathetic to how much LBJ was really calling the shots. In fact, after he left the job, he once asked a mutual friend, "Is Helen all right? She said something nice about me."

Waiting in the wings was a thirty-one-year-old wunderkind named Bill Moyers, the youngest person to hold the second-toughest job in the White House. He was an ordained Baptist minister, had degrees in journalism and theology, had done graduate work at the University of Edinburgh, worked on Johnson's Senate staff in 1959 and became associate director of the Peace Corps during the Kennedy administration—when he was twenty-six—the kind of accomplishments that bring to mind that old joke, "It's a sobering thought when I realize that when Mozart was my age, he'd been dead for three years."

He was different, but more important, he had a very different relationship with LBJ than Reedy had. Moyers not only spoke for Johnson, he also spoke *to* Johnson—frequently. He was less fearful of Johnson's wrath and, compared with Reedy, could be downright glib. I confronted him once with an answer he had given to one of my questions and he responded, "I may shade the truth a bit."

Like Reedy, Moyers was popular with reporters but began parting company with Johnson on the Vietnam War.

When Johnson underwent gallbladder surgery in October 1965, he made the announcement himself. Shortly after the operation, Johnson invited several reporters to Bethesda Naval Medical Center to see him. A pressroom had been set up in a ward that usually housed psychiatric patients. When Johnson asked Moyers what had happened to the patients, he quipped, "We gave them all press badges."

Johnson relied on Moyers as a trusted adviser, but his stock fell when LBJ felt he was getting too independent, and it didn't sit well with LBJ that Moyers was friendly with Bobby Kennedy.

As Vietnam dragged on, Moyers became more skeptical of U.S. involvement there, and when he entered the Oval Office, Johnson would say, "Here comes 'Mr. Stop the Bombing.'"

One of my favorite stories of their relationship came from Johnson himself. Moyers had had religious training and LBJ sometimes referred to him as "my Baptist preacher." As Johnson told me, Moyers was saying grace at a White House dinner one night. With his head bent and praying in a low voice, people could hardly hear him. "Speak up, Bill," Johnson commanded him.

"I wasn't talking to you, Mr. President," Moyers replied.

Moyers's problem with the press was the administration's credibility. He tried hard, but history and LBJ just weren't on his side. In private conversations he could be candid about his boss and the direction the country was going. In public, he defended Johnson's policies, his decisions and his choices.

But then, this is the burden of most press secretaries who find themselves in the predicament of speaking for the nation's chief executive/commander in chief/world's most powerful leader.

He left in December 1966 after seventeen months on the job with Johnson's credibility in worse shape than ever. Only the president could do anything and it was apparent he wasn't going to. In a 1971 PBS program on the Johnson presidency, Moyers said LBJ was a "complicated man who wanted the world to behave in a simple and straightforward way—his way . . . [he] didn't want anyone to know what he was doing until he was good and ready to tell them. And even when [reporters] caught him in the act [lying] . . . he denied it." It was the Johnson style to leave himself some wiggle room on the big questions.

Moyers went on to greater glory as publisher of *Newsday* and later produced some thought-provoking TV documentaries on America.

During Moyers's tenure, LBJ also came up with a handy ex officio press secretary, Robert Fleming. He was the Washington bureau chief of ABC and Johnson persuaded him to come to work at the White House. At a news conference, LBJ said Fleming's title was deputy press secretary but added he was "my press secretary."

This created a little confusion and a reporter asked Johnson if Moyers still had the title of press secretary. "Special assistant to the president. It has always been that," said Johnson. "You can call him press secretary, though, if it gives you any thrill. . . ." We knew then that the die was cast and Moyers's days were numbered.

But it was Moyers who continued to talk candidly with reporters, Moyers who had the close relationship with LBJ, Moyers who was familiar with top-level goings-on in the White House. LBJ knew all that. Fleming stayed on at the White House when George Christian came aboard and did garner the title deputy press secretary.

George Christian held the job of LBJ's press secretary for two years—to me, a real achievement. He had been a journalism student at the University of Texas, worked for International News Service from 1949 to 1956 and had served as executive assistant to two Texas governors, Price Daniel and John Connally. In one of those weird White House coincidences that one runs across from time to time, Warren Harding's press secretary was also named George Christian.

He seemed to understand Johnson best and had his confidence, but even Christian felt his master's wrath if a reporter did not get the story "right."

One day he came into the pressroom, his face ashen, to tell me I had messed up on a story. Johnson had been watching the UPI ticker and when he saw my story snapped at Christian, "You go tell that girl!"

I wasn't the only one. He once called AP's Frank Cormier after a bulletin cleared on the wire—and before the next take was filed—and told him, "You got it all wrong."

But Christian knew how to survive in the Johnson White House: don't say much. In fact, if you can get away with it, say nothing. Reporters called him "Old Blabbermouth."

He held no background sessions as Moyers had done. He didn't believe in follow-up questions at news briefings. He held the line at what he was told to announce and not one word extra. Our briefings were kept to routine business—if anything about the White House at the height of Vietnam could be described as routine. He was the first to perfect mumbling—an art Mike McCurry later imitated when the tough questions came along.

But in this era of leaks, I'll give Christian credit. He kept the secret that shocked the nation on March 31, 1968. In the summer of 1967, LBJ had first confided to Christian and to Lady Bird that he would announce that he wasn't going to run for reelection, but many months elapsed before he could bring himself to do it. In all that time, we never heard a word.

I had been to church with Johnson early that Sunday morning. Still riding in the presidential motorcade we stopped at Vice President Hubert Humphrey's apartment. It struck me as an unusual move, but I thought it might be to discuss what he would say about Vietnam in his momentous speech.

That night, LBJ walked into the Oval Office to deliver a televised address on Vietnam. Doug, Cliff Evans, a veteran broadcaster for RKO, and I were allowed to stand in the doorway and listen to the speech. Word had spread through the pressroom that Johnson was going to add a few thoughts at the end of his address that weren't included in the advance text we'd received.

On a hunch, a UPI deskman, hearing that Christian announced there would be an addendum to the speech, wrote a bulletin saying Johnson would not seek reelection. Actually it was a bell-ringing flash.

In an article for *Texas Monthly* magazine, Christian later recounted the chronology of events:

> The first time President Johnson told me he wasn't going to run for reelection, I thought he was pulling my leg. It was the late summer of 1967 and we were in his bedroom, where I went every weekday morning to discuss issues prior to my press briefing.

He instructed me to start working on a withdrawal statement. "You don't tell anybody; nobody knows but Bird and me," he said. "I don't know when, but I think we ought to do it before the first of the year."

His reasons for doing so, he said, were health-related. He had had a heart attack in 1955 that had almost killed him. But then he brought in other personal problems; his daughters had to be in the limelight, his wife had no freedom from the goldfish bowl, he couldn't politick while he was trying to find peace in Vietnam. . . . It became clear that he was thinking of anything to justify his decision. He wanted out, but he couldn't find the right way to get out.[2]

A few months after their initial conversation, LBJ sent Christian to Austin to see one of his most trusted advisers, Governor John Connally, with instructions to get from Connally a rationale for the decision to leave. The two spent a few hours "to develop some eloquent and credible prose," Christian wrote.

Just before Christmas, Johnson went to Melbourne, Australia, for the funeral of Prime Minister Harold Holt, a trip that turned into an exhausting marathon journey to Australia, Thailand, Vietnam, Pakistan, winding up at the Vatican for a brief audience with the pope and then back to Washington in time for Christmas. In Rome, the pope gave LBJ a fourteenth-century painting. Johnson gave him a twelve-inch plastic bust of himself.

Along on the trip was Horace Busby, a former aide who had helped Johnson write his most important speeches. Johnson asked him at one point what he thought he should do and Busby replied, "Not run."

According to Christian, LBJ had thought about making his announcement in January, to close out his State of the Union address. He told Christian afterward that he thought it was the wrong time to do it. "It just didn't fit," he said. "I couldn't go in there and lay out a big program and then say, 'Okay, here's all this work to do, and by the way so long. I'm leaving.'"[3]

He wrote in his memoirs that he had given the closing paragraph of the speech to Mrs. Johnson and had forgotten to get it back.

But adding to all his other problems was his nemesis: Bobby Kennedy had announced he would run for president. With the war, the riots, the campus turmoil and an increasingly hostile press, the die seemed cast.

Johnson scheduled the television address for Sunday night to announce the curtailment of the bombing in most of North Vietnam as a bid for peace talks. Another White House speechwriter, Harry McPherson, had written out the final draft and Johnson told Busby he would send it to him.

"'While the messenger is on the way out, you redo what you did in January and send it back down here,'" Christian quoted Johnson as saying.

" 'Don't mark "eyes only, secret, classified" on the envelope, because that way twenty-five people will read it before I see it. Just put L. B. Johnson.'

"The envelope made it to Johnson unopened and he handed the contents to me with the statement that 'this will be my peroration.' "[4]

The speech was scheduled for 9:00 P.M. and at 7:30 P.M., the five concluding pages Busby had written still weren't typed on the TelePrompTer.

The first two went on, then the next two, and finally, at 8:15, the last page with the words, "Accordingly, I shall not seek—and will not accept—the nomination of my party for another term as your president."

Bob Fleming was in charge of proofreading the TelePrompTer and "as he started reading the last page, he literally dropped his pipe right out of his mouth on the floor," Christian wrote.

When Doug, Cliff and I heard the words, I remember Doug gasped, "My God!" For a few seconds the three of us could just stand there in disbelief.

I remember Lady Bird embracing him as soon as the camera was turned off, and his daughters' eyes brimming over with tears. Luci, who was going to turn twenty-one later that year, sadly noted that she wouldn't be able to vote for her father.

Christian spent some time briefing us and, as he wrote, "I felt like saying, 'We taught you characters. We actually pulled off one that you didn't hear about.' It was the first time in history that nothing leaked."[5]

Later we were invited into the Oval Room in the family quarters to speak with Johnson. He was dressed in casual clothes and eating chocolate pudding from a goblet.

As we pressed him he kept repeating that his electrifying decision was irrevocable and we just kept pressing him more. Finally, with a bit of exasperation, he said, "My statement speaks for itself. I don't see any reason why we should have these high school discussions about it."

And as Christian later wrote about that mind-boggling evening, "Johnson was as happy as I ever saw him. . . . He had a midnight press conference, trying to portray the whole exercise as rather routine. And you know, 80 percent of what he told them was true."[6]

While Christian believed that Johnson was a "happy" man after the announcement, I believe that he had some misgivings about giving up the most powerful position in the world, even though he immediately found his popularity rising in the country and could finally go places without facing hostile crowds. I went with him to Chicago on the day after the announcement and picked up on a tremendous sigh of relief.

As the day approached when LBJ would step down, the joke around the White House pressroom was that we pitied his ranch foreman Dale

Malachek, who was destined to be ordered around by a restless, frustrated "boss."

Years later, I was asked to be part of a "roast" for Christian when a chair was endowed in his name at the University of Texas.

> He's never told an off-color story in his life [I began]. In fact, he's never told a story. George thinks a double-entendre is a two-base hit. George is a Bill Moyers without a divinity degree—or a network. . . . As I recall, George's only problem as press secretary was that he talked too much. That is how he endeared himself to LBJ. . . . He was able to enhance LBJ's suffering credibility with his forthright approach to our questions. For example, I came upon a White House transcript from the Vietnam era to demonstrate why we called him "The Great Leaker."
>
> Reporter: George, how does the president feel about DeGaulle's statement that foreign intervention in Vietnam must cease?
>
> Christian: I don't have any comment on it.
>
> Reporter: Does the White House confirm or deny that we are going back to the United Nations on the Vietnam problem?
>
> Christian: I was asked that yesterday.
>
> Reporter: Are you denying it?
>
> Christian: I didn't have a comment on it yesterday, and I don't have a comment on it today.
>
> Reporter: Has the president read the statement by the peace protesters?
>
> Christian: I don't know.
>
> Reporter: Does he have any response?
>
> Christian: I don't know.

As I wound up my remarks, I pointed out that a lot of his friends in Washington were dumbfounded that a chair would be named after him. And one wanted to know if it would be called "The Easy Chair."

After he left the White House, Christian went home to Texas and was one of the key figures in the Democrats for Nixon organization along with John Connally.

Richard Nixon made that transition I've mentioned from having a press secretary to employing a team of public relations officers and his came straight from J. Walter Thompson.

I think Nixon did try to remake his relationship with the press when he first came into office. But with H. R. Haldeman guarding the gate to the Oval

Office, distrust began to ooze from both sides of the West Wing. As Haldeman once put it, he didn't mind being Richard Nixon's "son of a bitch."

In the middle was press secretary Ronald Ziegler, who stayed on the job until his boss was forced to resign. A protégé of Haldeman's, he had worked at J. Walter Thompson—two of their accounts were Disneyland and Sani-Flush—and at first, he enjoyed an easy relationship with us. He was quick, bright and personable and able to joke and banter with reporters. But his credibility suffered greatly in the early stages of the Watergate break-in.

When he settled into his new job at the White House, he took the time to speak to some of the longtime reporters and ask their advice. Smitty told him simply, "Never lie."

A press secretary's job is a hot seat, but I don't think anyone felt the fire as much as Ziegler did as the Vietnam War dragged on and the Watergate scandal began unraveling—except maybe Clinton's spokesman Mike McCurry as headlines blasted daily about Paula Jones, Monica Lewinsky, Kathleen Willey and others. But McCurry was smart enough to have others hired to be the spokesmen as the allegations against the president and the court rulings mounted.

In the spring of 1973, at a press conference with Ziegler and Leonard Garment, a special consultant to Nixon, I asked who, if anyone, had reported to President Nixon the results of an inquiry into John Dean and what was the president's reaction:

> Garment: Helen, I followed a number of the briefings on this, and I think they accurately describe the situation that took place at the time.
> HT: You are not giving me an answer.
> Garment: I think you have had answers on this subject.
> HT: No. Who?
> Garment: Well, I think you have from Ron.
> HT: Tell us again what you know.
> Ziegler: The position is stated in previous briefings.
> HT: It was not stated in previous briefings.
> Ziegler: We went through this, Helen, in a briefing when you were on vacation.[7]

Ziegler had to live down his branding of the break-in of the Democratic National Committee headquarters on June 17, 1972, as a "third-rate burglary." Two years later he had to concede that everything he had said regarding the Watergate debacle was "inoperative."

Before that humble confession, we realized Ziegler was at a distraught Nixon's beck and call.

It was left to his deputy Gerald Warren to step out on the podium every day to take the heat and the zingers from reporters and respond to the head-lines about Watergate. And I will admit, we felt sympathy for the belea-guered Warren as the White House began circling the wagons.

After Nixon's resignation, both Ziegler and Warren landed on their feet. Warren went on to a slot at Copley Press in San Diego; Ziegler to heading various business associations from truck stops to chain drugstores.

At what point does a press secretary defy his boss, especially when he's told to make a statement he knows is patently untrue? In my opinion, a good press secretary doesn't check his morality outside the gate—or his integrity. Or as Jody Powell used to say to President Carter, "Mr. President, that dog won't hunt."

When Nixon stepped down on August 9, 1974, President Gerald Ford asked Jerry ter Horst to be his press secretary. Like Reedy, ter Horst had been a respected newsman, and we in the White House press corps felt—at long last—we would be getting straight information from someone who would level with us and give us the facts.

But his tenure was short-lived. At Ford's first news conference, I asked him what was in store for Nixon and got an evasive answer. While rumors of a pardon were circulating, ter Horst was asked if a pardon was in the works, and he replied Ford's counsel had assured him that that was not the case.

When Ford announced the pardon on September 9, ter Horst felt betrayed and that his credibility had been lost. He resigned.

Ron Nessen, who had worked for UPI and NBC, followed ter Horst and in his first statement to the press he told us, "I'm a Ron but not a Ziegler," giving rise to the phrase coined by Peter Lisagor, "Two Rons don't make a right."

We took him at his word—at least we had another newsman in the job who understood the process—but despite his intent to clear out any remaining post-Watergate vestiges of hostility, he began to clash with the press and would accuse us of being "blind" or "mistrustful."

I will say he brought off a now-familiar practice at presidential news con-ferences: establishing the format of a reporter being able to ask a follow-up question. (But later on, Clinton tried to evade follow-up questions unless the reporter insisted and stood his or her ground.) He also got in the habit of issuing memos about routine White House matters, which cleared up a lot of busywork.

Nessen knew his first priority was serving the president, but it seemed he thought his best defense was a good offense. Many others in his position tried the same approach and, invariably, met with little success because their hostility, defensiveness and attitude were hard to hide and reflected badly on the president.

Still, he gave a few stabs at sincerity. On the day he became press secretary, he told reporters, "I will never knowingly lie to the White House press corps. I will never knowingly mislead the White House press corps, and I think if I ever do, you would be justified in questioning my continued usefulness on this job."

Then there was that little flap about Henry Kissinger . . .

Kissinger had continued to serve in a dual role, as secretary of state and presidential national security assistant. On April 9, 1975, Bob Schieffer of CBS reported that there was some kind of covert operation to remove Kissinger from the national security post. White House aides told a few reporters that a few other White House aides, Nessen included, were trying to put "a little open space" between Ford and Kissinger.

Needless to say, the story created headlines. Reporters were told that Nessen had sent a note to Kissinger denying he was the source of the story. Around the same time, an assistant press secretary named Louis Thompson was dismissed. Nessen denied that Thompson had been fired to calm down Kissinger, who, when his back was up, required a lot of calming. But Schieffer and Thompson both denied that Thompson had been the source. And in a coup de grâce, Nessen told reporters that the story "had no relation to anything that is going on in the White House."

A few days later, at a regular briefing, he began his response to a question with "To tell you the truth . . ." The press corps burst into laughter.[8]

When Jimmy Carter arrived at the White House, along came Jody Powell, that fast-talking Georgian who was equally quick on the draw in any verbal duel with reporters.

He was thirty-three when he became White House spokesman. He was born in Cordele, Georgia, graduated from Georgia State University and worked for a while in insurance. Finding that line of work not to his liking, he enrolled at Emory University to study political science. He read about Jimmy Carter while doing some research, and in 1970, he volunteered to work for Carter's gubernatorial run.

He was smart, snappy and lightning-fast when it came to putting on the spin:

> Reporter: Will President Carter meet with Prime Minister [Menachem] Begin when Begin is in the country ten days from now?
> Powell: I don't know of any plans for a meeting.
> Reporter: Would you think it unlikely?
> Powell: All I can say is I don't know of any plans . . .
> Reporter: How about [Egyptian President Anwar] Sadat?

Powell: The same is true.

Reporter: Have you heard anything in the weeks that have passed . . .

Powell: If something does develop, I will let you know.

Reporter: Wouldn't . . . be strange for a president not to see these two?

Powell: Not necessarily. They are not [coming] here on official visits.

Reporter: Doesn't he [Carter] want to pursue efforts for peace in the Middle East?

Powell: No, we decided we are for war. . . .[9]

Jody wore only one hat in his job: to speak for the president and to defend him. He was sharp but he was approachable and, refreshingly enough, he freely admitted when he leaked stories—sometimes. Other times, he would attribute the leak to some low-level bureaucrat trying to make points or influence policy.

He kept two plaques on his desk. One said: "Believe it or not, I took this job for the romance and adventure of it." The other read: "If you can't dazzle them with brilliance then baffle them with BS."

No doubt about it: He was capable of both.

When reporters quizzed him about a report that the United States and the Soviet Union had collaborated on calling South Africa's hand on a secret nuclear test, Powell said, "I know because I leaked the story."

He was just as open at times about his boss. Once, at a softball game at Plains, Powell, within earshot of Carter, called him an "arrogant bastard." And in our briefings, he would occasionally remind us that Carter, known for his frugality, was "tight as a tick." He got away with it all.

Of the many press secretaries, he was among the closest in comparison to Jim Hagerty in terms of his ability to speak for Carter, as Marlin Fitzwater was for President Bush.

He said he believed in freedom of expression but not to the point of absurdity. An article about him in the *Detroit News* on April 3, 1977, described Powell's behavior one day when he went into a tirade against reporters.

A reporter who was not present for the flare-up came up and said, "I'm sorry I missed your daily snit."

"It was no snit," replied a grinning Powell. "It was calm, reasoned discourse with a couple of assholes of the press."

When President Reagan's press secretary James Brady was critically wounded in the assassination attempt on Reagan on March 30, 1981, deputy Larry Speakes took over the daily duties in the press office. Brady miraculously recovered from the bullet wound to his head but he was left partially paralyzed. Out of loyalty, Reagan had him retain the title of press secretary and Speakes remained a deputy his entire tenure.

But Jim Brady was and is a tough act to follow. He once complimented me as being the "professional's professional." I'll say the same about him. He usually was in his office at the same early hour as I and sometimes, when I'd be walking past his window, I'd tap on the glass.

Jim invariably would yell, "Woman, have you no shame? Get yourself in here."

So in I'd go and my response invariably would be something like, "Do you think I'd have gotten this far if I had shame?"

Ironically, when Brady arrived for his new job at the White House, he found a bulletproof vest in the closet. Ron Nessen had left it for Jody Powell and Jody had left it for Brady. Attached to the vest was a note: "It's not the bullets that get you in this job, it's the gnats and the ants."

After the shooting and his long recuperation, he came with Nancy Reagan to cut the ribbon on the newly renovated pressroom. I called out to him, "We miss you, Jim."

"I miss you too," he responded, and after a well-timed pause, added, "I miss *most* of you. We tried to run over Sam [Donaldson] in the street."

In an interview I gave to Mollie Dickenson for her book *Thumbs Up: The Life and Courageous Comeback of White House Press Secretary Jim Brady,* five years after he was shot, my feelings about him hadn't changed, and to this day the same assessment applies: "To meet Jim is to know him. He is always the same. Open and friendly. There's not a sinister bone in his body. And yet you know where he stands. He is a Republican and for Reagan. Although I don't think he is as far to the right as Reagan is."[10]

When things started getting out of hand at the Reagan White House—top aides being fired, Nancy Reagan's astrology turn, Iran-Contra—I think Jim would have handled those controversial issues with ease, professionalism and an adroit amount of skepticism.

As I also told Dickenson:

He would have kept the White House from getting out of kilter and obsessed. He would have been a great leavening agent. The way he would have expressed himself would have had the effect of moderating things. I think he would have softened this administration. Jim would have cajoled the president with something along the lines of "C'mon, Mr. President, get off this ideology, you and I are two boys from the Midwest." That sort of thing. I think it is inevitable that Jim would have made mistakes. Not catastrophic mistakes. But he would have rolled with the punches and would have created an atmosphere of tolerance and would have made the White House a friendlier place.[11]

Jim's sense of humor would have stood him in great stead with the press corps, but Reagan's other key staffers weren't so appreciative. As Reagan's press secretary during the 1980 campaign, Jim, looking out the window as the plane flew over the Great Smoky Mountains, said, "Look at those killer trees," referring to the candidate's comment about trees causing pollution. His remark got him kicked off the plane for two days.

Marlin Fitzwater, who was working for the Environmental Protection Agency, later wrote, "I later kidded Jim that the only people who truly appreciated his humor were at EPA, because his comment was the first indication of anything less than total disdain for the environment by the Reagan team."[12]

For myself, I'll take a comment and a mistake like that any day from Jim Brady.

Jim also on occasion would come into the pressroom in the morning and talk to us, find out what we were writing—or thinking—or just "troll," taking our queries so he could try to get an answer for us by the time of the morning "gaggle." And when reporters would begin to probe one lead or another, he would at least try to steer us in the right direction. He invited trust.

There was affection for Jim Brady I've never seen for a press secretary, ever. And it was too short a time—less than three months—too brief a period that we enjoyed his presence at the White House.

A banker's son raised in Merigold, Mississippi, Larry Speakes graduated from Ole Miss in 1961 and worked as an editor at several small newspapers. He got a job as press secretary to Senator James O. Eastland, a powerful southern conservative, in 1968. In 1974, he was assigned as press secretary to Nixon's Watergate lawyer, James St. Clair, and then was named a deputy in the Ford press office. He worked in public relations during the Carter administration and found himself as a liaison to Ford in the Reagan campaign.

When Speakes was informed, he could be helpful. When he was cut out of the loop, what resulted could be embarrassing and infuriating. As I once told him, "You didn't tell a lie, but you left a big hole in the truth."

Authentic information is one of the cardinal requirements for any press secretary, and in October 1983, Bill Plante of CBS went to Speakes to confirm a story. Plante said he had information that U.S. forces were preparing for an invasion of Grenada. Speakes went to Admiral John Poindexter, the deputy director of the National Security Council, and apparently was told the report was "preposterous" and reported that back to Plante. The U.S.

military did invade the island nation shortly thereafter, causing Speakes some serious credibility problems.

And there was someone else in the White House, another major survivor, who made life unpleasant for Speakes, or vice versa—David Gergen, the director of communications. He was close to the inner circle, especially to chief of staff James Baker. He had been a speechwriter for Nixon and director of communications in the Ford administration. He was from North Carolina and carried degrees from Yale and Harvard Law School.

The Reagan press office followed the Nixon pattern: Speakes dealt with the reporters who covered the White House daily and Gergen worked with newspaper editors, TV and radio station managers and other opinion-makers in and around Washington. In addition to his own turf, Gergen had authority over Speakes, the speechwriters and the Office of Media Liaison. So Gergen took the podium occasionally.

But Speakes had learned from his former master, Eastland, and he out-maneuvered Gergen in the eventual power struggle.

(Gergen, however, is one person I've met in Washington who should never be counted out. He got called in when the Clinton White House fell into disarray in its first term and proved a very helpful adviser. In fact, he turned around the press and public perception of the White House.)

After Jim Brady, it no longer mattered who was on the podium on any given day. There seemed to be a growing lack of civility, compared with Brady's easy badinage.

The Reagan White House wanted reporters to focus on what was right with the country, not what was wrong, and Speakes was one of the most vocal on the subject, telling us we should be more "upbeat" and spotlight the "good news" about the economy. Just as a press secretary wants to steer reporters to the positive side of the presidency, he also wants to steer them away from the negative side. But now and then, Larry seemed to exhibit a problem with perspective.

When the gross national product—what is now known as the gross domestic product—showed a slight increase one year, we got a briefing from the chairman of the Council of Economic Advisers. When the unemployment figures dropped a few tenths of 1 percent, Reagan appeared in the pressroom and declared to us that America was "on the mend."

Afterward, Speakes chastised us at an afternoon briefing.

"It seems that 10.8 percent unemployed is big news, while 89.2 percent of the Americans who have jobs and enjoy the highest standard of living in the world is not news," he said. "Does the public perception that things are bad come first? . . . Or is it that the public only thinks things are bad after they've seen the bad news night after night? Think about it before you talk to your next caller from a pollster."

Not only did he expect us to report only the good news, but I think he expected us to ignore presidential remarks or assume that the president didn't know what he was saying.

Such was the case when Reagan said one day that he knew he was going to "kick myself" for saying the corporate income tax should be abolished. But he went ahead and said it anyway—much the same way President Clinton was to confess in 1993 that he raised the corporate tax too high and there was hell to pay.

The next day, Speakes accused the press corps of "jumping up and down, clapping your hands and licking your chops over this statement." It took his boss to finally, gracefully, put the matter in perspective by admitting he goofed. He told us he said he would kick himself, "and I did."

Like Nessen, Speakes decided early on that he had to take on the press—the offense versus defense program. In that respect, he did not do Reagan or himself much good. He created a hostile atmosphere by targeting individual reporters, especially women.

He tried to deflect important questions by ridicule and by insult. When President Reagan was diagnosed with colon cancer, the orders were to keep it quiet. Speakes tried his best to keep reporters at bay but he was not up to the task. With all due respect, however, he was obviously doing his best to make sure the orders from Reagan's advisers and the first lady were carried out.

In 1985, Reagan checked into Bethesda Naval Hospital in Maryland for his annual physical. Doctors removed a small polyp from his colon and in the course of that procedure found another larger polyp, which they suspected could be malignant.

We were on stakeout at the hospital and shortly after the doctor announced "The president has cancer," we immediately started hounding Speakes for more access to the doctors. Sam Donaldson and I—of course—were being especially persistent and Speakes lost it slightly, telling us to "Go fly a kite."

I said something to Speakes along the lines of "You're very tired, Larry," to which he shot back he wasn't tired, just "tired of you people."

The rhetoric quickly escalated, and I indicated he should send in a pinch hitter. That was in the heat of the battle. In retrospect, I realize he was under tremendous pressure to say as little as possible.

Speakes left the White House in 1987 and took a high-paying job at Merrill Lynch as senior vice president for communications. He was riding high until he wrote a kiss-and-tell book as Reagan was about to begin his second term; in it, Speakes admitted he had deceived reporters, putting words in Reagan's mouth. Use of one's own words or thoughts instead of the president's usually results in an unhappy ending for a press secretary.

In his book *Speaking Out: The Reagan Presidency from Inside the White House,* he wrote of a Reagan-Gorbachev summit: "I polished the quotes and told the press that while the two leaders stood together . . . the president said to Gorbachev, 'There is much that divides us but I believe the world breathes easier because we are here talking together.' CBS had me on the news Wednesday evening . . . and Chris Wallace said, 'The talks were frank. The president's best statements came off-camera, aides quoting him as saying, "The world breathes easier because we are talking together." ' "

He also admitted to manufacturing quotes when the Soviets shot down a Korean airliner in 1983, killing all 269 people aboard: "I made presidential quotes out of [Secretary of State George] Shultz's comment about the incident pitting the whole world against the Soviet Union, as well as some of Shultz's suggestions about what retaliatory steps we should take. My decision to put Shultz's words in Reagan's mouth played well, and neither of them complained."

Well, as that plaque on his desk used to say, "You don't tell us how to manage the news and we won't tell you how to write it."

Members of the White House press corps are not the kind of people who break into applause, especially at briefings. That kind of move might be interpreted as falling below the objectivity radar. But we made an exception the day Speakes took the podium in January 1987 and announced Marlin Fitzwater would be his successor.

Max Marlin Fitzwater described himself as "the kid from Abilene, Kansas," but with more than twenty years of government service to his credit, he knew he wasn't in Kansas anymore. Fitzwater was a real professional who was respected because he played it straight with us since he had access to the White House inner circle. Marlin understood the needs of the press, and when he continued in the job under President Bush, we knew we could count on him. Or, as he put it, when someone asked him why Bush had decided to keep him on and not choose a "fresh face," he told us, "Well, I don't know. I mean, I'm willing to take a new face if anybody could give me one, that's for sure. I'll take Tom Selleck's."

Of course we tangled from time to time because Marlin hated to brief and we constantly reminded him that was his job, to brief us. Or, as he put it in his book *Call the Briefing!*: "The White House press corps gathers every morning like a pride of lions. It snarls and growls, sleeps and creeps, and occasionally loves, but it is always hungry. And although containing the most gentle-looking of creatures, it can be aroused to anger with the slightest provocation."[13]

But he did it, through six years and 850 briefings. And I think I detected a look of total relief each time one ended.

He began his career in government service working for the Appalachian Regional Commission and was a speechwriter at the Department of Transportation from 1970 to 1972, where he worked for Secretary John A. Volpe in the Nixon administration.

I liked the story he told about Volpe giving him eight themes he wanted in every speech: patriotism and pride in country, support for the president, religious beliefs, the role of family, the need for discipline in life and work, praise for his wife, humor and the need for a strong work ethic.

"What about transportation?" Marlin asked him.

"That too," said Volpe, without cracking a smile.[14]

He went to the Environmental Protection Agency in 1972, working his way up to press director in 1980, around the time the toxic waste site known as Love Canal was about to become a national issue. He moved to the Treasury Department to work for Secretary Donald Regan and then to the White House as Speakes's deputy in 1984. He moved on to be Vice President Bush's press secretary and in 1987 found himself back at the White House when Speakes left. One of the requests he made was that Jim Brady keep his title as press secretary and he be named "assistant to the president for press relations."

His first of those many briefings was on February 2, 1987. "It's obvious the president wanted an anchorman type," he told us in his first few days on the job, "thin, with a lot of hair."

Aside from that fine-tuned sense of humor, he also had a fine-tuned sense of politics, and all those years of government service gave him not only the knowledge of the inner workings of government but the inner workings of presidential spin. I remember when President Bush's "read my lips, no new taxes" line went out the window the day Marlin put out a little statement in some of the most obtuse language I've ever read. Reporters were doing double takes as they kept rereading "revenue enhancement"—until we figured out the way to read it was between the lines.

He also could tip you off in obtuse but effective ways. The United States was leading up to the conflict with Iraq, but it had been a quiet day—too quiet. I remembered other occasions in other administrations when nothing was coming out of the Pentagon, a lull before a storm.

My niece Suzanne Geha, who worked for a television station in Grand Rapids, Michigan, had set up an interview with me via satellite for 4:00 P.M.

to get my views on the tense situation in Washington and I had to go over to the Hay-Adams Hotel across the street, where the local affiliate had set up a place for the interview. I went in to see Fitzwater.

"Marlin, is it safe for me to leave?" I asked.

He asked where I was going and I told him.

"Well, you'll be safe for about a half-hour," he said.

The war against Iraq began that night.

But Marlin was not immune to gaffes, and one of the most notorious was when he referred to Soviet leader Mikhail Gorbachev as a "drugstore cowboy," an event that he called "the worst mistake of my career, calculated and wrong."

In 1989, Secretary of State James Baker had gone to Moscow and returned with the Soviets' promise to reduce their nuclear arsenal, but turning the promise into practice was proving difficult. At a briefing on May 16, Owen Ullman of Knight-Ridder asked the question that sparked the remark:

> Ullman: Marlin, since the election, Gorbachev gave conventional arms cuts in New York, plutonium factories, his latest offer handed to Baker, now this. And the president's been calling for deeds, not words, but what deeds has George Bush responded with? I mean, you've criticized Gorbachev here, but he's made a whole series of proposals. I don't recall that Bush has responded with deeds, but just words.

> Fitzwater: I think that's the essence of the PR game that he's playing here, and that is that the United States has been very careful and methodical in its examination of . . . our relationship with the Soviet Union . . . and the president has said that he is willing to change the way the United States had viewed the Soviet Union for the last 40 years. And that out of that could come any number of kinds of initiatives. We contrast that, which is an admittedly cautious approach, to the one of throwing out in drugstore cowboy fashion, one arms-control proposal after another. . . .[15]

Marlin went back inside his office but he couldn't hide forever. And as he later described it, he knew he had to tell the president what he'd said, why he said it and admit he made a mistake: "As I opened the door, they (the press) started to shout. Helen's screechy voice was first, or maybe I just always heard it first. 'Where'd you get that "drugstore cowboy"?' "[16]

I had to wait for my answer; Marlin had to tell the president first.

"Drugstore cowboy" wasn't the only "Marlinism" during his tenure.

In the 1992 presidential campaign—his first—I often thought his staff must have cringed when he said former presidential speechwriter/pundit/commentator/candidate Pat Buchanan had gone "Looney Tunes," or that Ross Perot was a "dangerous and destructive personality," or the one that gave the Clinton campaign fits, that vice presidential candidate Al Gore was an "environmental extremist" and "Mr. Sellout America."

President Bush stayed the course with Marlin and was "very understanding of my problems," Marlin once said. "A couple of times he will say, 'You might be a little ahead of my position there' or 'I'm not sure I'd use exactly that language.'"

And in that campaign, Marlin showed he could feint with the best of them. When reports were surfacing that Secretary of State James Baker would take charge of the Bush campaign, Fitzwater told us it was all speculation and "no decisions have been made."

He knew Baker was coming back—we all knew it—but it was part of the game and we all had to play along.

I have no doubt one of the most trying times for any press secretary is when the United States is involved in a military action, and Marlin's most trying time was the Gulf War. While American bombers were hammering Iraq, we zeroed in on our target: Marlin. He did briefing after briefing, day and night. Detail after detail, statement after statement. Early on in the game, the big question was when, exactly, President Bush decided to go to war. Three stories were circulating but all had variations in the timing. As we surrounded his desk demanding to know which one was right, Marlin the unflappable waved his hand. "Pick whichever one you want," he said. "I'll back you up."

Relief for Marlin was infrequent at best. One way he found it was disappearing at certain times when we were looking for him to confirm, deny or clarify something we had heard.

"The people's right to know is guaranteed by the Constitution," he said in an interview in 1990. "But it doesn't say when they get to know." He stuck by that principle through the war.

"Chances are when I can't be found I don't want to be found," he said. "In many ways silence is the only weapon I have, and I use it very carefully."[17]

But his honesty and professionalism were never questioned, especially when he conceded that "I'm afraid out there," when it came time for the war briefings. "I speak for the president and the margin for error is small."

That margin for error got lost in the heat of the 1992 campaign at one stop in Oklahoma when we were in the filing center, listening to Bush's speech over the public address system. Marlin thought the reporters should be in the hall listening rather than in the filing center and was getting a little angry.

He spotted Rita Beamish of AP and Kathleen DeLaski of ABC in a hallway and erupted, "I'm sick of you lazy bastards. Go out and cover the events."

It didn't take long for the two of them to come barreling back into the filing center and announce to all present, "Marlin called us 'lazy bastards.'" And that, rather than the campaign appearance, was the story of the day, with Marlin apologizing and, as he put it, "in full grovel by 6 P.M. But it was still a day lost for the president and it depressed me even further."[18]

My feelings for Marlin approximate those I've had for most of the pros who find themselves on the business end of my questions. He played it straight, kept his cool and took the job—but never himself—too seriously. I shall always fondly remember his love for cigars, his terrific hats—he started collecting and wearing them in 1971 after he was diagnosed with skin cancer—his battles with his weight, his penchant for napping and as then-ABC correspondent Brit Hume put it at the time, "the continuing saga of Marlin Fitzwater, eligible bachelor."

By the way, President Clinton was not the first White House habitué to have a fondness for junk food. At the economic summit in Venice, while we were all gorging on sublime Italian cuisine, Marlin sought more common fare and managed to find it at a Wendy's. During the Gulf War he remarked one day that Saddam Hussein had two victims, "the U.S. and my waistline."

On his last day at the White House, Marlin came into the pressroom and our last "official" encounter was not without its tense moments.

"Hi, Helen," he said. "What's happening?"

"What's happening?" I responded. "That's my line. What's happening with you? What's the president doing? Has he said good-bye to the help?"

With me, it's reporter first, foremost and always, I guess. But my respect for Marlin has never flagged. As I used to tell him, "We have the questions even if you don't have the answers." I don't think he liked it but he did respect our role and didn't try to manipulate.

Since the many brouhahas of the Clinton presidency, he's been sought out as a solid analyst of press relations and the inner workings of the presidency.

The picture that graces the back of his book had been hanging in the press office for some time. He called me and asked if he could use it—something he didn't have to do—and he even sent me an inscribed copy. There I am, peering into the window and inside is Marlin, looking out. The inscription: "To Helen 'Peeping Thomas.' It's been a great 10 years."

In June 1998, I was asked to participate in a "roast" of Marlin that honored him and the newly named Marlin Fitzwater Center for Communications at Franklin Pierce College in New Hampshire. I got to poke some good-natured fun at him, and I think Marlin took my remarks in stride.

"Marlin Fitzwater teaching students to communicate," I said, "you've got to be kidding.

"As press secretary," I recalled, "he spoke so softly I had the feeling that he did not want us to hear what he was saying. And quite frankly, there were times when we could not believe what he was saying. Not that he would lie deliberately—no, never. I'm here to say that Marlin never tried to manage, manipulate or control the news. He simply avoided it. Most of the time, Marlin kept his cool, even in trying times. And the trying times were every day. But later he got his revenge in his very forgettable memoirs *Call the Briefing!*—That was the signal when Marlin wanted to put on his hat and duck out the back."

As his White House days wound down, Marlin invited the new Clinton team to come in and spend some time with him, talk about how the media operations are run and get their bearings in their new posts. Dee Dee Myers sent an assistant who spent about a half-hour there. Someone told me later that Marlin shook his head and said that what the new administration needed was "a few old, bald, fat guys in the White House. We reassure people."

When I walked in to a Gridiron meeting as the club's first female member, someone said to me, "Well, the roof didn't fall in, the walls didn't cave in. I guess we'll be all right."

When Dee Dee Myers took the podium as the first female White House press secretary, there weren't any building collapses either. But talk about breakdowns . . .

Margaret Jane Myers of Valencia, California, a 1983 graduate of Santa Clara University, had worked as a press aide in several Democratic campaigns in California and hooked up with the Clinton campaign in December 1991. Almost immediately, she found herself on the front lines of political trench warfare. After a bruising campaign filled with Gennifer Flowers, draft-dodging controversies, inhalation and other relevant questions about the candidate, she got to the White House with the traditional title of press secretary. However . . .

The traditional rank that goes with the job is assistant to the president. She was classified as a deputy assistant. Her pay grade was a step below the traditional tier for presidential appointees, so she earned less money. She didn't get the office traditionally assigned to the press secretary with the fireplace and the bank of televisions on one wall. She also didn't get the responsibility of the daily press briefings, the job usually associated with press secretary. In the beginning that duty was reserved for George Stephanopoulos, the communications director, who also occupied the press secretary's office. In short, she was treated badly.

It's tough being the "first woman" anything, and I think Myers labored under some unnecessary handicaps. She deserved to be part of the power structure but instead she found herself out of the loop and a prime target when some serious gaffes occurred:

• The weekend before Thomas "Mack" McLarty was moved out as chief of staff and Leon Panetta was brought in, Clinton called McLarty, Panetta and Vice President Al Gore to Camp David to discuss the rearranging of personnel. Myers unknowingly said Clinton had not met with anyone at Camp David.

• The day before it was announced that Hillary Rodham Clinton was going to represent the United States at the Winter Olympics in Norway, Myers denied she was going.

• She had to admit she was unaware that Clinton had not been briefed on the Iraqi assassination plot against George Bush, and when she said there would be no news that weekend it was just before Clinton announced a military strike against Iraq.

For that I blame the president, who should have kept her informed.

In a May 3, 1993, profile of Myers in *People* magazine, I said, "We like her. We just need to know how close she really is to the president."

In that same story Myers retorted that "asking why I'm not in that office is such a Washington question. Where you sit is not what matters in this organization."

As it turned out, it did matter—not that there was much organization to speak of in the first Clinton administration.

After it ran one of the most effective Democratic campaigns of modern times, the Clinton White House seemed to go from the "rough and tumble" of election politics to the "rough and stumble" of daily governance. Their arrogant disdain for the daily press was already evident, but even that was overshadowed by some policy blunders I never thought I'd see. There was the firing of the White House travel office staff—and George Stephanopoulos acknowledging he urged the FBI to announce that it was conducting a criminal probe of the matter. But it was left to the benighted Myers to announce to the press that the FBI probe was taking place. It was a big faux pas and she took the fall for it.

And let's not even talk about that haircut in Los Angeles . . .

By May 1993, polls showed that Clinton's approval rating had plummeted to 36 percent, lower than for any American president at this point in his term, with 50 percent disapproving of his performance in office. Clinton ordered a top-to-bottom review of his staff after weeks of political pounding and made some changes.

To the shock and surprise of many in Washington, Clinton chose David Gergen as Ranger No. 1, that stalwart Republican who had served in three administrations. Gergen had been working as an editor-at-large at *U.S. News & World Report* and in that capacity had criticized Clinton for "lurching to the left."

In his new role as counselor to the president, he took overall responsibility for the communications department from Stephanopoulos, who gave up the daily briefings to become a senior adviser to the president.

Clinton made the announcement shortly after 7:00 A.M. in the Rose Garden before he flew off to deliver the commencement address at West Point, telling us that the "message here is we are rising above politics."

Gergen said that he took the job because he was convinced that Clinton "wants to run a bipartisan and fair government. Maybe I'm wrong, maybe naïve, but I think I can help with that."[19] Or, as many have learned, when a president calls, it's almost impossible to turn him down.

Just a few weeks before his appointment, Gergen had written: "Whoooshhh!! To paraphrase Ross Perot, that sucking sound you hear is the air rushing out of Bill Clinton's balloon as he ends his first 100 days in office."[20]

So Myers finally assumed the job she was hired to do and took her place on the podium every day.

Meanwhile, Gergen set about repairing some breaches with the press corps. His office might have been down in the basement—it was the old barbershop—but his fingerprints were everywhere. And I think Marlin was right. But it took a tall, savvy guy—in fact, "Tall" was the nickname Speakes had attached to Gergen—who knew how Washington worked and could provide a certain degree of reassurance.

He organized Clinton's first prime-time press conference on June 17. He even gave it his best effort to have his boss show up on time at events.

He had access to all staff meetings. He reported directly to the president and, in effect, taught him to understand and use the tools of the presidency to communicate his message and revive his faltering administration. Mainly, he helped move Clinton to the right politically.

It was a behind-the-scenes but important role he played, and he had many in Washington wondering how long he would last among the Democrats, who did not trust him, and the palace guard, who eventually succeeded in pushing him out.

Even after communications improved, chaos still plagued the White House. Discipline was at a premium and things were back to their constant state of confusion.

In June 1994, in rode Ranger No. 2: Leon Panetta, former congressman from California, former chief of the Office of Management and Budget and now chief of staff. By September, Myers made a personal plea to Clinton to keep her job after Panetta made public his plans to replace her. Clinton overruled Panetta and she hung on till December, and was even able to move into the office, briefly, that was rightfully hers.

But she was frustrated in her struggle to get more information from Clinton's inner circle. When I would ask her why we could not cover certain events involving the president, she would bark, "Why do you always ask why?"

"Why not?" I would shoot back.

At her last briefing on December 22, 1994, Clinton made a surprise visit, telling her he wanted "to get you out of hot water since you always do that for me."

She had a few words of advice for her successor, "Keep a sense of humor. Never take it seriously" and quipped, "The press corps is a joke."

She then launched into her rendition of a David Letterman "Top 10" list by outlining the things she would not miss about her job:

10. "Helen Thomas." (To which I responded, "I thought I'd be first." "Just wait a minute," said Myers.)

9. "Air Force One food."

8. "Twenty-four-hour-a-day paging, late-night phone calls and those early morning baggage calls."

7. "The soft, quiet and reflective questioning of Sarah McClendon."

6. "The fact that my busy social calendar has made it often difficult to get back to the president and to all of you—busy returning those phone calls."

5. "Bureau chiefs, editors and especially headline writers."

4. "The ongoing and breathtaking attention span of certain network correspondents, who can simultaneously question and do crossword puzzles." (ABC's Brit Hume)

3. "That daily crush to make it to my briefing on time so as not to miss the opening." (Like her boss, Myers was late on a daily basis for scheduled briefings.)

2. "Did I mention Helen Thomas?"

"Finally, the number one thing that I will not miss. All of this." She paused for a moment and then added, "That's only half true."[21]

I don't think she was given a fair shake and I cannot help but feel that the old boys' network worked against her. She acknowledged that she occupied a "still-male-dominated profession" and that "women have gone far but we still have a ways to go" before achieving full equality.

But I did not appreciate an interview she gave to *Vanity Fair* magazine in which she called us "the beasts." Funny thing, after her White House experience she slipped right into an editor's job for *Vanity Fair* magazine and co-hosting a talk show on CNBC, "Equal Time," with Mary Matalin, who was deputy director of George Bush's reelection campaign. And she can tell it like it is.

Following Myers was Mike McCurry of Charleston, South Carolina, a graduate of Princeton and Georgetown Universities. He made one condition before he took the job: unfettered access to the president and full access to all White House meetings, including the 7:30 A.M. staff meeting.

He grew up in Redwood City, California, and had considered journalism as a career. But his main interest was politics, and in 1976, he wrote press releases for Jerry Brown's 1976 presidential bid. He spent five years as press secretary to New Jersey senator Harrison Williams, until it fell to him to call the senator one day in 1980 and tell him that the *New York Times* was preparing a front-page story that Williams and eight other members of Congress had been implicated in an FBI bribery investigation known as Operation Abscam. Williams was convicted and went to jail.

McCurry then went to work for Senator Patrick Moynihan of New York. He worked on Senator John Glenn's 1984 presidential campaign, then on Arizona governor Bruce Babbitt's short-lived presidential bid in 1988 and on vice presidential candidate Lloyd Bentsen's campaign in 1988. In 1992, he worked for one of Clinton's rivals for the Democratic nomination, Senator Bob Kerrey of Nebraska.

After the Clinton victory, Secretary of State Warren Christopher tapped him for the spokesman's job and he proved more than deft at diplomacy with a penchant for puns. Referring to an incident in Iran, where the government had beheaded twelve thousand pigeons in a crackdown on gambling on illegal bird races, McCurry called it "news most fowl, from a regime most foul."

We got a hint of the McCurry wit the day Clinton introduced his new press secretary in January 1995 and a reporter asked if he had any reservations about taking the job, given his association with Kerrey. "Well, I think, as everyone said here, I've worked for a very long list of losers in my time," he responded, thought for about a second and then retook the high ground: "It's nice to be working for a winner now, yes. Thank you for feeding me that line."

He was smooth, articulate and nimble in his answers, impressing the C-Span audience far and wide. And I really can't recall the last time a press secretary began a news conference wearing a paper bag over his head and billing himself as an "anonymous source."

McCurry brought a new spirit to the White House pressroom when he first came aboard. I told him one day that we were tired of being treated with contempt by the press office. "Anyone who does that will not be around here long," he said, and he kept his word.

He put together a staff that did not view reporters as the enemy or as intruders—a refreshing change from the recent past.

Like all press secretaries he jousted with the press corps, but he also tried to accommodate reporters while working within the constraints laid down by the senior staffers, who wanted to plant the "story of the day" and keep us away from any other idea of what news was. Still, when he was asked whether he would ever lie, he said, "No, but I might speak very, very slowly."

While he was a key member of the Clinton team and served his boss well, I never felt he and Clinton had the kind of relationship that existed between Carter and Powell or Bush and Fitzwater. But that saved him from a greater grief.

When the allegations arose that Clinton had had an affair with a then-twenty-one-year-old White House intern, Monica Lewinsky, McCurry took himself out of the access loop, stayed uninformed and could plead ignorance. He was able to take the self-protective stance of "see no evil, hear no evil" since Clinton's defense of the allegations was in the hands of his lawyers, who set the strategy and demanded silence. Or, as he told us on January 30, 1998, when he was avoiding all conversations re Monica: "I'll refer you to my transcript yesterday, which referred to my transcript the day before."

He also was able to avoid the blizzard of subpoenas engulfing the White House. "It was a good approach for me personally, a good approach for the institution of the presidency and a good approach for Bill Clinton personally," he said after the announcement on July 23, 1998, that he was stepping down.[22]

Even though he was accused frequently of stonewalling, he could turn that hellish situation to his advantage as well. When the scandal broke, the networks began broadcasting the afternoon briefings in the pressroom. On one occasion, he brought out a number of officials who then proceeded to explain Clinton's policy proposals. After a particularly coma-inducing session of a school modernization plan, he grinned and said, "Note to stations down the line. We're now returning to your regularly scheduled program."

During all the revelations and allegations about the president's sexual conduct, it became more impossible to explain and McCurry expressed to a reporter at one point that impossibility.

The tiny fissure in the stone wall was an interview published in the *Chicago Tribune* on February 18, 1998, in which McCurry said that if there were a "simple, innocent explanation" for the Lewinsky matter, "I think we would have offered that up already." That sparked a new round of speculation that the White House was trying to offer at least some kind of description of what had gone on. However, the usually adroit McCurry said later that his remarks were just answers to hypothetical questions and not based on facts or opinions.

The McCurry touch was on display when he met with the press corps for the afternoon briefing:

Q: . . . I wanted to ask you about this story we asked you about this morning.

McCurry: Which one was that, Sam [Donaldson]?

Q: This is the Chicago Tribune story.

McCurry: Chicago Tribune?

Q: And you know what the quotes are. I just wondered what you were trying to get across.

McCurry: I think what I was proving was that only fools answer hypothetical questions. And I don't know that there's anything to say beyond that.

Q: Well, if you just clear up one point. The story seems to suggest that you are saying that the policy is to reveal the truth, but slowly, or in degrees or stages.

McCurry: That's an observation I've made on other occasions that I applied inappropriately to this matter.

Q: Are you trying to retract your interview?

McCurry: No, I said what I said. I just shouldn't have said it.

McCurry decided to leave while the grand jury was still hearing testimony about the Lewinsky situation. When President Clinton stepped up to the podium on July 23 and announced, "The long-awaited coup in the press office is finally taking place. It's rare that I get to announce my own personnel decisions!" it marked one of the best-kept and worst-kept secrets of the Clinton White House—but I'll give them points that the news did not leak, especially when compared with the way details of what was going on in the grand jury had all the security of a leaky sieve. His departure had been rumored for months and Mike had intimated to me and others that he was looking to move on.

President Clinton said McCurry would be "the standard by which future press secretaries will be judged." From where I sit, that remains to be seen. However, when McCurry was asked what he considered the key to his survival in this most difficult of jobs, he responded: "Just keep your eye on what matters most, remember that your first and foremost obligation is to the truth and the American people, and to get everyone to that point sooner or later. And if you can keep the crowd entertained on the way, that's all the better."[23]

By October 1, 1998, independent counsel Kenneth Starr had made his report to Congress accusing President Clinton of impeachable offenses stemming from his alleged lying and cover-up in what the president acknowledged in August was an "inappropriate relationship" with Monica Lewinsky. The House Judiciary Committee was weighing the evidence to determine whether to open a full-blown impeachment inquiry—and after 539 briefings, Mike McCurry was stepping out of the line of fire. His last session with reporters was a mix of candor, humor, melancholy and a repeated defense of his decision to keep himself away from any information about the president's affair for the seven months he stood at the podium before Clinton finally admitted it:

> Of the millions of pieces of information that I stuffed in this pathetic brain of mine every day, I segmented out on matters related to Monica Lewinsky, questions that would jeopardize the president's attorney-client privilege, if I had direct knowledge of actions by the president. You asked me questions about the president's actions—if I had got those answers from him, he would have in effect forfeited his attorney-client privilege. And he would have been an open sitting duck for Ken Starr because he could have subpoenaed me and I wasn't interested in being subpoenaed. . . . The one thing I was determined, when that story broke back in January, was to never come here and do what some of my predecessors unfortunately did, which was to lie to you and mislead you. And I know that puts you in a tough position too. It's better than consciously misleading people—you know, I know, that at times I came up short. I know there were times that I didn't have the right information. Frankly, the president misled me too. So I came here and misled you on occasion, and that was grievously wrong of him. But he's acknowledged that. But you know, did I ever come here and send you folks in the wrong direction—I did not. I'm confident of that.

It was also my last chance to get in a parting shot. "You've done a good job, Mike, under the circumstances," I said, stressing the "under the circumstances" part.

I should have known he would get in a shot as well.

"Thanks, Sweets," he said to me and then told the group, "Helen and I have always had a thing for each other."

Enter Joe Lockhart, thirty-nine, born into a family of journalists—his parents both worked for NBC News—a former television journalist himself, a Bruce Springsteen and a New York Mets fan who served as press secretary in the 1996 reelection campaign. So far, so good. Like many of his predecessors he seemed to rely on humor to deflect the touchier situations of the scandal enveloping the Clinton White House.

On a trip to Moscow in September 1998, he overslept and missed his ride aboard Air Force One to the next stop in Belfast, Ireland. When he did catch up to the group, he offered a mock apology that smacked of his boss's mea culpa in his August televised address.

"I take responsibility for my own actions," Lockhart told the press corps. "I deeply regret it. I'm dealing with the people I have hurt the most. And I'll have nothing further to say."[24]

He has stepped into what can be an uncomfortable pair of press secretary's shoes, and for the most part, is a straight shooter in a complicated White House, handling the job with refreshing candor. These days, I often run into two special friends, Tom Johnson and Neal Ball, who served as deputy press secretaries in the Johnson and Nixon administrations, respectively. They always remind me that I greeted them on their first day in the job with the caveat, "Always tell the truth."

Both of them did and they also, like their superiors and colleagues, understood that "no comment" was also acceptable when they could not break a White House confidence. I have to admit that Salinger confessed that, in his time, "no comment" was nearly always tantamount to "yes," but unless that "yes" came flat out, we obviously couldn't report it as such.

I believe all the press secretaries started out with the best of intentions, if perhaps not fully cognizant of the worst of the pitfalls. A high-profile spokesman for the president walks a tightrope and is in an impossible situation. The bottom line is: No one speaks better for the president than the president himself.

To that end, weekly news conferences would be the ideal and would be rewarding for both sides. The sessions would give the president a forum to explain his policies and actions through our questions. Some presidents have said the feedback is good for them since they get to know what the press, and hopefully the public, is asking.

And I think the press secretaries I've confronted over these many years might even agree with me, because I've seen that look of relief when the president is the one standing in front of the podium in the pressroom and the press secretary is standing off to the side—and off the hook.

Or, as Marlin Fitzwater put it, "It's the greatest job in the world and worth taking no matter how much trouble your president is in. Now, you may die in the job, it may ruin your life, and your reputation. But it still will have been the greatest experience of your life."[25]

NINE

On the Road

Next to the Oval Office, I think it's the most important symbol of American power in the world.

—Marlin Fitzwater

I'm really going to miss SAM. Through good times and bad times, SAM was a real constant in my career. Big and imposing, SAM was a memorable figure, especially at sunset, standing there majestically, the last rays of the sun bouncing off that presence.

And when Donaldson was on board, it was pretty interesting too.

SAM—Special Air Missions—26000, known by its more popular name Air Force One, was the Boeing 707 that served Presidents Kennedy, Johnson and Nixon. It was the first jet-powered presidential plane. Another aircraft, SAM 27000, came in during Nixon's administration and was used by Ford, Carter and Reagan. The two planes were used simultaneously for a while, serving as backup planes to each other.

SAM 26000 was retired in 1998 because the Air Force decided it was too expensive to maintain. But up until that time, it was in use for various missions. Secretary of State Henry Kissinger used it in the final days of the Vietnam War for thirteen secret meetings with officials of Communist North Vietnam. It also ferried "Miz Lillian" Carter when she led the U.S. delegation to Israeli prime minister Golda Meir's funeral.

On November 22, 1963, SAM 26000 bore home the body of a slain president and was the site of the swearing-in of a new one. SAM 27000 flew President Nixon to China in 1972 and carried him home to California after his ignominious resignation.

Vice President Al Gore often used SAM 26000 as Air Force Two and in 1997 it flew two hundred missions to fifty-eight countries, one of its last being Secretary of State Madeleine Albright's trip to Hong Kong for ceremonies marking the end of British rule in the colony.

There have been many planes designated for presidential use, as far back as Franklin Roosevelt's administration. Roosevelt was the first chief executive to travel by air when he boarded the *Dixie Clipper,* a "flying boat" furnished by Pan American World Airways, on a trip from Miami to Casablanca to meet with British prime minister Winston Churchill and Allied military leaders to plan the invasion of southern Europe.

As Jerry ter Horst and Colonel Ralph Albertazzie point out in their book *The Flying White House,* that trip, while having its own historic significance, "accomplished one other thing of importance to the presidency and the future of aviation. It gave birth to the idea that there ought to be at least one airplane with the specific and primary mission of transporting a president of the United States."[1]

Since then, many special planes have carried presidents to the far corners of the globe with a trip's duration measured in hours rather than days. For example, there are about 3,900 miles between Washington and Casablanca and a Boeing 747 can complete the journey easily and comfortably in about seven hours. When Roosevelt made that trip in 1943, it required three stopovers, changing planes, crossing the equator four times and spending more than 90 hours in the air. But that trip gave the president his wings and all who have followed have made air travel an integral part of the presidency.

"Air Force One" is not the name of a specific aircraft but the radio call sign of any aircraft carrying a president. The Douglas DC-4 that became Roosevelt's official plane was dubbed *Sacred Cow* and the backup aircraft was known as *Guess Where II.* The same plane and the Douglas DC-6 that followed it for Harry Truman's use was called the *Independence.* For Dwight Eisenhower, it was a Lockheed Constellation known as *Columbine II* and later a Lockheed Super-Constellation designated *Columbine III.*

John F. Kennedy used a Douglas DC-6 and then the Boeing 707—SAM 26000—was commissioned for presidential use. With that, the name Air Force One worked its way into the lexicon. It was the chief means of transport for Lyndon Johnson and early on in the Nixon presidency until the arrival of SAM 27000.

In 1971, Nixon named it *Spirit of '76* in honor of the country's bicentennial. President Ford retained the name but still continued to refer to the plane as Air Force One, as did nearly everyone involved with its maintenance and operations.

Kennedy decided the aircraft needed a distinctive look and enlisted Jackie's help on the project. She worked with the designer Raymond Loewy, who eliminated traditional military markings, put together the distinctive blue and white color scheme, the seal "United States of America" emblazoned on both sides of the fuselage, and an American flag painted on the tail. That basic design hasn't changed much on the outside. The interior design has been altered over the years, but creature comforts for the first family have always had priority: living room, bedroom, bathroom, offices and a conference room. One room does double duty as a medical clinic.

When Lyndon Johnson became president, he rearranged the interior to suit his taste. The plane could accommodate about forty people but LBJ wanted room created for several dozen more. He had the seats reversed so they faced toward his own compartment. The cherry-wood panels were torn out and he installed clear plastic dividers. He ordered a chair duplicating the one in the Oval Office that went up and down at the press of a button—the Secret Service dubbed it the "throne"—and he put in a large kidney-shaped table complete with telephone console that served as his meeting room. The table also could be elevated and lowered.

Johnson liked to have news conferences aboard Air Force One, most of them off the record, which was just as well, as we strained to hear him above the engine noise. With his "captive audience" of press people, he would go on for hours.

I can recall the many, many times he would pour himself a drink, prop his feet up on the table and say to his press secretary George Reedy, "Bring the boys in here." And equally so, I recall the many, many times I walked into his cabin and reminded him, "We're not all boys, Mr. President."

Two trips with LBJ will always be with me. One was to Chicago on April 1, 1968, the day after he announced he would not seek a second term; the other was when he left Washington and headed home to Texas after Nixon was inaugurated—Texas, he used to say time and again, a place "where they know when you're sick and they care when you die."

On that trip to Chicago, where Johnson addressed the National Association of Broadcasters, I think I saw him at a frail moment, for lack of a better term—an unlikely characteristic that no one ever would have associated with LBJ. He had stunned the nation with his electrifying announcement the previous night, and we were all hoping he might be willing to talk about it. On the trip to Chicago, he stayed out of sight. On the way back, he was more than willing to talk.

We almost didn't get a chance to hear what he had to say. Because of a traffic snarl, our shuttle to the airport was late as we had exceeded our "filing time" on the ground to get our stories out about his speech.

But Lyndon must have been in a good mood. He held the plane for us and even invited us to join him in his cabin for lunch. The group included Doug, Dan Rather, Max Frankel of the *New York Times,* Jack Sutherland of *U.S. News & World Report,* Cliff Evans of RKO and myself.

I noticed he seemed more composed, relaxed and at ease than he'd been in a long time. He had a certain lightness about him.

After lunch, we asked him if he felt relieved, and he said, "Yes, I think so. I don't think there's anything unusual about it or newsworthy. When you're speaking to a TV audience that size on a subject of that consequence, there is always a certain tenseness. Grant or Lincoln said that they never addressed more than one person that their stomachs did not feel like a rolling ship."

He went on to tell us he had tried "to get the right phrase to convey my thought." He talked, and he talked and he talked, about how Vietnam had divided the nation and how "this division hurts our men a great deal. They don't understand draft card burners saying that it's being done in the name of free speech and dissent.

"It seemed to me that I am becoming more of an object of contempt and controversy than I thought to be in the interest of the men and women I have to serve. It was getting to the point where a man could no longer be president. Yes, I feel I made several errors in the past. I came to the conclusion if I signed the Lord's Prayer it would be objected to."

As we all sat and wrote furiously, he conceded that he didn't think Lady Bird "believed I was going to say it until I actually read the line. But I knew it. George Christian knew it."

John F. Kennedy, he rambled on, "said I was the best one for him. He wanted me. Mr. Sam [Rayburn] said 'Let's give the people of this nation a chance to vote for a man from Texas.' We can't do a thing for the country if Nixon is president.

"Franklin D. Roosevelt was slandered as much as anyone could be. I think Eisenhower is very much underestimated. He's done things without regard to self or political party. I grew up in a school where I had to be prudent, but there was a time when you had to put the whole stack in and let everything ride on it. I did that with the civil rights bill. I think we are unjust to our presidents. Truman. Living out there, quietly, unnoticed. Things that I did came out of Truman's basket. Medicare is one example."

He then went on to remark on his negative image and coverage, and the familiar LBJ surfaced. "There's always someone disruptive. Is criticism and carping inherent in the presidency in the future? I suppose after a time you develop barnacles. If we had listened to the columnists years ago in the thirties and forties . . . today we'd be slaves.

"I don't need the job . . . the salary. I don't need your approval. I'm going to live a full, happy life. I don't give a particular damn what you think. But I do think this country is going to be better for y'all, for the things I've done."[2]

When the plane landed, I asked Johnson to autograph a copy of his address to the NAB for me. He complied and even added a personal note. The other reporters handed him similar documents for his signature and he shook hands with all of us before leaving the plane.

It's a relatively short trip from Chicago to Washington, but that day, I felt like I'd traveled a million miles. I had learned not to expect such forthrightness from presidents—or their staffs. For me, it was a revelation to see and hear LBJ this way. And ironically enough, I understood what Hubert Humphrey had said when he described being around LBJ as "sometimes you felt as if you were sitting at the feet of a giant."

After his inauguration in January 1969, Nixon permitted the Johnson family to use the plane for their ride back to Texas. Saul Pett of AP and I went along to spend a few days with them as they settled into their newly quiet life on the ranch. I filed a story, "LBJ Goes Home," that UPI later published as part of *Selections 1969*, an anthology of stories and pictures that "gave distinction to the UPI news and picture services in the course of the year." Wrote editor Roger Tatarian:

Washington—He had surrendered the presidency to Richard M. Nixon less than five hours earlier and the deep shadows of the chill winter afternoon were reaching across Andrews Air Force Base in nearby Maryland when he finally left.

There had been the traditional ride with the new president to the Capitol for the swearing-in ceremony, followed by the nostalgic farewells of friends and political associates. There was a surface air of gaiety. But underneath was the solemnity—and occasional tears—which inevitably must mark the end of an era.

After five years and two months in the world's most demanding job, Lyndon Baines Johnson was going home to his rolling Texas hill country, unsure of the exact details of his future and hauntingly uncertain how history would evaluate his record at the White House.

The 36th president of the United States was expansive, even ebullient, as he boarded the same Air Force plane which brought him here from Dallas on Nov. 22, 1963, following the assassination of John F. Kennedy.

The familiar Johnson juices, which took him alternately from the pinnacles of optimism to the canyons of despondency and which confounded those who try to characterize him with any certainty, were running high. People, he said, "are good."

The mood persisted during the two-and-a-half-hour flight to

Bergstrom Air Force Base and then on to Stonewall, Texas, and the LBJ ranch.

Johnson got a rousing welcome from his rancher neighbors, who still call him "Lyndon." But there seemed to be one of those subtle changes in mood. Although basking in their affection, he told them, somewhat poignantly, "I have been a little too small for every job and I've always had to try harder."

Questioned in Washington shortly after Nixon was sworn in, Johnson said he felt a sense of relief almost the moment the ceremony began. In the first few days at the ranch, he discovered truly how many responsibilities he had left behind.

There no longer was the inevitable man with the black satchel containing the nation's nuclear attack codes. There were no business or ceremonial deadlines to meet. The war and peace decisions with which he had wrestled so long had passed to Nixon.

Johnson and Lady Bird launched their retirement with long walks and miles of horseback riding in the brilliant sunshine which bathed the range and the Pedernales River. The former president said of those first few days that it was "like having a day off."

The atmosphere changed at the Johnson place the moment he relinquished the presidency. Barricades were removed and the gatehouse guards departed. Security became minimal although Johnson still has Secret Service protection as an ex-president. Souvenir shops still sold rocks from the LBJ ranch and crockery embellished with Johnson's portrait. But there was a "for sale" sign on a new Johnson City motel.

The center of Johnsonian activity has shifted to Austin where the former president's offices are being organized to handle the 2,500 letters and 200 telephone calls he has been getting every day. . . .

His legislative accomplishments included a new civil rights law, Medicare, education for all, from 4-year-old Head Starters to 74-year-old adult students. A broad housing bill was passed and "open housing" became the law of the land. He paid high praise to the "fabulous" 89th Congress.

But it quickly became obvious that he was more at home in the war against poverty, illiteracy and hunger than he was in the jungles of diplomacy where even the world's most powerful nation could not impose peace.

Vietnam was Johnson's Waterloo. He has told visitors that he might have sought reelection had it not been for that conflict and the national disunity it created. . . .

Johnson was a man besieged but righteous in his cause. He appealed for patience and perseverance during a "time of human testing."

. . . One of the things he took home with him to Texas was the belief that he had succeeded at least in part. Johnson feels he was so mistrusted that it took a complete act of personal sacrifice to be believed.

The former president acknowledges that he suffered from a "credibility gap" but he attributes it to his failure to communicate rather than to his credibility. Others close to Johnson believe his need for secrecy led to suspicion and misinformation.

Johnson has kept his personal opinion of Nixon a secret. He has told friends, however, that he ran for the vice presidency because his beloved friend, the late Speaker Sam Rayburn, could not bear to see Nixon as president in 1960.

"I wanted to be vice president about as much as I wanted to be the Pope," Johnson once said glumly.

But now that he has experienced the power and frustrations of the presidency, Johnson has only compassion for the man in the White House. Equally, he obviously cherishes his membership in the world's most exclusive club—the presidency of the United States.

(Jan. 30, 1969)

When President Nixon came on board, nearly $800,000 was spent on refurbishing the interior of SAM 26000. The floor plan had at its heart a three-room suite of private quarters for the president and his family in the forward section: a combination office and sitting room for the president, a smaller sitting room for the first lady and a large lounge that could be used as a conference room. Another change was a special aisle along the left side of the interior affording movement but not disturbing the first family's privacy.

Forward of the presidential suite was the seating area for the Secret Service agents and to the rear a staff compartment with workstations for the secretaries. Behind that was an eight-seat guest area followed by the press cabin and another cabin for Air Force One's security guards.

Despite the changes to the layout, Pat Nixon decided to keep the desert color scheme Lady Bird had used: soft beiges, sand tones and golds, accented here and there with a splash of green, orange or yellow.

Then again, the Nixons pretty much started out with a clean slate. When the plane returned from Texas, Colonel Ralph Albertazzie recounted, "I found an empty larder. We had no presidential china, no Air Force One silverware, no cocktail napkins, no towels—not even any paper products like toilet tissue. All these items were not stamped LBJ either but were imprinted 'Air Force One.' But they were all gone.

"Even LBJ's special executive chair—the one we called 'the throne'—was unbolted from the floor and taken away. The presidential stateroom was bare of pillows, blankets, everything that bore the presidential seal. I couldn't believe my eyes."[3]

All the items had been carted off for eventual display at the LBJ Library in Austin—where you can see most of them today. As it was, the Nixons had ridiculed "the throne" and were probably glad LBJ's people had saved them the trouble of throwing it out.

But LBJ wasn't the only one to pick a presidential plane clean. After SAM 27000 arrived in December 1972, Henry Kissinger made great use of SAM 26000 for his many secret meetings in China, Vietnam and Paris. And like LBJ, he began to think of it as his plane. Bill Gulley, former director of the White House Military Office, recounted that Kissinger's staff knew of his attachment to the plane, and when they were planning a farewell party for him, one of his aides called to ask if there was some memento from the aircraft they could present to Kissinger.

"I called the Air Force One office, got [Colonel Les] McClelland, the pilot of Air Force One and asked him to have something sent over. He said, 'Christ, Bill, Kissinger's already taken everything off the thing but the landing gear. Does he want that too?' "[4]

After their trip home, LBJ and Lady Bird traveled twice more on Air Force One. President and Mrs. Nixon invited the Johnsons to fly with them from San Clemente to Arcata, California, for the dedication of the Lady Bird Johnson Redwood Forest, commemorating her efforts to beautify America. After the ceremonies, Nixon, instead of putting the Johnsons aboard the private plane that had brought them to California, ordered the crew to take them back to Texas aboard the presidential aircraft.

Several days after Johnson suffered his fatal heart attack on January 22, 1973, Air Force One was dispatched to the Texas ranch and his body was brought to Washington where it lay in state at the Capitol.

As they were traveling back, Albertazzie said he felt a tap on his shoulder. "Good to see you, Ralph," said Lady Bird. "Lyndon would have been happy to know you were flying him home on his final trip."[5]

With the delivery of SAM 27000, Nixon transferred the name *Spirit of '76* and made his maiden voyage on it on a trip to California in February 1973. He apparently liked it but his family felt otherwise. When the plane's layout was being planned, Mrs. Nixon was shown a floor plan and asked, "Is this the way Dick wants the airplane?"

"Well, this is the way [H. R.] Haldeman said the president wanted it," Albertazzie told her.

"I don't think Dick is going to like it," she said.[6]

Haldeman's plan called for the big staff compartment—his territory—to be built directly behind the president's office and before the first lady's sitting room. That meant that the presidential lounge, where Mrs. Nixon, her daughters and their husbands liked to gather, would no longer be adjacent to the presidential suite. It also meant the first family had to walk through the staff compartment every time they entered or left the lounge. Construction proceeded according to the Haldeman plan:

> From his big swivel chair at the first table in the staff section, he had easy access to the president's door, noting whom he summoned in and how long they remained together. It was all part of Haldeman's modus operandi. He wanted Nixon under tight surveillance. Haldeman's deputies, Dwight Chapin and Larry Higby, were under orders to keep a log of everything Nixon did aboard the plane, with whom he talked, how long they talked, and if possible, what they talked about.[7]

However, stories were beginning to surface about Mrs. Nixon's dissatisfaction, and within a few weeks the White House Military Office sent a memo to Andrews, instructing the personnel that the next time SAM 27000 was out of service for maintenance, Nixon wanted the same floor plan installed as was in SAM 26000. That was accomplished for about $750,000.

When the maintenance period—and the renovation—was scheduled, Mrs. Nixon met with interior decorators to come up with a color scheme. She chose shades of blue, from the deep blue of her husband's personal chair and desktop to the crushed velvet upholstery in Wedgwood blue chosen for her sitting room and the presidential lounge. The staff tables were inlaid with leather and muted blue plaids and textured materials were chosen for the Secret Service compartment and the press cabin. Blue-gray carpeting was laid throughout.

Whatever the color scheme, it's a great plane. Granted, air travel is not the only mode of transportation I've endured covering the presidency. Cars, trains, boats, buses, helicopters, aircraft carriers—you name it. But flying on that aircraft carries a special charm—although when I'm at Andrews Air Force Base at 5:00 A.M. I may think otherwise.

For the reporters, photographers, technicians and other media personnel assigned to a presidential trip, the day usually begins before dawn with the trip to Andrews. If the presidential trip is overseas, our luggage has already been turned in, screened and put aboard the day before. When we arrive, we begin a series of check-ins. The transportation officer checks names against one list, the Secret Service agent hands out identification tags or "trip passes."

These passes can range from small color-coded tags to breastplate-sized medallions. The passes also have an identifying photo that sometimes looks as if it were taken from a police mug shot. With our names checked off and our tags affixed around our necks, we board buses to be driven across the tarmac to the plane.

When Franklin Roosevelt traveled, his total entourage numbered about twelve. The designated core press pool that travels with the president still hovers around that number. The bulk of the press corps flies on a press charter.

But on President Clinton's trip to Africa in 1998, there were sixty-eight people attached as part of the White House delegation, sixteen members of Congress and a twenty-four-member "citizens' delegation" ranging from bank presidents to investment corporation representatives to foundation executives to civic leaders—not counting the members of the press, the Secret Service personnel, the military aides, the advance team, the airplane security team and the flight crews.

So is it any wonder I say that traveling with the president is like traveling with the circus?

During World War II, news blackouts were common on the president's comings and goings. Reporters knew that the president was going to be out of town, they just couldn't report it, and what's more, there was no official "press pool" to accompany him, since the trip was a secret. The appropriately named Steve Early would prudently pass the word to the press corps with something like "If I were you, I'd be in Quebec tomorrow."

Since then, preparations for any trip, from a jaunt to Philadelphia to deliver a speech to a two-week sweep of European capitals, have become like something I'm sure Ike planned when he was putting together the Normandy invasion. There is an increased demand for coverage of the president, an increase in the number of people doing the covering and a consequent growth of security measures.

We fill out visa applications; we fill out forms from the White House press office as to our needs for hotels, space in the filing center, telephones, laptop hookups; our supervisors write letters certifying we are "Members of the Working Press" assigned to cover the trip; we pack our bags and hand them over to the Secret Service for inspection.

Once we're there, be it overseas or a campaign stop in Duluth, we're running on pure adrenaline. The days are long, the nights are short and sleep is fitful. One of the constant fears that plagues the press is the thought of over-sleeping and missing the bus that takes you to the plane that takes you to the next stop, so you can hit the deck running all over again.

On long trips that cover several cities, our bags usually are due in the hotel lobby long before we are—well, maybe an hour or so before us, like 4:00 A.M. On one campaign trip, my UPI colleague was Steve Gerstel, who truly liked to "unwind" at the end of a long day. After he "unwound" for several hours, Steve still remembered to put his bag outside the hotel room to be picked up. About two or three hours later, he sat bolt upright in bed and realized he'd packed all his clothes in the bag for pickup. Fortunately, he was able to retrieve his luggage or he would have had to leave the hotel and board the press bus in his pajamas.

After we've boarded the press bus—hopefully in the correct attire—we head back to the airport for another leg of a journey and the same routine: get on the plane, land at the next stop, leave by the back door, run to the designated spot and watch and wait for the president to come down the gangway. After this leg of the journey is done and if we've spent the night, we board the buses again the following morning for another trip to the airport to get on the plane and land at the next stop and on and on.

We watch the president come down the ramp and shake hands with the welcoming party. Then we run for the buses to get to the press center to file our stories, or hop into the buses that become part of a presidential motorcade.

In my early days, my colleagues and I would be running out the airplane exit loaded down with portable typewriters and tape recorders. Those items have given way to cellular phones and laptop computers, but I haven't noticed them getting all that much lighter over the years. All in all, when you think about going through this routine over and over on a fourteen-day trip, you get the idea of the kind of endurance test covering a president can be, not to mention the strength and agility required.

President Bush, who must hold some kind of record as the No. 1 Traveling Man, flew to Pearl Harbor in December 1991 for commemoration ceremonies and we reached Honolulu after 8:00 P.M.—1:00 A.M. Washington time. Most of the press pool was then up by 4:00 A.M. (Washington time) covering the morning's events. Then we had about ninety minutes to write and file our stories before we got back on the plane at 1:00 P.M.

Sometimes I thought if it weren't for the honor of the thing . . . But I also knew I was happy to be along for the ride.

One ride I could have done without, though: I was on a short trip with

President Reagan from Topeka, Kansas, to Ogden, Utah. A valve got stuck and the air-conditioning went out in the back of the plane, sending the temperature into the nineties where we were sitting. Up front in the VIP cabins, all was well. In fact, deputy chief of staff Mike Deaver covered himself with two blankets when he dozed off.

When the jet landed at Hill Air Force Base near Ogden, the military police who travel aboard Air Force One cited "security reasons" and would not let the mechanics from the base repair the defective valve.

Where have I been and how many times have I been there? To tell you the truth, after thirty-eight years and a few million miles, I think I can safely say "just about everywhere and three times." And each time I boarded that plane, I was always ready for a lot of work, a lack of sleep and a grand adventure.

Even in the air, you don't stop working. On the old plane, the press section was located near the rear—right near the lavatories. When officials would walk by us we nabbed them for what came to be known as the "men's room press conferences."

While we didn't necessarily pick up many hot tips in those situations, I did manage to buttonhole someone who could have spilled the goods—if he had been a little older. We were on our way back from the Democratic National Convention in New York in 1980. Jimmy Carter had clinched the nomination but only after a painful and trying time with Senator Ted Kennedy of Massachusetts.

The scene everyone remembers at that confab was Carter following Kennedy around on the "victory podium" after the nomination, trying to get him to raise his arms in solidarity with everyone standing there.

On the plane, the Carter family kept to themselves in the family quarters until Chip Carter came out with his three-year-old son, who wanted a soft drink. I grabbed my notebook, gestured to the little boy and said teasingly, "So tell me, what did your granddad have to say about Senator Kennedy?"

Some reporters have preferred riding in the second plane, known as the press charter or, in more common parlance, the "zoo plane." But it's good to be on Air Force One in case someone decides to "make news." Sometimes the White House makes an official statement while we're airborne and then we make what is known as a "pool call" back to the home office. The operator contacts all three wire services simultaneously and one wire service reporter aboard the plane is designated to read the information over the phone to the desk editors in Washington. The editors in turn file a story with the dateline "Aboard Air Force One."

Sometimes, though, the younger reporters just don't get it. As UPI's senior White House correspondent and bureau chief, my rank has its priv-ileges. I can assign one of the other reporters to a trip—with a little instruction.

Ken Bazinet was covering President Clinton on a trip to California solo and as such was the designated UPI correspondent traveling aboard the presidential aircraft. For their last stop before returning to Washington, they were headed to Charlotte, North Carolina, so Clinton could watch the NCAA basketball championship. Word had spread that it was going to be much more fun on the charter on that leg of the trip, given the high antici-pation over the game. Ken, one of the most rabid basketball fans I've ever known, called and asked if he could ride aboard the "zoo plane," which would have left us out of the loop if anything was said aboard Air Force One.

Drawing on my years of experience of the necessity of being wherever the president is—and slightly flabbergasted at his suggestion—I said, "Ken, let me put it this way: If that plane goes down, I want you on it."

To this day, I insist I was trying to be funny, but he thinks otherwise.

I'd had my own close calls with missing the presidential aircraft, which likely prompted my rather blunt response. In the Kennedy days, we'd wrapped up our "body watch" of him and his family on vacation in Hyannis Port, Massachusetts, and the press pool boarded the bus for the ride to Logan Airport.

We got stuck in Boston's busy traffic and by the time we got to the airport, we saw the presidential plane had taxied out to the runway and was ready to take off. We stood there stranded, forlorn and wondering (1) how we were going to get back to Washington and (2) how we were going to explain this to our editors once we got there.

Suddenly, we saw the plane slowly turning around and coming back to the terminal. Pierre Salinger had told Kennedy that his band of White House reporters had arrived late and the president ordered the plane to head back and pick us up.

I wonder what the chances are of that happening today?

On another trip, I remember Kennedy wandering back to the press cabin to chat. We had hit some turbulence on the trip and the flight had had its rocky moments. We asked him what he thought the reaction would be if the plane ever crashed. He looked over to where I was sitting, grinned and said, "I know one thing. Your name will be just a footnote."

Incidentally, it's not a free ride. Media outlets pay handsomely—some-times the equivalent of first class plus—for their reporters and photogra-phers to travel. The cost is prorated according to the number traveling on board, but consider a trip that will take them from Washington to Hawaii to

Australia to the Philippines to Thailand and back to Washington—with a couple of refueling stops—and the price escalates accordingly.

Traveling at taxpayers' expense are the president, his family and any special invited guests, along with the staff and flight crew. Staffers who travel with the president are in the top pecking order and seats are highly coveted. It is quite a coup for "ordinary citizens" to travel aboard the presidential aircraft, but some big campaign donors have been afforded the privilege in several administrations.[8]

SAM 27000 had room for 69 passengers. After his first ride, President Reagan jokingly pronounced it "rather small, but it will do." Around 1982, the Air Force began preliminary planning on a Boeing 747 to replace the presidential jet and its backup plane. The new aircraft was ready for Reagan's flight home in 1988 after he left office. It seats 70 passengers and has 87 phones, 16 video monitors and 11 videocassette recorders. It can fly 9,600 miles without refueling, has a maximum speed of 701 mph, can be refueled in midair if need be and has special antiattack capabilities.

As George Bush once noted in a statement to the *New York Daily News,* "It was reassuring to have a device that would fend off heat-seeking missiles."

Before that, however, four 747 jumbo jets known as "Doomsday" planes were already operational as part of the presidential fleet along with the helicopters that are kept for White House use. The four planes each bear the official name National Emergency Airborne Command Post. They were designed to serve as a presidential command center in a war. At least one is on standby at all times at Andrews Air Force Base. The plane, about three-quarters the size of a football field, contains six areas for planning and directing military action in times of emergency and can stay aloft for seventy-two hours without refueling.

Jimmy Carter used a prototype of the aircraft for his first trip home to Plains after he took office in 1977. He called the experience "very sobering."

Ronald Reagan made a few trips in a newer, more sophisticated model, once for a three-day trip to Texas to do some turkey hunting. He said he was "highly impressed" with the plane's capabilities.

George Bush made full use of the new 747—estimated cost $181.5 million—when he took office, or, as he used to joke, "Have plane, will travel." Barbara Bush said the 747 was so big she could "exercise in it." In an interview on September 10, 1990, with me, Chris Connell of AP and Gene Gibbons of Reuters, she lauded Nancy Reagan's choice of interior colors, said it was "tastefully done" but she thought it "needs pictures on the wall. That's all. It's so big it needs pictures on the wall, masterpieces."

One of us asked her, "You don't think people will see this massive jet coming in and say 'Boy, we've got a king for a president now?' "

"No, I don't think so," she said. "I think people will think the press will be a little less grumpy now that they're more comfortable sitting in that wonderful plane, have all those good refreshments and being treated—paying all that you pay for it and then being comfortable. They'll be pleased for you."

We reminded her that her husband had said "Have plane, will travel."

"He said that?" she said. "Oh, dear. Well, that's better than 'Have cook, will invite over.'"

And travel he did. According to a summary from President Bush's library, from January 20, 1989, to August 1, 1991, he had racked up 326,927 miles aboard a presidential aircraft. He visited 45 states, 126 different U.S. cities, 3 national parks, and made 43 visits to 32 different foreign countries.

Dwight Eisenhower traveled a little over 300,000 miles too, but it took his entire eight-year presidency to hit that mark.

The service, without a doubt, is first-rate. Even though there's only so much you can do with food at forty thousand feet, the Boeing 747s came equipped with two modern galleys complete with ovens, broilers and microwave units. It reduced the need for frozen precooked meals and gave the flight crew a chance to prepare meals in-flight. The newer planes have even more sophisticated appliances aboard, but by and large, everyone seems to agree that in-flight food is in-flight food.

When it was announced that SAM 26000 was retiring, I called Master Sgt. Howard Franklin—"Howie" to presidents and anyone else who was privileged to ride aboard Air Force One. He had spent twenty-nine years in the Air Force, twenty-four of them as a steward aboard the presidential aircraft, beginning with the Nixon administration and ending with his retirement in 1994. We got to reminiscing about some of those mass-produced meals aboard the plane—and a few other experiences as well.

One of Howie's first assignments was as a member of the flight crew for Henry Kissinger during his secret shuttle trips to Vietnam and his more public journeys to Paris for the interminable peace negotiations.

Kissinger, he said, played his cards close and his travel plans even closer. He liked to keep everyone in the dark most of the time—especially the State Department correspondents—and rarely announced where he was going and how long he would be gone. Once he planned a sixteen-day tour that turned out to be a thirty-four-day marathon of eighteen-hour days that left everyone exhausted: the flight crew, the press corps, his staff and the Secret Service agents assigned to him.

"It made us all a little crazy," said Howie, "but I remember him telling us something like 'If you think working in government leads to paranoia try working in academia.'"

On those secret trips all the food had to be brought on board and nothing could be purchased locally as a safeguard against tampering. The crew got used to planning for Kissinger's trips: If he hinted he would be gone for ten days, they laid in supplies for twenty. But their best-laid plans sometimes went awry when the trip lasted even longer.

Toward the end of one of those marathon trips, supplies were running low, tempers were running high and Kissinger was hungry. Howie managed to cobble together a fruit salad with sour cream and brown sugar, but when he put it down in front of the secretary, Kissinger blasted him.

"What is this shit?" he shouted.

Howie blasted back, "Eat it, it's good for you!"

Kissinger, he said, proceeded to eat the salad and pronounced it indeed good.

A sense of humor was more than necessary on those trips, Howie recalled. Kissinger once told his Secret Service agents of his fear, with all these secret comings and goings, that he might be kidnapped.

"Don't worry, Dr. Kissinger," one of the agents quipped, "we'll never let them take you alive."

Kissinger's eyes popped at that one but then he started to laugh, Howie said, defusing what could have been a tense moment—and the possible end of an agent's career.

Another time, a steward was bringing breakfast to the flight crew and had to pass through the area Kissinger was using. The steward hemmed and hawed, not wanting to risk the possible wrath of Kissinger, until finally Howie just grabbed the tray and started walking—just as Kissinger was changing his clothes.

"Oh, I caught you with your pants down," he said, and continued on to the flight deck.

He said only President Bush exceeded the kind of travel schedule Kissinger put flight crews through, but he was a "hardworking guy, very businesslike.

"The joke aboard the plane used to be, 'Hey, doesn't this guy have a secretary of state?' But he was great," said Howie.

Then again, I reminded Howie, there were all those trips we had taken with Nixon, who was inside the White House for only four of the forty-four weekends of his second term. The press corps was tempted more than once to begin their stories with: "The president arrived in Washington today for a brief visit."

Some members of the first family knew how to enjoy a trip, Howie said. When "Miz Lillian" Carter led the delegation to Israel for Golda Meir's funeral, "She had a poker game going on in front with all the members of Congress and she had a poker game going on in back with the Secret Service agents," he recalled. "The whole flight, she would go back and forth between the two games—and she was winning all their money."

Serving the presidents was always a pleasure, he told me, and most of them went out of their way to acknowledge the tough jobs the stewards had on those many, many trips.

"Reagan had a real gift for being president, but he was always personable," Howie said. "There was never a time you brought him anything, not even a glass of water, that he didn't acknowledge you or say 'thank you.'"

And despite all the myths, he said, first families weren't too demanding when it came to food and drink. Usually it was some member of the White House staff who gave the crew a hard time, like when the menus had to be submitted to Nixon's staff for approval. And there was one time . . .

"One steward, Charlie Green," Howie said. "I think Lyndon Johnson fired him eight times and hired him nine times. And once it was for that root beer thing."

Johnson had developed a taste for a certain brand of root beer and the flight crew had packed enough on board for Johnson but for no one else, since nobody else ever ordered the stuff, Howie said. As it was, Master Sgt. Joe Ayers, who had been LBJ's personal steward aboard the plane, requested and got a transfer because of a root beer incident. Johnson had consumed all six bottles aboard and Ayers unfortunately was the one to tell him they were out of it. "How many times do I have to tell you that I want diet root beer on this plane at all times?" Johnson screamed. "It's not a difficult transaction. You can buy the fuckin' stuff anywhere, Sergeant. I want an order sent out to all Air Force bases: stock root beer!"[9]

The crew learned to stock as much as they thought was necessary, Howie said, until one trip, LBJ ordered his usual root beer and then told the crew to serve it to the rest of the staff and the press pool.

"Then LBJ called for another one and Charlie told him 'We don't have any more.'"

"That's funny," said Johnson, "I just talked to the company president yesterday and I didn't get the impression they were going out of business."

Nixon and Ford did prefer cottage cheese, he said, but Nixon did not cover it with ketchup as was reported over and over. Ford, however, was known to dash a little A-1 Sauce on his. LBJ liked chili and Bush "wanted Texas barbecue morning, noon and night." Reagan liked having meat loaf and macaroni and cheese and lemon meringue pie.

Such a gourmet trip down memory lane, I said, until Howie reminded me: "You, Helen, how could I forget? Always a bologna sandwich and black coffee."

Well, sandwiches and coffee might have been a better menu on June 12,

1996, when President Clinton was flying from New Mexico to South Carolina. My colleague Paul Basken was aboard that flight and I couldn't figure out why he showed up for work the next day looking a little pale and squeamish. Then Paul gave me a copy of the pool report that had been filed for the trip:

Pool Report
Air Force One, Albuquerque to Charleston
Shaken, not stirred

Approximately 30 minutes into the flight, 30 miles west of Lubbock, Air Force One hit a patch of severe midair turbulence that sent passengers and food flying during a terrifying few seconds of zero gravity. The president was sitting in a large armchair in his office cabin reading when the clouds attacked. Meal service had just begun but the president did not yet have his New Mexico fiesta platter of tamales, frijoles, rice, guacamole and salsa. After the first jolt Clinton fastened his seat belt, said [White House press secretary Mike] McCurry, just in time for the whopper.

The rest of the passengers weren't so lucky. Your pool and Secret Service agents were thrown two to three feet, in some cases more, into the air as the plane lurched violently—and loudly. Mexican food, plates and broken glass were sprayed all over the aisles and galley. (Wire photos have good shots of galley wreckage.) One agent reportedly suffered a cut hand from a broken bowl. Others were shaken but unhurt except for a few bumps and bruises. The president dispatched Bruce Lindsey to the military aide to get a report on the situation from the cockpit. The cleanup began almost immediately, with an aroma of salsa wafting through the cabin as stewards picked up glass shards and tamale remnants.

Clinton, dressed in jeans, sneakers and a Boston Marathon T-shirt, came back about 20 minutes after the incident to make sure everyone was OK and to survey the cleanup efforts. (He offered no federal funding.)

When asked if he was strapped in when the turbulence hit, Clinton responded, "I was holding on, holding on. That sure was a character builder." The president seemed amused that the pool might go without dinner but judging from the green gills in the back of the plane there would have been few takers.

One acrobatic note: McCurry caught his Scotch & soda midair—Apollo 13 style—imitating a Bugs Bunny feat he's long studied. "I was sitting there with my drink and I managed to catch it as it came back down," he said. The salsa-drenched agents were not quite so amused. Most have no change of clothes, since they were [scheduled] to return to Washington Tuesday night. They were trying hard to scrape dinner from their suits and pick rice from their holsters before landing.

A few technical notes: the pilot had just deviated from the flight path and was heading south, climbing from 33,000 feet to 37,000 to avoid storms in the area when the incident occurred. It felt as though the plane dropped for several seconds, but according to McCurry, the pilot said Air Force One, a modified Boeing 747, did not drop. It was buffeted by midair turbulence. 46 passengers and 26 crew members were aboard for the cloud rodeo. Some likened the experience to an earthquake at 33,000 feet.

. . .

That's it from your well-shaken pool who are growing fonder by the minute of Tower Air.

Karen Breslau, Newsweek
John Harris, Washington Post

So much for the food. I will say that after he got bounced around on that flight, the green-gilled Paul managed to get off the plane, walk into the office at Andrews, hook up his computer and file a story about the incident to the copy desk.

My former colleague Cheryl Arvidson reminded me of the one—and perhaps only—time I ever ordered a drink aboard Air Force One.

We were flying back from Tokyo with President Reagan after the economic summit in 1986. Cheryl was the designated print pool reporter, Tom Raum of AP the wire reporter and Sheila Kast of ABC was the television pool.

We first stopped in Los Angeles after leaving Washington, then had a brief stopover in Hawaii, then on to Guam and Bali, Indonesia and finally Tokyo.

We were just getting ready to leave Hawaii when the news broke of a nuclear accident at Chernobyl. "We literally started off on our trip toward that section of the world not knowing how serious the accident was or how dangerous the cloud of radiation might be that was headed toward the very places we were going," Cheryl said. "The cloud was being pretty much dismissed as a threat to us by the time we got to Indonesia, but people weren't sure that was right and the media certainly were not totally comforted at the prospect of what might be ahead."

But we continued on our journey under that uncertain cloud.

When we got to Tokyo we assembled for the traditional welcoming ceremonies by the host nation in which each visiting dignitary is received with the flag and national anthem of his or her country. This ceremony was being held at the presidential palace so the traveling press climbed aboard buses and got herded onto risers to witness the event.

As we stood there, we heard what sounded like explosions in the distance; figuring it might have been a military salute of some kind we didn't pay much attention.

Later we found out that the police had arrested some terrorists who were throwing crude bombs at the palace grounds from an apartment in downtown Tokyo. Not a big deal on its own, but given the surrounding events, this summit was turning into a bizarre situation even before it started.

Our stories that day not only covered the start of the summit but a nuclear cloud that could have been drifting our way and some bombs over Tokyo.

And as Cheryl put it so well, "Complicating the story was the fact that in Japan we were thirteen hours ahead of Washington, so just when our day was wrapping up, the U.S. news cycle was just beginning, meaning that you could literally find yourself working around the clock because your deadlines were coming at a time when all you wanted to be doing was sleeping, and when D.C. was sleeping, the big news of the day was going on. So by the time the pool got on Air Force One, we were pretty tired and stressed out."

We all wearily boarded the plane and the stewards came by and offered us something to drink. "I remember several of us thought a drink might be just what was needed," Cheryl said. "The steward took our orders and then turned to Helen, who ordered a glass of red wine.

"He was clearly astonished and exclaimed, '*Miss Thomas?*'

"I will never forget that look, and I knew right then that that may have been the first time Helen had ever ordered a drink while flying on Air Force One."

For historic moments aboard the presidential aircraft, probably none will ever compare with Lyndon Johnson's swearing-in as the thirty-seventh president, taking the oath flanked by Lady Bird and the bereaved Jacqueline Kennedy in that crowded sweltering compartment.

U.S. District Judge Sarah T. Hughes, a friend of Johnson's, administered the oath of office. Johnson repeated the simple oath: "I do solemnly swear that I will faithfully execute the office of President of the United States, and I will to the best of my ability preserve, protect and defend the Constitution of the United States, so help me God."

Lady Bird Johnson recalled that at that incredibly difficult time, it was necessary to telephone the grief-stricken Bobby Kennedy for the correct wording of the oath, as no one could remember.

And a search for a Bible, which is not legally required as part of the oath taking, had everyone scrambling. Steward Joe Ayers remembered that Kennedy always carried a personal Bible and went to look for it. According to Secret Service agent Emory Roberts, it wasn't a Bible but a Catholic missal, a book of prayers and masses in English and Latin. As recounted in *The Flying White House,* the book "probably had been presented to the president shortly after arriving in Dallas. [Roberts] reports that the book was still cellophane-wrapped in a cardboard box when found for the ceremony and obviously had not been opened."[10]

Unfortunately, after administering the oath, Judge Hughes said she gave it to "an official-looking person" as she left the plane and it has never been found.

Smitty was aboard, and as he recounted in *A White House Memoir,* no room has ever seemed smaller than the compartment in which LBJ took the oath:

> The room is used normally as a combination conference and sitting room and could accommodate eight to ten people seated.
>
> I wedged inside the door and began counting. There were 27 people in this compartment. Johnson stood in the center with his wife, Lady Bird. . . . The compartment became hotter and hotter. Johnson . . . urged people to press forward, but a Signal Corps photographer, Capt. Cecil Stoughton, standing in the corner on a chair, said if Johnson moved any closer, it would be virtually impossible to make a truly historic photograph. . . .[11]

I was back on the ground in Washington, but given the miles I've logged and what I've witnessed on my travels, that singular moment probably stands alone as the time of greatest anguish aboard the president's plane.

In all my travels, the most significant, most interesting and most incredible trip was China in 1972.

Nixon's strong suit was foreign affairs and he always seemed happiest when he was boarding the plane for a trip out of the country. George Bush probably surpassed his mileage-per-trip ratio, but Nixon always liked to stress he was the first U.S. president to visit some foreign land.

I can't say the press corps, or even some heads of state, were thrilled with this proclivity. Several summers found us sweltering in the heat of some tropical clime. One summer when Nixon visited India, Prime Minister

Indira Gandhi, responding to Nixon's remarks about the warmth of his welcome, said, "Well, sir, you came at the wrong time of the day and the wrong time of the year."

Henry Kissinger has been identified with scoring the historic diplomatic breakthrough with China. He made all the preliminary trips that eventually paved the way, but Nixon was the point man. They worked well together: Both of them seemed to equate diplomacy with secrecy.

Yet secrecy was crucial in this instance, and they covered every track until Nixon announced the visit to China, which we called Red China back then, on July 15, 1971, and said that he would visit Peking, now Beijing, before May 1972.

We were on "body watch" in Laguna Beach, California, when word spread that Nixon was flying to Burbank to broadcast a nationwide address. We took off down the highway to pick up the press helicopter to accompany Nixon and when I saw the president and Kissinger get off the helicopter together—Kissinger wearing a broad smile—I figured it was a piece of good news the American public was going to hear, possibly a move toward peace in Vietnam.

But his announcement made the room rock. I remember Nixon looking elated when he came out of the studio. The trip was set for February 1972.

In the preliminary talks, Chinese premier Chou En-lai hinted at the difficulties involved in accommodating the usual number of press that accompanied a president on his travels and suggested perhaps ten reporters and a couple of camera crews. The White House received more than two thousand applications for press credentials.

The negotiations that took place to have more reporters, photographers, camera crews and technicians attached to the trip probably could have used Kissinger's mediating skills. The number first got increased to twenty-eight, then eighty and finally eighty-seven. Nixon handpicked the press corps and the Chinese reserved the right to veto any one of us. I was one of three women chosen along with Barbara Walters of NBC and Fay Wells of Storer Broadcasting.

Beyond the number of bodies, there were enormous technical considerations. Communications from China to the outside world at that time consisted of a few radio channels. The White House first suggested converting a plane into a giant mobile broadcasting studio and parking it at the airport, from which the networks could send TV signals to a communications satellite. The Chinese vetoed the idea as they considered it an infringement on their sovereignty. In the end, the White House turned over a building plan for a broadcasting facility and it was built in Peking.

The three networks got twelve correspondents and twenty-five cameramen and producers—three of whom, it turned out, were network vice presidents; public broadcasting got one correspondent, no cameraman; the wire services got three reporters and two photographers each. The rest of the pool broke down to six magazine writers, four radio broadcasters, two magazine photographers, two photo technicians, twenty-one newspaper reporters, three syndicated columnists and a correspondent from the Voice of America. At that time, it was the largest contingent of U.S. media ever allowed into China all at once.

President and Mrs. Nixon were in an expansive mood when they boarded the plane. One of the pool reporters handed Nixon an elaborate-looking atlas of China, which bore the seal "Central Intelligence Agency" on its cover.

"Do you think they'll let me in with this?" Nixon asked.

"This will probably show how much we don't know about China" was the response.

As it was, the plane turned into a flying library for most of the press corps as we immersed ourselves in books, monographs, position papers and other research, just as we'd begun doing when the trip was announced.

Chopsticks were provided for our first meals on board and a red rose was placed on each of the meal trays served to the women during the trip. Nixon had said earlier that based on his many travels he needed no instruction on the use of chopsticks, "but," he joked, "she does," pointing to his wife, Pat. That was far from the truth. She was extremely adept with them.

I asked for a fork and got one.

Our first stop was Hawaii, at the Marine Corps Air Station in Kaneohe Bay. There, the Nixons stayed in a seventeen-room house belonging to a Marine general. It had a commanding view of the sea and the nearby islands.

Hundreds of people showed up the next day to see the president off. As he left he told them, "Tomorrow I will be in China. I think it is most appropriate that this journey begins in Hawaii, a state where East and West really do meet."

The journey had been timed to accommodate the jet lag that comes with flying across many time zones and the International Date Line. After an overnight stop in Guam, we continued on.

At the Rainbow Bridge Airport in Shanghai, 8:55 A.M., Richard Nixon became the first U.S. president to set foot on Mainland China.

For me, I felt like I'd landed on the moon. When you cover a president, you get used to throngs of people turning out. Premier Chou En-lai greeted the Nixons at the airport and hustled them off in a limousine with lace curtains on the windows. From the press motorcade trailing behind, I noticed there weren't many people about, and of the few who were, even fewer either turned their heads or slowed their bicycles when the limousines passed.

At the airport, there had been forty-two Chinese officials, the Chinese Army band, an honor guard of five hundred military personnel and the American press corps and advance party, which had come earlier to await Nixon's arrival. There were no foreign diplomats. Aside from airport employees, press bus drivers and the limousine chauffeurs, there were no "typical citizens" on hand.

The Nixons stayed in a government guest house called Taio Yu Tai, "The Fishing Terrace," made of yellow brick and surrounded by mainly empty gardens and bare willow trees surrounding a small frozen lake. I think the biggest assembled crowd of "ordinary" Chinese citizens the president might have seen on his entire visit was on the morning of February 24, his fourth day, when groups of schoolchildren and soldiers showed up outside the compound where he was staying to shovel and sweep away the snow that had fallen overnight. As soon as the snow was gone, so were they.

Of course, there were the preprogrammed crowds we came into contact with when President and Mrs. Nixon toured the historic sites and attended official functions. They were always exceedingly polite and friendly. But trying to gauge the reaction of the hotel clerks, the interpreters, the minders, elevator operators and store clerks was an exercise in futility. There was no such thing as "public opinion" back then. People were told what to think and so they did.

Newswise, it was equally silent. Press secretary Ron Ziegler had briefed us that we would be getting little in the way of hard news until the final communiqué was issued. All the sessions were conducted in secret and the most secret of all took place shortly after we arrived.

We'd been taken to wait outside the guest house to accompany Nixon to a scheduled meeting with Chou En-lai. Meanwhile, Chou, Nixon and Kissinger slipped out a back door for another meeting—a private one with Mao Tse-tung at his home. So secretive were the Chinese about Mao's residence that afterward Ziegler refused to describe it or its location—the southwest corner of the Forbidden City.

Nixon spent fifteen hours in formal business meetings with the Chinese leaders. The schedules we received looked like this:

Monday, Feb. 21: Meeting with Chairman Mao at his residence. Only Kissinger accompanied Nixon. One-hour meeting.

Tuesday, Feb. 22: Restricted meeting between Nixon and Chou. Three hours, 50 minutes.

Wednesday, Feb. 23: Restricted meeting between Nixon and Chou. Four hours.

Thursday, Feb. 24: Restricted meeting between Nixon and Chou at Nixon's residence. Three hours. Chou also stayed for dinner and they continued their conversation for about another three hours.

Friday, Feb. 25: Restricted meeting between Nixon and Chou. One hour.

Saturday, Feb. 26: Plenary meeting at Peking airport before departing for Hangchow. One hour.

For the members of the press, we found ourselves in a curious position. While Nixon and Chou were behind closed doors, the Chinese had worked out a meticulous schedule and our guides and interpreters sometimes became distressed when we wanted to change the program. But there was so much to see, so much to do and eight days just wasn't enough.

It was exhausting and exhilarating and a culture shock like I've never known, starting with the hotel. Our rooms were spare but comfortable. On the desk in my room when I checked in were Chinese stamps, a canister of tea, a thermos of hot water, fresh fruits and a dish of chocolate and hard candy.

Candy, strangely enough, was a big deal with the Chinese. Shortly before Nixon arrived, two members of the advance party became ill and had to be sent home. James Pringle, the Peking correspondent for Reuters, heard about it and filed a brief report. The Chinese got a little miffed, as they had imposed a ban on leaking news before Nixon's arrival. As punishment, they took away the bowls of candy that had been placed in the working quarters of a couple of American technicians.[12]

But our guides, minders and handlers tried to be helpful, sometimes a little too much so. In our hotel, the toilet seats had been refinished with a lacquer containing an extract of sumac, which caused poison ivy–like boils in the sensitive areas of twenty-three American advance people and seven Chinese interpreters. The U.S. Public Health Service was able to diagnose the problem and word got around to "beware of the seats."

There was no litter anywhere. One male reporter kept throwing away a pair of thermal underwear in the wastebasket in his hotel room and every day they came back, freshly laundered. The same thing happened to a woman reporter and a certain pair of stockings. I ended up carrying around tangerine peelings in my purse for days, not wanting to know how those might be returned.

Wake-up calls were indeed that. Instead of "Good morning, Miss Thomas, it's five A.M.," I would answer the phone and a voice kept repeating loudly and insistently, "WAKE UP. WAKE UP."

Accompanying Mrs. Nixon was one of the best parts of the trip for me, as her schedule, packed as it was, was orderly and a little less frenetic. Pat had done her homework to prepare for the trip, including reading *Quotations from Chairman Mao,* and her diplomacy skills matched her husband's. She managed to avoid dialectical discussions with her guides, most of whom were women from the ranks of the Revolutionary Committee, but when the topic began to veer toward the political, she would smile and say, "Oh, yes, I'm acquainted with his philosophy."

We traveled one day to the Evergreen People's Commune, a short distance from Peking, where she told the smiling members of her days growing up on a farm in California. As we walked through we passed a pigpen and she wondered aloud, "I wonder what kind of pigs they are."

"Male chauvinist," I said. Mrs. Nixon looked a bit startled but everyone started laughing—except our Chinese hosts.

We visited a clinic where she witnessed two young girls performing acupuncture on a frail, elderly woman. We went to classrooms and the Peking Children's Hospital, where she donned a white physician's smock and hugged the youngsters with affection. She toured the Peking Hotel and got a lesson in the art of Chinese cooking. In fact, I think the fine art of food preparation began to wear her down a little. Her hostesses seemed preoccupied with cooking and whenever there seemed to be a few minutes to spare in the schedule, they hustled her off to yet another demonstration.

Like any tourist, she also wanted to shop. She bought a pair of off-white silk pajamas with green piping for her husband, a dozen cups and saucers in the blue and white rice pattern and gold silk brocade. "I couldn't go back without gifts for the girls," she said.

She met once with Chiang Ching, Mao's wife, when they attended a ballet called *Red Detachment of Women,* extolling the peasants' revolt against landlords.

She met twice with Chou En-lai's wife, once upon arrival in Peking and then at the ballet. But Pat sat next to Chou every night at the banquets and teased him into speaking English. "He's a charmer," she said later. "He's a man who knows the world. He has a delightful sense of humor."[13]

Chou accompanied the first couple on their visit to Hangchow, and in a park on West Lake, he paused before a cage of lovebirds. The birds began embracing with their necks and beaks and Chou gave Mrs. Nixon a slightly flustered look. She smoothed over the situation by giggling and saying "Lovey dovey." As they moved to another cage, Chou said something in Chinese to the birds. "I talk to my bird like that too," she told him.

After days with Pat going out to this site and that, there were banquets every night with most of the dinners in the twelve-course range and always accompanied by a lethal-tasting alcohol known as Mao Tai, what we called the Chinese version of "white lightning." There were frequent toasts at every banquet, and on those occasions, everyone got into the spirit of the new relationship between China and the United States.

When Nixon joined his wife to view the Great Wall, press secretary Ron Ziegler's stage management of the event took a rather zany turn. While we waited at a teahouse where the Nixons and their hosts were relaxing, Ziegler came up to us and said, "If you ask the president how he likes the Great Wall, he will be prepared to answer."

Well, since we'd seen so little of Nixon we jumped at the opportunity. Charles Bailey of the *Minneapolis Star* got tapped to ask the question: "How do you like the Great Wall, Mr. President?"

"I must say that the Great Wall is a great wall," Nixon recited.

Finally, the day for some "hard news" arrived, and for that I had UPI's own secret weapon, State Department reporter Stewart Hensley. Stu's parents had been missionaries in China and for him the trip had held a special significance. When the communiqué was released, I relegated myself to holding open a phone line between Peking and Washington—at $14 a minute—so Stu could dictate the story, which he did accurately and flawlessly.

He was handed the communiqué, flipped through it for a few seconds and dictated a lead that said in effect, there is one China and Taiwan is a part of it:

> The U.S. side declared: The United States acknowledges that all Chinese on either side of the Taiwan strait maintain there is but one China and that Taiwan is part of China. The United States government does not challenge that position. It reaffirms its interest in a peaceful settlement of the Taiwan question by the Chinese themselves.[14]

All in all, I have to agree that it was, in Nixon's words, "the week that changed the world." The prospects for formal diplomatic relations were vastly improved and history has been built upon some of the groundwork that was laid in 1972. Or maybe, as Pat commented on the long ride home, "People are the same the world over. I think they're good people. It all depends on the leadership."[15]

Two and a half years later, on August 9, 1974, Richard Nixon delivered his emotional farewell address to distraught staffers in the East Room, and then walked to the South Lawn where the helicopter "Marine One" was waiting. He climbed the stairway, turned at the top of the stairs, stretched out his arms and gave the Churchillian *V* for victory with both hands.

At Andrews, he boarded Air Force One, and at 10:17 A.M. it lifted off for his last trip as president. No press pool was allowed to accompany him.

At 11:35 A.M., back in Washington, a letter on White House stationery was delivered to Secretary of State Henry Kissinger:

Dear Mr. Secretary:
    I hereby resign the office of President of the United States.
                                                        Richard M. Nixon

At that same time, Air Force One was eight miles northwest of Salem, Illinois.

At the stroke of noon, over Jefferson City, Missouri, the plane radioed Kansas City, notifying them of the change in call sign from Air Force One to SAM 27000. Richard Nixon became the nation's only living former president and was now a guest aboard an airplane on loan from President Gerald Ford.

As the plane continued its journey to California, Nixon decided to stroll the length of the plane. When he reached the section reserved for the press—members of the Secret Service were occupying the seats—he remarked, "Well! It certainly smells better back here!"[16]

Not that Nixon ever spent a lot of time talking to us when we traveled, unlike Kennedy and Johnson. But he liked Doug and Smitty and once, when Doug was celebrating a birthday, he surprised everyone on a flight back to Washington by bringing back a cake and champagne into the cabin for a little celebration.

What stays in my mind, though, was the time we were flying across the Pacific to meet the Apollo 11 astronauts. Nixon strolled to the rear of the plane and we were more than a little shocked to see him standing there. The shock turned to befuddlement at one of the strangest conversations I've ever heard between the president and the press.

None of us said much as Nixon began rambling on in a free-form way, just standing there, looking no one in the eye.

I did get in a question about Vietnam while Ron Ziegler shifted nervously and H. R. Haldeman, whose dislike for the press was visceral, gave me a menacing glare.

But the president looked off, as though he were pondering the question, then he said brightly, "You know, the Senators and my friend Ted Williams have gone into a little slump. What they ought to do is make some trades. They could get a lot for Epstein."

As Dan Rather of CBS recounted, "It's fair to say that there were several people at the press table who didn't know who Epstein was."[17]

I certainly had no idea. My colleagues generously explained to me that

Mike Epstein was a first baseman for the Senators, a left-handed power hitter. So much for Vietnam.

Like LBJ's famous off-the-record press conferences aboard, the plane often is where the old "trial balloon" gets floated now and then, when the president or an aide will make some remark that turns into a story quoting a "high-placed official."

I was on board when President Reagan made his first trip to his California ranch after he was elected. White House counselor Ed Meese, who later would become attorney general, was traveling with us after having appeared on a Sunday talk show in which he sounded rather bellicose about the U.S. military role in the Caribbean.

He indicated that the United States was going to take on the Communists in Central America and I asked him when the American people would have a say in foreign policy, especially if a war were involved.

"Every four years, when they elect a president," he said.

I decided then and there it would be best to fasten our seat belts for the uncertain ride ahead.

Other times, it's the president himself floating the "trial balloon," or even more rarely, making the kinds of statements you can't believe he's making. In May 1989, we were traveling with President Bush through Mississippi and Kentucky and he called the press corps in for an impromptu chat.

Panama's Manuel Noriega had been giving the United States more than a few serious diplomatic migraines over the past few years. In 1987, two U.S. grand juries indicted him on multiple counts of drug trafficking and money laundering.

The indictments had touched off efforts, first by Reagan and then by Bush, to remove Noriega from power. Economic sanctions and attempts to build support for Noriega's opposition hadn't worked. In the 1989 Panamanian presidential election, Bush sent nineteen hundred U.S. troops to reinforce the eleven thousand U.S. forces already in place to protect American citizens in the zone. Noriega nullified the election, marred by fraud and violence against the opposition candidates.

On the plane, Bush leaned forward in his chair and told us that the Panamanian people ought to rise up and, in so many words, throw the bum out.

"They ought to do everything they can to get Mr. Noriega out of there," he said. "The will of the people should not be thwarted by this man and a handful of these Doberman thugs."

This was kind of startling to hear: Was the president of the United States seriously advocating a rebellion in a sovereign country? I remember catching the eye of AP's Rita Beamish and the looks on both our faces reflected the fact that we just couldn't believe what we were hearing.

"If I were speaking to the Panamanian people, I would tell them that the affection of the American people for the people of Panama is very much intact, strong," Bush went on, as our jaws dropped farther. "Secondly, I would say to the Panamanian Defense Forces . . . they have a useful role to play and they will in the future of Panama have a useful role to play. The problem is not the PDF per se. The problem is Noriega."

We asked him specifically if he was urging the PDF forces to overthrow Noriega and he said, "I would love to see them get him out. Not just the PDF—the will of the people of Panama. I'm not about to get into proposing a three-point plan of action for the people of Panama. All I want them to know is that if they get rid of Noriega, they will have an instant normalization of relationship with the United States and there will be a useful role for the Panamanian Defense Force."

Was there anything he wanted to add to temper the call for revolution in another country, a reporter asked? "No, I would add no words of caution," Bush responded.

Noriega survived a coup attempt that October.

But in early 1990, Bush began the second year of his presidency by wrapping up an eleven-day vacation as the biggest military offensive since Vietnam entered its second week. In Panama, U.S. soldiers hounded the refuge-seeking Noriega with rock 'n' roll songs like "Nowhere to Hide." In Texas, Bush shot quail, played golf, fished, attended some private dinners.

"The president isn't on vacation," Marlin Fitzwater insisted. "He is on holiday. The president works every day. He will continue to receive regular updates on Panama and briefings on world affairs."

The president finished up his "holiday" on New Year's Day by going fishing with Barbara on a private lake outside Montgomery, Alabama. On the flight back, Fitzwater came back to brief the press corps and announced the withdrawal of the first U.S. troops from Panama—and that Barbara had hooked a six-pound bass.

There have been tense moments, funny moments, strange moments and bizarre moments aboard Air Force One. There have even been a few bomb scares, three that I know of during the Nixon administration.

The first one was on February 27, 1969, when we were getting ready to leave Berlin for the trip back to Washington. The plane was ready for takeoff and the control tower asked the pilot, Colonel Ralph Albertazzie, to hold his position. Someone at the Berlin airport had received a telephoned threat to blow up the plane. There had been a similar threat in Dublin on a trip to Europe. Both times, the threat was delivered via an anonymous phone call saying a bomb had been placed aboard the president's plane.

Taking the necessary precautions, the crew rechecked all the packages that had been brought on board. Packages are usually X-rayed before they go on the plane, but this time each one had to be unwrapped and examined. No trace of an explosive was found.

Another incident occurred in April 1971, Albertazzie said. "Some man anonymously called American Airlines reservations at Rockefeller Center in New York, of all places, and said, 'We are going to blow up the president's plane.'"

The airline immediately called the Secret Service in Washington, who alerted California, where the president was staying.

"My first reaction was that the man was going to have to travel all the way from New York to California," said Albertazzie. "But then I remembered the backup plane, painted the same as ours, was in New York getting some work done, and I realized he could be referring to it. So we tightened up our security. We do tighten things up considerably."

When it comes to putting in late nights and long hours aboard the plane, there's that old cliché: The only thing worse than being on a presidential campaign is not being on a presidential campaign. I'm here to say not true. Actually, there are days I think I'm still recovering from the Johnson-Goldwater race of 1964.

Huge crowds turned out to see LBJ and he wanted to meet each and every person who was there to see him. He campaigned eighteen to twenty hours a day. He made speeches until his face turned red and his voice gave out. He was always in motion. For those of us following him around, it always seemed to be three o'clock in the morning. Then he would race back to the plane, glad-hand the crowd at the airport and come bounding up the steps of the plane. He would rip off his sweat-soaked coat and shirt, toss them with a "Here, Bird," to his wife, head to his compartment, and we would take off again, into the darkness for another city, another stop, another speech.

"Some men are born to campaign," Lady Bird once said. "Lyndon was."

We had been on the road before the Democratic National Convention opened in Atlantic City on August 24, 1964, and were actually looking for a little easement after the rocky road the Republicans had carved two weeks before in San Francisco. But LBJ was not about to have any moribund tribunal nominating him. No, he was still pulling the strings and livening things up as he went along. He kept everyone in suspense about his choice for vice president until the last minute, and then flew to the convention with Hubert Humphrey at his side, making the vice presidential nomination himself right after the delegates chose him by acclamation.

We began traveling in earnest at the end of September. Johnson spent forty-two days straight on the stump, covering sixty thousand miles and making nearly two hundred speeches. He gloried in the mobs of people who showed up wherever he went. He would halt the motorcade, speak off the cuff through a hand-held bullhorn and then leave the car to shake hands with people. His right hand often got swollen and began to bleed after hours of handshakes and had to be bandaged. But he didn't stop. He was in a hurry for a landslide and for an elected legitimacy.

I longed for the days of Harry Truman traveling civilly and gracefully by train. I got a chance to do that to some extent when President Clinton decided to travel by rail on a series of campaign stops before he arrived at the Democratic National Convention in Chicago in 1996.

When a reporter is on the ground like that, they tend to get a better sense of what is really happening in the country and how the electorate may really be feeling, despite all the polls that get taken every day. Reporters who covered Truman's famous whistle-stop campaign of 1948 noticed that at stop after stop the crowds seemed to be getting bigger while, at the same time, everyone seemed to be reporting that Thomas L. Dewey was going to be the next president.

In that grueling stretch in 1964 that I spent hopping on and off the plane, I longed for a decent meal and a few more hours of sleep. What I longed for most of all was a different speech from the candidate. It's something I've longed for through *every* campaign that I've covered.

"The speech." You hear it several times a day, seven days a week for at least twelve weeks. You can recite it by heart. And yet it could be very dangerous to tune out the candidate and "the speech" in case he inserts a few new paragraphs.

Finally, in 1996, I pulled rank and let my younger colleagues chase the candidates across the country.

There were two big movies that summer that played aboard the president's plane. One was *Air Force One,* starring Harrison Ford as the president who battles terrorists aboard the aircraft. While the Republicans were busy nominating Bob Dole to be their standard-bearer in the race, President Clinton and his family vacationed in Wyoming, where the actor lives. Clinton and Ford had dinner one night and the president offered Ford and the film's director, Wolfgang Petersen, a tour of the real thing.

On a trip back to Washington from a West Coast campaign swing in July, *Air Force One* played on Air Force One. My colleague Lori Santos later filed a report that the film didn't get an overwhelming thumbs-up from some of the people who operate and ride on the real plane.

> While many of the Air Force personnel, White House staff and media on the plane agreed the flick was action-packed, most took issue

with various depictions of the plane where some obvious creative license was taken. There was no word available from Air Force pilots in the cockpit, but some other personnel quibbled with the alleged galleys and supplies shown in the movie.

Reporters noted that their actual cabin was a good deal less spacious than pictured on the big screen, and staffers wondered if they would ever be called on to parachute out of the back of the plane like in the movie. It wasn't a welcome thought.

Each section of the plane—the first family's quarters, the Secret Service area, the press cabin and so on—has an overhead TV connected to a VCR operated by Air Force communications staff.

Upon boarding, passengers get a booklet listing the various movies available, and they can pick up a phone near the seats and give their movie choice to the crew. Each separate section—presidential, military, Secret Service, press—can be watching a different movie, but everyone in the same section has to watch the same film, so many times, the one who gets to the phone first is the one who picks the movie.

For me, usually when the movie goes on in the press cabin, I put a blanket over my head because the movie inevitably is not my kind of entertainment—there's usually too much sex and too much violence.

There was one movie shown on a trip to Europe, though, *The People vs. Larry Flynt,* that piqued my interest. I had already put the blanket over my head when I heard the words *First Amendment* and I peeked over the top of the blanket. Can't say I enjoyed those rather raw scenes, but I thought the courtroom scenes were pretty good and it did have a lesson or two about rights guaranteed under the Constitution.

The other movie featured during the 1996 campaign got a much better reception on Air Force One than *Air Force One.* While the movie menu changes frequently, I believe the film *Fargo* is the record-holder of Longest-Playing Film Aboard Air Force One—in the press cabin, anyway.

It started on a campaign swing in August, when the press corps watched *Fargo* and a disagreement emerged between a photographer for Agence France-Presse and a photographer for Reuters, over a certain line in the movie. They made a $20 bet on the exact phrasing of the line and asked that the movie be shown again.

At the end of the second showing, Ken Bazinet later related, of the fourteen people in the cabin, thirteen agreed with the line according to the photographer for AFP. The lone holdout was the Reuters photographer.

So it was agreed they would watch it a third time and settle the bet once and for all.

Thus was born the "*Fargo* campaign cult" aboard Air Force One.

"We all started requesting that it be shown," said Ken. "By the time the campaign was about over, we were calling the communications department and saying things like 'release the hounds' and they would play *Fargo*. We watched it about three times a day traveling to three different cities."

As the campaign progressed, a race developed between the reporters and photographers to see who could phone for *Fargo* first. Of course, there were a few dissenters—who were unsuccessful in their efforts to ban the film from the press section.

All told, *Fargo* played to a packed house in the press compartment about three dozen times. "Maybe twelve viewings into it, it really took on a life of its own," Ken told me. "About a half-dozen of us watched it without the headphones and recited all the lines. From there it progressed into something like *The Rocky Horror Picture Show*—people would respond to scenes with stuff like 'No! Don't go into that room!'"

And what did the first family think of all the *Fargo* mania?

President Clinton came back at one point and he said he had liked the movie, said Ken, "but I hear you guys watch it all the time. That's weird.'"

It was First Lady Hillary Rodham Clinton who stole the show. NBC's Clare Shipman, then with CNN and a full-time *Fargo* watcher, brought Mrs. Clinton to the press cabin on the last leg of the long trip that would bring them home to Little Rock in November.

"She went along with the joke and started talking in that excessive way [in the movie] saying things like 'Yah, yah, you betcha,'" said Ken.

She spent a few minutes talking with reporters and at one point someone asked her what she thought of the movie. Mrs. Clinton, who had been taking heat from the Republicans for her book *It Takes a Village,* paused for a moment, then looked at the assembled press and said, "Well, there's room in my village for a wood chipper."

"She brought the house down," said Ken.

After being regaled with this story by the many reporters who pushed the envelope of the innocent but psychotic fun that invariably goes with a campaign season, I could understand how and why something like that would happen. As Ken mentioned later, "When you think about it, we should have been watching *Groundhog Day,* because that's what covering a campaign is like. You know, same speech, different day."

Yes, traveling aboard Air Force One has its cachet, be it a state visit or a campaign swing.

It also can be a place where former opponents meet on common ground. In 1981, President Reagan invited Presidents Nixon, Ford and Carter aboard to represent the United States at the funeral of Egyptian president Anwar

Sadat. Rosalynn Carter also made the trip and later told me that when they got on board, the atmosphere between them and Gerald Ford was "tense." But the ice was broken later, she said, and as they got settled Ford "couldn't have been nicer." But Nixon surprised her the most, she said, by his friendliness.

Well, there's common ground and then there's common ground. On trips of such international importance does it really matter what door you leave by? You've got to get off the plane anyway. But apparently, a perceived snub on board the plane bound to another state funeral was enough to shut down a government.

I belatedly heard of the assassination of Israeli prime minister Yitzhak Rabin, but I called the White House immediately and assigned Ken, who had been working that Saturday, to make the trip.

The White House and Congress at the time were deadlocked in negotiations over the budget that had led to the first government shutdown. As Ken described it later, "Air Force One was packed for the out and back flight for Rabin's funeral," with the usual contingent of White House staff, Secret Service personnel, the military who guard the plane and a host of congressional leaders, including Senate Majority Leader Bob Dole and House Speaker Newt Gingrich.

Gingrich and Dole sat in the staff conference room, which is in plain sight of the seat assigned to UPI since all the cabin doors are open. "Dole and Gingrich faced the press cabin so their expressions, body language, was easily detected," said Ken. "All I had to do was lean to the left about two inches to see how they were doing."

From what the press pool could gather, they weren't doing well. "Dole was leaning on his left arm and had a look of misery on his face. Gingrich talked, and talked and talked. It didn't even look like Dole was responding." Eventually, all the reporters checked up on the two from time to time, peering through the doorway.

"It was the same thing," said Ken. "Gingrich talking and Dole looking like he'd like to parachute to safety and silence. This pretty much went on the entire flight. We never saw Clinton in the conference room."

After the trip home, Gingrich went on full offensive of how he was denied a chance to talk about the budget with Clinton and how he was made to leave through the rear door of the plane.

He went on to complain about his shabby treatment to reporters, saying that it "was unfortunate that here was an opportunity when we were together for some twenty-five hours, and we might have at some point in that process made a little progress."

About the rear door exit, he said, "You wonder where is their sense of manners, where is their sense of courtesy."

The press jumped all over that one and among the resulting news coverage linking the continuing government shutdown to Gingrich's peevishness at his perceived slight was the classic headline from the *New York Daily News*: "Crybaby."

Democrats had a field day, the Speaker's popularity plummeted while the president's soared as poll after poll came out. There were other reasons for the shutdown and the ongoing budget battle, but Gingrich's blooper caused the Republicans considerable embarrassment.

What was even harder to understand, Ken said later, was that "no one could have known" Gingrich's reaction about getting off from the back of the plane because "it's the usual protocol. The exit at the rear of the plane is much closer to the staff conference room" where the two GOP leaders had sat for the entire flight and "cabinet secretaries and other guests who ride Air Force One in that cabin almost always exit the plane from the rear."

In December 1995, Democratic senator Christopher Dodd of Connecticut accompanied Clinton on a five-day trip to Europe. When they arrived home, Dodd used the front exit to leave the plane.

"I think I just walked off," Dodd told reporters afterward. "Other than seeing the president for the first couple of minutes on the flight, I spent most of my time talking to you guys and others.

"I never saw him. And I'm his Democratic national chairman. Newt's got to stop worrying about that, huh?"

No matter where we may be or what the occasion, the president's arrivals and departures are set up so that no one else is allowed to steal the show.

But on one trip to Spain, I got a royal welcome and lots of teasing afterward as a result of the pool report written by Nancy Mathis of the *Houston Chronicle* and Ken Walsh of *U.S. News & World Report*:

Pool Report #1
July 4–5, 1997: Air Force One arrival to Palma de Mallorca

Flight aboard Air Force One was uneventful. Arrived on time at about 2 p.m. Mallorca time. The first sighting of King Juan Carlos and Queen Sofia was as they made a beeline to the press area to shake the hand of . . . Helen Thomas.

They then took their place at the head of a long receiving line. President Clinton, wearing a dark suit and a red tie, and Mrs. Clinton, wearing a pale green dress suit, deplaned. The president came down the stairs slowly and deliberately, holding on to the rail with one hand and Mrs. Clinton's hand with the other.

The King and president shook hands heartily. The Queen and first lady shook hands and bussed cheeks. After Clinton worked the receiving line, the foursome later huddled for some time talking intently. Then everyone left to tour some fort or castle or some darn old thing.

After all these years and all those miles, I still get asked from time to time, "Have you ever ridden aboard Air Force One?"

"Many times," I reply and once again realize that riding on the president's plane is very special. For all the history I've witnessed on all those trips, I still don't take it for granted, nor have I ever considered it routine. It has always been a thrill to be welcomed aboard.

TEN

"She Told the Truth"

The funeral wreath was made of white chrysanthemums, decorated with white ribbon, sent by two unidentified men from Pasadena, California. The flowers spelled out the message: "Martha was right."

Martha Elizabeth Beall Jennings Mitchell died of bone cancer on Memorial Day 1976. Many considered her little more than a cartoon of a cabinet wife. Some considered her a caricature of life according to Washington's rigid social protocols. A few, after a while, considered her dangerous.

But she was one of the most unforgettable and phenomenal women in public life I've ever encountered. She began causing a sensation the minute her sling-back pumps hit the ground in Washington.

Once she began talking, and talking and talking, a familiar joke in Washington used to be: "My, but Martha Mitchell certainly is outspoken."

"Really. More outspoken than whom?"

In December 1971 a wire story ran about Vice President Spiro Agnew's gag Christmas gift list. Included on the list were: "For Martha Mitchell, a brand-new Princess phone. For John Mitchell, a padlock for a brand-new Princess phone."

"Why did Martha Mitchell call you?" someone asked me after I filed my first story based on one of her many telephone calls in which she expressed her outrage a few days after the Watergate break-in.

I wasn't the only reporter she called, but I did take her seriously and I wrote about what she told me. Sometimes the stories made it to the wire and sometimes they got spiked. But Martha perhaps put the answer best herself when she told an interviewer, "Helen knows me well enough to know I'm not going to give her a line of bull. We just kind of fell into each other's arms. Several other reporters had been recommended to me, but when I talked to them they were cold fish. They were calculating, and, I thought, unwilling to stick their necks out. Helen Thomas, I knew, would print the truth no matter what it cost her personally, and I wanted the truth to be known."[1]

I don't think the dust will ever entirely settle on the Watergate scandal, but I do think Martha deserves more than a footnote in its history. She should be remembered as the woman who tried to blow the whistle on what was going on, but sometimes her stories seemed so out there, it was close to impossible to get anyone to listen. However, I listened and I wrote and I'll let history decide.

I do remember her telling me early on in her time in Washington, "Politics is a dirty business," and I remember equally well a memorable remark her husband made shortly after they arrived: "Watch what we do, not what we say."

Martha grew up in a fairly well-to-do family in Pine Bluff, Arkansas, where her father, George Beall, was a cotton broker and her mother, "Miss Arie," an elocution teacher who loved the theater. She was popular with both men and women and loved to have fun. Her lifelong friend, Clifford Kunz, whom she met at the University of Arkansas, used to tease her that she would not date anyone in college unless he had a car.

She taught school for a brief time and then worked as a secretary in wartime Washington. Working as a receptionist with the Army Chemical Corps, she met a handsome Army captain, Clyde Jennings, whom she married in 1946.

Jennings, it was reported, told an acquaintance, "Everything was fine in the first part of the marriage, but as we were leaving the church ceremony . . ."

They had a son, Jay, and were divorced in 1957. On December 30 of that year, she married John Mitchell in Elkton, Indiana. Mitchell, who also was divorced, had been born in Detroit, Michigan, grew up in Long Island and Queens, New York, attended Fordham University Law School and joined the firm of Caldwell and Raymond, which specialized in municipal and state bond financing. Their daughter, Martha, was born in 1961.

They had a lovely redbrick Colonial home in Rye, New York, and lived the sublime suburban life when Mitchell was offered a job with Richard Nixon's New York law firm. Martha urged him to take it—a move she later regretted.

Mitchell left his $225,000-a-year job as a municipal bond trader to work as Nixon's campaign manager in 1968 and after the election was named U.S. attorney general, a $60,000-a-year post back then. I don't think Martha really wanted to leave that country club life in Rye and come into this vast unknown, but she gamely packed up their belongings and moved them to the nation's capital. She did try to live up to her belief, as she said, that a "person in the Cabinet should let the people know who is representing them. If you're in the Cabinet you shouldn't be invisible. Before John took this job he said, 'Honey, if we're going to be in government, we're going to do what's right—we're going to let the people know who's representing them.' People often don't know they have a contact in government because they haven't bothered to find out, number one, and number two, the government hasn't told them. And that's the reason the government's been run so slipshod." [2]

They rented a plush six-room apartment at the Watergate.

When he took over the Justice Department in 1969, Mitchell said, "I am first and foremost a law enforcement officer." In his first week in office, he permitted his department to drop an antitrust case against El Paso Natural Gas, which had paid the former Nixon-Mitchell law firm more than $770,000 over a six-year period. It was considered such a blatant political act that the Supreme Court, in an unusual move, took over jurisdiction of the case.

New to Washington, Martha was not familiar with the long-standing edict, albeit broken a few times, that political wives should be seen and not heard—especially cabinet wives who must defer to the first lady and follow her cue. And if she eventually did learn that rule, my guess is she just decided to ignore it. "Washington is so staid," she complained her first summer here. "Protocol is so outmoded. It's just ridiculous. Because I'm the wife of the attorney general, I have no right to express my opinion. The only thing I can compare it with is the way the Negroes are treated." [3]

But she never seemed to have any trouble exercising her right to express her opinions, and in the early years obviously enjoyed the attention she got for expressing them. At one function she cut her finger and someone passed her a Band-Aid. "Where am I supposed to put this—over my mouth?" she asked.

In Nixon's first administration, she was known as the loud defender of the president, who, despite outward appearances, got a kick out of her vivacity amid that buttoned-down administration. He liked to tell a story of how his admiration for Martha mirrored his admiration for Jessie Wilson, wife of Defense Secretary Charles Wilson under President Eisenhower.

Remember that Eisenhower was the kind of president Americans revered to the point of deification. At a White House party for newswomen, Nixon recalled how Eisenhower had rebuked Wilson for his remark that during the Korean War the National Guard was harboring draft dodgers. Eisenhower called Wilson's statement "unwise." Mrs. Wilson then denounced Ike, saying his comment was "uncalled for" and that she was "indignant."

Now there, Nixon said, was a spunky cabinet wife, and he often was fond of saying, once he learned of her latest outrageous remark, "Give 'em hell, Martha."

Martha was affectionately called Nixon's "secret weapon" in the beginning. Her husband referred to her as his "unguided missile." She brought an aura of excitement to the Nixon administration. Pat Nixon, who knew the pitfalls of politics, was highly disapproving. A longtime student in the protocol of political life, Pat sometimes confessed to being aghast at Martha's behavior and it became apparent Martha was getting the cold shoulder from the East Wing of the White House, the first lady's bailiwick.

In November 1970, Martha, still complaining about the artificiality of Washington's social life, did try to go along. She gave a cabinet-wives luncheon for Pat Nixon at Blair House, only to have Connie Stuart, Mrs. Nixon's chief of staff, tell reporters that Pat was merely attending a luncheon without any mention of the hostess.

Martha was furious and telephoned reporters, charging that Stuart "is trying to get rid of me. How can anybody take over my party? It's just unbelievable. I cried my eyes out today. Somebody should get down and bleed for me. I try so hard."

Still, it was Pat Nixon herself who gave Martha an early lesson in life in the nation's capital, telling her shortly after she arrived, "Just remember, Martha, your best friends will become your worst enemies." [4]

Part of Martha's charm in the early Nixon administration was her willingness to speak out on any subject that caught her attention. Mrs. Nixon defended Martha's right to speak freely but, she said, "As for myself I only talk on subjects of [sic] which I am really informed."

Being uninformed never stopped Martha. She admitted being generally ignorant of economics with this breezy description: "The only thing I remember is 'law of diminishing marginal utility.' The reason I remember the law is because in order to explain it to us they used ice cream sodas and I've always adored chocolate ice cream sodas." [5]

And when Nixon asked cabinet wives to speak out in support of the administration's economic policies, Martha put the wage-price freeze in terms a homemaker could identify with—if the homemaker were Gracie Allen. "With this freeze a woman knows exactly how much she is going to have to spend," she said. "Now she can plan before she goes to the grocery store because she knows what each item's going to cost. And instead of $25 just buying one little sack of groceries, now, if the freeze hadn't gone on you probably wouldn't even get a whole sack." [6]

In plainer terms, she also advised American women to "go out and spend money and enjoy yourself. . . . I think everybody should have a good time." [7] And she did, for a while.

In September 1970, on a trip aboard Air Force One, she was sitting with some White House aides and wives in the VIP cabin of the plane. Her husband and Secretary of State William Rogers were up in front with Nixon, his pal Bebe Rebozo and a few others. It was a long flight from California to Washington and many were asleep or reading quietly, including us in the press corps in the back.

Martha looked around, pronounced her group "the dullest bunch I've ever seen," and headed back to the press compartment, where several reporters were sitting around a table playing cards. She ordered a Scotch and asked one reporter if he knew how to play gin rummy. He said yes, dealing six cards instead of ten. She grabbed the deck. "Hell, you don't know how to play," she said.

Well, here was a cabinet wife in a chatty mood so why not ask her a few things, I thought—but best to ease into the strong stuff. I asked her what she thought about midi-skirts, the latest fashion travesty out of Paris that year. "Oh, Helen, why don't you ask me something important?" Martha sniffed.

"OK," I said, "what do you think of the Vietnam War?"

"It stinks," she said, and looking around to see if some reporters were taking notes—and noting that a few of them weren't, added, "Now, you take this down..." The war, she said, "would have been over sixteen months ago if it hadn't been for [Senator William] Fulbright." Fulbright, who was chairman of the Senate Foreign Relations Committee, had steered the Gulf of Tonkin Resolution through the Senate for Lyndon Johnson. But he became convinced he was being lied to about the depth, gravity and the inability to win in Vietnam and on January 24, 1968, announced his opposition to a resumption of the bombing over North Vietnam. Like Martha, he was from Arkansas; unlike Martha, he was a Democrat.

And with that, the rest of the press cabin put down their cards and picked up their notebooks.

"If this country would stick together ... if everyone felt a common cause in Vietnam, we would have been out sixteen months ago, and it makes me so mad I can't see straight," she went on and then started a quick mambo through a political minefield. "We shouldn't have gotten into the war in the first place," she said. "The Nixon administration inherited it and they're trying their best to get out of it."

A few minutes later Mitchell came back to the press cabin and I asked him if he wanted to hear what his wife had just said. "Heavens no," said Mitchell. "I might jump out the window."

Secretary Rogers, however, did get a summary of Martha's diatribe against the war when he came back to the press compartment. He sat down, started dealing the cards for a round of bridge with Martha and a couple of reporters, looked over at her and said, "Why don't you stick to law and order and I'll take care of foreign policy?" Not too long after that, Mitchell said he would only allow his wife to give interviews in Swahili.

And after that, I noticed she never flew aboard the presidential aircraft again but was instead relegated to the second plane. She told me later she never was officially informed of being banned from the plane, but she did hear that the order came from H. R. Haldeman, Nixon's chief of staff.

I met Martha along with the rest of the Nixon cabinet wives at the White House in early 1969 and I was struck by her warmth, her vivaciousness, her wit and her quick smile—she was definitely spring to the Nixon White House winter when it came to atmosphere.

Nixon wanted the cabinet wives to be active and Martha quickly jumped into that side of Washington life, immersing herself in several worthy projects. She enlisted the wives of Justice Department officials in a national narcotics education program for parents and teenagers, taking them on tours of the city's riot-damaged ghettos. When Nixon wanted the wives to help promote the administration, Martha wasted no time. One of her first interviews—and first set of headlines—came from an interview with CBS's Marya McLaughlin:

> As my husband has said many times, some of the liberals in this country, he'd like to take them and change them for Russian communists. I don't think average Americans realize how desperate it is when a group of demonstrators, not peaceful demonstrators but the very liberal communists, move into Washington. This place could become a complete fortress.[8]

She became an instant celebrity and a hot property for the Republican Party, which had no qualms in sending her on the road to promote the cause.

There has been endless speculation over the years about how much Martha did know about Watergate and the subsequent cover-up. I think her innate sense told her there was something larger going on than just a "third-rate burglary," and her public insistence that her husband leave the White House should have been a cue for reporters that something larger indeed was going on.

Did she know everything about Watergate? I think she knew things around the edges and was smart enough to put the pieces together. And I think she did have some kind of intuition for danger. Her son, Jay, was serving as an Army lieutenant in Vietnam and several months had passed with no word from him. Martha grew more agitated and worried as time passed and would call me in tears, wailing, "They won't tell me anything." She called me twice when I was in Laguna Beach, California, at the press center when we were covering Nixon at San Clemente, to ask me to find out what was happening to Jay, insisting she knew he was in trouble.

"But Martha," I finally said, "you can find out in a minute. Why don't you call Laird at the Pentagon?" referring to Defense Secretary Melvin Laird. But she kept insisting that when she called she couldn't get anyone to speak to her.

I ended up sending a message to UPI's bureau in Saigon. Finally, word came back that Jay was safe but had been in a combat zone that had endured heavy fighting and a number of casualties.

So maybe it was that intuition that kept me listening when she would call and rail about Watergate.

Once Jay made it home safely, she began focusing on her husband, who was put in charge of the Committee to Re-Elect the President—CREEP. She wasn't happy about it—from cabinet wife back to the campaign trail. She used to quip that "the president and I haven't decided what to do with him," but privately she raged about it.

The day Mitchell resigned from Justice to accept the campaign position I telephoned her to get a comment, but a secretary informed me there would be "no comment."

"Martha Mitchell . . . no comment?" I said. "You've got to be kidding."

She also worked at campaign headquarters for a while, and was called on to speak at campaign rallies and other events. She and Jeb Stuart Magruder were among the first to work in the office. A short while later the committee hired a security director named James McCord.

In June 1972, the Nixons and the Mitchells were on vacation in Key Biscayne, Florida. The Mitchells had leased a house on an island owned by Rebozo. It was in that house that Martha later told me she heard some campaign planning going on. She also recalled to me much later that, one night, her husband was sitting in his favorite armchair in their Washington apartment reading a campaign strategy book and later said to her, "This is foolproof."

In mid-June, Martha was getting ready for a quick trip to New York for a dental exam and a physical. Fred LaRue, an associate of Mitchell's, asked her to postpone her plans so she and John could fly to California for the weekend. She said she didn't want to go but LaRue insisted that his wife could only go if Martha did. After they arrived, the Mitchells and their daughter Marty, then eleven, stayed in a villa reserved for government officials at Newport Beach. Traveling with them were Lea Jablonsky, Mitchell's secretary, and Steve King, a bodyguard assigned to them by CREEP.

It was the weekend of June 16, 1972, during which five men were caught breaking into Democratic National Committee headquarters in the Watergate.

On Sunday night while still in California, the Mitchells attended a party at the home of Mrs. Donald K. Washburn. Other guests included John Wayne and his wife and Nixon's personal attorney, Herbert Kalmbach. John and Martha got into an argument at the party over John's insistence that they leave early; finally he announced that he had an important meeting to attend the next day and hustled her out.

John suggested Martha stay in California for a few more days and caught a late-night flight back to Washington, but not before leaving orders that Martha was to have no newspapers delivered to her for the next few days.

Even though the break-in story played on television and radio, somehow Mitchell managed briefly to keep Martha from hearing about it.

But the following Monday morning, Martha asked for a newspaper, saw McCord's picture and became furious. For three days she tried to call UPI, but later told me that the switchboard operator had told her that the "campaign security staff had embargoed any calls out" of the villa.

On Thursday at about 9:00 P.M., Doug and I were at home, just finishing dinner, when the phone rang. It was Martha. She sounded calm, sad and uncharacteristically subdued. We chatted for a little while and I asked her about Watergate.

"That's it," she said. "I've given John an ultimatum. I'm going to leave him unless he gets out of the campaign. I'm sick and tired of politics. Politics is a dirty business."

Then suddenly, her voice became more agitated and she yelled, "You get away. Just get away," and the line went dead.

I tried to call back several times without success and then called the switchboard operator. I was told that "Mrs. Mitchell is indisposed and cannot talk."

I then called Mitchell, who had returned to Washington, at their Watergate apartment and told him what had happened during my conversation with Martha and that I was a little concerned. He sounded rather blasé but tried to ease my fears. "That little sweetheart," he said. "I love her so much. She gets a little upset about politics but she loves me and I love her and that's what counts. I'll tell you a secret: I've promised Martha I'll give up politics after this campaign."

The more we talked, the more bizarre his attitude struck me, but he kept assuring me that Martha wasn't in any danger. I telephoned UPI's desk and dictated a story to Bob Taylor, who decided it was credible and ran it. Later I heard that along with Mitchell, White House counsel John Dean and a few others were in the apartment at the time of my "distress call" to him at home and they had quite a laugh over it.

The story got a fair amount of play—mostly on the women's pages. Maybe editors thought it was just another case of Martha being Martha and newsworthy only because it revealed a rift in a very public marriage. Back in Washington, administration aides began hinting that Martha was hallucinating, that she was deranged or that she was just drunk.

In an interview later, Martha told me, "I want to be sure my side is revealed and that people know I'm not sitting here a mental case or an alcoholic."

What happened in that villa? She later told me a hair-raising story: "They threw me down on the bed—five persons did it—a doctor, a nurse, Lea Jablonsky . . . pulled my pants down and stuck a needle in my behind, the longest needle you ever saw. I've never been treated like this before." She had a gash in her hand that she said required eleven stitches.

In 1986, Steve King was interviewed by Rob Zaleski, a reporter for the *Capital Times* in Wisconsin. King was chairman of the state Republican Party and the general manager of a chemical manufacturing company. King, a former FBI agent, told Zaleski only that he was the Mitchells' security guard at the time and that the wound to Martha's hand was self-inflicted—and that he regretted ever getting involved in the Nixon campaign.

"Obviously, Martha Mitchell's version isn't true and I've said that many, many times," he said. "The right people know that. But quite frankly, I've chosen not to hang the Mitchells' laundry—their personal problems—out in public. And even though it's been fourteen years and probably wouldn't hurt anybody now, I still choose not to talk about the problems that family had. Despite all the things that have been said and done to John Mitchell . . . I have enormous respect and admiration for the man."

He described Martha as "an absolutely charming, typical southern belle type of woman. But she had some deep-seated personal problems. And they manifested themselves in a number of different ways. If you recall, she was grabbing a headline every other day during those times."[9]

About a year after the incident, columnist Jack Anderson reported that friends of John Mitchell said King was merely following orders: Martha had been close to a nervous breakdown and her husband, for whatever reasons, wanted it kept quiet.

The following weekend I was covering Nixon at Camp David. The press corps was staying at a motel about six miles away from the presidential retreat. On Sunday morning I called my office, only to be told that Martha had been trying to reach me. I called the number she left and discovered she was at the Westchester Country Club in Rye, New York. She sounded distraught and furious, saying she had become a "political prisoner." "It's horrible. I don't like it. Martha isn't going to stand for it," she told me. I was used to her referring to herself in the third person so that didn't make me wonder about her mental state, but she did sound desperate. "When are you coming home?" I asked her. "I am home," she replied.

I filed a story, and this time it got more play than merely to divide the gardening tips and recipe columns. Reporters and photographers converged on Rye as well and I tried to make a few follow-up calls to her. The operator would only take messages and when Martha returned to Washington and I was able to speak to her again, I asked her why she never returned any of my calls. She told me she never got the messages.

On July 1, Mitchell resigned from CREEP, citing the need to sacrifice his career "for the happiness of my wife and my daughter," and back then, we all wanted to believe him. Martha was happy, while Mitchell saw he was going to have to remove himself from a nasty situation. He didn't succeed on several fronts.

Apparently the White House was taking her phone calls a little seriously by this time as well, or so it would seem:

> Sunday, June 25, 1972
>
> At Camp David. . . . Got into the Martha Mitchell problem. Apparently she called Helen Thomas the other night and said if John didn't get his ass out of politics she was going to kick him out of the house, but her phones were then pulled, either by her or someone in the room. She's demanded that they be reinstated, and the phone company has delayed on it, and now she's threatened to the phone man that if they don't get her phones in, she's going to blow the whole Republican [deal], whatever that means.[10]

So Mitchell left the campaign, right. White House tapes later revealed that Nixon and Mitchell decided Martha's rants for her husband to resign would be a convenient cover to evade the public eye, and Mitchell became even more enmeshed in CREEP. His law office was in the same building as the campaign headquarters. Martha later said, "If I hadn't heard those tapes, I would have gone to my grave thinking he left the campaign for me."

Mitchell still had the most clout with Nixon and he was still the number one adviser. He was a frequent guest aboard the presidential yacht *Sequoia*.

Meanwhile, Martha went underground for a while, and during the Democratic National Convention that summer of 1972 in Miami, the most sought-after button was one that read "Free Martha."

She stayed quiet until after Nixon's landslide victory and then the phone calls to me resumed, and this time, their tone made me more than uncomfortable. "If you don't hear from me, call the police," she told me in November 1972.

In the spring of 1973, the family was ready to move into an opulent fourteen-room apartment on New York's Fifth Avenue and Martha threw herself into overseeing its renovation and decoration. People may have talked a lot about Martha's talkative side, but everyone always agreed on her great taste, her marvelous eye for interior design and her wonderful capacity as a hostess.

She seemed happy to be away from Washington as the Watergate noose started tightening around the president and his staff, but every now and then I'd still hear from her.

"Mr. Nixon knew all about the whole goddamned thing," she told me in one call around February. In mid-March, as the tapes later showed, Mitchell was summoned to the White House for a conference and it was suggested he take the rap for the cover-up. He declined and returned to New York. I got another phone call from Martha. "John Dean wasn't big enough," she said. "They want John to take the rap."

Over the next several months, when Martha wanted to expound she found me no matter where I was.

Once I was in Oklahoma. J. R. Wilson, who was the bureau manager in Norman, wrote a wonderful account of that weekend when, as he put it, the UPI brass "somehow blackmailed" me into attending the infamous UPI Editors of Oklahoma annual weekend gathering at a lodge.

I was trying to be a good sport about the whole thing, especially when they told me we would be getting up at 5:00 A.M. for the traditional fish fry and Bloody Mary breakfast. The night before, a Saturday, there was a huge party and everyone was having a great time when, about 2:00 A.M., the phone rang and Jerry answered it.

Jerry said the call was for me, a "somewhat bleary female voice, heavy of southern accent" and she was demanding to speak to Helen Thomas. Jerry asked who he should say was calling and the response was, "Tell her it's Martha Mitchell and I have to talk to her *now*."

I wondered aloud how she had managed to find me in this rather remote spot of America—I think perhaps the desk in Washington might have had something to do with it—but when I took the phone a silence fell over the entire group and they listened to me. There wasn't that much for them to hear. Martha was on another tear about the machinations to make her husband the fall guy for the Watergate cover-up—I think the sum total of my side of the conversation consisted of "uh-huh," "yeah," "you don't say. . . ."

"They're not going to get away with this, Helen," she said, and once again, "Martha won't stand for it."

I finally managed to end the conversation and, facing the rather goggle-eyed group, did my best to explain that I had become used to such things—if Martha wanted to talk, neither time, location, distance nor ritual fish fry was going to stand in her way.

In May 1973, I was giving a speech in Madison, Wisconsin, and her telephone call was blunt and to the point. "Nixon should resign," she said. "He has lost his credibility in the country and in the Republican Party. I think he's let the country down."

I called the Washington bureau and dictated a story of what she'd just told me. Nixon was spending the weekend in Key Biscayne but his aides wasted no time with a barrage of phone calls to Mitchell, who then issued a statement that it would be "ridiculous" for anyone to take his wife's suggestion seriously. "Martha's late-night telephone calls have been good fun and games in the past," he said. "However, this is a serious issue. I'm surprised and disappointed that a 'news organization' would take advantage of a personal phone call made under the stress of the current situation and treat it as a sensational public statement."

He added that under the circumstances he thought Martha was entitled to some consideration, "particularly from a reporter whom she considered a personal friend."

I guess what he didn't understand was that with all those phone calls, Martha was simply trying to convince her husband to tell what he knew and stop "protecting King Richard," as she described Nixon. She loved her husband, plain and simple, and I think by making her views known publicly, she believed he would come to his senses. But by that time the game was too far gone and she never could break his unshakable loyalty to the president.

"I love him very much," she told me. "He loves me because I've stood up for him. But he is defending the president who planned the whole goddamned thing. I'm under surveillance day and night. I'm no fool."

I was getting it from all sides around that time. Martha's calls were newsworthy so I reported them, but I was still covering the White House and taking a fair share of abuse for what stories about her I reported.

One day, a White House aide—a former associate of Mitchell's—taunted me. "Why don't you show some class, Helen, and hang up on Martha Mitchell?"

The inner sanctum at the White House apparently didn't think I was showing much class either:

Transcript, June 19, 1973, Oval Office: The president, Rose Mary
Woods, Al Haig, 11:04 a.m.–11:17 a.m.

Nixon: . . . the one item I don't remember talking about is Helen
Thomas. For her to print another story on that poor sick Martha
[Mitchell] . . . and you know what she did by that story? She convicted
John. She said that John told the Prez . . . Well, for God's sakes, John's
denied it.

Woods: I know.

Nixon: . . . denied his own involvement. Unbelievable.

Woods: Well, she's [Martha Mitchell] a nut. She is a nut, you know,
as far as I'm concerned. . . . Helen Thomas is bad. . . . Martha called
other people. She called [*Washington Star* reporter] Betty Beale a lot of
times. She doesn't call her because Betty won't print [that talk]?

Nixon: No. Betty's a decent person.

Woods: That's right.[11]

Rose Mary Woods might have thought I was a bad person, but I realize
she was one of the few remaining loyalists from that dwindling band of
beleaguered aides who were forced to stick it out, knowing it was all over.

It was getting worse by the summer of 1973, and the phone calls increased
in number and intensity. She again said Nixon was going to have to resign or
be impeached, and she repeated that the White House was trying to get her
husband to shoulder the blame for the whole, sorry mess.

Mitchell apparently was listening in on the extension and interrupted.
"Are you willing to take the blame?" I asked.

"Any attempt to make me do it isn't going to work. I've never stolen any
money. The only thing I did was try to get the president reelected. I never did
anything mentally or morally wrong," he insisted.

So I filed that story and the White House began circling the wagons ever
tighter, now thinking that Mitchell might blow the whistle on them.

The White House was getting more interested in my conversations with
Martha as well. The White House tapes that have been released so far contained this conversation between Nixon, Alexander Haig and Fred Buzhardt
before John Dean testified before the Senate committee:

Nixon: They didn't pay any attention to Martha's crazy crack—I
mean, Helen Thomas (unintelligible) should be weird but covered
(unintelligible).

Haig: I'm working her over, goddammit.

Nixon: No, I will never (unintelligible) ever again (unintelligible) I won't speak to her anymore because she knows Martha's sick. For her to crack those terrible stories and Martha calls up and says, "John (unintelligible)"—Christ, she'd convict her husband. You realize it? He's denied it.

Buzhardt: I know.

Nixon: She's out (unintelligible) talked to me about this.

Buzhardt: Never?

Nixon: Never, never. Of all people. Huh?

Buzhardt: (Unintelligible) she hasn't got sense enough to know she's even doing him in.

Nixon: What?

Buzhardt: She's even doing him in with these things.

Nixon: I know. How are you working Helen Thomas over? I don't know either (unintelligible) can't work over one individual but God almighty, I'd just say that's unconscionable (unintelligible).[12]

The phone calls continued and on August 26, 1973, I filed a column:

San Clemente, Calif. (UPI)—Martha Mitchell says she has seen a campaign-style book written by President Nixon and H. R. Haldeman and that it included plans for Watergate-style operations.

She said the Senate Watergate committee should call her to testify.

She said Mr. Nixon's news conference denial that her husband, Attorney General John N. Mitchell, had told him the details of Watergate, was "a damned lie."

Her husband shielded Mr. Nixon in his testimony to the Ervin committee because he hopes Mr. Nixon will pay him back with executive clemency if Mitchell is convicted of crimes, Mrs. Mitchell said in a telephone interview with this reporter.

"I saw the leather-bound campaign strategy book for 1972 that was written by Nixon and Haldeman," she said. "It included the whole procedures of everything that has happened. I saw it with my own two eyes, when I was trying to press John not to go into the campaign.

"It was at least 2 inches thick," she added. "Everything was there from A to Zeta." She said she read part of the book and for that reason she should be called to testify.

She angrily disputed Mr. Nixon's statement that Mitchell had never told him about the Watergate break-in, and that he had not asked Mitchell about it.

"For God's sake, he used to call John at 2 o'clock in the morning and he said he didn't call his attorney general? He called him every night. I've got proof from Julia (her housekeeper).

"Nixon was aware of the whole damn thing," she said angrily.

Mrs. Mitchell watched the presidential news conference last Wednesday and was particularly irate with Mr. Nixon's statement that "throughout I would have expected Mr. Mitchell to tell me in the event that he was involved or that anybody else was. He did not tell me. I don't blame him for not telling me. I regret that he did not because he is exactly right. Had he told me, I would have blown my stack. . . ."

Mitchell testified that if he had told Mr. Nixon, he would have "blown the lid," a different expression, meaning expose the facts.

Mrs. Mitchell surfaced after a nearly month-long silence to express her views.

She said she fears "John Mitchell will never get out of it."

She indicated that there was friction between her and her husband because of "what Watergate has done to our lives. We have been suffering."

She also described Mr. Nixon as the "most egotistic person I have ever met in my life. He has a temper like I do if I get mad at something."

"The president has assaulted both John and me in taking everything we had or wanted."

At several points during the conversation, she insisted that her telephone was tapped. She made two calls from her New York apartment and a whistling sound could be heard at intervals.

In another telephone call, Mrs. Mitchell said she tried Friday night to communicate with the Western White House on her husband's relationship with President Nixon but she was told to "call UPI," she said.

"I'm so damned mad," Mrs. Mitchell told the UPI news desk in New York in a 3 a.m. telephone call. "I asked them to let me speak to the president. I wanted to tell him something. They told me, 'Why don't you call Helen Thomas?' "

On September 10, 1973, about seven months after they'd moved into their New York apartment, Mitchell moved out and took their daughter, Marty, with him. As he left, he told Martha, "You are the most wonderful woman I ever met." According to friends, it was Mitchell's refusal to break with Nixon that destroyed the marriage. They separated in 1974 and Martha said, "He fell into the clutches of the King."

At his trial in late 1974 on charges of conspiracy, obstruction of justice and three counts of perjury, Mitchell's own lawyer echoed Martha, maintaining that Mitchell had done what he did because he "believed in and trusted and he was completely loyal to Mr. Nixon." Mitchell was convicted on all counts on January 1, 1975, along with Haldeman, White House domestic adviser John Erlichman and Robert C. Mardian, who had been appointed assistant attorney general and put in charge of the Justice Department's internal security division; he had worked with Mitchell to orchestrate the cover-up.

Mitchell was given a thirty-months-to-eight-year prison sentence and quipped, "It could have been a hell of a lot worse. They could have sentenced me to spend the rest of my life with Martha." He was released from prison in 1979.

Martha picked up the pieces of her life in New York after Mitchell moved out. The divorce proceedings were acrimonious and news stories from time to time detailed how Martha had either tossed his clothes and belongings out the window, out the door or down the elevator shaft. Martha originally was awarded $350 a week when they had separated and that amount was increased to $1,000 after the divorce, but Mitchell didn't hold up his entire end so money became tight.

But she was most devastated, she said, with the estrangement from her daughter, Marty. The youngster had stopped by in October 1973 to pick up some clothes, and Martha later recounted, "She said to me, 'My father told me a child needs only one parent. You don't have a car and a chauffeur and you can't take care of me. My father says you're running around with a wild set of people and you'd better watch your step.'" Martha admitted that through the years she had spoiled her daughter, "but he has brainwashed her against me. I have tried to see her at school, but the teachers say they have orders from him not to let me in. In the beginning she used to call me at night, but not anymore. It's the ugliest, cruelest thing in the world—they've used Marty to get even with me."[13]

After Nixon resigned in August 1974, Martha found herself in demand for talk shows and interviews and "the voice that launched a thousand quips" was back in action. She traveled, visited friends, and began writing a book and making plans to host a television show.

She came back to Washington in the summer of 1975 for a visit and over Labor Day weekend, at a friend's house, she fell when opening the refrigerator door. Unable to cope with the severe pain in her neck and back, she was taken to Northern Virginia Doctors' Hospital. X-rays showed she had two broken ribs and a broken neck vertebra. But other tests revealed something worse. Martha had multiple myeloma, a painful bone marrow cancer that leaves the victim's bones brittle and full of holes.

She called me from the hospital and I sat by her bedside that day while doctors explained the illness to her, drawing diagrams and using words like *malignancy* instead of *cancer*. She listened quietly, her eyes round and wide, but it was as if she were listening to them describe someone else's condition. I went back to my office and, sadly, began to write the first news story of her illness. The next morning, Martha watched the news on the "Today" show. Shocked and tearful, she spoke to her friend Diane Auger. "They say I have cancer." As far as I know, she never used that word again. Friends and strangers alike flooded the hospital with get-well cards. Her son, Jay, who was working as a congressional aide, and his Mississippi-born wife, Janice, visited her often.

By early October, she was anxious to leave the hospital. "Get me out of here," she'd tell everyone who came to see her. Jay brought her to an apartment leased by Diane and her husband, Tom Beury, near the Shoreham Hotel. Martha saw other doctors who confirmed the diagnosis.

She tried to keep her spirits high and her outlook positive. However, of the hundreds of letters she received, she could not bear to read those from people who also suffered from the same disease, even though many of those letters went on to offer encouragement, telling her she could live a long life.

In mid-November, Martha went home to New York. She spent one night in the apartment and then entered Sloan-Kettering Memorial Hospital and was put under the care of Dr. Klaus Mayer, the stocky, graying chief of hematology.

"When I first saw her, she was so ill, I thought she wasn't going to last a week," Mayer said later. "But she responded beautifully."

He confirmed she had a "very progressive myeloma" and her bones were eroding rapidly. Her skull, he said, looked like Swiss cheese in places. He began an aggressive chemotherapy series during which Martha's personality seemed to undergo a transformation.

I spoke to Dr. Mayer periodically to check on her progress and he told me something astounding: "At first she was difficult to handle," he said. "She was paranoid. She accused me of working for Nixon. Once she suspected her disease was brought on by the injection she had forcibly received in California—a highly inaccurate supposition.

"But then her attitude changed rapidly and we became good friends. I think it was mainly that she learned to trust me. But she never gave up the lingering idea that 'those guys' had induced her illness."[14]

Dr. Mayer said the nurses became very attached to Martha and Martha became attached to some of the other patients, roaming the corridors either in a wheelchair or using a walker. "She'd sit out in the solarium and talk to visitors," he said. "I remember one black man who had to go home to the

South to take care of his kids—his wife was very ill—and she told him, 'Don't worry, I'll visit her every day.' And she did. She couldn't have been nicer."

She knew she had a very serious illness, Mayer told me, "but she hoped to live. She hoped to be able to do things, appear on television, write a book, that sort of thing. I didn't discourage her. She would say 'I wish I could live. There are so many interesting things to do.'"[15]

Mayer stayed in close contact with Mitchell, who was dividing his time between New York, where he maintained a suite at the Essex House, and Washington. They talked many times about Martha's illness, he told me, and Mitchell was "concerned about her health and upset about her sickness." But after giving what was described as "considerable thought," Mitchell decided that visiting Martha would serve "no useful purpose."

"It's not that he had hostility and didn't care," said Mayer. "The last thing he wanted was another blowup."[16]

Mayer did bring up the idea of a visit to Martha; at first she had no interest, but later indicated she would be willing to see her ex-husband. However, "she was very upset about her daughter," he said.

Marty, while not hostile to Martha at this point, shared her father's well-known reserve and apparently also decided that visiting was not in order. Perhaps she hoped to avoid a repeat of another high-voltage scene when Martha went to Sacred Heart Convent Academy in Greenwich, Connecticut, and tried to take her out of school.

Jay visited her regularly and when he couldn't get to New York, telephoned her every week; Clifford Kunz, her longtime friend from Arkansas, also came often.

Martha remained at Memorial until January 1976, when she moved to the Hospital for Special Surgery for an operation on her hip. She stayed there until March 7.

Finally, she returned home and was cared for by two nurses, Linda Francis and Katherine Foster. To everyone's amusement, she insisted on calling Mrs. Foster "Elizabeth" and got everyone to do the same.

One night she fell, broke her arm and returned to the hospital for more surgery, where she stayed until May 14. When the time came for her to leave, she said that the hospital staff was the only "family" she had.

"When she first came, she was lonely and upset," said T. Gordon Young, the hospital's administrator. "We liked her. She was a lady. She got a lot of mail. I was so disappointed that her family didn't care to visit her."

As she left the hospital for the second time, Martha flashed her famous smile at Young. "You know, I may fool them all yet," she said. [17]

But in addition to her deteriorating health, her financial troubles were mounting. John Mitchell had her covered under his health insurance, which took care of the hospital and doctor bills, but he had stopped her weekly $1,000 alimony checks. Martha's lawyer, William Herman, went to court on May 18, filing papers saying that she was "desperately ill, without funds and without friends."

In an interview, Herman told me his attempts for an out-of-court settlement went nowhere. Eventually, the State Supreme Court awarded Martha a judgment of $36,000 in back alimony.

William Kilbride, the assistant manager of the Security National Bank branch that had Jacqueline Kennedy Onassis as a customer, also had befriended Martha. Through him, Martha arranged for the payments of her apartment maintenance bills of $2,300 a month, but funds were dwindling. As her plight became public, small donations showed up in the mail from time to time.

On May 28, Herman, Kunz and Kilbride arrived at the apartment. Martha had decided she wanted to sell some jewelry to pay her caregivers, including her engagement ring and a diamond necklace in her safe-deposit box.

She had always resisted giving her power of attorney to anyone, but this time she felt there was no alternative. She also hinted there were papers and letters in the safe-deposit box that would have made for "interesting reading." Ironically, she died two days later and her safe-deposit box was sealed.

Her arms were black and blue from the wrists to the elbows from the painkiller injections she had been given and as the three men went over her financials with her, she looked at them for a long moment and then said, "Don't worry, you won't have to put up with it long."

The next day, when he went to visit, she seemed to be her "bright old self," Kunz told me. "She was in better spirits than I had seen her in a long time. I think she knew she was not going to get well, but she thought they had arrested it. There were signs she was getting better."[18]

However, she had also begun to get huge blisters on her arms that turned into welts. She asked that her doctor be called.

Another old friend from Pine Bluff, Ray West, Jr., had been with her on Thanksgiving Day in 1974 when she began talking to him about where she wanted to be buried. "She said 'You're my family,' " he recalled. "I wonder how long she had known?"[19]

When Katherine Foster came on Saturday, she called Dr. Mayer and asked him to come by. He said he would stop the following morning. During the night Martha began to cough up blood.

The next morning, Dr. Mayer said she had hemorrhaged during the night from stress ulcers. She was very sick but quite conscious. He thought of putting her in his car and taking her to the hospital but said she "knew better how sick she was" and asked for an ambulance.

Just before the ambulance arrived, Martha went into cardiac arrest. They resuscitated her but her kidneys had shut down and Mayer, who had gone ahead to the hospital to wait for her, said, "it was pretty hopeless."

She did not regain consciousness. Mayer called Mitchell and later recalled, "He was fully informed she was in very critical condition. God knows there wasn't anything he could have done. He would have been in the way. She was unconscious. Also, he didn't express any desire to see her at that point."

Martha died on Monday at 4:25 A.M.

Mayer called Mitchell at 4:27 A.M. to give him the news and said Mitchell was "very upset" when he went to see him later in the day. "He obviously cared for her at one time or another. He was very somber, serious, sad."

Jay had been visiting his father and stepmother in Philadelphia and did not receive the message on Sunday that his mother had taken a turn for the worse. His father heard the news in the coffee shop of their hotel and went upstairs to break the news to Jay.

William Herman, her attorney, had been given the key to the apartment and on the day she died, he and Kunz went over to pick up Martha's favorite yellow dress for her burial. The superintendent would not allow them to enter and told them Mitchell had given the order.

Mitchell then called Ray West and they made the funeral arrangements. Martha would be buried in Pine Bluff at the foot of her mother's grave.

Mitchell, Marty, Jay and a few friends from Washington converged on Pine Bluff. Some viewed the body before the silver casket was closed. Her hair was done up in that familiar upswept style and she wore a pink peignoir. Jay could not bring himself to look at his mother that way.

Mitchell controlled the funeral and barred press coverage but that didn't stop reporters and photographers from covering the story. Riding in the limousine between Marty and Jay to the services at the First Presbyterian Church, he and Marty maintained their stoicism. Jay had difficulty controlling his tears. In church, Marty was overheard hissing to her half-brother, "Don't talk to the press."

After the funeral, Mitchell clapped Jay on the back and told him to buck up—and then began talking about his concern over the thirty-six lawsuits he faced. A few days later, he went to San Clemente to visit Richard Nixon.

Also attending the funeral was nineteen-year-old Piper Dankworth, the daughter of June Dankworth, one of Martha's friends to whom Martha had entrusted her handwritten will. June sent copies of the document to Jay, William Herman and Mitchell. William Kilbride of Security National Bank was notified that the bank had been named executor of the estate. Her holographic will, dated May 1974, said simply that the estate was to be divided between Jay and Marty, and that anyone who contested it would be left $1.

But the will's validity came into question because two witnesses had not signed it. Mitchell said Martha had left a later will, also handwritten, and he informed the bank that under the state's Tenancy Survival law the apartment would revert to him. But he later indicated he would not contest the will.

In early June 1976, Mitchell, Kilbride, Marty and Jill Reed, Mitchell's daughter from his first marriage, went to the fourteen-room apartment. It was Mitchell's first visit since he'd left in September 1973. [20]

Marty headed straight to her old room and stayed there with the door shut. One friend of hers told me that after Martha died, she took out her mother's picture from a "hiding place" and put it on her bureau. "She wanted to remember the good old days," the friend said. Another friend recalled that Marty broke into a wide smile when he told her, "You'll be as pretty as your mother someday."

Strolling through the apartment, Mitchell seemed nostalgic. When he walked into the dining room, he noticed Martha's portrait, and a blank space where his own portrait had hung. "What did she do with it?" he wondered to those gathered. Then he paused and said, "Wait a minute, didn't that go down the elevator shaft too?" He later found the empty frame, a metaphor for what their lives had become.

Also missing, when he checked the vault, was the family silver.

Mitchell noted the elegant furnishings had been appraised at six figures. "The wife buys and the husband pays for it," he said, but he recalled Martha's flair for decorating, the fresh flowers every day and how she had worked to make it a home for the three of them.

He mentioned he was looking for "certain papers" that Martha had "released to writers" and told Kilbride the bank should reclaim them. "They're certainly salable," he said and taking a long slow look around, he smiled. "Woodward and Bernstein would have had a field day in here."

He walked to the door of his former study and found it locked. He reached into his pocket, pulled out a key, slipped the key in the lock and opened the door. He asked about the status of Martha's safe-deposit box and, one person in the room noted, seeing him standing there, puffing on that ever-present pipe, "he looked like a grandfather—with a bit of the fox in him."

I spoke to Jay sometime afterward and asked him how he felt about his mother and how he was dealing with her loss. "How do you describe the pietà?" he said. "She's happy now, she's at peace. She is still alive in the hearts of many."

When Martha died, a few in her family and some friends had hoped a memorial would be built in her honor. These days visitors can view her girlhood home and the folks of Pine Bluff named its main traffic artery the Martha Mitchell Expressway after their favorite daughter.

For me, it was a fitting memorial that George McGovern made Martha a part of the *Congressional Record*. On June 3, 1976, McGovern stood on the Senate floor and after making his own brief tribute said: "The distinguished reporter, Helen Thomas, has written a fitting tribute to Martha Mitchell which appears in the June 1 issue of the *Washington Star*.

"I ask the unanimous consent that the article by Ms. Thomas be printed in the *Record*." [21]

There was no objection. I had titled the article "Martha Mitchell: She Told the Truth" and some parts follow:

> As the parade passes by, I salute Martha Mitchell.
>
> Perhaps it is fitting that she died on Memorial Day, the holiday of tribute to the nation's war dead. In a sense she was a personal victim of the political war of Watergate, and one of its very few heroines.
>
> She loved her country and she proved it. Her epitaph might read: "She told the truth." No, she shouted it from the housetops. And at the end, her credibility stacked up better than that of some recent presidents.
>
> Knowing Martha as I did, she probably did not go gently into the night.
>
> There were so many things she wanted to do. She was working on a book to be titled "Martha, Martha." She was planning to write a column. She would have her own television show.
>
> "I'm going to live the life of Martha Mitchell," she once said, and live it she did before fatal illness struck her down. . . .
>
> Martha did not discover the telephone as some believed. But her late-night telephone calls to reporters became legendary. She never phoned unless she had something to say and she stressed she had learned "never to lie.". . .
>
> Somewhere along the way, someone told Martha that if she talked to a wire service reporter, the story would get out quickly. She wanted that. . . .
>
> She knew a lot and she was not going to be shut up. She began to call reporters and say her husband would be made "the fall guy" and the "goat" for Watergate.
>
> Martha begged her husband to make a clean break, but she failed. "I don't think he's going to get out of it," she told me.

She was one of the first to accuse Nixon. She said he knew everything her husband knew.

She also was one of the first to demand Nixon's resignation. "Mr. President should resign immediately. I think he's let the country down," she said early in 1973. "It's going to take a hell of a lot to get him out...."

Washington will remember her fondly....

And so will I.

ELEVEN

Doug

At the White House there's a hallway leading from the Rose Garden back toward the offices of the press secretaries. On the walls are pictures of the White House pressrooms in their many incarnations and some pictures from press conferences of long ago. There are some drawings there too: The artist Norman Rockwell once visited Franklin Roosevelt and made a series of illustrations depicting what he saw on his visit. There is a wonderful one of Smitty, sitting on top of that Philippine mahogany table in the West Wing pressroom—the one he sometimes made full body contact with as he barreled out of the Oval Office—and he's sitting there quietly, staring into space. (I guess it was either a slow news day or Rockwell took some artistic license.)

There's another picture, a photograph, of Roosevelt in an open car, surrounded by the twelve or so members of the press corps, all with their notebooks and pens, all taking notes, inches from the president. No "bubble" limousine with bulletproof glass, not a Secret Service agent in view.

Standing close to the car is a man with a small mustache, wearing a rumpled shirt and an intense look. That's Smitty.

Also standing close to FDR is the reporter for the Associated Press, a handsome young man with slicked-back hair, wearing pleated trousers.

That's Douglas B. Cornell. He was my competition for ten years and my husband for eleven.

Whoever plans on falling in love? I certainly didn't have a two-track mind back then when I first started covering the White House. I didn't think it was possible to do the kind of work I loved to do and still be a wife. I was hard-driving, competitive and convinced that no one could ever understand how important my career was to me. Besides, in those days, we "ladies of the press" were busy breaking down the gender-specific walls, either fighting for the "hard news" assignments or trying to kick in the door at the National Press Club. So who had time, anyway?

How wrong—and how lucky—I was.

Douglas B. Cornell was born in St. Louis, Michigan, in 1906 and grew up in Falls City, Nebraska. His father was an osteopath and Doug watched him work tirelessly to save lives during the 1918 influenza epidemic. His father wanted Doug to follow in his footsteps, but medicine wasn't his career choice. He began working for the *Falls City Daily News* while he was still in high school—an English teacher had encouraged him to be a writer—and went on to get a journalism degree from the University of Missouri in 1928. He worked at the *Moberly Monitor-Index* in Missouri, the *Des Moines Register,* the United States Daily and the General Press Association. He arrived in Washington and joined AP in 1933, six months after FDR was inaugurated.

He covered the Army-McCarthy hearings, the firing and farewell speech of General Douglas MacArthur and every national political convention from 1936 to 1968. In World War II, he and Smitty accompanied FDR on trips, some of them so secret they couldn't write a line.

FDR used to refer to Doug, Smitty and Bob Nixon of International News Service as "the ghouls," that tight band of reporters assigned to watch his every move. One day he said to them, "You're just waiting for something to happen to me, aren't you?" "No, sir," said Smitty. "We're just here *in case* something happens to you."[1] Not much on that score has changed, as President Clinton learned full well.

Doug admired FDR very much and never forgot the one year, when his campaign train passed through Nebraska, Roosevelt invited Doug's parents aboard. And before the war, Doug covered some of Roosevelt's eloquent speeches and a few Roosevelt probably wished he hadn't delivered.

I recently ran across a copy of one dated October 20, 1940. The pages are brittle and yellow, the print is fading, but there are Doug's notes scribbled in the margins, still readable. Roosevelt was in Philadelphia and had announced he would seek a third term. Around this passage Doug left a number of question marks: "Tonight there is one more false charge, one more outrageously false charge—made to strike terror in the hearts of American citizens. It is a charge that offends every political and religious conviction that I hold dear. It is the charge that this administration wishes to lead this country into war."

On December 7, 1941, the Japanese attacked Pearl Harbor and Roosevelt went to Congress to seek a declaration of war. As part of the press pool, Doug recalled the story that FDR expressed some concern about rhetoric regarding the war.

"What will I tell the people?" Roosevelt asked. An aide quipped, "Tell them you were never in Philadelphia."

Along with his coverage of the White House, Doug was known as the "big story man," the one to turn to when dispatches flooded in from all over the world and the task was to skim them quickly, decide what to use from each dispatch, put it all together mentally and dictate a story—known as a "roundup"—with a powerful lead paragraph. He rarely sat at a typewriter. Instead, if he was working on one of his own stories, he would leaf through his notes and any releases that had come out, call the office and dictate flawlessly. His longtime colleague Frank Cormier would often tell the story of how, after John F. Kennedy's funeral, Doug walked into the bureau to write the roundup that would be filed in time for the morning newspapers. But he didn't sit down in front of a typewriter. He walked over to a telephone, dialed a colleague sitting across the room and began dictating: "November 25, 1963, Washington—The peace of eternity came in an Arlington grave today to John F. Kennedy, whose quest for enduring peace in a dangerous world was cut short by an assassin's bullet."

Doug and Smitty had that unerring ability to spot the most important point in a news release or a speech transcript—hence, the lead paragraph—before most reporters had finished thumbing through the pages.

I once saw a White House aide hand him a Kennedy speech that ran into many pages. Doug grabbed it, did a quick search, put his thumb on one of the middle pages, picked up the phone and quickly dictated the lead that was buried inside: Kennedy had predicted that millions would die in a nuclear war.

In the Roosevelt days, he told me about a similar instance when he was hunting for "the story" somewhere inside a multiple-page speech. "I looked at the start, nothing there. I looked at the end. Nothing there. I opened it in the middle and there was a paragraph that sort of indicated that Roosevelt might be willing to run for a third term, although he was sort of reluctant about it.

"So I started with that, desperately thumbing all the time in the hope of finding the spot when he would definitely come out and say: 'Okay, I'll take the nomination for a third term.' But he never did and it turned out the part I lit on was the nearest thing to it and just what I should have used all along. Whew!"

Sometimes the White House reporting game sounded like the "Perils of Pauline." One day, FDR's press secretary had a copy of what the reporters considered a "hot speech" and they were itching to get their hands on it. Sitting at his desk, Steve Early began handing out mimeographed copies one by one, but the press guys, impatient bunch that they were—and are—lunged for the copies in Early's hand, knocking over everything on the desk and pressing him until Early was sitting in a corner with a chair on top of him.

Early was "the maddest man you ever saw," Doug said. Then he added with a smile, "I don't know if anyone else got their copies, but I got mine and I ran."

As I've said, there is so little give-and-take between presidents and the press these days as to be nonexistent compared with the freewheeling banter Smitty and Doug enjoyed with FDR.

Doug once asked Roosevelt: "How old are you, Mr. President?" FDR replied: "According to the calendar, my age is sixty-two, but when there is work to be done, I am thirty-five."[2]

Another time, at a press dinner, Roosevelt was signing autographs freely. One reporter tried to trick him into signing his name to a document appointing the reporter to be ambassador to the North Pole and passed it on to Roosevelt. When the document got back to the reporter, Roosevelt had initialed it but had crossed out "North Pole" and written in "South Pole" along with a note: "Sorry, the North Pole is already occupied."

Doug's writing was admired by both his peers and by the people he covered. It was careful, meticulous and precise—just like his legendary expense reports. Once he submitted a report that listed "Ruler to aid in tearing copy off Teletype, 7 cents. (10-cent ruler on sale.)" Another time, he was called away from a backyard chore to cover a president at Camp David. His expense report included the cost of the wasted concrete that had hardened and the price of renting a jackhammer to remove it.

My first encounters with Doug were when he and Smitty would come sweeping into Georgetown Hospital as part of President-elect Kennedy's media pool when the new president made twice-a-day visits to Jackie after she had given birth to their son John Jr. AP's Fran Lewine and I were assigned to cover the hospital full-time and our jobs were to feed the two big guns whatever news we had turned up that day for them to include in their stories.

I saw Doug nearly every day after JFK's inauguration when I began working full-time at the White House. After all, the AP desk was directly across from the UPI desk in that old White House pressroom in the lobby. We covered the same stories and ran together into the Oval Office as part of what Kennedy called "the thundering herd."

Doug and Smitty were the yin and yang of the White House press corps. Where Smitty was flamboyant, Doug was subdued. Where Smitty was brash, Doug was courtly. When Smitty screamed, they could hear him in Akron. I never saw Doug lose his temper except when an error got edited into his copy.

Once, when we were covering Lyndon Johnson in Texas, an editor inserted the word *sprawling* to describe LBJ's ranch. Doug fired off a message: "It isn't sprawling. If it was, I would have said so."

When Smitty would hold forth in the pressroom, telling stories that would have us all in stitches—and embroidering those stories as he went along—Doug would be sitting in a chair, working a crossword puzzle. Every now and then he'd look up at Smitty, shake his head and give a bemused smile, knowing the details weren't *exactly* the way Smitty, the great raconteur, described them. After all, he'd been there too. But Doug, like the newsman he was, stayed out of it, detached and quiet—and immensely tolerant of his colorful friend. On the other hand, Smitty was the first to admit that Doug could outwrite him any day of the week.

I'm equally sure that in those early days, I too struck Doug as brash, loud, opinionated and passionate about a lot of things. Those opinions never showed up in my copy, but in the pressroom, like my boss, I had no qualms about expressing a few things now and then, admittedly throwing in some expletives when the spirit moved me.

Doug sometimes would talk about the guilt he felt when his job took him away from home for weeks at a time, away from his wife, Jenny, and his son, Doug Jr., who later became an architect for the National Park Service. In 1950, in order to spend more time at home, he left AP and took a job with *U.S. News & World Report.* He lasted about eighteen months. He couldn't stand the slow pace, he said. Jenny, who had suffered with cancer for many years, passed away in 1966.

Wire service reporters were always chasing the same stories; it's the nature of the business. The wire services back then were the first to break the news, so the competition was fierce—we all kept an eye on what our competition was up to. And covering the Kennedys—at Middleburg, Virginia, where Jackie would flee to her beloved horse country, or at Palm Beach, or at Hyannis Port, Massachusetts, or at Newport Beach—we got thrown together all the time. The press corps hung out together, dined together and did our watchdog routine together—on the first family and on one another. If someone disappeared from the group for more than a few minutes, the group started worrying if whoever had disappeared had found a telephone and we were all getting scooped.

Doug and Smitty were the big White House guns; I was still learning my way around in the Kennedy years. But we were all friends and often went out to dinner together on those many trips through three administrations. We were all over the country, all over the world. People can get to know one another.

After Jenny passed away, Doug and I began to see each other socially, but we were very discreet. After all, we were private people and professional competitors. But by 1971, Doug had reached retirement age; my career was cooking along and we decided to get married after he retired. Unbeknownst to us, however, our quiet little romance was about to become quite public.

Doug was going to retire October 1 and President Nixon decided to give him a surprise retirement party. A few days before that, I had told Mrs. Nixon's press secretary, Helen Smith, that she would be getting a wedding invitation soon but to please stay mum. She knew we were seeing each other—and that we were nervous about being discovered.

The retirement party was held in the State Dining Room and Nixon had prepared a presidential citation for Doug. I was standing in the back of the room, taking notes as usual, when suddenly I was getting pushed to the podium where Nixon asked me to read the citation. It was a very touching and emotional moment as I read:

> The President of the United States of America to Douglas B. Cornell, Reporter extraordinary, White House correspondent with six presidents and friend of many years: As you retire after more than four distinguished decades in Washington journalism, you take with you the abiding respect and admiration not only of your colleagues but also of those whose activities you have chronicled—including especially that House freshman from California whom you began covering 24 years ago, and who has prized your fine reporting ever since. Associated Press readers, newsmakers, and news professionals across America will miss the Cornell by-line. So will I. All of us join in warm tribute to a consummate professional.[3]

I thought that was the end of that, but then Pat Nixon came up to the platform and grabbed the microphone. Calling it "the biggest news of the century," the first lady announced our engagement.

After the gasps and the applause died down, the president quipped that "the best marriages are made in heaven but the press marriages are made in the White House."

And as the blubbering bride-to-be, between tears and laughter, I tried to take notes. Pat Nixon, with a broad grin on her face, said, "At last, I've scooped Helen Thomas."

Later on, someone asked Doug what he considered the high point of his career. "This is it," he said. "No president ever gave me a party before."

Me, I got to have lot of showers and receptions given by my many long-time friends: Dorothy and Gloria Ohliger, Dorothy Newman, Eleni Epstein, my cousin Julia Rowady and Helen Smith. And Pat Nixon, truly gracious after her big "scoop," held a postwedding luncheon at the White House.

We were married on October 16, 1971, in a small simple ceremony in St. John's Episcopal Church, bordering Lafayette Park across from the White

House. It is known as the "church of the presidents" and every president since James Madison has attended services there.

All my brothers and sisters attended—my brother Matry walked me down the aisle and my sister Barbara was my matron of honor—along with a few friends from Detroit. Ayesha was there, of course, and had a fine time reminding me in later years how nervous I was.

We had two receptions. The first one was at the American News Women's Club, which Eleni had decorated with white flowers and white satin ribbon. Our guests included Tricia and Ed Cox; Herbert Klein, Nixon's director of communications; Ron Ziegler; Martha Mitchell and many other friends from the press corps and government. Liz Carpenter, with whom I'd logged so many miles when she worked as Lady Bird Johnson's press secretary, came from Texas bearing a gift from President and Mrs. Johnson, a silver cup that was inscribed, "To Helen and Doug: Happiness always from the LBJs."

The other reception, at Ayesha's restaurant, was a little more informal and a little more raucous. There we feasted on stuffed lamb, watched a belly dancer, listened to Arabic music and drank a lot of champagne.

Of all the congratulatory notes I received then, those I enjoyed most were from my women friends, expressing happiness for me and saying I had renewed their hopes—that my getting married was a most encouraging sign for them.

Doug and I moved to a two-bedroom condominium near the Shoreham Hotel. He planned to write his memoirs and spend more time at the cabin he and his son had built and named "Boulder Lodge" in Rappahannock County near Sperryville, Virginia. My life returned to its usual frenetic pace at the White House.

I suppose it takes a wire service reporter to understand another wire service reporter's life. In that respect, I couldn't have wished for a more understanding, amiable, cooperative companion. In an interview for *Parade* magazine, I think Doug, in that elegant way of his, put it best as to why we "worked" as a couple: "Living with Helen has changed my orderly life into something of a catch-as-catch-can existence. I never know when she goes to work in the morning where she'll wind up at night, or when she will get home for dinner, or whether she will. Someone who hasn't been a wire service reporter probably couldn't stand being married to someone as energetic and devoted to her job as Helen, but I can. I think she's a terrific reporter. I hope she never gives it up."[4]

But I did make time—something I was fairly unused to—in my married years for a little r 'n' r now and then. The lodge was our weekend haven when we could steal away. It was idyllic, with a wall-to-wall, floor-to-ceiling window overlooking a waterfall and a fireplace made of stone indigenous to the area. While it had all the modern conveniences, I did insist—and Doug submitted—to having a telephone installed. Doug's favorite times were spent working on the place.

We invited friends in from Washington for weekends—the menus were heavy on the barbecues—and made many friends among our neighbors who numbered retired bankers, diplomats and authors.

On the window that looked out on the waterfall and the hills Doug had tacked a small piece of yellow paper torn from a legal pad on which he'd written the biblical phrase, "I look to the hills from whence came my strength." It stayed there for years, a testimony to nature and "Old Rag," the mountain everyone loved in the Blue Ridge.

He also loved to travel, and for those adventures we had our dearest friends Jean and Bob Baldwin of Austin, Texas.

I met them on my first trip to Texas with Lyndon Johnson. For many years, Jean and Bob were active in the Headliners Club, the quasi–press club at the Driskill Hotel where the press corps stayed. When LBJ came to town, Jean and Bob loaded up their house with enough barbecue, wine and whiskey to keep a military battalion happy, and their parties for the press corps were legendary. They made Texas the welcomest place in the world for my colleagues and me.

I was a fish out of water on my first trip to Texas. LBJ had decided to attend a football game and as Jean remembered when I visited with her a year ago, said, "I saw you getting on the bus and you looked like one of the most forlorn, saddest people I've ever seen, like you were going to your own execution."

No sports fan am I. Jean, who never met a stranger, took me under her wing when we all piled onto the bus to go watch the Longhorns play. We became close friends from then on.

After Doug and I were married, we traveled with Jean and Bob quite a bit. One of the wildest vacations we ever endured was a little jaunt we made through Guatemala and Mexico in October 1974. The long Watergate nightmare was over, Nixon had resigned and Doug decided I needed a break.

So down we went to enjoy ourselves for a few weeks to get some sun, do some sight-seeing and just relax. We'd been in Guatemala a couple of days and one night were sitting in a restaurant having a fine time with margaritas in hand when a woman approached our table. "Aren't you Helen Thomas?" she asked me.

I answered in the affirmative, and she immediately launched into a diatribe against "you reporters," railing about Watergate and shaking her finger at me. "You've destroyed the greatest president who ever lived," she yelled.

I just looked at her and said, "Madam, have you heard the tapes?" That didn't stop her and she got louder and more abusive. Doug and Bob got on either side of her and escorted her out.

That night, at about 3:00 A.M., we woke up to the most god-awful rumbling—like a freight train was headed directly for the hotel. Doug looked out the window, saw the volcano erupting and started throwing clothes in the suitcases. I ran out to the hallway and started pounding on Jean and Bob's door. Jean opened the door and looked at me as if I'd gone off the deep end. "Get your stuff together, we're getting out of here, there's a volcano," I babbled. Jean kept standing there and I realized I might not be connecting. She did go to the window, looked out and uttered a long, drawn-out expletive. Bob woke up, saw what was going on and started packing.

Bob and Doug packed the car as volcanic ash began drifting down over it. Meanwhile, Jean had made it down to the front desk and was arguing with the clerk about the bill. I met her in the lobby.

"Look at this," she said. "There's all this stuff on here we're being charged for. It's like they took my phone number, my Social Security number and my address and put a dollar sign in front of it all. I'm not paying this." She then turned to the desk clerk and continued arguing as the volcanic ash continued to fall and the noise got closer.

I finally erupted myself. "Jean, are you going to let money stand in the way of saving your life? Let's go!"

With black clouds overhead, the three of us finally managed to get her in the car—still complaining about the bill—and we drove through the night to Mexico. We checked into a hotel, exhausted, and later that afternoon grabbed the beach chairs and carried them down to the lake. We'd just settled into our chairs when we noticed the water looked a little roily but we just kept sitting there, talking, glad to be away from the volcano.

Then Bob noticed the waterspout forming on the lake. We hustled back to the hotel and didn't come out for twenty-four hours.

A few days later we were walking around sight-seeing and a well-dressed but kind of distant-looking woman was sitting outside a cantina and started talking some kind of gibberish. Some college-age students noticed the woman pointing to me and walked up to Jean. "Is that Helen Thomas?" one of them asked. "Yes it is," she said. "Well, that woman," he said, "keeps repeating her name and saying things about her."

We decided it was time to come home and after that, as Jean joked to me years later, "We just started calling you Mary Jane for a while."

Our lives were happy, complete, fulfilled. I was busy with my job and Doug was my anchor. His understanding never flagged; he never got annoyed with my crazy hours. He had always personified that phrase *grace under pressure* for me and I could always rely on his quiet perspective when I needed to vent about whatever strain the White House was imposing on the press corps.

His unflappability was phenomenal. One night we got out of our car on a tree-shaded street, only to be accosted by a man brandishing a gun, demanding our money. I was doing my best to keep my hysteria under control and with shaking hands, handed over my heavy leather handbag, which contained my wallet, my keys and what I missed most later on, my passport that bore the entry visa from Nixon's historic breakthrough trip to China. Irreplaceable. The thief then waved the gun over in Doug's direction. Very calmly, Doug reached into his back pocket, took out his wallet, removed a $20 bill from his wallet and handed it over. The thief ran off.

In 1974, I was having one of my best years professionally. After thirty-two years as a member of the Wire Service Guild I was promoted to a newly created management post, White House bureau chief, becoming the first woman to serve in that capacity for a wire service. A year later, I was elected the first woman president of the White House Correspondents Association, was invited to join the Gridiron Club as its first female member and my book *Dateline: White House* was going to be published.

Doug had planned a surprise anniversary party for me and invited a number of friends. Toward the end of the evening, he turned to a friend sitting across the table and said, "Do I know you? Can you tell me your name?"

In 1976, my sister Isabelle came for a visit and we went with Doug to the doctor. He told us Doug was losing his memory, but when Isabelle, who had been a public health nurse, described Doug's symptoms to her doctor in Detroit, he said it sounded like Alzheimer's disease. I had no knowledge of the heartbreaking, devastating condition. For years, though, Doug had always expressed the fear that he would suffer from senility, as his mother did in her declining years.

Slowly, agonizingly, my husband of too few years began to slip away from me. He would become disoriented and, finally, things reached the point where he had to have constant supervision. My two "guardian angels," Isabelle and my housekeeper Nellie Wigginton, bless them, came to the rescue.

I would get him ready before I left for work every morning and Nellie would watch over him until I got home at night. When Isabelle retired in 1977, she came to Washington to help out as well. We all worked to keep him alert and active, going for long walks, visiting some of his favorite spots.

But his disease got worse and he required more and more care. Isabelle had to return home and with that, we made one of the most difficult decisions I hope I never have to face again with anyone close to me. Doug accompanied Isabelle back to Detroit where she and the rest of my family all pitched in to take care of him. I was determined not to send him to a nursing home. But there were long presidential trips that would take me away.

Some friends thought I was too protective, but I wanted them to have remembrances of the real Doug, the Doug who was their friend and colleague, whom they had known, respected and admired.

After being in Detroit several months, Doug suffered a bout of pneumonia and was rushed to the hospital. He was put on life support but nothing could be done. I was at his bedside when he died at age seventy-five on February 20, 1982.

He left a big hole in my life. He was a wonderful husband, wise and good and a great friend.

For the many differences I had with the Reagan administration over those eight years, I still will remember the kindness of the president and Nancy's condolence call when Doug passed away and the beautiful basket of flowers they sent. Years later, when President Reagan disclosed after he left office that he too had been diagnosed with Alzheimer's, I could empathize with Nancy and understand the road that lay ahead of her.

We held a memorial service a few days later in Washington where friends and former colleagues gathered to pay tribute with grief and laughter. His colleagues Frank Cormier and Marvin Arrowsmith gave eulogies. And the music included some of Doug's favorite songs: "My Buddy," "I'll See You Again" and Victor Herbert's "Ah, Sweet Mystery of Life."

His obituary, written by AP's Harry Rosenthal, recapped a few of Doug's more memorable opening paragraphs. AP had always dispatched Doug to the funerals of great statesmen. He was their top writer when it came to sentimental journeys and when AP celebrated its 150th anniversary this year, my "competitor" Larry Knutson, who had researched some of Doug's more memorable leads, shared them with me:

From Bonham Texas, 1961: Speaker of the House Sam Rayburn, a small man of great national stature, died today in this little Texas town he loved.

Nov. 10, 1962: Hyde Park, N.Y: This was a gray, somber, glowering day, this day of the funeral of Eleanor Roosevelt—and scarcely in keeping with the vivacious spirit of the great lady who was gone.

Washington, 1968: Robert F. Kennedy was buried on a gentle hillside Saturday in the uncertain light of a full moon and the flame flickering eternally over the grave of martyred President John F. Kennedy.

One of the highest compliments we heard was a response to an editor at the *Los Angeles Times* who had written to inquire who had written an especially elegant story, one that had run without a byline. The details are lost to time but Frank Cormier remembered the newspaper editor was told: "Oh that's Douglas B. Cornell—and he always writes that way."

Several years earlier, Doug and I had planted a blue spruce seedling at the cabin, a Christmas gift from Lady Bird Johnson to the White House newswomen as a memento of her beautification trips.

When we planted it, I recalled a story John Kennedy used to love to tell. It seems a nobleman asked his gardener to plant a certain tree. The gardener protested: "But, monsieur, it will take a hundred years to grow."

"In that case," the nobleman replied, "we must begin immediately."

After the services I carried out Doug's wishes and had him cremated. With a few friends I made the trip to the cabin and carried out another wish, scattering his ashes at the base of the tree and in the Hazel River in front of the house.

Years later, I was sitting in Ayesha's restaurant with a friend. She was admiring my rings and asked where they all came from. I pointed them out: one from Ayesha, one from my dear friends, the Nine family. One from Doug that had belonged to his mother. On my left ring finger, three bands of baguettes; one is my wedding ring and two are gifts from Doug.

"Did you like being married?" she asked.

"It was probably the most unexpected and wonderful thing that ever happened to me," I told her.

"Well, it must have been something," she said. "You were so busy covering the White House and he was retired. I mean, I'm sure he understood having been a wire service reporter and all."

Yes, he did understand. And I told her of those many moments of getting late-night phone calls from the copy desk, being told to rush back to the White House when a story had broken, or racing around getting ready to leave on yet another presidential trip, and before I was out the door, out of the corner of my eye, I would see my husband sitting there in his favorite chair, with that bemused smile on his face, enjoying the latest performance of "hyper Helen" and her White House adventures. And each time, before I sailed out the door, I would stop, turn around and say, "I love you, Doug."

And still, with that bemused smile, he would look at me and say, "Sometimes."

No, Doug. Always.

The Smallest Sorority

It's hell.
—Eleanor Roosevelt, responding to a reporter's question on what it was like to be
the wife of a public official for more than thirty years

There have been only forty-three of them in the nation's history. They came from places as variegated as America itself—New York, Texas, Illinois, Michigan, Missouri, Vermont and Georgia. They have had lives of poverty or lives of privilege or somewhere in between. They have been oldest daughters, youngest daughters, middle daughters and only children. And up until the twentieth century, we didn't hear much about them because reporters didn't scrutinize their lives.

Their fame, notoriety and attention is by association since they've all been married. But each has left an indelible mark on America in one way or another in modern times, to the point where referring to Jackie or Lady Bird or Nancy or Hillary doesn't even require a last name. Our first ladies have been admired, imitated, criticized, revered and reviled. For reporters, they're the second-biggest story in the White House every day—and there have been days when they've taken the top spot from their husbands.

How the term *first lady* worked its way into the national vocabulary is a little cloudy. Some have attributed it to Lucy Hayes when she accompanied her husband, Rutherford B. Hayes, on the very first presidential cross-country trip and newspaper accounts referred to her as "the first lady of the land."

Having covered many first ladies, I know there were times when the White House must have seemed like a prison, or as Harry Truman once described it, "the crown jewel in the penal system." While the Constitution doesn't spell out the duties, assignments or responsibilities for the wife of the chief executive, I don't think anyone would argue these days that whatever the definition one may choose when using the term first lady—a title, a role, a job—it has evolved into one of considerable power. In fact, Nancy Reagan used to list "first lady" in the spot marked "occupation" on her income tax forms.

A woman automatically takes on the title when her husband takes office; the familiar role of hostess/wife/diplomat goes with the territory as well, but what she does with the job is entirely up to her.

It's hard to believe that until the twentieth century first ladies were just about invisible. Even no less a figure than Edith Kermit Roosevelt once remarked, "A lady's name should appear in print only three times: at her birth, marriage and death." But the explosion of mass media and the change in thinking about a "woman's place" in society has forever altered the public perception of what a first lady should be. A first lady is a newsmaker no matter how hard she may try to stay out of the picture—and oh, how some of them have tried.

As a reporter, I've admired all of those I've covered, from Jacqueline Kennedy to Hillary Rodham Clinton, for their activism, their dedication and their sheer grit in moments of crisis—and they all have endured them. In modern times, each in her own way has followed a pattern set by that most famous of first ladies, Eleanor Roosevelt, whose activism in so many causes—not to mention her service as her husband's eyes and ears in her travels across the country—has become the role model for so many since. If you don't believe me, just ask Hillary, who has been known to have had a few imaginary conversations with her.

Eleanor went everywhere her husband couldn't: poverty-stricken cities in the Great Depression, sweatshops, migrant labor camps and jails.

One of my favorite stories about the indomitable Eleanor was when she set out on a tour to inspect conditions in the nation's prisons. At a staff meeting, FDR asked an aide, "Where's Eleanor?"

"She's in prison," was the reply.

"I'm not a bit surprised," quipped her husband, "but what's she done now?"

I think each of them understood that we reporters came with the turf in their new lives, and while some did their best to accommodate or at least tolerate us, a few did their best to ignore and elude us.

Privately, I am sure at times most of us were called everything in the book for a question we asked or a story we had written. I can still recall Lady Bird giving me the cold shoulder after I wrote about Luci's engagement; Pat Nixon looking me straight in the eye and saying "I love my husband" as I questioned her about the Watergate scandal enveloping the White House; and even the grandmotherly Barbara Bush rapping me on the head, twice, when I asked her how her husband could have sent emissaries to China after the bloodshed in Tiananmen Square.

But I also recall their good works, their energy and their commitment. Someone who never did become first lady, Muriel Humphrey, actually put it in an interesting way. I asked her during the 1968 presidential campaign why she would want to take on that formidable role, and she said, "Because I can wave a magic wand."

In a way, she was right. But I think the magic wand is more like a spotlight, and wherever the first lady has decided to focus it—on a cause or a project close to her heart—the nation has responded.

We've seen that spotlight shed on many areas: historic preservation, beautifying America's natural landscape, volunteerism, the elderly, the Equal Rights Amendment, foster grandparents, literacy, children and various aspects of health care such as breast cancer, mental health, the needs of the disabled and drug addiction. Results have been mixed but the abiding lesson is they planted these issues in the public consciousness and we continue to see the fruits of their labors long after they've returned to private life.

Beyond their public causes and projects, the first lady is the nation's number one hostess. She's also an administrator. While her husband is running the country, she's busy running the White House. There is a huge staff at her disposal but she's the one who makes the decisions. There is a social calendar to be scheduled months in advance—we may marvel at those gorgeous Christmas decorations every year but there are thousands of people who've been laboring on them since June. When there's a state dinner, she selects the menu, goes over the invitation list, consults on the flowers, the seating arrangements, the entertainment and a few other thousand details. And oh yes, she picks out a dress.

She's an activist, she's a hostess, she's a wife, a mother, and a fashion touchstone, probably the least-liked part of the package. As Eleanor Roosevelt described all the unsought attention to her clothes, "Sometimes I feel like I'm dressing the Washington Monument."

"All the talk over what I wear and how I fix my hair has me amused," another first lady once said, "but it also puzzles me. What does my hairdo have to do with my husband's ability to be president?"

Hillary Clinton, you might say? No, try Jackie Kennedy, after she received a number of letters during the 1960 campaign telling her she should change her hairstyle.

She also got so annoyed on that campaign when her style and taste became such a big issue that she told Nan Robertson of the *New York Times* that if all the reports of her spending were true, "I'd be wearing sable underwear."

Contrast that to a White House dinner I was covering when someone complimented Barbara Bush on the lovely gown she was wearing. She grinned and said, "Same old dress. I've worn it once before."

Each first lady undoubtedly would have preferred that we not cover the social events at the White House. We were an irritant, buttonholing the president and guests of honor, intruding—or was it crashing—their parties.

On the other hand, they also realized the social events were news, not just by virtue of the guest of honor but also to highlight the many celebrities who entertained, and maybe to let the American people share vicariously in the glittering evening for which they were paying.

Tape recorders were ruled off-limits at those glittery events. But there is no doubt that there have been times at social occasions when all bets were off, when there's breaking news and there's access to the president. Those moments cannot be passed up—protocol notwithstanding. In cases like that, we never got the feeling we were welcome, tolerated perhaps.

But I did get invitations to at least one state dinner in each administration and several invitations to other special social events—teas, receptions, picnics, along with the Yuletide parties for the press corps.

Going to a state dinner at the White House has always been a thrill. It marks a chance to dress up and leave my usual fashion accessories—notebook and press credential—at home. I was there to have a good time and I did. Even the first ladies' press secretaries dropped their glares and smiled. They would hold me harmless. After all, I was a guest and would so behave.

But that did not mean I could not pick up a tidbit or two here and there for future reference.

At one dinner I sat next to General Alexander Haig, President Reagan's first secretary of state, and from his disenchanted comments, I knew that his days in the cabinet were numbered. Reagan advisers were out for his scalp.

Then there was the disapproving look I got from Barbara Bush at a state dinner in honor of Russian president Boris Yeltsin. He was seated at the table next to mine and, thinking of my nieces and nephews and wanting to come up with some historic memento of the occasion, I asked Yeltsin to sign my menu card. Sitting next to me was the wife of James Billington, head of the Library of Congress and a renowned Russia scholar. When she saw what I did, she asked me to get an autograph for her husband. So I again defied the gods of protocol and approached Yeltsin. He graciously obliged. He was having a great time, and enjoying being the center of attention. When I caught Mrs. Bush's look, I felt a bit uncomfortable. But I was not sorry I had gotten the autograph, especially for the nation's top librarian.

When I was at these events as a member of the working press, the first ladies' press secretaries and staffs were given the impossible task of controlling us. We would be allowed to mix and mingle with the guests after dinner during coffee and cognac but we were still under the watchful eye of White House aides. Sometimes we managed to give them the slip and would sidle up to the president and often get introduced to the guest, a president or a prime minister. Sometimes I thought our intrusion was a welcome relief, obtuse as that may sound. But when the guest did not speak English, we may have given the president a momentary break from interminable translations.

All of the first ladies had some trepidation and some insecurities in adapting to their high-profile position on the national scene, but all of them expressed in one way or another a singular advantage to living in the White House. As wives of political figures they have been well acquainted with life on the campaign trail and the many separations between them and their husbands. Barbara Bush once said, after she moved into the White House, "Now I see George," adding she could wave to him from the Queen's bedroom when he headed for the Oval Office. Betty Ford said she was happy because "now I know where Jerry is these days," and Hillary Rodham Clinton said in a speech in 1995, "It's also kind of nice to have your husband live, as it were, above the store. He's actually home for dinner a lot more than he was in our previous life together, so there are many more things about the circumstances and the opportunities that are just wonderful."

They obviously went into the White House with lots of advice from friends and supporters. But no one could prepare them for the road ahead.

The magnitude of the role of first lady cannot be exaggerated. Furthermore, they knew they had to measure up. Each woman knew she would inevitably be compared to those who had preceded her and that the public would be her judge. None could have felt prepared for the exalted status she would attain or the attention she would command. They had married very ambitious men and they had to find their niche. Some decided to pull strings behind the scenes. Others took a more up-front approach and incurred a lot of resentment and some political fallout.

Some were ambivalent about living in the White House. But they all knew they had gained a national identity and a place in American history just by virtue of their address. Their lives took on a dimension on the world stage that demanded so much but in turn gave their lives so much meaning in terms of what they did for their country.

First lady: so many roles, so many jobs, so many responsibilities. They have to do it all and they have to do it all well. I think they did.

Jackie Kennedy

On a trip back to Washington from Hyannis Port, Jackie Kennedy brought along her latest pet, a German shepherd puppy her father-in-law had given her for her birthday. She had named it Clipper, and while traveling back to Washington, the press corps sent up a note asking her what she would feed it.

She sent back a one-word reply: "Reporters."

That pretty much was the stuff and substance of what it was like to cover—or try to cover—my "first" first lady in my early tenure at the White House. She waged a three-year war of independence with the press and, looking back, I would say it ended in a draw. We won a few, she won a few, but her army included the Secret Service.

Still, the women of the White House press corps owe her a vote of thanks. In large measure, she made our coverage hit the front pages more often than not, and she set the tone for full-time coverage of first ladies that persists to this day. It was a melding of the right person at the right time in the right place in history.

At the age of thirty-one, I don't think she was enthusiastic about becoming a celebrated figure on the world stage when she moved into the White House. But given her background, she was well prepared for the role she would play, and I think she warmed to the public side of it eventually. Her children were another matter.

In early 1960, the press perhaps got its first insight of what it might be like to cover her as first lady. Someone asked her where she thought the Democratic National Convention should be held and she replied "Acapulco."

Up to that point, I had covered diplomats, politicians and other government officials and found them by and large pretty much down-to-earth and well acquainted with the rules of the journalism game.

So nothing prepared me for the job I had ahead of me covering the 1947 Debutante of the Year who had attended private schools, spent summers in Newport, went to Vassar, spoke French and treated the press corps like so many foreign invaders.

What was puzzling about the way she treated us was that she herself had been in journalism for a time, working as the "Inquiring Camera Girl" in 1952 for the *Washington Times-Herald*. She would scoot around town interviewing people, taking their pictures and writing up their answers for a daily column. One of her first interviews was with Pat Nixon, wife of then–Vice President Richard Nixon. Another was with Nixon himself, and later on, she interviewed a junior senator from Massachusetts named John F. Kennedy. She also staked out the Eisenhower grandchildren and one time talked to a youngster named Tricia Nixon, who told her she didn't like her daddy being away from home so much.

In any case, she intrigued and captivated the nation, partly because of her personal history and partly because she held herself aloof from everyone save her family and close friends. I don't think any of the reporters who covered her ever got the full picture and I think that is clearly the way she wanted it.

One of my early encounters was in November 1960 as I stood outside the Kennedy home in Georgetown and the door opened. A very pregnant Jackie, looking a little confused and unhappy, bid her president-elect husband good-bye as he was leaving for a trip to Florida to rest up from his campaign. She gave birth to her son, John Jr., shortly after, curtailing her husband's trip and giving us our first inkling of the hide-and-seek game she would be playing with us for the rest of his administration.

When she and her infant son came home from the hospital she went in through the front door and slipped out the back for her meeting with Mamie Eisenhower and the traditional incoming first lady's tour of the White House. Jackie, an aide told me later, started crying after she left the home she would be moving into in three months. She said she thought it looked like a hotel decorated with year-end clearance items from a discount store.

That fit of tears, though, gave rise to one of her most significant contributions to American history. She was determined to remake the White House into a national historic treasure, and she succeeded beautifully. She persuaded Congress to designate the building as a national museum and then put together committees of historians, art experts and museum directors to aid in the project, soliciting funds for the restoration and for the paintings, furniture, sculptures and other items with a historic and artistic connection to the White House.

When the restoration was complete, she helped to prepare the book *Historic Guide to the White House,* the first of its kind ever published. As a result, tourists began flocking in greater numbers to see the results of her handiwork. She also allowed television cameras in, a striking departure from her now-famous penchant for privacy. In February 1962, she conducted a televised tour, explaining the work that had been done and answering questions from interviewer Charles Collingwood about White House history. The show drew an estimated 48 million viewers.

Her interest in historic preservation extended beyond the walls of 1600 Pennsylvania Avenue, and as first lady she also helped to halt the demolition of an old building once known as the War, State and Navy Building. She once said it reminded her of the grand opera house in Paris. It is now known as the Old Executive Office Building, located next to the White House. After she left the White House, she lent her support to such causes as saving New York's Grand Central Station and preserving Central Park.

She had another goal in the White House: shielding her children and protecting their privacy. Aside from the tall rhododendron bushes she had planted along the fence, she went to great lengths to keep Caroline and John Jr. out of the white glare of publicity, though her husband often sabotaged those efforts. When she was out of town, Kennedy would invariably allow photographers into the Oval Office when the children were there visiting their father.

Three-year-old Caroline gave the press corps some of its best laughs in those rare times we spotted her. One day she was wandering around and someone asked her, "Where's your daddy?"

"He's upstairs with his shoes and socks off, doing nothing," she replied.

Her mother, on the other hand, spent a lot of her time trying to figure out how to elude us, even if she was in the same room. During her first year in the White House, she gave a press luncheon and arranged the seating so that she was sitting near her friends and women writers who did not cover her on a daily basis. At a press reception in Paris, she snubbed the American newswomen while giving interviews to the foreign press.

While it was obvious she would have liked—as she once suggested—to keep the women reporters assigned to her at bay by agents armed with fixed bayonets, it seems that she should have known a smile, a wave or a few words would have alleviated a lot of resentment on both sides.

Although she never reconciled herself to the invasion of privacy that is part and parcel of a first lady's life, she did discover that being the president's wife enabled her to use her special skills and interests in ways the White House had never seen. Dinner party lists bore names like Carl Sandburg, Leopold Stokowski, Igor Stravinsky and Pablo Casals. She replaced the formal U-shaped tables so familiar at state dinners with the small round tables that are a hallmark of White House entertaining to this day. White tie was out, black tie—the most her husband would tolerate, we heard—was in. After dinner, the men no longer retired to a separate room for their brandy and cigars; everyone mingled for an after-dinner drink or coffee.

Still, there was, in the words of former White House aide Dave Powers, that familiar ring of "the boss can't do a thing with her" when Jackie wanted to stay out of sight. She always pleaded "family duties" when she retreated into privacy—or what became known as the PBO: polite brush-off.

She refused to attend a Congressional Wives' brunch in her honor and it later came out she remarked she couldn't stand "those silly women." Instead, she went to New York to catch a performance of the Royal Ballet. Lady Bird Johnson substituted for her.

JFK himself pinch-hit for his wife when she refused to attend a Distinguished Ladies' Reception in her honor, shortly after his inauguration. And she was a no-show at a reception for exchange students one summer on the South Lawn. Her social secretary Letitia Baldrige told us Jackie was under the weather with the "same old sinuses." It later was discovered she was in the family quarters peeking through the window at the scene below.

Trying to understand her desire to have it both ways—seeking press coverage when beefing up the image demanded it, shutting us out when it suited her—was a constant conundrum for us. We retaliated in a variety of ways, mostly involving working our sources and using long-range binoculars.

I was one of the few who managed to get an interview with her—not face-to-face, as I have with every other first lady since—but she consented to answer a list of questions I submitted. That was considered a journalistic coup back then.

I also got a chance to poke a little fun at her in 1962 at the annual show given by the Women's Press Club. I donned a pink evening gown and had my hair done bouffant style by Jackie's hairdresser, Jean Louis. I sang a little song, written by newswoman Gwen Gibson, in that breathy, little-girl voice that America's ears often strained to hear:

> If I want to give a ball
> For just me and Charles DeGaulle,
> I have absolutely, all the gall I need
> I'm . . . Jahh-keeee!
> If I like to water-ski
> and maintain my privacy
> Am I to blame?
> You would do the same
> If you were me
> I'm Jahhh-keeeee!
> If I want to fly away, without taking JFK
> Or if I'm fond of French champagne
> And I'd rather not campaign
> That's me . . . Jahh-keeeee!

The next day, Kennedy came up to me in the Rose Garden with a wide grin on his face and said, "I've been reading all about you. Some party."

So we eventually became accustomed to her Friday-to-Tuesday trips to the family home she was designing in Virginia and her secret trips to New

York, and she became, I think, accustomed to us trying to second-guess her every move.

When she became pregnant in January 1963, we figured she would be even more determined to stay out of sight.

But none of us was prepared for what had to be one of the saddest days of the Kennedy presidency. In August we were covering her, or rather staking her out the best we could—on Squaw Island near Cape Cod where she was spending the summer. Earlier that spring, her doctor had told her to cancel all of her official activities in an effort to ensure a healthy birth for their third child.

On August 5, Pierre Salinger burst into the West Lobby announcing that Kennedy was leaving in five minutes for Hyannis Port. Jackie was on her way to the hospital at Otis Air Force Base for a cesarean section.

Patrick Bouvier Kennedy—weighing four pounds, ten ounces—was born suffering with a lung ailment known as hyaline membrane disease. He was rushed to Children's Hospital in Boston. I covered the hospital during two tense days as Kennedy spent time with his infant son; he was with him when he died.

The outgrowth of such tragedy is hard to predict, but it was obvious the first couple had grown closer to each other—and more affectionate in public—afterward. Jackie's depression seemed to linger and a concerned JFK conveyed that message to his family and friends.

Thus came an invitation via her sister Lee Radziwill for a two-week vacation in Greece, cruising the Aegean aboard a luxurious yacht owned by a shipping magnate named Aristotle Onassis.

Even though JFK had encouraged her to make the trip, the stories that filtered back of Jackie's sight-seeing tours, her water-skiing, her dining and dancing till the wee hours of the morning were not exactly the kind of first lady image he had planned on as he was preparing to launch his reelection campaign. A cable was sent and a penitent Jackie came home.

A few weeks later, plans were under way for a political trip to Texas in advance of the presidential campaign, and much to JFK's surprise and delight, Jackie agreed to accompany him—the first such trip she would be making since 1960.

On the morning of November 22, 1963, the president was up early while Jackie took her time getting ready for the Dallas motorcade. She recalled years later that "JFK picked out that suit" that she wore, a pink Chanel.

It began November 21 in San Antonio, followed by two appearances in Fort Worth and wrapping up in Dallas.

Her world and America were shattered by the bullet that killed her husband as she sat next to him in the open car in the motorcade.

Back in Washington, I got tipped off that Kennedy's casket would be brought back to the White House after midnight, and I was further told that when Jackie got off the plane, chief of protocol Angier Biddle Duke asked her if there was anything he could do.

"Yes," she replied, "find out how Lincoln was buried."

On the day of the funeral, I was assigned to stand on the steps of St. Matthew's Cathedral holding what passed for a "portable" telephone in those days—about the size of an automobile battery and just as heavy—calling in to the desk and dictating the running story of the national figures and dignitaries who entered. Bob Andrews, one of UPI's best rewrite men, took the details and shaped the story. After the service, I found myself standing near Jackie as she emerged, holding her son's hand, and saw her lean down and whisper to him. The small boy lifted his hand into a military salute and I had a hard time choking back the tears as I dictated the details to Bob.

I remember her courage and control over those four days; how she supervised the funeral arrangements and told the family, "We must just get through this."

After the service in Arlington National Cemetery, where she lit the eternal flame at her husband's grave, she received the dozens of visiting heads of state in the Red Room. After the state leaders left, she hosted a birthday party for John, who had turned three that day.

In her final days at the White House, she cleaned out the Oval Office, gave some small possessions of her husband's as gifts to the staff, oversaw the packing of their belongings and prepared to take her leave. On December 6, she called for the staff to say her good-byes before she left and one remarked later that "it was so wonderful seeing her smile—to be able to smile."

She had one more official duty, an East Room ceremony for the presentation of the presidential Medal of Freedom, which she and JFK had redesigned.

She slipped out before the ceremony ended, collected her children and left the White House. She wouldn't return until several years later at the invitation of Pat Nixon when her official first lady portrait was unveiled.

Jackie lived for a time at the home of Ambassador Averell Harriman in fashionable Georgetown, but soon her temporary home became a stop for tour buses. She moved her family to New York where she purchased a Fifth Avenue apartment and furnished it in comfortable and tasteful "Jackie" style.

In New York, she shopped incessantly and one of the favorite jokes among the late-night talk-show hosts was "Where does Jackie go when the stores are closed?"

She refused to write her memoirs, but later became a respected editor first at Viking and then at Doubleday.

In 1968, she married Aristotle Onassis as the public gobbled up stories of the jewels he showered on her. That romance was short-lived and she found the beautiful Greek Islands not as idyllic with the sophisticated, suave, but bored "Ari."

She returned to New York and they lived separate lives until Onassis died. Her share of the Onassis wealth as a result of a temporary standoff with Christina Onassis, Ari's daughter, left her a very wealthy woman.

For fifteen years, Jackie's constant companion was Maurice Templesman, an international gem dealer, who helped her invest her money well.

At the age of sixty-four, Jackie was diagnosed with a virulent cancer. Always a woman of great courage, she summoned her family, including her former in-laws, to her apartment where she said good-bye.

I never saw her again after she left the White House. She had closed the door on that part of her life. About a year after she was gone from Washington, I wrote her a note requesting an interview and received a note back: "I'm still in mourning."

I believe she was happy living her life out of the spotlight. But when she did venture out in public, she always stopped the show.

She remains a unique and mysterious woman to the American people, which may have added to her appeal. I would have liked to have known her better. But she was not about to reveal herself, leaving others to assume and guess with unrequited curiosity who she really was.

Jackie showed in life and in death that she had, as Lady Bird Johnson put it to journalist-author Ruth Montgomery, a quality extolled in JFK's book *Profiles in Courage*: "The most admired of human virtues is courage, which is grace under pressure."

The real Jackie was a very private person who rose to public and signal occasions.

Lady Bird Johnson

On August 28, 1970, Lyndon and Lady Bird Johnson stood with President and Mrs. Nixon in a magnificent redwood forest in Northern California to commemorate Nixon's signing of a proclamation declaring the three-hundred-acre tract the Lady Bird Johnson Grove, in honor of her tireless efforts to preserve America's natural landscape.

As the four stood together, Nixon observed the similarities between himself and LBJ in their respective political histories: congressman, senator, vice president, president.

Johnson remarked to Nixon, "Presidents are lonely people. The only ones they are sure of all the time are their women kinfolk."

Nixon responded, "Yes, and we're both fortunate in the fact that we married above ourselves."

No truer words were ever spoken. Lady Bird Johnson and Pat Nixon were the traditional consummate political wives, devoted to their husbands' careers—partners, confidantes, helpmates.

She was born Claudia Alta Taylor in Karnack, Texas, in 1912. Her nickname, Lady Bird, came about when she was a small child and a family employee described her as "purty as a lady bird." Her mother, Minnie Patillo Taylor, died when Lady Bird was five and she was raised by her father, Thomas Jefferson Taylor, an aunt and a retinue of family servants. She attended the University of Texas and earned a degree in liberal arts and journalism.

In 1934, she met Lyndon Baines Johnson, then a congressional secretary, who was visiting Austin. He asked her for a date; she accepted and when he returned to Washington he barraged her with letters, telegrams and telephone calls. As she remarked many times, "Sometimes Lyndon simply takes your breath away." They were married in November 1934.

During World War II she helped keep his congressional office operating while he served in the Navy, and in 1955, when LBJ suffered a severe heart attack, she kept that office running until he returned to his post as Senate majority leader.

After several miscarriages, she gave birth to Lynda Bird in 1944 and to Luci Baines in 1947.

I remember running into her in a Los Angeles hotel in 1960 when LBJ was one of the many contenders for the Democratic nomination. With all the hubbub and mad dashing going on around her, she had decided to take her daughter to an afternoon movie. Later that evening, when it was becoming clear that Kennedy had the nomination sewed up, there were several observations that the Johnson family had been seated far, far away from the action in the convention hall while the Kennedy contingent sat in a box near the stage.

After Kennedy won the nomination, negotiations began to get LBJ to take second place on the ticket. Speaker Sam Rayburn acted as a go-between and eventually gave up his opposition to LBJ taking the second spot. Not Lady Bird. As pols ran in and out of their suite through the long night, she repeatedly told Lyndon he would be letting his Texas friends down if he accepted the number two spot.

It was probably one of the rare disagreements in their longtime partnership when Lyndon poked his finger at her and said, "Don't you know I'll be one heartbeat away from the presidency?"

Liz Carpenter, who worked as Lady Bird's chief of staff, press secretary and a thousand other jobs that defied pigeonholing—I often thought of Liz as sort of a combination Broadway impresario and battalion commander—once described her boss as "a touch of velvet with the stamina of steel" and that description probably never was more on point than November 22, 1963.

Lady Bird was riding in the motorcade in Dallas with her husband and later said that when she heard the crack of a rifle, she thought it was a firecracker—until Johnson's Secret Service agent Rufus Youngblood threw himself on top of LBJ and screamed at her to get down. In the race to Parkland Hospital, she recalled, she heard the nervous voices on the Secret Service radio channel and knew something terrible had happened.

She later told journalist-author Ruth Montgomery that as she watched LBJ take the oath of office aboard Air Force One, "I felt that I was stalking across the stage in a Greek tragedy, just putting one foot before the other. There was a sense of unreality, yet there was also the sense of wanting to take in, and remember, everything that was going on."

When she moved into the White House, she later told reporters, she "walked on tiptoe and talked in a whisper." She also faced the problem of making her mark following one of the most publicized first ladies in modern history. But the day Jackie left the White House, she left a small bouquet and a note addressed to Lady Bird.

"I wish you a happy arrival in your new house, Lady Bird," said the note from Jackie, and it ended, "Remember—you will be happy here."[1]

Media reports used to hint that Jackie snubbed Lady Bird; there was that remark attributed to Jackie that Lady Bird would "crawl down Pennsylvania Avenue on broken glass" for Lyndon. But they did stay in touch over the years, and after she moved into the White House, Lady Bird visited her a number of times at the Harriman home in Georgetown and tried to coax her back to the White House for meetings concerning White House preservation. Jackie always declined. She later said the Johnsons invited her to nearly every state dinner, but "it was just too painful for me to go back to that place."

In 1964, when Lady Bird decided to rename the landscaped East Garden the Jacqueline Kennedy Rose Garden, Jackie sent her mother to the dedication. Jackie later said, "That was so generous of Mrs. Johnson to name the garden after me. . . . So I suppose they [the media] were saying how awful of me not to come, I can see that was an uncomfortable position for her."[2]

They corresponded for many years and Lady Bird was a luncheon guest at Jackie's home on Martha's Vineyard every time she visited the island. Lady Bird recalled one luncheon in 1993: "We talked about authors and the books coming across her desk and into her life and the children, now grown of course. We did not reminisce about the past. In all of that, in looking back and remembering now, I have a feeling of ineffable sadness."[3]

Still, Lady Bird must have felt not unlike Bess Truman in those early days. She told us newswomen, at one point, that she felt she was suddenly onstage for a role for which she had never rehearsed, "but like Lyndon, I will do my best." She also said early on that "I will try to be a balm, a sustainer and sometimes a critic of my husband. As for myself, my role must emerge in deeds, not words."

Those "deeds" she spoke of kept the newswomen who covered her constantly on the go. Lady Bird may have gingerly stepped into the most public of all her public roles, but like the sign she kept on her desk— "Can Do" — she probably will go down in White House history as one of the most remarkable first ladies in terms of achievement.

Covering Lady Bird had its own exhaustion threshold: While we had exhausted ourselves just trying to eke out news of Jackie and her secretive comings and goings, we exhausted ourselves just trying to keep up with Lady Bird.

We had more access, and not only at the Texas ranch. When Lady Bird launched her historic "beautify America" project, we all got to go along for the ride. And what a wild ride it was.

Let me say for the record that my idea of a "nature hike" is a ten-minute walk, maybe, through some carefully landscaped gardens. Lady Bird and Liz had other ideas. I probably never was in better physical shape than when Lady Bird was around. We logged over 100,000 miles on those beautification trips with this "secretary of the exterior."

We climbed mountains. We trudged along the Comanche Indian Trail in Texas. On a raft trip through the Snake River in Wyoming, I was assigned to a raft called *Martini*. I quickly dubbed it "Martini on the rocks" because that seemed to be where I spent most of our time. When her press entourage was photographed on that trip for a picture in *Sports Illustrated* magazine, you can spot me fairly easily: I'm the most miserable-looking one of the bunch.

We poked around historic houses all over the country, including the birthplaces of John Quincy Adams in Massachusetts, Andrew Jackson in Tennessee, Thomas Wolfe in North Carolina and Robert Frost in Vermont. I will admit, I got a little tired on the road.

In Vermont, Lady Bird stopped to read a plaque that contained the lines from Frost's poem "Mending Wall," and I couldn't help but counter with a paraphrased line from "Stopping by Woods on a Snowy Evening," saying aloud, "yes, and we have miles to go before we sleep." Lady Bird turned around, saw me standing there, and must have been able to read the exhaustion in my face. She laughed heartily and I think we were able to call it a night then.

Still, we reporters were proud participants in the Lady Bird brigade. We felt we were part of a great adventure, promoting conservation and preservation of this land we love. And her actions eventually turned into legislation, a bill known as the Lady Bird Bill focusing on cleanup, scenic landscaping and removing billboards. However, there was some backlash. On a trip to Montana we spotted a billboard bearing the slogan "Impeach Lady Bird."

In addition to her beautification trips, we also hit the road when Lady Bird visited sites where her husband's Great Society programs had been implemented. She was the chairwoman for Head Start, a national preschool program for underprivileged children, and traveled across the country on behalf of that initiative. For LBJ's War on Poverty program, she went to meet what she described as "the people behind the statistics" from rural Appalachia to urban slums.

The most incredible trip, though, was a political one: the Lady Bird Whistlestop Campaign, at that time the most active public campaigning ever by a first lady. Our four-day journey aboard the "Lady Bird Special" train began in Alexandria, Virginia, took us through North Carolina, South Carolina, Georgia, Florida, Alabama and Mississippi and ended up meeting Lyndon in New Orleans. We made 67 stops and completed 1,682 miles over 4 days.

We knew it was going to be a rough trip as many in the South opposed the civil rights bill, and she met that challenge head-on in her first speech:

"I know that many of you don't agree with the civil rights bill, or the president's support of it, but I do know the South respects candor and courage and I believe he has shown both. It would be a bottomless tragedy for our nation to be divided."

She never faltered or lost her composure as we chugged deeper into Goldwater country. Up to that point the receptions had been friendly with a few catcalls and some signs saying "Fly away, Black Bird," but things took a definite rude turn in South Carolina. Signs in front of the lovely antebellum homes in Charleston said, "Sold on Goldwater" and at a rally in Columbus, a group of hecklers tried to drown her out by shouting "We Want Barry." Lady Bird summoned up that now-familiar southern gentility, held up her hand and said in a calm but terse voice, "In this country we have many viewpoints. You are entitled to yours. Right now, I'm entitled to mine."

There was no telling, not until November, how many votes she swayed but there was no doubt she'd won admiration from every stripe of Democrat. There were politicians who didn't support her husband's policies, but they couldn't ignore the first lady and still be considered gentlemen. Along the campaign route, House Democratic leader Hale Boggs of Louisiana urged his constituents to attend a rally. Even Governor George Wallace of Alabama sent her a large bouquet of roses.

When we finally reached the end of our grueling, grimy journey, Lady Bird awarded each of us a certificate lauding us for our endurance:

> Having partaken generously of eight states of southern hospitality from Alexandria to New Orleans, day on day, daze on daze, eyeball to eyeball, elbow to elbow, weaved and wiggled the crowded aisle of the Lady Bird Special in pursuit of the better story; having kept attentive to the primary mission of 1,682 miles—an objective crowd estimate and correct analysis of those events that alter and illuminate the political world; and having lost composure only when necessary to file and beat the deadline by phone or telegraph or ESP —
>
> Now, therefore the above individual is awarded this certificate of journalistic perspicuity.

She used to tell us that "Lyndon stretches your mind," but after that trip, I never had any doubt that with him or without him, Lady Bird was one of those women who would make a mark on society. We are better off for the fact that she did it on a national scale.

As busy as she was, she had another all-abiding, all-important job in the White House—being a mother to nineteen-year-old Lynda and sixteen-year-old Luci, two very different young ladies caught up in what Luci used to call "this presidency situation." And with both of her daughters, she was the mother of the bride in their time at the White House.

In an interview with Lady Bird, she told me that she asked Luci if she felt there was enough "home life" for them despite their very public lives. Luci, she said, told her, "Well, Mother, we have to. There's just four of us and that's all we've got . . . there's only us who really understand."

Of her daughters, Lady Bird described them as oil and water. "When Luci begins a speech, I hold my breath," Lady Bird once said. She never had that problem with Lynda because Lynda seemed to have taken a page from Jackie's "avoid the press" instruction book.

I always enjoyed talking to the straight-on, strong-willed Luci. As her mother once put it, "Luci does not bend with the wind. She is not always flexible. The rest of us may wobble about something but not Luci. She is the one person I know who makes up her mind and sticks by it."

Luci kept the White House a lively place, but after she began dating Pat Nugent, she seemed to ratchet down a bit. However, she made big headlines when she converted to Catholicism and when she became engaged to Pat.

I had picked up a tip that Luci was taking religious instruction and called Liz Carpenter, who said something about religion being a private affair. When I found out the exact date she was going to be baptized I reluctantly agreed to hold back the news so the family could have its privacy at the ceremony. Luci gave me an exclusive afterward in which she told me, "I cried. Just about everybody cried. Five years ago, I, like all young people, began to question, began to wonder. I found my answer in the Church."

After I broke the story of Luci's engagement to Pat Nugent, she chided me, telling me that was "a terrible thing to do" to her father. "Pat and I felt the pressures on him were so great we didn't even mention the subject all weekend."

On August 6, 1966, nineteen-year-old Luci married Pat Nugent in an event that was billed as a "simple family affair." The ceremony took place at the National Shrine of the Immaculate Conception, featured a one-hundred-voice choir, twelve bridesmaids and was televised live by all three networks. Her seven-tiered wedding cake weighed three hundred pounds. As one pundit described it, "they invited only the immediate country."

Lynda, on the other hand, at first gave us the cold shoulder at every opportunity, especially our interest in her romances. When she married her Marine fiancé Charles Robb in a private ceremony in the East Room, she took a moment to glower at us as she glided down the aisle because she thought we were standing too close.

But those romances and weddings provided the Johnsons a happy respite from the divisiveness in the country that was emerging over the Vietnam War and the escalating racial conflict. And Lady Bird was more than aware of the stress her husband endured.

One of the starkest examples of Lady Bird's composure in the face of the growing anti–Vietnam War protests occurred right in the White House. She had begun sponsoring what was known as "woman doer" luncheons honoring women who had made significant contributions to their communities. The luncheons stopped after singer Eartha Kitt, who had been invited to one event, loudly criticized the administration right in the Blue Room.

"You send the best of this country off to be shot and maimed," Kitt shouted. "They rebel in the streets. They will take pot . . . and they will get high. They don't want to go to school because they're going to be snatched off from their mothers to be shot in Vietnam."

It was a stunning moment, and I watched Lady Bird slowly rise with tears in her eyes to face Kitt. In a shaken but firm voice, she said, "Because there is a war on—and I pray there will be a just and honest peace—that still doesn't give us a free ticket to not try to work for better things such as against crime in the streets, better education and better health for our people."

There is no doubt that Lady Bird was the one counselor her husband could not ignore when she tried to persuade him not to seek a second term. He had already had one heart attack and she did not think he would be able to survive another four years of the pressures that faced him daily.

It was all reminiscent of the time when Franklin D. Roosevelt was trying to decide whether to seek a fourth term in 1944. The tide was turning in favor of the Allies, but Roosevelt's family knew his health was failing.

The family had gathered to watch the movie *Wilson,* the biography of the World War I president who suffered a stroke while in office. His wife, Edith, tried to cover up the extent of his incapacity and took over some of the reins of power. While viewing the film, Anna Roosevelt stood up in the darkened room and said in anguish, "Dad, that's you, That's you."

After Johnson made his announcement, Lady Bird said, "I felt ten pounds lighter, ten years younger and full of plans."

Lady Bird was one of the most remarkable women ever to grace the White House. Her integrity and understanding, along with her tolerance and compassion have been constants in her life. Although her experiences seem inextricably entwined with her husband's, she cut her own path. Her beautification efforts continue today, helped with her creation of the National Wildflower Center near Austin.

"Life," she told me after she'd left, "is richer and fuller because I tried harder and did things I never thought I could do and was scared to do. I'm glad for all the things I did and only regret some I did not do."

One day in the spring of 1998, the phone rang in the UPI booth at the White House and I picked it up. There was no mistaking that soft drawl.

"Hi, Helen, it's Lady Bird. What's going on over there?"

We chatted like old friends, and afterward, it brought back two memories for me. The first is a now very faded snapshot on a bulletin board that sits in Jean Baldwin's kitchen down in Austin. In it are two women sitting and relaxing on a park bench just having an ordinary conversation. One is Lady Bird. The other is me.

The other memory is from a day down at the LBJ ranch, when the president and Lady Bird were hosting one of their famous picnics. One of the guests was a young man who was a member of the Congolese delegation to the United Nations.

"Is she a 'lady'?" he asked me, puzzled by her first name. Maybe he thought she came from British royalty.

"Heavens, no," I said. "It's her nickname."

"Well," he said, "she *is* a lady!"

And again, truer words were never spoken about Claudia Alta Taylor Johnson.

Pat Nixon

I can still see President Nixon sobbing uncontrollably at the funeral of his wife, Pat. Her onetime press secretary Helen Smith later remarked to me that she had never seen Nixon more distraught.

I thought about what she said and about that incredible day when I stood in the East Room and listened to him bid farewell to his staff after he'd resigned. I went back and looked up that speech to see if he'd made any references to his family and this is what I found:

> And I say to them, there are many fine careers. This country needs good farmers and good businessmen, good plumbers, good carpenters. I remember my old man; I think that they would have called him sort of a—sort of a little man, common man. He didn't consider himself that way. You know what he was? He was a streetcar motorman first, and then he was a farmer, and then he had a lemon ranch. It was the poorest lemon ranch in California, I can assure you—he sold it before they found oil on it. [Laughs] And then he was a grocer. But he was a great man because he did his job—and every job counts—up to the hilt, regardless of what happened.
>
> Nobody will ever write a book, probably, about my mother. Well, I guess all of you would say this about your mother—my mother was a saint. [Pause] And I think of her two boys dying of tuberculosis, nursing four others, in order that she could take care of my older brother for three years in Arizona, and seeing each of them die. And when they died, it was like one of her own. Yes, she will have no books written about her. But she was a saint.[1]

I could find no reference to the woman standing next to him who had stood by him for his entire political career, nor could I find any reference to the two daughters they had raised and who were standing by their father as well.

Why not? I'm still trying to figure that one out. But maybe that would have been too much for them to bear.

Pat had endured so much in the roller-coaster life she had with Richard Nixon, and I think she was probably the most underrated first lady I've covered. She was warm, kind, lively and in my heart I will always think of the time she got to be a reporter with a breaking story—when she revealed that Doug and I were getting married.

But Nixon and his palace guard never understood what an asset she could have been, although all of us who covered her saw her courage and devotion to her husband and family, to her great credit.

One of the few times I got an inkling of what she might be feeling was when a reporter asked her if she would want her daughter to marry a politician.

"I would feel sorry for her if she did," Pat replied.

"Well, you married one," countered another reporter.

"Yes, but I don't tell everything," said Pat.

Thelma Catherine Ryan was born on March 16, 1912, in Ely, Nevada. Her family moved to California and settled on a small truck farm near Los Angeles. Her mother, Kate, died in 1925, so at thirteen, young Pat took over the household for her father and two older brothers. When she was eighteen, her father passed away. Determined to continue her education, she worked her way through the University of Southern California as a salesclerk, a telephone operator and a bit player in the movies. She graduated cum laude in 1937 with a teacher's certificate and took a job at Whittier High School teaching typing and shorthand.

Richard Nixon had returned home to Whittier after completing his studies at Duke University Law School and set up a practice.

In 1938, Pat decided to try out for a part in a play being put on by the Whittier Community Players. She won the part—as Daphne in the Alexander Woollcott–George S. Kaufman play *The Dark Tower*—and met another cast member: Richard Nixon.

It was love at first sight for him, but she was a little less impressed. Dick Nixon, who believed in never giving up, pursued her for two and a half years. They were married on June 21, 1940.

World War II brought the young couple to Washington when Nixon got a job with the Office of Price Administration before he left to serve in the Navy; Pat also worked at OPA. After the war, Nixon decided to enter politics.

Pat Nixon was a quick study of the requirements of political wives, and in six years, she saw him elected to the House, the Senate and the vice presidency. Through it all, she stayed by his side on the many long and grueling campaign trails.

"It takes heart to be in political life," she once observed, and I think the high regard and acknowledgment of her many contributions to her husband's career did not go unnoticed.

In 1960, women delegates to the Republican National Convention wore buttons with the slogan "Pat for First Lady."

When Nixon was defeated by John F. Kennedy and conceded on election night, the cameras caught a poignant scene of Pat, tears streaming down her face. I think she felt personally repudiated and went into seclusion, inconsolable. Usually meticulous about answering her mail, she let thousands of letters pile up without a reply.

She had a few "vacations" from political life, as she called them: After the presidential campaign the Nixons returned to California, where Nixon joined a Los Angeles law firm. Her first "vacation" ended when her husband told her he was mulling over a bid for the governorship in 1962.

It was a tempestuous campaign, and when Nixon was clearly losing to Edmund G. Brown, some reporters observed that a frustrated Nixon shouted at his wife when she stopped their motorcade at a hamburger stand so everyone could grab a bite to eat.

She enjoyed another "vacation" when they moved to New York in 1963 after the gubernatorial election and Nixon went to work for a Wall Street law firm. Until 1968, Pat Nixon was a happy woman, riding the Fifth Avenue bus taking her daughters sight-seeing and on museum tours.

When 1968 rolled around, and Nixon had his sights on the White House again, she balked. But then she realized how important it was to him to make another run for the presidency and supported his decision. She did little campaigning on her own this time though, leaving it to her daughters to make individual trips on their father's behalf. And this time I'm sure her election night tears were tears of joy at her husband's victory.

I think to her delight and surprise, she really enjoyed being first lady. She loved being a hostess, not just at state dinners or other "official" events but opening up the White House to everyone. We in the press corps found her more relaxed and at ease than we'd ever seen her in the vice presidential days. Her Secret Service code name was "Starlight" and it fit her well.

She turned her attention to the White House, making it more accessible, instituting special tours for the blind and the disabled, and she helped prepare a booklet about the exterior gardens. She restored the Map Room, reinstated the exterior lighting that LBJ had ordered turned off and added more antiques to the state rooms.

She had never been inside the family quarters when her husband was vice president. When she arrived, she had the walls repainted a bright yellow. It was said she was never happy with the antique wallpaper depicting Revolutionary War scenes that Jackie had chosen for the family dining room, but given the expense, she left it alone.

But it was Jackie herself, when she and her children came for a private visit in February 1971 to view her official first lady portrait by Aaron Schickler, who told Pat not to be afraid to make her own mark on the White House, and that "every family that lives here should put its own imprint here." In a note to Pat after the visit she wrote, "I have never seen the White House look so perfect. There is no hidden corner of it that is not beautiful now. It was moving, when we left, to see that great house illuminated, with the fountains playing...."[2]

As an aside: I had been tipped off to Jackie's visit and confirmed the information with Helen Smith, who then asked if I would please hold off on the story until after Jackie and the children had left. I agreed to do so but not before extracting a promise of more information. After they were gone, I filed my story, and sure enough, the White House switchboard lit up. The next day I covered a reception Pat was giving and she made it clear how unhappy she was that I had broken the story even though I'd agreed to the ground rules. But I reminded her that news doesn't always break "at what you think is the proper time" and I think she understood. Her big fear, I suppose, was that Jackie might have thought the Nixons themselves leaked the story.

Pat not only focused on being mistress of the White House—the one role where H. R. Haldeman and company seemed not to interfere—but she kept up the goodwill tours she had first embarked on when Nixon was vice president.

When an earthquake hit Peru in 1970, she insisted on making a trip down there, bringing tons of relief supplies and touring the devastated areas.

Still, the president's aides seemed to view her as an impediment. Perhaps with her good sense and devotion to her husband, she was. Many times her staff would receive memos from the West Wing notifying them of a presidential trip that excluded Pat. Rather than working to build a significant slot for her on some project that would complement her husband's work, they seemed determined to exclude her at every opportunity.

Pat never stated outright that she had a personal project she would try to highlight as first lady, but if she had, undoubtedly it would have been volunteerism. "Government is impersonal," she once said, "and to really get our problems solved we have to have people too. We need the personal touch."[3]

In 1969, she went cross-country visiting various community projects, organized by volunteers to help the poor, the disabled and the aged. She did champion the Right to Read program and helped bring about the Parks to People program for the disadvantaged.

In the early 1970s, some of us thought we were witnessing the transformation of Pat Nixon. She seemed to be expressing her opinions a little more readily, and in 1972 she did something totally unexpected: She went on a campaign tour by herself through several midwestern and western states.

Flying back to Washington, she was upbeat, confident of Nixon's reelection and surprisingly talkative with us. "I don't think in such a short period, we ever had such a change in our history, and I think the days ahead, and the years ahead under this great president—I don't take any credit, but listen, I kinda love him—and I think he's going to do a great deal for our country."

One of the reporters on board teased her that we had never heard her speak so eloquently about her husband. But she caught us up. "I've done so much for twenty-five years but I've never boasted," she said. "I cannot boast for my family."

However, I think she was entitled to a little boasting when she helped daughter Tricia plan her wedding to Edward Cox on June 12, 1971. There was no evidence of mother-of-the-bride jitters and she told us during the whirlwind of preparations, "Anyone who can't plan a wedding in a month just is not worth her salt." Tricia had chosen the Rose Garden for her wedding, marking the first time an outdoor wedding was ever held at the White House.

I admit I contributed to the hubbub by hosting a wedding shower for Tricia and inviting the women reporters who covered the first family. We gave her a few gag gifts, like a red wig and oversize sunglasses so she could come and go "in disguise," along with the traditional things any new bride—first daughters included—needs when she is setting up housekeeping.

On the day of the wedding I was part of the small press pool covering the event, and it appeared the weather was conspiring against Tricia's wish for an outdoor ceremony. Rain delayed the service for a few hours, but at 12:30 P.M., Connie Stuart, Mrs. Nixon's chief of staff, announced that the wedding would proceed outdoors.

One of the guests, Alice Roosevelt Longworth, also had had her wedding at the White House—in 1906. Someone asked her if Tricia's ceremony reminded her of her own nuptials. The ever-tart, ever-feisty Longworth replied, "Good God, not a bit. I was married twenty years before Hollywood. This wedding was quite a production."

I must say, I had never seen President or Mrs. Nixon look happier than they did that day. They even made their own "first" at the wedding—dancing for the first time in public. Later, when asked if he would dance again at a White House party, Nixon quipped, "Never again."

But Watergate soon destroyed any pleasure she may have taken in all those years as first lady. At first she seemed convinced it was a Democratic plot to get her husband, and she must have felt we were being disloyal when we approached her with our questions. But in tribute to her, and today I marvel at the fact, she always tried to answer, and I remember, at one point, she told us, "We're going to fight, fight, fight" against calls for her husband's resignation.

Even after the House Judiciary Committee voted articles of impeachment, her loyalty was unshakable. I'll never forget her clenched fists when I asked her a question and she said, "You know, I have great faith in my husband. I happen to love him."

But the strain on her must have been excruciating, and one incident stands out for me. It was Valentine's Day 1974 and no one had seen the president for weeks. The next thing I heard, Pat and Dick had shown up at Trader Vic's restaurant a few blocks from the White House.

Lesley Stahl of CBS and I hooked up and we got a table within range of the Nixons and their friend Bebe Rebozo. We thought we had the scoop on the rest of the Washington press corps, and when the Nixons got up to leave, we ran out ahead of them, hoping to spring a few questions.

However, our little secret had quickly spread, and when we got on the outdoor escalator, we saw what had to be every television and still camera in the Washington area waiting outside.

As the couple came out, Lesley and I got pushed farther and farther to the back away from the president as the cameras closed in. We were standing there on the outside of the circle. As we looked to our left we saw that someone else had been pushed aside as well. There was Pat, standing all alone.

She must have been glad to see a familiar face because when I asked her, "How are you?" her eyes welled up with tears. "Helen, can you believe that with all the troubles Dick has had, all the pressures he's been under, he would do this for *me*?"

Personally, I thought he owed her a lot more than one night out to dinner.

Up to the very end, though, she stood by her husband and urged him not to resign. She later said she thought he should have burned the tapes, comparing them to private letters.

On that fateful day, the family gathered in the upstairs quarters to say their good-byes to the household staff. They then came downstairs for Nixon to deliver his farewell to the rest of the White House personnel, and I was roped off with the rest of the press in the East Room. As they entered and Pat saw the television cameras, she said, "Oh, no." But Nixon had given the OK for the address to be televised, so again, she stood and endured her particular place in history.

On the eve of her husband's presidential inauguration in 1969, a reporter had asked Pat if she had encouraged him to enter politics.

"No," she said, "I did not. Politics was not what I would have chosen for him because, after all, you don't see as much of your husband as you would like and it's a hard life."

But, she went on, Nixon was convinced that politics was his duty, "so what could I do? There it was, what my husband wanted and there was a part for me to play. So I dug in and I played it. I found I really liked it."

Gerald and Betty Ford walked out of the White House with the Nixons as they boarded the helicopter that would take them to Andrews Air Force Base, where they would board Air Force One for their trip home to California. Betty Ford, who was trying to make conversation, noted that the red carpet had been rolled out.

Pat looked at her and said, "You'll see so many of those . . . you'll get so you hate them."[4]

Long-suffering Pat Nixon had seemed to understand her role from the start, unlike some of her predecessors, who learned the hard way. She never spoke against the man who had taken her on a ride to the top and had caused her so much pain and anguish. And she was able to maintain her dignity through it all and gain the admiration of the nation. Her loyalty was never questioned, nor was it self-serving.

In July 1976, Pat suffered a stroke that left her partially paralyzed. She stayed in the family compound in San Clemente and refused many requests for interviews. In 1980, the couple moved to New York City to be closer to their children and grandchildren, and in 1981, they moved again to Saddle River, New Jersey.

Her public appearances were few. In 1990, she attended the opening of the Nixon Library in Yorba Linda, California, and in late 1992, she again traveled to California for the opening of the Reagan Library in Simi Valley, California.

She developed lung cancer and passed away on June 22, 1993, and was buried at the Nixon Library. At Pat Nixon Elementary School in Cerritos, California, flags were lowered to half-mast and students planted a rosebush next to the wishing well that she had dedicated when the school opened in 1975.

I hope it was a yellow-rose bush. That was always her favorite color.

Betty Ford

In the fall of 1978, I was sitting in the makeshift pressroom in a VFW hall in Thurmont, Maryland, waiting for news of a breakthrough in the Middle East peace negotiations taking place at Camp David between President Carter, Egyptian president Anwar Sadat and Israeli prime minister Menachem Begin. My phone rang and it was Bob Barrett, one of Gerald Ford's aides, telling me Betty was about to undergo facial surgery.

I asked if the procedure were cosmetic and there was a long pause. "Let me have her tell you," he said, and put her on the line.

"Are you going to have a face-lift?" I asked.

"Yes," she replied. "Isn't it wonderful? I'm sixty years old and I need a new face."

That was so typical of Betty Ford—forthright, honest, candid as they come.

She was born Elizabeth Ann Bloomer in April 1918 in Grand Rapids, Michigan. When she was eight, she enrolled in dance classes and by fourteen, began giving dance lessons herself. Her father died when she was sixteen, and to help make ends meet, Betty added modeling to her after-school jobs, working at the local department store.

She spent two summers at the Bennington School of the Dance in Vermont, where she became acquainted with Martha Graham, and in 1939 traveled to New York to study with the renowned dancer and choreographer.

She returned home six months later and started her own dance company and became fashion coordinator for the local department store. In 1942, when she was twenty-four, she married William C. Warren, a Grand Rapids insurance salesman, but they divorced when Betty was twenty-nine.

In August 1947, she met Gerald Ford and he proposed in 1948 in a rather unusual way. "I'd like to marry you," he told her, "but we can't get married until next fall and I can't tell you why."[1] He was planning to run for Congress, but his candidacy was being kept secret until June, when he put himself into the race.

They were married on October 15 and settled into suburban life in Alexandria, Virginia, where Betty ran the household and raised their four children. When he became House minority leader in January 1965, the time he spent away from home increased even more. "The Congress got a new minority leader and I lost a husband," she said. "There followed a long stretch of time when Jerry was away from home 258 days a year. I had to bring four kids up by myself."[2]

A health problem developed in August 1964 when she strained her neck, resulting in a pinched nerve that put her in traction for several weeks. She also developed arthritis, and thus her dependence on painkillers began. By 1970, the physical ailments and exhaustion she suffered from the pressures of her life as a congressional wife and raising the family alone led her to seek psychiatric help. She found the therapy helped and became more self-confident and able to speak her mind—something that we all got to know quite well when she moved into the White House.

What was ironic is that she had decided it was time for her husband to retire from politics, and they had tentatively agreed that he would leave after one more election in 1974.

Those plans came to a grinding halt in 1973 after Vice President Agnew resigned and Nixon named Ford his vice president. Betty found herself immersed even more in political life, but she seemed to enjoy her new role. Eight months later she was catapulted into the all-consuming job of first lady.

From the outset, it was apparent to us that she was unique. She was not afraid to speak about her divorce, her psychiatrist or anything else we asked.

After the Fords left the White House the family succeeded in a difficult intervention and she agreed to undergo treatment for substance abuse. This ultimately led to the creation of the Betty Ford Center for Drug and Alcohol Rehabilitation, which opened in 1982 in Rancho Mirage, California, where she works hard giving aid and comfort to the patients, be they celebrities or just plain working folks.

But most of all I remember her as a first lady who somehow trusted that the American people would always understand. Some of her remarks were considered explosive, as when Morley Safer asked her in a "60 Minutes" interview what she would do if her daughter told her she was having an affair.

"Well, I wouldn't be a bit surprised," she said. "I think she's a perfectly normal human being, like all girls. If she wanted to continue it, I would certainly counsel and advise her on the subject. And I'd want to know pretty much about the young man."

When we asked President Ford about her remark he said he thought he had lost 10 million votes. "Then when I read about it, I raised it to 20 million," he said. But he stood by her and supported her.

Her remarks first prompted a hostile, angry response and letters and telegrams flooded into the White House. But in about a week, the mail turned friendly and a Harris poll showed her ratings higher with the public than her husband's. And her ratings kept soaring to the point where Ford wondered if his would ever equal hers. "Frankly," he said at one point, "I think we're going to have to run Betty for president."

She became one of the most articulate proponents of women's rights ever to reside in the White House, and her activism was expressed in a variety of ways. She urged that women be appointed to high office and was vigorous in her support of the Equal Rights Amendment, which was anathema to most Republicans at the time.

One of my favorite stories about her ERA advocacy involved her complaining about the lack of a flag on her car. "I have a nice car but no flag," she told Rick Sardo, one of the president's military aides. "If the president gets flags why not the first lady?"

About a week later we noticed she did indeed have a flag on her car. It was lace-trimmed blue satin, with red, white and blue stars. In the middle was a pair of red and white bloomers, in honor of her maiden name. Above was the phrase "Don't tread on me," and below the letters *ERA*.

Although she was in hot water a lot of times by virtue of making comments off the top of her head, throwing the right wing of the GOP into a tizzy, she called them as she saw them and she never retracted.

Newsweek magazine chose her as its Woman of the Year in 1975, pointing to her honesty and candor as her most remarkable traits. "I don't like to dodge a question," she said, "and I guess I'm not astute enough to walk around it."

She said what she thought and with no apologies and her critics did not prevail. After headline-making remarks that even made her staff cringe, her popularity polls shot up.

Her courage and her candor were never more in evidence than in late September 1974. She had invited Lady Bird Johnson and her daughters to come to tea after the dedication of the Lyndon B. Johnson Memorial Grove on the Potomac. As soon as the Johnsons left, Betty left for Bethesda Naval Medical Center to undergo a biopsy.

I was in the pressroom on September 27 when Ron Nessen called a briefing and informed us that Betty had entered the hospital and would undergo surgery the next morning. I quickly called in the story and left with the motorcade that took President Ford to the hospital.

The next morning the hospital issued a two-line statement: "The results of the biopsy on Mrs. Ford were unfavorable. An operation to remove her right breast is under way."

After she left the hospital and recovered, she spoke frankly about it before a number of groups and emphasized the need for regular exams for early detection of breast cancer. I think her willingness to discuss her condition so openly removed a stigma and paved the way for the kind of public attention and increased research we see today.

Afterward, she said that the night before the surgery, she told her husband and children to go home because she did not want them worrying, assuring them that she would be fine.

In the early days of Ford's presidency, she urged him to pardon Richard Nixon, something he was inclined to do. She undoubtedly felt a great sympathy for the family, especially Pat.

In July 1975, when Ford announced his intention to seek the presidency in his own right, she campaigned both with her husband and independently, and for once, the GOP considered her a powerful drawing card. There were Betty as well as Jerry campaign buttons, bearing such slogans as "Keep Betty in the White House," "Betty's Husband for President."

Her husband's defeat by President Carter hit her hard, but her courage prevailed as she was the one to stand before us in the pressroom on election night. Ford was suffering with laryngitis after the exhausting last push of the campaign and it fell to Betty to read the concession telegram that he had sent to Carter.

Then, in November 1987, she underwent a six-hour open-heart operation to clear four clogged arteries. She recovered and was soon her active self again.

I'll always have a special place in my heart for Betty Ford. She was always kind to me. One year, out of the blue, the phone rang and it was Betty, inviting me to Thanksgiving dinner with her family out in Palm Springs.

I had to decline this most gracious invitation. But it reminded me of how down-to-earth Betty Ford is and how lucky we all have been to benefit from the refreshing honesty of this most fascinating first lady.

Rosalynn Carter

The "steel magnolia" may be remembered as the first lady who attended cabinet meetings, and annoying as it was to some, it was because her husband wanted her there. If any presidency to date reflected the phrase "full partnership" in terms of White House operations, the Carters were the first to exemplify it publicly.

Rosalynn not only sat in on cabinet meetings, she and her husband met for lunch once a week to discuss policy and coordinate their work. From the Iranian hostage crisis to the Camp David peace accords, she was kept informed of all developments.

"Her influence on her husband was considerable," said Carter's national security adviser Zbigniew Brzezinski, "and was exercised almost openly. Carter—at least to me—was not embarrassed to admit it."[1]

That was nearly unheard of in first lady history. Liz Carpenter, no stranger to "steel magnolias" in her tenure with Lady Bird Johnson, once described Rosalynn to *Washington Post* writer Myra MacPherson as having "the manner of Melanie and the efficiency of Scarlett." For myself, I would substitute "strength" for efficiency.

She was born August 18, 1927, the oldest of four children on the family farm outside of Plains, Georgia. Her father died when she was thirteen and her mother, with a family to support, worked a number of jobs while Rosalynn helped run the household and looked after her younger siblings.

She had known the Carter family casually and was friendly with Jimmy's sister Ruth. When the three of them went on a picnic in June 1945, while Jimmy was on home leave from the Naval Academy, he ended up asking her for a date for that evening. Later, she learned that Jimmy told his mother that night, "She's the girl I want to marry."

In February 1946, she visited him at Annapolis and he proposed. They were married in July when Jimmy graduated. She was nineteen years old.

Over the next seven years as a Navy wife she adapted to a life that meant many separations and running the household and raising the children alone. But she took pride in her accomplishments and in her organizational skills. She gave birth to three sons—Jack, Jeff and Chip—in those years as well.

She became more assertive and independent and when her husband told her he was giving up his Navy career to return to Plains—his father had died and Jimmy was going to take over the family business—she blew up.

"I didn't want to go back," she said. "I had been so independent. I didn't want Mother and Jimmy's mother to tell me what I was doing wrong. I wanted to keep our life the way it was. We had a battle that lasted for days. I screamed and yelled and did everything to make him change his mind but I couldn't do it." [2]

Then she began working a few days a week in the office, and in a few years she knew as much about the business as her husband did. Their marriage gradually had evolved into a full partnership.

In 1962, Carter ran for and was elected to the Georgia State Senate. Rosalynn did all the requisite campaigning, but when he was in Atlanta for legislative sessions, she was home in Plains watching the family business. Their daughter, Amy, was born in 1967.

When Jimmy was elected governor in 1970, she again had a new role and a new challenge: first lady of Georgia. She took a special interest in conditions for the mentally retarded and worked to improve the state's services for them. She visited hospitals and helped put together a list of recommendations to upgrade facilities for the handicapped.

She played a key role in the 1976 presidential campaign. Governor Carter was an unknown figure nationally, so she embarked on a solo trip, visiting more than thirty primary states, mustering support in countless speeches and interviews.

After his inauguration, Rosalynn plunged into her new task as first lady. At the top of her list of projects was mental health. Though she often complained that reporters in the White House didn't cover the topic because it "wasn't sexy enough," she persuaded her husband to appoint a national commission on mental health and served as its honorary chairman. She helped craft legislation designed to improve mental health programs at the local, state and national level, and on February 7, 1979, appeared before a

Senate Resources subcommittee to push for increased federal spending for mental health programs.

Congress passed the Mental Health Systems Act in September 1980, but her victory was short-lived. Within weeks, Ronald Reagan had won the election and the act was repealed. "The funding for our legislation was killed by the philosophy of a new president," she wrote in her memoirs. "It was a bitter loss." In an interview in October 1981, she told me she considered the action "incredible" and a "tragedy." [3]

She didn't stop with one project. She also took on the needs of the elderly, working to improve health services for older Americans in rural areas, helped in devising legislation to reform Social Security and contacted state legislators to drum up support for the Equal Rights Amendment.

At one point the *Washington Star* summarized her activities in her first 14 months in the White House: visited 18 nations and 27 American cities, held 259 private and 50 public meetings, made 15 major speeches, held 22 press conferences, gave 32 interviews, attended 83 official receptions, and held 25 meetings with special groups in the White House. [4]

When a reporter commented that Rosalynn was trying to take on "all the problems that we have," her press secretary Mary Hoyt responded, "So what's wrong with that?"

While she worked hard to develop what she termed a "caring society," she didn't neglect her duties as White House hostess. Like first ladies before her, she took an active role in planning state dinners, seeking to tailor them to the guests' interests. However, she later recounted in her memoirs that "real protocol" was "warmth and putting your guests at ease, an important part of traditional southern hospitality, not just rules."

One of the "rules" that fell by the wayside was allowing the young Amy to attend state dinners. I remember one in particular—in honor of a visit from the president of Mexico—that caused some public consternation. Amy sat down at a table filled with dignitaries, pulled out a book and began to read.

But the Carters were intent on making the White House a home for their young daughter and every now and then, Amy and her friends could be found roller-skating in the East Room. I heard later that the Carters were deeply hurt after his defeat by a remark from a *Time* magazine columnist, "Now at last we're going to have some class in the White House."

With double-digit inflation and the seizing of the Iranian hostages plaguing her husband's presidency, Rosalynn took the lead in 1980 on the campaign trail. She crisscrossed the country and maintained high hopes for her husband right up to the end, despite the gloomy predictions of the pollsters. When she arrived in Plains on election day and her husband's defeat was all but guaranteed, someone said to him, "Mr. President, you make a great example. You don't seem bitter at all."

Rosalynn interjected, "I'm bitter enough for both of us."[5]

On November 18, 1980, she met with a group of women journalists for an informal news conference at the White House to discuss her future plans.

She told us that after the election "I went into my room and cried a little bit but I came right out and that was it. I think you accept it. When you've done all you can possibly do, that's all you can do. It was out of our hands. You go from one phase of your life to the next phase of your life. I think it's going to be exciting."

Since her White House years, Rosalynn has certainly had an exciting few phases in her life. She became immersed in planning the Carter Library in Atlanta, writing her autobiography and helping her husband raise money for Habitat for Humanity, a nonprofit organization that builds low-cost housing for the poor.

In April 1984, I saw her again when she was on her book tour. I asked her, in looking back on her White House years, if she would have done anything differently. "I don't know," she told me. "Jimmy has taught me you do the best you can and you don't look back with regret. I have never looked back."

Nancy Reagan

In 1980, I was sitting on a campaign plane with Nancy Reagan and we began talking about the possibility that her husband was going to be the next president. I asked her what project she was thinking of pursuing and she said, "I'm going to take care of Ronnie."

I was a little shocked at that response and said, "If your husband is elected, you will have a platform given to very few people. You should think about what you want to do with it. You'll never be given this kind of opportunity again."

I also mentioned to her that being first lady carries enormous pressure and Nancy nodded and said, "I'm sure you're right, but there will always be a part of me that's private, that's mine."

"You may think so," I said, "but you have no idea what it's really like. I don't see how you *can* know till you get there."

It took her awhile but eventually, she did figure out what I was talking about.

The name "Nancy" is actually her nickname. She was born Ann Francis on July 6, 1921, in New York City, the daughter of Kenneth Robbins, a New Jersey automobile dealer, and Edith Luckett, a professional actress. Her parents separated when she was two and her mother pursued her acting career, placing the youngster with an aunt and uncle in Bethesda, Maryland. When Nancy was seven, her mother married Dr. Loyal Davis, a Chicago neurosurgeon, and Nancy went to live with them in an apartment on Lake Shore Drive.

She graduated from Smith College and decided to follow in her mother's footsteps and pursue an acting career. In 1949, she met Ronald Reagan. They became engaged in February 1952. Many times she has said that her life "really began with Ronnie."

Nancy Reagan may be remembered for her high style and her campaign to get the nation's youth to "Just Say No" to drugs. But to me, she has a special place in history for influencing her husband to take a softer line toward the Soviet Union and to seek a peaceful rapprochement with what he had branded the "Evil Empire."

Those moves no doubt led to a breakthrough in superpower relations. Her nudge outmaneuvered the conservative hard-liners in the Reagan administration and led to summit meetings on nuclear arms reduction between Reagan and Soviet leader Mikhail Gorbachev.

But of all the first ladies I've covered, this one got off to the worst start. She was first depicted as a frivolous clotheshorse who preferred to hang out with her wealthy California friends.

Her first meeting with the White House newswomen after the budget-busting inaugural gala did not get off to the most auspicious start. Much was made of her inaugural wardrobe—a red Adolfo dress, a black formal dress by Bill Blass and a white, beaded gown by James Galanos, all topped off by a full-length mink coat by Maximilian.

Things only got worse when she solicited donations from wealthy friends and spent $800,000 to redecorate the family quarters in the White House, prompting stories that donors were buying influence. Another eruption of hostile headlines broke out when she purchased a 220-piece set of gilt-edged china, again through private financing, for $209,508.

Shortly after Reagan was elected to his first term and just before they moved into the White House, Maureen Santini of AP and I were granted a joint interview. We asked for her views on gun control and she disclosed that her husband had given her a "tiny little gun" that she said she kept in a nightstand drawer for protection.

Not even the attempted assassination of her husband in March 1981 seemed to silence the criticism. She spent days and nights at the hospital and appeared before the cameras regularly to deliver updates on his recuperation. For months afterward, she could only refer to it as "that thing that happened." An admitted "worrier," she said she could not hear a siren after the incident without suddenly freezing. Still, the public held her sincerity suspect.

By December 1981, her image problem had reached the point where Republican strategists were beginning to consider it a liability. A *Newsweek* magazine story that month described how she seemed to be an "idle rich, queen-bee figure" obsessed with fashion and appearances. A poll in the same magazine showed 62 percent of Americans thought she put "too much emphasis on style and elegance" while an economic recession was going on.

Under the wise guidance of her outstanding press secretary, Sheila Tate, Mrs. Reagan's public image slowly began to undergo a transformation. She again took up the cause in which she had been active when her husband was governor of California, the Foster Grandparents Program. She also took up the problem of drug addiction among the nation's youth, visiting rehabilitation centers, attending antidrug conferences and making television appearances.

She narrated a PBS docudrama on addiction called "The Chemical People," delivered an antidrug message on the NBC sitcom "Diff'rent Strokes" and appeared on "Good Morning America" interviewing recovering addicts. By 1986, Reagan joined her antidrug campaign, appearing with her to launch the National Crusade for a Drug-Free America.

With the press corps, she took a different tack. One day in March 1982, I got a call from Tate, who sounded me out about the possibility of the first lady appearing in a skit at the annual Gridiron dinner. I quietly passed the word along and what happened later made no small number of headlines.

At the dinner, she was seated a few seats away from her husband. Gridiron member Maureen Ribble had just finished a number as Nancy to the tune of "Second-Hand Rose."

> *Secondhand clothes*
> *I give my secondhand clothes*
> *To museum collections and traveling shows*
> *They were oh, so happy when they got 'em*
> *Won't notice they were ragged on the bottom.*
> *Secondhand dress*
> *Good-bye you worn-out old mess,*
> *I never wear a frock just more than once*
> *Calvin Klein, Adolfo, Ralph Lauren and Bill Blass*
> *Ronald Reagan's mama's going strictly first-class*
> *Rodeo Drive, I sure miss Rodeo Drive*
> *In frumpy Washington.*

After the number Nancy got up from her chair and slipped out. A few guests began murmuring that she had been offended by the lyrics. What really happened was that Nancy had ducked out to change into her costume for her own number.

The curtains opened and there she was, decked out in an aqua cotton skirt with red and yellow flowers, a navy polka-dot blouse and short-sleeved red sweater, white pantaloons decorated with blue butterflies, a big feathered hat, white feather boa, yellow rubber boots and big red earrings.

She began to sing her own lyrics to the same song:

> *Secondhand clothes*
> *I'm wearing secondhand clothes*
> *They're all the thing in*
> *The spring fashion shows*
> *Even my new trench coat with fur collar*
> *Ronnie bought for 10 cents on the dollar*
>
> *Even though they tell me that I'm no longer queen*
> *Did Ronnie have to buy me that new sewing machine?*
> *Secondhand clothes, secondhand clothes*
> *I sure hope Ed Meese sews . . .*

The audience, including her husband, was astonished at her self-deprecating, self-mocking performance; gave her a standing ovation and yelled for an encore. She was only too happy to comply and when she finished, she picked up a china plate and threw it on the floor. It was supposed to break but it didn't. No matter.

In his remarks later, Reagan told the crowd, "I was surprised when I learned I was coming here as a happy husband and leaving as a stage door Johnny."

White House political advisers have often said the Gridiron show marked the turning point in public perception of the first lady.

By 1985, her polls showed her popularity at a high point, even higher than her husband's.

There's no question that she took a more active role in her husband's administration after he was elected to a second term. Her sole concern, she said repeatedly, was her husband's welfare. And his second term was rife with crises: his colon cancer operation in July 1985, the Iran-Contra scandal that began heating up in November 1986, his prostate surgery in January 1987. She herself developed breast cancer and underwent a mastectomy on

October 17 of that year, and ten days after her surgery, her mother passed away. She was extremely courageous.

Her deep concern for her husband resulted in a bitter confrontation with White House chief of staff Donald Regan that kept Washington buzzing for months. Staffers knew her wrath when they overbooked her husband's appearances. However, many first ladies had been protective in the same way, causing presidential aides to run for cover. And like the able Tate, her second-term press secretary, Elaine Crispen, always did her best to cooperate with us and give us as fair a reading as she could of what was going on.

From the beginning, when Regan assumed the job after James Baker, there was friction. After Reagan returned to the White House following his prostate surgery, Nancy wanted to ensure he had enough rest and recovery time before plunging into a full presidential schedule. Regan, on the other hand, tried to get his boss to assume as full a schedule as possible to show the public he was in good shape and calm in the face of the Iran-Contra scandal. He reportedly hung up on Nancy a few times and the last time he did was the last straw.

She reportedly began pushing for his ouster at the end of 1986 to the point where the *Washington Post* reported that Reagan finally yelled, "Get off my goddamn back!"

She denied that account to me in an interview on December 17, saying, "You know, the thing that is annoying about that is they called to get a confirmation of that. And we denied it and then they went ahead and printed it. So you have to say to yourself, 'Then why bother to call?'"

She went on to say that "they happened to pick the one word that Ronnie never uses, ever. He'll say 'damn,' but he will never put those two words together, ever. He feels very strongly about it. He feels that you are damning God, and I've heard him stop people and say 'Please don't use that.'"

When I broached the subject of the Iran-Contra scandal, she got a little teary-eyed and said her husband had "tried everything" to get Lt. Colonel Oliver North and National Security Adviser John Poindexter "to tell the truth" about the clandestine operation.

"He's disappointed in not having been told the truth," she said, "and that's upsetting to him. He wishes the two men would come forward and talk. Those are the only two men who know anything, really know what happened."

In the same interview, I broached the question of her influence and she explained, "I think if you're married, particularly if you've been married a long time, you care what happens to your husband."

Regan later wrote the book *Behind the Scenes,* revealing that Nancy for years had consulted Joan Quigley, a San Francisco–based astrologer, concerning the president's travel schedule and other matters.

But after the Iran-Contra affair broke, that was the least of her troubles. With widespread talk of impeachment, her main goal was to save her husband. Reagan made few appearances in 1987 when his political fate was at stake and Nancy stepped into the breach. I was amazed that she stepped out in front and took questions.

But again she let the self-deprecating humor come through when the dust settled. In a speech she gave to the American Newspaper Publishers Association in May 1987, she obviously felt comfortable enough with her behavior to discuss it in public. She told the audience she almost had to cancel her appearance. "You know how busy I am," she quipped. "I'm staffing the White House and I'm overseeing the arms talks. I'm writing speeches."

She also defended her role as her husband's protector. "Although I don't get involved in policy," she said, "it's silly to suggest that my opinion should not carry some weight with a man I've been married to for thirty-five years. I'm a woman who loves her husband and I make no apologies for looking out for his personal and political welfare. We have a genuine sharing marriage. I go to his aid, he comes to mine. . . . I have opinions, he has opinions. We don't always agree. But neither marriage nor politics denies a spouse the right to hold an opinion or the right to express it."[1]

Her guardianship was evident as her husband became more hard of hearing and she would prompt him or answer the question herself. Once, on an outing, Reagan was asked what the administration was doing about the environment. She whispered, "Doing all we can," and he repeated her words—except that a microphone had picked up her whisper and it became a crescendo when it was replayed on TV.

In the interest of disclosure, however, I must say that Nancy's protective nature even extended to me once. We were in Moscow for a summit between Reagan and Gorbachev and the Reagans, on the advice of their son Ron, decided to visit the Arbat, a pedestrian mall in the city made up of several blocks of shops and street vendors, where merchants sell everything from fur hats to wooden dolls. The Arbat is about two blocks from the American embassy residence, Spaso House.

The Secret Service was opposed to the Reagans being in such an open area but they were adamant. It was a Sunday afternoon, they had some free time and they wanted to see the Arbat, so they climbed into their car for the two-block ride to the area.

Once the crowd of Sunday strollers realized who was there, they applauded and cheered and rushed up to the Reagans. Reagan shook hands as they walked along but soon enough, the crush of the crowd prompted some overreaction by Soviet security. It had taken only a few minutes for the crowd to form and the Secret Service started moving toward the president and first lady—but the crowd moved along with them.

Things were getting fairly confusing and the press pool began running after the president with KGB agents elbowing people out of the way and knocking some of us to the ground. About a hundred yards from Spaso House, two KGB agents grabbed me and started dragging me down the street. I started screaming and Nancy stepped back three or four steps, grabbed my coat and began yelling, "She's with us!" The agents let me go and Nancy and I walked to where Reagan was standing and we all walked toward the residence. "You owe me one, Helen," she said.

Marlin Fitzwater later joked that the White House had lost another chance to get rid of me.

But it's not like that hadn't happened to me before in Moscow. I'd learned my lesson that lung power was a good way to get rescued. I was following President Nixon and Soviet leader Leonid Brezhnev as they walked down the street, trying to eavesdrop on their conversation, when several KGB agents closed in on me and started pushing me around. I started yelling and quickly got the attention of the Secret Service who came to my aid.

Despite the ongoing relationship between Reagan and Gorbachev, there was one person I think Nancy could have done without—Raisa Gorbachev. Politely put, I'd describe their relationship as "difficult." You could have stored meat in the room when those two were together. Raisa always seemed intent on trying to upstage Nancy and Nancy always appeared at the end of her diplomatic rope. She was less than pleased with Raisa's behavior in 1987, when the Gorbachevs visited Washington, and after Raisa reportedly lectured Reagan on the Soviet system, Nancy reportedly snapped, "Who does that dame think she is?"

On the trip to Russia in 1988, Nancy had asked to see the icons at the Tretyakov Gallery and they were supposed to tour the place together. Raisa showed up early and informed the media gathered to cover their tour, "Our guests are late so I'll tell you about the gallery." She moved the press upstairs and proceeded to hold a news conference.

Nancy, who had arrived at the gallery at the scheduled time, was told plans had changed. She went upstairs and when Raisa spotted her, she turned away from the press and started escorting Nancy out of the gallery. Bill Greenwood of ABC said to Nancy, "Mrs. Reagan, Mrs. Gorbachev has been talking with us and we all think you should have equal time. She said there was no religious significance to the icons."

"I don't know how you can neglect the religious implications," Nancy replied. "I mean, they're there for everyone to see."

By the end of Reagan's term, they appeared to mellow a bit, and in the summer of 1989, after Nancy left the White House, she received a note from Raisa. "I keep in my heart the warmth of our previous contacts and meetings," she wrote. Also enclosed was a Soviet book on drug abuse, an ironic touch since when Nancy had hosted a White House meeting for first ladies of other nations on the topic, Raisa had made clear there was no drug problem in the Soviet Union.

All through the years I covered the Reagans in the White House, one situation always remained a mystery to me: their family, which many considered dysfunctional. Their daughter, Patti Davis, wrote an unflattering roman à clef novel with characters who resembled her parents. But after the Reagans moved back to California, she reconciled with her mother.

Their son, Ron, was close to his mother when she lived in the White House but was rarely on the scene. Later on he became estranged from his parents. As first lady, Nancy frankly acknowledged a rift with Reagan's son, Michael, who was adopted when Reagan was married to Jane Wyman. But Maureen, Reagan's daughter from his first marriage, became very close to Nancy during the White House years.

The Reagans moved out of the White House on January 20, 1989, turning over its stewardship to George and Barbara Bush.

I stayed in touch with Nancy through the years and was deeply saddened, along with the rest of the nation, when Reagan released his letter disclosing that he was suffering from Alzheimer's disease.

I saw her several years later when I was invited to deliver an address on first ladies at the Reagan presidential library. It was a wonderful day for me, filled with nostalgia, and after my speech, Nancy gave a luncheon for me and those of my close friends who had accompanied me, Abigail Van Buren, her daughter Jeanne and my longtime pal Margaret Kilgore, who had worked with me at UPI and later went to the *Los Angeles Times*.

Before the lunch, Nancy and I strolled around reminiscing, and she took me out on the balcony and pointed to a barren stretch of land below.

"That's where Ronnie and I will be buried," she said sadly.

I recalled one of our last interviews before Reagan left office and asked her what was the toughest part of living in the White House.

"Being under a microscope," she said. "Nobody is prepared for being under the kind of magnifying glass that you're under. I don't care how long you've been in public life. You just learn to handle it."

Then I asked her what had been the best part about being first lady. "Being able to use that platform and doing something you care about and are concerned about and hopefully can do something about, and I think I have," she replied.

Barbara Bush

When George Bush made a run for the White House in 1980, eventually ending up as Ronald Reagan's running mate, one of Barbara Bush's sisters-in-law told her that the family had been asking, "What are we going to do about Bar?"

As she recounted years later, "That really hurt. They discussed how to make me look snappier—color my hair, change my style of dressing, and, I suspect, get me to lose some weight. I know it was meant to be helpful but I wept quietly alone until George told me that I was absolutely crazy."[1]

It's hard to imagine Barbara Bush having doubts about anything. By the time her husband was inaugurated, she was showing off her stylish new wardrobe to groups of Republican women, and when the compliments flowed about her appearance, she said simply, "What you see is what you get." I think that line was the touchstone of her tenure as first lady, and she is bound to go down as one of the most popular ones we've ever had. And while she may have insisted that "nobody noticed what I wore," let me say that in the twelve years she spent as the second and then first lady, we *all* noticed.

Her nonthreatening, "just a housewife" demeanor put her in high regard with Americans who had just finished eight years with the high-flying Nancy Reagan. Barbara went with the image of serene, loyal wife who was content to run the East Wing and be "everybody's grandmother" who walked her dog in her housecoat at 5:00 A.M. on the White House grounds. It's no coincidence that the Secret Service gave her the code name "Tranquility," and it's no surprise she won the hearts of Americans. With her three strands of faux pearls and the $29 pair of shoes she purchased to go with her inauguration gown, she seemed down to earth, accessible and easily likable.

But benign and passive she was not. She had a keen wit and a disarming, direct way about her. Feisty, breezy and fun are the words that come to mind when I think of her. But there was a core of strength and purpose beneath all that—as a friend of mine once described her, an iron fist in a velvet glove. She knew who she was and she has always been true to herself, her husband and her family.

She was born Barbara Pierce on June 8, 1925, in New York City and grew up in Rye, New York, in a family that listed one president in its genealogy. She was the third child among Martha, Jim and Scotty. Her father, Marvin, became president of McCall Corp., which published *Redbook* magazine, among others, and her mother, Pauline, was the typical suburban matron of those times.

When she was sixteen, she met George Bush at a Christmas dance in

Greenwich, Connecticut. He was a senior at Phillips Academy Andover and he asked her out on a date for the next night. They began corresponding after he returned to school and he invited her to his senior prom that spring.

After the dance he walked her home and ended their night with a kiss on her cheek. "I married the first man I ever kissed," she often said years later. "When I tell this to my children they just about throw up."

They were married on January 6, 1945, during his service as a Navy pilot in World War II, and as a military wife, she moved around the country with him for eight months. After he left the service, they settled in New Haven, Connecticut, while he attended Yale. In 1948, after he graduated, they relocated to Texas where he joined Dresser Industries. They moved again to California, where his work took him, and then back to Texas in 1950, where he and a partner started their own oil company. All told, she has said, they have moved about twenty-eight times in the course of their marriage.

They had six children but lost their four-year-old daughter Robin, who was stricken with leukemia and died in 1953. Barbara described the experience as "trying to be strong" for her family and her daughter in the months she was hospitalized, but when the youngster died, "I fell apart." Her husband, she said, would not let her retreat into her own grief. "I wanted to get back to real life, but there is a dance you have to go through just to get there," she wrote. "When I wanted to cut out, George made me talk to him and he shared with me. What a difference that makes. He made me remember that the loss was not just mine."[2]

With Bush's first successful bid for a seat in the House of Representatives in 1966, her life as a political wife began, and she and the children followed as his career accomplishments piled up: U.S. ambassador to the United Nations, chairman of the Republican National Committee, chief of the U.S. Liaison Office in Beijing, director of the CIA, vice president and president.

The typical press deconstruction and the raising of her profile began when she and her husband stumped the country when he ran for vice president. Most reports focused on her openness and friendliness. A little hint of the iron fist, however, surfaced in the 1984 Reagan reelection campaign. Fritz Mondale, the Democratic presidential candidate, had been making comments about the surfeit of finances in the Bush family, and Barbara was getting a little annoyed with those news reports. One day it was reported that Geraldine Ferraro, Mondale's running mate, and her husband, John Zaccaro, were worth at least $4 million.

Sitting in the press section of the campaign plane with Terry Hunt of AP and Ira Allen of UPI, Barbara was asked for her reaction and she said, in what she thought was an off-the-record remark, "That rich . . . well it rhymes with rich . . . could buy George Bush any day." After the consequent media hoopla about her statement, she called Ferraro and apologized for referring to her as a "witch."

"I do not blame the press for reporting it because I should have known better," she wrote years later. "But they should know I never again felt free to be relaxed with them."[3] I think that incident set the tone for her approach to the White House press corps after she became first lady.

In her White House days, there was a feeling among many that she exhibited a touch of distance when dealing with her staff, and where the press corps was concerned, I got the impression she thought we were an unruly bunch. But surprisingly, she gave us wonderful, candid interviews. She also put up with us in good humor most of the time and maintained that, as first lady, she "had the best job in America."

She approached her role in a way that seemed a throwback to earlier times. She was not interested in discussing policy, sharing power or making her influence felt. Being "just a spouse" was fine with her. Once, my UPI colleague Lori Santos was invited to a movie screening in the White House theater and she brought her husband, Craig Schwed, an editor for Gannett News Service. Upon meeting the first lady, Craig told her, "I'm just a spouse." She put her arm around him and said, "My favorite kind."

But when she was asked to deliver the commencement address at Wellesley College in 1990, the "just a spouse" image almost backfired when a group of graduating seniors signed a petition protesting her appearance, noting that Barbara "has gained recognition through the achievements of her husband" while they had spent four years at a school that "teaches us that we will be rewarded on the basis of our own merit, not on that of a spouse."

She managed to turn that around and her speech was an unqualified hit as she stressed the importance of making choices and noting the challenges that faced women and men.

Accompanied by Raisa Gorbachev, whose husband was in Washington on a state visit, she faced the doubting audience and told them to "believe in something larger than yourself" and "to get involved with the big ideas of your time." Early in her life, she told them, she had made a choice and she hoped they would do the same. Her last line, I think, was another exhibition of how this first lady was made of tougher stuff than anyone had surmised. "Who knows?" she said. "Somewhere out in this audience may even be someone who will one day follow in my footsteps, and preside over the White House as the president's spouse. I wish him well!"

In an interview with several wire service reporters a few months after that speech, she told us, "Nobody booed us there. Everybody was very nice. They didn't mean they didn't like me, Barbara Bush. What they meant was they wanted someone who lived and worked in the world and coped with life's problems that girls have—women have today. That's all they meant. And I understood that. The only thing I did feel they should remember was I didn't ask Wellesley to have me; they asked me. So it all worked out fine."

Her project as first lady—literacy—was something she had hit on in 1978, long before she arrived in the White House, but now it became a mission she could trumpet from a national platform. "I realized everything I worried about would be better if more people could read, write and comprehend," she said. And she'd had a family experience tangentially connected to her cause. Her son Neil had been diagnosed with dyslexia as a youngster but had overcome the disability with the help of his mother, through a program of reading and special instruction. She worked with a number of literacy foundations before the Barbara Bush Foundation for Family Literacy was launched in 1989. One of its greatest underwriters was an English springer spaniel named Millie, her dog, and, according to her husband, probably the only creature his wife has ever indulged. Under the auspices of her owner, Millie decided to "write" a book "as told to Barbara Bush."

Actually, it was the second time Barbara had assisted a family pet in a writing project. She had been considering ways to raise money for literacy causes, and in 1984, the family cocker spaniel C. Fred wrote a book with her help. *C. Fred's Story* raised about $100,000 for two programs, Literacy Volunteers of America and Laubach Literacy Action. C. Fred died in 1987 and replacing him was Millie, who was unfairly described as an "ugly dog" but was without a doubt a breed apart as a best-selling author. *Millie's Book* sold an estimated 500,000 copies, hit a number of best-seller lists and earned close to $1 million for the literacy foundation. At one point, the book was number one on the *New York Times* best-seller list and it outsold President Reagan's memoirs.

Between her hectic schedule as first lady, her foundation work, her appearances and her travels with her husband, she lost a lot of weight and the press took notice. She attributed the loss to eating smaller portions and staying active, along with her exercise routine of swimming every day and playing tennis whenever possible. In fact, she was suffering with Grave's disease, or as she put it, her thyroid "just went wacko." Her eyes became swollen and irritated, her vision blurred and she finally sought medical treatment that consisted of doses of radioactive iodine to slow down the hyperactive gland. Several months later, she underwent a ten-day course of radiation therapy. Oddly enough, her husband developed the same disease later on and also underwent treatment.

While she was receiving treatment she decided to play an April Fool's Day joke on the press corps at the annual Gridiron dinner. She showed up impeccably dressed, as usual, but on top of her head was a strawberry blond wig. "So much had been made of my white hair, I thought this was the perfect joke," she said. [4]

Her joke caused more concern than laughter, though, as dinner guests wondered if she were more ill than she had been letting on and wore the wig to cover some hair loss.

While she minded her political P's and Q's as first lady and said repeatedly that she stayed out of her husband's business, early in his term, when AP's Terry Hunt asked her if she favored a law that would prohibit the sale of military assault weapons to the public, she answered "yes." After the tragic shooting of five schoolchildren in Stockton, California, she said she never dreamed her response would make such big news:

> The press interpreted this to mean I disagreed with my husband! It seemed so clear to me that there was absolutely no need for anyone to have an assault weapon and frankly, I assumed it was already against the law. . . . However, in March, George did expand the ban against importing assault weapons, including the AK-47, which had been used in California to kill five schoolchildren. [5]

Yet the day after she had responded to that question, she issued a retraction.

We also tried to elicit her views on abortion, but she told me repeatedly, "I think what George thinks." It wasn't until her husband was out of office that she wrote that the decision was up to "the mother, the father and the doctor." [6]

In September 1990, as the crisis with Iraq was heating up, I asked how she was coping with the interruptions, the late-night phone calls and the distinct air of apprehension that engulfed her home. "That goes with the job, I guess," she said. "We're not complaining about that."

When the war broke out in early 1991 she fulfilled her supporting but significant role by traveling to military bases to visit the families of soldiers stationed overseas. When she was asked whether she felt the war would hurt her husband politically, she responded that she couldn't care less because she knew he was "doing the right thing."

In one of my last interviews with her before the election, I got the impression she was kind of ambivalent about her husband seeking another term. "We love being here," she said. "It's been wonderful," but when I pressed she finally conceded she "could go either way."

With rare exception, she kept her feelings and her opinions to herself about the hot-button issues that arose during George Bush's presidency, and in the 1992 election cycle, she campaigned as diligently as any first spouse;

her support of him never wavered. I don't think anyone outside her circle knew the depths of her bitterness toward the press until long after her husband's defeat:

> Why did we lose? George Bush says it was because he didn't communicate as well as his predecessor or successor. I just don't believe that....
>
> And the press. I honestly believe that most of them wanted Bill Clinton to win....
>
> Yes, many reporters do a fair job of covering the campaign—in fact, too many to mention. But I will be honest in telling you that the overall experience has left a bad taste in my mouth about the media, and makes me question what I read. I hate that. I respect and like many members of the press. I just wish I could respect more of what they do.[7]

I always suspected the velvet glove would come off sooner or later. And in her post–White House years she seems more at ease and more ready to let her opinions fly when asked. I saw her most recently in the summer of 1998 when she attended the "roast" for Marlin Fitzwater, and when I walked over to say hello, she was warm, cordial and friendly.

These days, it looks as if she may be gearing up for another campaign cycle, with two sons in high-profile political careers and one being mentioned as presidential timber. Whatever she decides, I'm sure she will be true to herself and we all may enjoy hearing "what you see is what you get" all over again.

Hillary Clinton

> There is no formula that I'm aware of for being a successful or fulfilled woman today. Perhaps it would be easier ... if we could be handed a pattern and cut it out, just as our mothers and grandmothers and foremothers were. But that is not the way it is today, and I'm glad it is not.
>
> —Hillary Rodham Clinton

On April 25, 1998, at the White House Correspondents dinner and for the second time in my career, a first lady was complicit in a successful attempt to "scoop" me on a story.

The first time was when Pat Nixon stood before a microphone in the East Room and announced my engagement to Doug. The second time it was Hillary Rodham Clinton on videotape.

The dinner had been proceeding with all the requisite brouhaha that one of those Hollywood-on-the-Potomac events tends to generate, especially since everyone seemed more intent on the moves of one guest—Paula Jones—than anything else going on that night.

After the dinner I was sitting there enjoying myself, watching all the awards handed out for news coverage. Then the association's president, Larry McQuillan of Reuters, said there was one more award to be given, but first, he directed everyone's attention to the giant TV screens at the front of the room on either side of the dais. The room darkened and I heard Ed Bradley's voice, "She began her career with . . ."

Oh, no. As I was contemplating crawling under the table, the audience watched highlights of Ed's 1987 interview with me for "60 Minutes." Somehow, all of my colleagues had managed to keep a key bit of news from me: The association had instituted a new Helen Thomas Lifetime Achievement award for White House reporting and guess who was going to be the first recipient?

The highlights from Ed's interview ended and the first lady appeared on the screen. Her remarks were as follows:

> Now, Helen, I know that your colleagues are hoping that this tribute comes as a surprise. But I think we all know by now how impossible it is to keep a secret from you.
>
> Generations of Americans owe you a debt of gratitude for the relentless and honest way you have brought us the news of the day.
>
> Helen, this may be the one and only time your colleagues get the last word. So we're using this rare opportunity to say one important thing:
>
> Thank you. Thank you for the work you do every day, for your humor and commitment and for the example you set for the rest of us.
>
> Congratulations, Helen.

What kind words. And to think it only took me nearly six years to get her to sit down for an interview.

Who is Hillary Rodham Clinton? She is unlike any first lady who ever arrived at 1600 Pennsylvania Avenue, and she has paid a high price for being who and what she is. But I think she has set a new example for those who will succeed her. Just as the country had to eventually accept women professionals, working mothers and women activists in other quarters of the country, so will we eventually have to accept a woman who may choose to be all these things—and be a first lady as well.

Just as the rest of the Clinton administration, in its early days, was intent on doing end runs around the White House press corps to get its message out, Hillary seemed to go along with that game plan. The wall went up early. She would talk to the media but her press lunch guests were largely women columnists from outside Washington. I started lobbying early on for an interview, only to be told by her then–press secretary Lisa Caputo that I could interview her if I traveled with her.

I hit the ceiling. "I'm here every day," I said, "why do I have to travel with her?" Lisa repeated the ground rules: no travel, no interview.

Another time in my lobbying efforts, one of her aides told me, "She is afraid of what Washington reporters will ask."

If you look at the litany, maybe she's got a point. She made it clear she was not going to be a traditional first lady, but no presidential wife in modern history, except perhaps Eleanor Roosevelt, has weathered such a steady barrage of opposition, criticism and just plain "Hillary hating."

The anti-Hillary swell reached one apogee when *New York Times* columnist William Safire—a former speechwriter in the Nixon White House— referred to her as a "congenital liar" in a January 9, 1996, column and White House press secretary Mike McCurry said if President Clinton weren't the president, "He would have delivered a more forceful response to the bridge of his [Safire's] nose."

Later in the day, Clinton himself commented, "You know, when you're president, there are a few more constraints on you than if you're an ordinary citizen. If I were an ordinary citizen, I might give the article the response that it deserves. Presidents have feelings too."

Granted, I've been known to take a few shots at presidents, but in my long years at the White House, I never saw anything like this. As trial upon travail has hit the Clinton White House with tidal regularity, there were times I could only marvel—from a distance, of course—at Hillary's inner strength: the Gennifer Flowers debacle of the 1992 campaign, the White House travel office flap, the still-ongoing Whitewater investigation, the suicide of deputy counsel Vincent Foster, the "lost" billing records, her torpedoed national health care plan, the Republican takeover of Congress in 1994, the behavioral gurus, the conversations with Eleanor Roosevelt, the appearance before a federal grand jury, the hours-long depositions, the Dick Morris "situation," the campaign finance allegations, the Paula Jones/Monica Lewinsky/Kathleen Willey questions of sexual misconduct concerning her husband. Not to mention the commodities market windfall. On a lesser note, there used to be a Web site devoted to the many hairstyles she adopted over the years.

I think Mike McCurry put it well when he told reporters one day that some people thought Hillary was "responsible for the weather outside."

When we finally sat down in the Map Room for our interview in 1998, I heard a familiar refrain, one I'd heard from a number of first ladies.

"Nothing can prepare you for living in the White House, at least that has been my experience," she said. "And I've been reading about other people. Presidents and their families that have been here . . . but you bring with you your whole lifetime of experience and values. And then you encounter the pressure, which is inevitable living here, you have to fall back on the most basic values that you were raised with."

With all the tumult during her tenure as first lady, I think her "most basic values" have served her well, yet I can't help but think what a long, strange trip it's been for her.

Born on October 26, 1947, she was the first child and only daughter of Hugh and Dorothy Rodman. When she was three and shortly after the birth of her brother Hugh, the family moved to Park Ridge, Illinois. Brother Tony arrived seven years later. Her father ran a textiles business while her mother stayed at home, but both parents knew the value of a college education. She entered Wellesley College in 1965, where her budding activism found a home, at first as a Republican. She and her colleagues in the campus Republican club worked for various candidates. But by 1968 her views had begun to turn and she campaigned for Eugene McCarthy in the primaries. That summer, however, she worked as an intern for the House Republican Conference chaired by Melvin Laird, then a congressman from Wisconsin who eventually became President Nixon's secretary of defense. When a group of students asked Wellesley president Ruth Adams that someone from their graduating class be allowed to speak at commencement, she nixed the idea at first. Hillary met with her and asked what the prime objection was to having a student speak, only to be told "It's never been done."

"Well, we could give it a try," she told Adams.

Hillary ended up delivering the "student address" at commencement and her remarks consisted of rebutting the speech of Republican senator Edward Brooke of Massachusetts, whose campaign she'd worked on in 1965. While Brooke told the graduates that "resort to political action is anathema," Hillary responded, "Every protest, every dissent . . . is unabashedly an attempt to forge an identity in this particular age. . . ."

She was one of thirty women who entered Yale Law School in 1969 and in 1970 attended the League of Women Voters national convention in Washington. The keynote speaker was Marian Wright Edelman, then a noted civil rights lawyer and advocate for disadvantaged children, and for whom Hillary would work in 1991 when Edelman founded the Children's Defense Fund.

When Edelman spoke months later at Yale, Hillary approached her and asked to work for her that summer. Edelman said she was welcome to come to work but there was no money to pay her. So Hillary found a grant from the Law Student Civil Rights Research Council that supported students working in civil rights.

"Meeting someone like Marian, who had a passion about helping children and had a lot of the same values I had, was a turning point in my life," she said.[1]

She spent her time monitoring Senator Walter Mondale's subcommittee, which was studying migratory labor. She said she returned to law school "with a growing commitment toward children, and particularly, poor children and disadvantaged ones."[2] Her relationship with Edelman changed, however, when President Clinton signed the welfare reform act, which Edelman had strongly opposed. Edelman's husband, Peter, left his post at the Department of Health and Human Services. I did notice that on the day of the signing ceremony, Hillary was present but stayed very quiet.

Another interest she developed at law school that year was in a fellow student: Bill Clinton. That oft-told story of their meeting in the library has taken on a life of its own. As she described it to me, "We started talking twenty-five years ago and we've never stopped talking. So he talks to me a lot about what is on his mind. I think that would be true with any marriage, but I am lucky because he and I have always been interested in the same things. We have always shared our ideas. We love to argue when an argument is called for about what we believe, [or] what we don't believe. So this is just something we have carried on in the White House and I imagine that in another fifty years we will still be having conversations. . . ."

They worked in Texas for George McGovern, and in January 1974, Hillary was chosen as one of three women to work for the House Judiciary Committee in its investigation of Richard Nixon. After Nixon resigned and her job ended, she got an offer to teach at the University of Arkansas Law School, where Bill Clinton was already on the faculty and launching his first political campaign, challenging John Paul Hammerschmidt for the House of Representatives seat in Arkansas's Third District.

Everyone thought Hillary was bound for the fast lane and a high-powered if not high-profile position with a legal firm in New York or Washington. When she accepted the job, she recalled, "My friends and family thought I had lost my mind. I was a little bit concerned about that as well."[3]

Bill Clinton captured 48.2 percent of the vote and Hillary went home for a while to wrestle with her life plan, but she did return to Fayetteville. When Bill picked her up at the airport he asked if she remembered a house in the area she said she liked. While she had been away, he bought it. They were married on October 11, 1975, about two weeks before her twenty-eighth birthday.

In early 1977, less than a month after her husband was sworn in as

Arkansas state attorney general, she went to work as an associate for the Rose Law Firm. She was promoted to partner in 1979 after having become, in 1978, the first lady of Arkansas. Daughter Chelsea was born on February 27, 1980. The Clintons moved out of the governor's mansion after his defeat in 1980 and back in after his reelection in 1983. In 1991, they gathered a few friends around a table in the governor's mansion and discussed the idea of Bill making a run for the presidency.

Hillary entered the national political limelight when her husband ran for president in 1992 and she said that the American people would be getting "two for one" if Clinton was elected—an impolitic statement leading to speculation, particularly by her detractors, that she would try to be a copresident.

When she made the remark about not "staying home and baking cookies," the public interpreted it as a slap against Barbara Bush.

When Gennifer Flowers went public about her alleged affair with the candidate, the soon-to-be first couple appeared on "60 Minutes" and Hillary managed to alienate another constituency when she said, "You know, I'm not sitting here as some little woman standing by my man, like Tammy Wynette. I'm sitting here because I love him and I respect him and I honor what he's been through and what we've been through together. And, you know, if that's not enough for people, then, heck, don't vote for him."

Some groups of women considered that remark another slap at their choice to stay at home and Hillary ended up apologizing to Wynette as well. But in later years, as we all saw, for whatever reason, she did "stand by her man."

And voters stood behind Bill Clinton in 1992. Before they moved into the White House, Hillary went to New York to visit the quintessential paragon of privacy, Jacqueline Kennedy Onassis, to seek her advice on how to keep daughter Chelsea out of the limelight and enable her to have as normal a childhood as possible even though they would be living the most public of lives.

"I felt like she was someone who sort of saw the world in the way I did, was concerned about protecting her children and gave me good advice about how to create protection for my daughter," she told me. "And she didn't give me any specific advice about, oh, you should go do this or go do that, she just said that, you know, at the end of every day, at the end of every week, you have no idea how long you'll be here, try to feel that you've done something you've loved, that you think is important, that you care about. Nobody can say what that is for another person, but the general advice was very helpful to me."

The press corps did honor her request to give Chelsea a wide berth, but some news now and then just couldn't help but spill out, and one incident seemed to illustrate just how much the first lady wanted to accomplish. When she was attending the Quaker-founded Sidwell Friends School, Chelsea developed a rash on her wrist one day and told amused school officials, "Call my father. My mother is too busy."

But sometimes the Chelsea privacy issue has gone a little over the top. When the Clintons visited China in the summer of 1998, I called the first lady's office with what I thought was a pretty noncontroversial question: Would Chelsea be sticking with her parents through the trip or did she plan on going to a few places by herself?

There was a gasp at the other end of the line. "Do you want me to lose my job?" was the nervous reply.

In Clinton's first administration, one aide said that Hillary seemed "targeted since the day she arrived here." I do think that by establishing her office near the Oval Office in the West Wing, she mixed the signals. Former chief of staff Leon Panetta admitted that he consulted with her at least once a week.

I do know she can be witty and charming, and there are times she can be downright funny. But no one could blame her for keeping her guard up.

She took a lot of knocks when her husband put her in charge of developing a universal health care plan. Her panel accumulated voluminous data on the needs and deprivations of millions of Americans, but when she insisted on total secrecy until the plan was ready, she bought a lot of opposition. One day I asked her aides if I could cover a White House session she had planned with Hispanic health care providers. They denied my request, telling me that there was "no room" available for reporters. The session was held in the spacious State Dining Room, which can accommodate a few hundred people. I later found out that only twenty health care providers attended the meeting.

With the luxury of hindsight in our interview, she noted that if she had to do it all over again, things would have been different. "I would try to learn more about what the press expected of me, because I really didn't understand that at all," she said. "And I would try to just be more sensitive to how anything I did might be interpreted or perceived. I just never thought about how somebody standing on the sidelines might interpret what I was doing differently than how I intended to do it.

"And so my lack of experience in that arena of public opinion and press coverage is something that I had to learn the hard way. So if I could have [had] either more experience or asked for help or gotten better advice from people around, I think that would have eased my transition."

But at the time, she gave the impression that she neither needed nor cared for any kind of advice. So while her staff was busy putting together the thirteen-hundred-page blueprint, the insurance lobby was busy trying to demolish it—before it ever got released with its now-legendary "Harry and Louise" commercials.

She retaliated on that score in March 1994 when she and her husband—with a little help—put together a video for the annual Gridiron dinner spoofing those commercials. The Clintons, portraying "Harry and Louise," had Hillary thumbing through a thick manual—the health care bill.

> "This thing scares the heck out of me," she said. "It says here on page 3,764 that Americans could get sick."
> "That's terrible," her husband responded. "You mean people will get sick under the Clinton health plan?"
> "And look, it gets worse," said the first lady. "On page 27,655 it says that eventually we are all going to die."
> "Wow!" said the president. "That is scary. You mean after Bill and Hillary put all those new bureaucrats and taxes on us, we are still going to die?"
> "Uh-huh," said Hillary. "Even Leon Panetta."

The video closed with the first couple looking into the camera and saying in unison, "There's got to be a better way," and a voice-over stating that the video was paid for by the "Coalition to Scare Your Pants Off."

I think if that video had run nationally as a counterweight to the real commercials her health plan might have gone farther. The plan eventually ended up being pronounced dead on arrival on Capitol Hill. But her efforts were not all in vain. She managed to highlight some of the most glaring shortcomings in national health care, including the denial of insurance to people with preexisting conditions and loss of insurance by people who either lost or changed their jobs. Into that breach stepped Democratic senator Edward M. Kennedy of Massachusetts and Republican senator Nancy Kassebaum of Kansas, who devised the Kennedy-Kassebaum bill covering those two failings, and it was enacted into law.

After the health care debacle, she was held responsible for the backlash created by "angry white males" who went to the polls in November 1994 and gave Republicans control of both houses of Congress for the first time in forty years.

By this time the phrase *lame duck* was being thrown at her husband and the Clintons went into a tizzy of soul searching. The president began consulting secretly with motivational gurus and Hillary held sessions with behavioral psychologists, who urged her to talk her troubles out with Eleanor Roosevelt, leading to a rash of jokes on the late-night talk shows.

But she was able to top them with her own self-deprecating humor, starting her speeches with the line, "As I was saying to Eleanor Roosevelt . . ."

But just like the Nancy Reagan situation, the Clintons had major political
worries in looking ahead to the next election and the possibility that the first
lady might be a liability in that effort. Mrs. Clinton decided that the solution
would be to summon strategist Dick Morris, who had helped Clinton to victory in his comeback 1983 gubernatorial campaign.

The net result of Morris's advice was to lower Hillary's profile, subsuming
her into the background to be seen and not heard, and moving the president
to what Clinton later called the "vital center." We got a softer, quieter Hillary
who stayed on the margins and made her suggestions quietly.

But in 1995, she even spoofed that image, again at the Gridiron show,
with another video portraying her as "Hillary Gump," even though she
skipped the dinner to travel to Asia.

Costumed as the heartwarming but dim hero of the movie, she discussed
her fascination with government bureaucracy, her habit of dispensing political advice and her ever-changing hairstyle.

Like the film, the video began with a feather floating down, leading to a
shot of the White House in the background. The camera panned down to
Hillary waiting at a bus stop in front, holding a box of chocolates on her lap.

> Hi, my name's Hillary—Hillary Gump [she said]. You can call me
> Hillary Rodham Gump. That's what everyone calls me, except on the
> Connie Chung show. You know, that's my house back there. My mama
> always told me the White House is like a box of chocolates. It's pretty
> on the outside, but inside there's a lot of nuts.
>
> My mama always gave me good advice. She told me life is like a
> regional health care alliance. If you pool your risks with a community
> health purchasing cooperative, and mix in a prospective payment
> review, you can reach an ideal cost-containment ratio. . . . My mama
> told me, Hillary, Hillary Gump, life is like a hairstyle. You just keep
> changing it until you find something that works.

In the video she sported long blond hair, a brown beehive and a black
bouffant as she recounted her charmed life advising a procession of Democratic standard-bearers.

To the 1972 nominee George McGovern she said, "Wait until two A.M. to
give your speech" and to Jimmy Carter she counseled, "Give a speech about
mayonnaise. Everybody loves mayonnaise. But he misunderstood my accent
and he gave a speech about malaise."

The video ended with a sport-shirted Bill Clinton sitting down next her and accepting her offer of a chocolate by grabbing the whole box. "You got any French fries to go with these chocolates?" he asked.

The crowd loved it, and in his remarks afterward, Clinton said, "The first lady wishes she could be here tonight. And if you believe that, I've got some Arkansas land I'd like to sell you."

Even Robert Novak, a constant critic of Clinton, said if that video had been released publicly, many of Hillary's image problems would have vaporized.

After the 1994 elections, Hillary slowly found her voice again when she traveled to Beijing in 1995 and made headlines at the U.N.'s Fourth World Conference on Women. It was a tense time in U.S.-China relations and some had argued that she should skip the conference.

At the conference, her speech was a stinging rebuke of human rights abuses. "It is time to break our silence. It is time for us to say here in Beijing, and the world to hear, that it is no longer acceptable to discuss women's rights as separate from human rights," she said.

She didn't mention China specifically but then recited a litany of abuses there and in other parts of the world, such as forced abortion and sterilization, and the denial of political rights and free speech. When she finished, the delegates leaped from their seats and the applause didn't die down for twenty minutes.

Still, she has been resented for being smart, savvy and steadfast. She's been attacked for being a "feminazi," for being the Tonya Harding of first ladies and for not confining herself to what Americans associate with that traditional role. And when the campaign for her husband's reelection rolled around, she did exactly that, being born again as the "little woman" who cared mainly about the problems of women and children. No surprise there. She'd been working on children's issues for years.

One historic "first" she gladly would have foregone was to be the first wife of a president to be compelled to testify before a federal grand jury, which she did in the Whitewater land investigation. After her grueling hours-long appearance, the word around the federal courthouse was that the jury was ready to indict special prosecutor Kenneth Starr. She's done many depositions since. In fact, the night of that correspondents' dinner when she and my colleagues surprised me, she had endured another five-hour session at the White House.

But every now and then, the old Hillary comes back into play. When the name Monica Lewinsky entered the political lexicon, she went on national television to defend her husband against the allegations and blamed the situation on a "politically motivated" prosecutor who was allied with a "vast right-wing conspiracy." Even after the president was forced to admit he had lied about the affair, she encouraged him to challenge Kenneth Starr when Clinton made his televised apology.

I don't think of her up-front demeanor as a liability. I think she is right to be outspoken on women's rights and children's rights. I think she has brought a lot of special talents, special skills and discrete experiences to Washington. But when she's been strong she's been accused of being pushy, strident and lacking in femininity.

"We can't stereotype anybody in this experience," she told me. "We should make it possible for everyone, particularly the spouses of presidents, to do what they are comfortable doing. If the next spouse of a president, male or female, says I don't want anything to do with politics, that's not my cup of tea, fine. Why do we have to have a cookie-cutter mold?"

For Hillary, politics is a way of life and I think she paid a price for being a demonstratively political first lady.

"If my husband weren't president, I would be involved in politics, I would be supporting candidates, I would be advocating for issues," she said to me, "just like I did before he was president and I will do again when he is no longer president. And I love it because I think politics, with a small 'p' . . . is how democracies make their decisions. . . . So for me I thought that I had some idea of politics at the national level. But I had no idea."

When I reminded her that she had a reputation for being hostile to the press, she responded, "No, I don't think that is valid," but she said it with a smile.

"I think I had a big learning curve that I had to really catch up on, because I was not that familiar with the mores of Washington and what people said or didn't say or thought or didn't think," she said. "And for me I have a great admiration and respect for the press. I sometimes feel like a disappointed advocate of the press because I feel so strongly how critical the role of the press is in our country. I go around the world giving speeches about the importance of a free press."

She seemed sanguine about the many slings and arrows she had endured as first lady, noting that "every life has its challenges.

"I've always believed it is a real mark of who you are as a person as to how you deal with the unexpected events of your life, the disappointments, the setbacks. And if you are lucky, as we have been, you have a lot to fall back on because you were well prepared as a child and as a young person and I don't think we do anything different. Our religious faiths are important to us, our family permanent to us."

Despite her incredible schedule—she has made fourteen solo trips abroad since 1997, including journeys to Africa and Asia, as well as official state visits with her husband—she also wrote a best-selling book, *It Takes a*

Village and Other Lessons Children Teach Us, describing the role a community must take in raising a child. She also joined the ranks of journalism, much in the same vein as Eleanor Roosevelt, when she took to writing a syndicated newspaper column.

Mrs. Clinton has acknowledged often in interviews that she and her husband have had their ups and downs and argued at times, but they have always been on the same wavelength in their optimistic view of politics as the way of achieving a better world. As she wrote in her book, "My strong feelings about divorce and its effect on children have caused me to bite my tongue more than a few times during my own marriage and to think instead about what I could do to be a better wife and partner."

After seven months of legal volleying, President Clinton told the nation in an address on August 17, 1998, that he misled his wife, his staff and the public and admitted he had had a relationship with Monica Lewinsky that he described as a "critical lapse in judgment and a personal failure on my part for which I am solely and completely responsible."

He went on to say that "Now, this matter is between me, the two people I love most—my wife and our daughter—and our God. It's nobody's business but ours. Even presidents have lives."

The next day, the first family left for a vacation on Martha's Vineyard, and through her press secretary Marsha Berry, the first lady issued a statement: "She is committed to her marriage and loves her husband and daughter very much. She believes in the president, and her love for him is compassionate and steadfast."

The nagging question for many was when did Hillary know of her husband's infidelities? Some said she was "misled" along with everyone else; others said she suspected; and still others said she knew for some time. Whatever and whenever she knew, she went to work helping her husband write the speech he delivered to the nation. While many of Clinton's aides reportedly argued for a softer tone, it is said that she told her husband that it was his speech and he should say what he wanted to say.

Ironically, her favorable ratings in the polls shot up during that most personally humiliating time.

There is no way to assess what she was thinking or feeling when the independent counsel's report hit the nation's airwaves and the Internet. In the weeks that followed the release of the report and all its seamy details, she kept to her vigorous schedule of travel and public appearances, campaigning for congressional candidates in 1998, and kept away from everyone but her closest friends. Her appearances on the hustings were a great boon to Democratic candidates, and she won great admiration for standing by her man, along with the sympathy vote. After the release of the report and all of the surrounding publicity leading to the impeachment inquiry, I was asked over and over, when I would speak around the country: "Do you think the Clintons will stay together after the Clinton presidency is over?" I think the answer may lie in what she once said about marriage:

> You've got to be willing to stay committed—to someone over the long run, and sometimes it doesn't work out. But often, if you've been real honest with yourself and honest with each other, and put aside whatever personal hurt and disappointment you have, to really understand yourself and your spouse, it can be the most wonderful experience you'll ever have.[4]

But who knows?

When I walked to the podium to accept my award that night at the White House Correspondents dinner, I could only think of a one-sentence acceptance speech: "You're only as good as your last story"—a line I had heard for years from the pros.

The story is still being written on Hillary Rodham Clinton. But if there's a "last story" to be written, I think she'll do what any independent woman would do and what some of her predecessors have done. She'll write it herself.

Hillary and her mother-in-law, Virginia Kelley, were worlds apart in lifestyle when they first came together as a family. But they grew to admire and respect each other greatly.

The first lady recalled that when Mrs. Kelley was battling cancer, "She never wanted anyone to feel sorry for her, and as with every other adversity she faced in her life, she'd get up at the crack of dawn, put on her lipstick and false eyelashes and go out to celebrate life.

"She was a great inspiration to all of us who knew and loved her. And I remember the sampler she kept on her nightstand that read, 'Lord help me to remember that nothing is going to happen to me today that you and I can't handle.'"

I think the quotation on that sampler personifies Hillary's own feelings during the devastating personal crises that she has endured.

And regarding her endurance, I'm reminded of what she told the Arkansas delegation at the 1996 Democratic National Convention. A friend, she said, had warned her to be careful; she would probably have everything thrown at her but the kitchen sink.

"Well," she said, "I just saw it go by."

THIRTEEN

"A Splendid Misery"

Kennedy used to say you don't make new friends in the White House. It appears you do make a lot of enemies. It also proves to me that if you want to go into public life you should decide at the age of five and live accordingly.
—Helen Thomas, speech to the National Federation of Press Women, Orlando, Florida, 1991

I have always considered myself privileged to be a witness to instant history at the White House. I have watched eight presidents so far with their triumphs and defeats, their highs and lows, their joys and sorrows. Each has wanted to put his stamp on the presidency and each hoped to be endowed with a special place in history. But greatness demands courage, and sometimes, albeit rarely, a president has risen to that challenge.

"A splendid misery"—that was how Thomas Jefferson once described the presidency. It is the highest political mark anyone can achieve in this country; it can be the loneliest spot in the world.

I can still hear Lyndon Johnson saying to us, "It's easy to do the right thing—if you know what the right thing is." The moral "right thing" is pretty apparent, but then there's the "political right thing" and the "expedient right thing" and any number of other "right things" that can push someone down the wrong path—and he often regrets it. I do not mean to sit in pious judgment. It's not easy up there. It takes a lot of courage to make a judgment call that could be politically unpopular but nevertheless morally right.

A president has to make his decisions independently. He can and should seek and get all possible advice, pro and con, and bring people in on the big decisions, "the takeoffs as well as the landings," as LBJ used to say. But in the end, the decision is his alone. As the sign on Harry Truman's desk said, "The buck stops here." Some presidents have tried to pass the buck and some have tried to spread the blame around. But the responsibility belongs to the president.

Teddy Roosevelt personified the presidency as a "bully pulpit" to achieve his goals, and those goals included persuading, convincing and arm-twisting if necessary the people from whom he needed support. I think the real lesson of the presidency—as in anyone's life and certainly in my field—is that you are accountable for everything you do. Without credibility—meaning honesty—a president cannot govern.

If I were to broad-brush the presidents I have covered, I would say:

• John F. Kennedy brought a new spirit to the country. I am always asked who was my favorite president of the eight I've covered on a daily basis and Kennedy is always my reply, despite the passage of years and the many historical events that followed his uplifting era. He understood the past and he cared about the future. After all, who else set a goal to land on the moon in a decade? He did not live to see it but we did it, and set the course for further exploration of the universe.

• Lyndon B. Johnson was the most successful in promoting the domestic agenda he called "the Great Society" that was to lift the quality of life for the less fortunate. In the aftermath of Kennedy's assassination, he also moved toward equal treatment of the races through the Civil Rights Act of 1964 and the Voting Rights Act of 1965.

• Richard Nixon made the breakthrough trip to China in 1972 that ended a twenty-year impasse in relations with the United States.

• Gerald Ford lived up to the awesome challenge that faced him when fate decreed that he would become president in the wake of the Nixon resignation after the unraveling of the Watergate scandal.

• Jimmy Carter made human rights the centerpiece of American's foreign policy and took concrete steps toward peace in the Middle East with the Camp David accords.

• Ronald Reagan turned the country to the right in the "Reagan Revolution" and planted the seeds for the fall of communism.

• George Bush was a forceful diplomat who understood the use of foreign policy and military power in turning back the Iraqi invasion of Kuwait during the Persian Gulf War.

• William J. Clinton balanced the budget, restored prosperity in the country and put education and training at the top of his domestic agenda as the United States moves into the twenty-first century.

These were the positive legacies that each president bestowed on the country, but each one also stumbled—from Vietnam to Watergate to the Iran hostage crisis to Iran-Contra to Monica Lewinsky. Acknowledging blunders is another story.

Before Vietnam or Watergate, the gentlemen's agreement in the White House was that presidents got a pass where their personal lives were concerned. People heard a lot, saw some and didn't report it. The resulting disenchantment with America's leadership after those two seminal events changed the course of presidential news coverage forever—along with the major changes in the media itself. But back then, the accepted attitude was that if a politician's lifestyle did not affect affairs of state, it was not reported.

I've been asked many times over the years, "Why didn't you write about Kennedy and his girlfriends?" Let me explain that presidents had more privacy then and the press was not privy to their sexual activities—only if those liaisons ended up on a police blotter or, as in one infamous incident, if a congressman followed a fan dancer into the Tidal Basin.

Now, presidents—and presidential candidates—put their privacy into a blind trust when they take office.

As more books are written about those presidents and more revelations about their personal lives come to light—true or not—I can only think of their families and the first ladies who have to endure the fallout.

Years after LBJ's death in 1973, in an interview on NBC's "Today" show, Lady Bird characterized her husband's reputation as a flirt and a ladies' man by saying, "Lyndon was a people lover and that certainly didn't exclude half the people in the world—women. I hope I was reasonable and if all those ladies had some good points that I didn't have, I hope I had the good sense to learn by it."

Her language could always finesse touchy issues. I think she nailed it when she told Muriel Dobbin, a reporter for the McClatchy newspaper chain, "You don't get to be president without [there being] some things you are ashamed of."

John Kennedy

Veterans Day, November 11, 1963: It was a short trip with President Kennedy over to Arlington National Cemetery to cover the traditional Veterans Day observance. Along for the ride was his young son, John. When the ceremonies were about to begin in the amphitheater, Kennedy realized his son was still outside where a military aide had been teaching him how to salute and march like a soldier. Kennedy told one of his Secret Service agents, "Go get John-John. I think he'll be lonely out there."

Two weeks later, JFK was buried at Arlington.

The vibrancy that John Kennedy brought to the presidency reflected his own spirit and refracted all across the nation. I always had the impression he was a young man in a hurry and I also felt that he sensed his time was short, after his two close brushes with death: one in World War II when his PT boat was rammed and again when he underwent back surgery in 1954.

Having known so much illness and tragedy in his life, I was struck by the fact that he wanted to live every moment to its fullest and that there was not a moment to lose. He was in a race against time.

In the exciting days shortly after he was elected in 1960, I found myself bundled up and spending hours outside his Georgetown home, watching the comings and goings of the new president-elect, his family, campaign aides, politicians and friends—anything that moved. UPI had installed a telephone in the backyard of a very kind and friendly woman who lived across the street and was equally caught up in the excitement of the new administration, with its accent on youth and "viguh."

Kennedy, who won by a very slim majority, was unable to hide his own tremendous sense of exhilaration and that feeling that lightning had struck. When he would emerge from his home, stand on the front steps and announce the appointment of yet another cabinet official, he exuded the feeling that America was on the march again.

Kennedy got used to seeing me and the other regular reporters and photographers standing on the sidewalk in front of his home in those post-election days. When I was assigned to the hospital after Kennedy's son was born, I got pulled off "baby duty" one day and was sent back to the N Street house. My assignment was to phone in as soon as Kennedy left the house to make the traditional visit to the White House for his big postelection meeting with outgoing President Eisenhower. Presumably, that is when Ike told him about plans for the CIA and a group of Cuban exiles to overthrow Fidel Castro with an invasion at the Bay of Pigs.

My first presidential trip was to Palm Beach, Florida, with Smitty to cover the Kennedy family over the Christmas holidays. The new first couple graciously threw a Christmas party for the press corps at their home but mostly we spent our time sitting in a motorcade for hours as they partied with their friends all over Palm Beach.

A blizzard the night before inauguration day 1961 made it a memorable one: The weather was unbearably cold but crowds still turned out in record numbers to witness the occasion and to listen to Kennedy's memorable speech. That was also the start of my working full-time at the White House. I couldn't have asked for better timing in that unbelievable era of hope.

I was low man—low person—on the totem pole for UPI at the White House but loved every minute and learned a lot from Smitty and Al Spivak, who took a "kinder, gentler" approach to the new kid in the booth.

In those days, reporters went in and out of the Oval Office and I became a familiar face to JFK as part of the UPI team. One day the press pool was summoned in and it turned out that I was the only print reporter on hand. Kennedy took one look at me and said, "Well, if it isn't Miss Thomas of the Universal Press."

Every new administration comes into the White House with a cocky self-confidence that begs to be deflated, and it doesn't take that long.

In April 1961, Kennedy sanctioned the invasion of Cuba at the Bay of Pigs, an operation quickly crushed by Castro. Operating on the better part of valor, Kennedy stopped the invasion, thinking better of it when he was asked to provide air support. It would have meant a full-scale intervention to depose Castro and he was not prepared for that.

In that brief time, the new president learned a lot about reading the fine print. He had a sharp lesson in understanding the consequences of his actions in the early days of his administration. After the Bay of Pigs fiasco, his polls dropped. But he learned a valuable lesson: that when he took full responsibility the American people were ready to forgive and give him another chance. His popularity rose immediately and his administration was back on track.

Reporters for the *Miami Herald* and the *New York Times* had learned of the impending invasion and Kennedy asked the editors to hold off on publishing anything until after it began. Later he expressed the thought that if those stories had been published, he might have realized the folly of it all before giving the green light to the invasion.

The situation with Cuba had another interesting sideshow, according to Pierre Salinger. One night Kennedy called him into the Oval Office and said, "I need your help." Salinger's mission was to purchase as many Petit Upmanns, Cuba's finest cigar, as he could; Kennedy needed them by the next day. Salinger and a team of aides visited every tobacco shop in the greater Washington area, laboring far into the night.

The next morning Salinger was called into the Oval Office.

"How did you do?" said JFK.

"I got about twelve hundred," said Salinger.

A delighted Kennedy reached into his desk drawer, pulled out a piece of paper and signed it. It was the Cuba trade embargo.[1]

When the Cuban missile crisis occurred in October 1962, Kennedy was more prepared for making a decision and knowing what was at stake. Presented with the evidence that the Russians were delivering missiles into Cuba capable of reaching major cities on the East Coast, he made a televised address detailing his order to impose the blockade of Cuba.

The day he sent an ultimatum to Soviet leader Nikita S. Khrushchev to remove the missiles, Smitty buttonholed Kennedy as he was walking through the West Wing lobby.

"It's been a very interesting day," JFK told him.

Fortunately, reason prevailed. Although Kennedy went on "red alert," Khrushchev "blinked"; the two leaders obviously did not want to blow up the world.

In 1964, when I was covering Lyndon Johnson on the campaign trail, he spoke of those terrifying hours and remarked, "Kennedy was the coolest man in the room, and he had his thumb on the nuclear button."

There had been a chill between Kennedy and Khrushchev dating back to their first meeting in Vienna in 1961, when they collided over several issues and Kennedy left the meeting shaken, asking his aides whether "the bastard is always that way."

The confrontation evoked much speculation that it was going to be a long cold winter. But by the time of the missile crisis, Kennedy gave Khrushchev some leverage so that he would not lose too much face, and compromised by agreeing to remove U.S. missiles from Turkey. I was struck in those days and hours that Washington seemed so calm, like the eye of a hurricane, with no panic among the people.

All the presidents I've covered have demonstrated a sense of humor honed from years in politics, but none was able to use wit with such dead aim as Kennedy. In that respect, he was the master. Nothing escaped him. In short, he struck me as a rare combination of the intellectual and the street-smart pol. He always used to say that I would be a "nice girl if she'd ever get rid of that pad and pencil."

Before I arrived at the White House and when he was a senator in 1958, he read a telegram from his father at the Gridiron dinner: "Dear Jack: Don't buy a single vote more than is necessary. I'll be damned if I'm paying for a landslide."

There was a lot of criticism and cries of nepotism when he named his brother Bobby as attorney general, to which he responded, "I was criticized about appointing my brother attorney general, but I don't see what's wrong with getting him a little experience before he goes out to practice law."

In 1961, when the women reporters were still banished to the balcony to cover speeches at the National Press Club, Venezuelan president Romulo Betancourt came to town and made a speech at a press club luncheon. Afterward, he met with Kennedy, and as they were walking through the lobby, the women reporters gathered asked for a comment.

Betancourt, a bit sheepishly, said he had told the press club that it might be a good idea for women reporters "to join their club activities."

Kennedy pointed to me and said, "There's one of your revolutionaries right over there. Here she is, trying to bring her own revolt into the White House."

His Roman Catholic religion was a controversial campaign issue in 1960, but he also managed to tweak that after he got into office. At another Gridiron dinner he said, "I asked the chief justice of the Supreme Court whether he thought our new educational bill was constitutional and he said, 'It's clearly unconstitutional. It hasn't got a prayer.'"

I often covered Kennedy when he went to Mass on Sunday and he always seemed a bit embarrassed to have the press along. Maybe it was because we always noticed that he rarely carried a lot of "walking around money" and he always put the bite on his Secret Service agents when the collection plate was being passed.

He also never forgot that early in this century being Irish was considered a handicap in Boston. He often spoke of his Irish roots and he never failed to mention the signs that he used to see at job sites when he was growing up: "No Irish need apply." No one was prouder of his Irish heritage and when visiting Ireland he thrilled the crowds with his ability to recite the works of famous Irish poets and the words to the song that was always played on official departures, "Come Back to Erin."

Although it lasted only a thousand days, his administration was marred by many crises and enjoyed many breakthroughs. He dealt with the atomic bomb question, getting the genie back in the bottle, as someone put it.

On June 10, 1963, he delivered one of his most memorable speeches. It was a commencement address at American University and he used the occasion to call for a limited nuclear test–ban treaty with the Soviet Union. Within four months he would sign that historic pact into law.

"What kind of peace do I mean?" he said to the audience. "Not the peace of the grave or the security of the slave. I am talking about genuine peace, the kind of peace that makes life on earth worth living, the kind that enables men and nations to grow and to hope and to build a better life for their children—not merely peace for Americans but peace for all men and women—not merely peace in our time but peace for all time."

On civil rights he was often accused of dragging his feet and of being too cautious and too hesitant.

The day after Kennedy's speech at American University, two black students tried to enroll at the University of Alabama and were blocked by orders from Governor George Wallace. That night, Kennedy delivered a televised address and called civil rights "a moral issue as old as the Scriptures and as clear as the American Constitution."

On August 28, 1963, Martin Luther King delivered his famous "I have a dream" speech on the Mall between the Washington Monument and the Lincoln Memorial before the 200,000 people who had marched in a nonviolent demonstration calling for equality among the races.

That evening, King was invited to a White House reception and when Kennedy saw him, he extended his hand and said, "*I* have a dream."

One of Kennedy's great contributions was to create the Peace Corps, which is still going strong, with people of all ages teaching and working on everything from public health to bridge-building in countries all over the world.

His own health problems—he also suffered from a mild form of Addison's disease—and the deaths of a sister and a brother during World War II may have given him a sense of melancholy or foreboding, but I think it also added to his feeling about the way life was to be lived.

He was always recommending books to us and one he kept bringing up was *Pilgrim's Way* by John Buchan, about a young man dying in World War I. The poignancy of youth and death seemed to preoccupy him.

Jackie recalled in an interview in *Look* magazine on November 17, 1964, the poetry he loved, especially Tennyson: "I am a part of all that I have met" from "Ulysses."

In the aftermath of his death, many books have been written that denigrated his personal life and questioned his accomplishments. But I think he left a great legacy: the fulfillment of his prophecy that the United States could put a man on the moon in a decade. He left us with the conviction that the sky was not the limit, that it was our destiny to keep exploring the universe, and in the words of that Tennyson poem, "to strive, to seek to find and not to yield."

So when I reveal the name of my favorite president, and explain why, inevitably, the reply would be a nod and the comment: "I knew you would say that."

When Carl Sandburg died, his wife said, "He belongs to the world." I think I can say the same thing of Kennedy.

Lyndon Johnson

My first job after college was as a teacher in Cotulla, Texas, in a small Mexican-American school. Somehow you never forget what poverty and hatred can do when you see its scars on the hopeful face of a young child. . . . I never thought then, in 1928, that I would be standing here in 1965. It never even occurred to me in my fondest dreams that I might have the chance to help the sons and daughters of those students and to help people like them all over this country.

But now I do have that chance—and I'll let you in on a secret; I mean
to use it.
            —Lyndon B. Johnson, address to a joint session of Congress, March 15, 1965

As Air Force One traveled from Dallas to Washington on November 22,
1963, Lyndon B. Johnson, the new president, walked over to Smitty and
Newsweek's Charles Roberts, who were trying to compose the stories they
would file when they landed.

"God knows the last thing I wanted was to become president this way," he
said to them. He paused for a moment and added, "Now that I am president,
with God's help, you're going to live long enough to write that I was the best
president this country ever had."[1]

In many ways he was an outstanding president, comparable to his hero
FDR, in his accomplishments in domestic policy, based on his determination to improve the quality of life of all Americans. But he could not pull
himself out of the quagmire of Vietnam.

He kept believing that more troops and military power could win the
war, while at the same time he was open to peace negotiations. But he was
obsessed with the fear, as was Nixon, that he might become the first president to lose a major war. His presidency ended with his loss of credibility.

He used to remind us, "I'm the only president you've got," and when
we asked him what his vision was, he liked to say he wanted to be "progressive without being radical" and "prudent without being reactionary." There
were times I wanted to shout, "Just be yourself!"

That was a pretty tall order. His gigantic ego was matched by his gigantic
inferiority complex. He was complex, coarse, courtly, cruel and compassionate. He had big ambitions and big appetites. He could preach honesty and
practice deception. He could be vindictive one minute, the soul of generosity the next. He could love and he could hate. But he also could be forgiving.

I think I can safely assure you that every story you have ever heard about
Lyndon Johnson is probably true—and then some. But for all the ego and all
the vanity, he had a tremendous sense of democracy. He understood all too
well that a president had to have the support of the people. Otherwise, he
had nothing—and that was never more in evidence than in his announcement that he would not seek a second term.

When it came to his goals, I am reminded of the story he used to tell
about Mrs. Lurana Fidelia Stribling, who in the early 1900s amassed one of
the largest ranches in Texas. She kept buying up ranch after ranch and one
day, one of her lawyers asked her, "Mrs. Stribling, how much land do you
want? Do you want all there is in the county?"

"No, I don't want it all," she said. "All I want is my own and all that joins it."

In his five years in office, Johnson racked up a brilliant legacy of "Great Society" social legislation: the antipoverty programs, the civil rights bills, Medicare, air and water pollution controls, urban mass-transit programs, education aid including Head Start, wilderness preservation, public housing, child care.

On the other side, there was his obsessive secrecy, the finagling with the budget, the credibility gap—and over it all, Vietnam.

When he ran for the presidency in 1964, he made as many as fourteen speeches a day. We reporters would be dragging and he would be repeating his line: "Whose finger do you want on the button?"

I was on Lady Bird's whistle-stop train when it met up with Johnson's campaign train in New Orleans. It was a remarkable reunion. "All I ever hear you say is 'nigger, nigger,'" Johnson told the stunned southern crowds.

Southern backlash or not, the voting public gave Johnson a landslide victory in 1964 when he defeated Senator Barry Goldwater with 61.1 percent of the popular vote, beating Franklin Roosevelt's 1936 record of 60.8 percent.

But his vast popularity gradually evaporated as the Vietnam War escalated. By 1967, more than 500,000 U.S. troops were deployed in Southeast Asia and hundreds of thousands of protesters kept demanding to know why.

Johnson, forgetting Eisenhower's warning against getting involved in a land war in Asia, kept upping the ante and fudging the body counts. Short of dropping a nuclear bomb, the American people began to realize that the war could not be won and its purpose became less acceptable. The antiwar protests grew louder across the country, and as time went on I was covering the White House inside and outside, standing on Pennsylvania Avenue as hundreds of demonstrators shouted, "Hey, hey, LBJ, how many kids did you kill today?"

In retrospect, I think if Johnson, and later President Nixon, had taken the advice of Vermont senator George Aiken—"Declare a victory and leave"— Johnson would have been a hero for bowing to the inevitable. But he would never back off from the stance that he would not be the first U.S. president ever to lose a war. He always carried with him a copy of the Senate vote on the Gulf of Tonkin resolution, and he would take it out whenever we asked him pointed questions about Vietnam, noting to us that the Senate had voted 88–2 and the House gave its unanimous support, 416–0.

It is often said he listened to the generals and they told him what he wanted to hear. But he also listened to the cabinet he inherited from Kennedy, including Defense Secretary Robert McNamara and Secretary of State Dean Rusk, who thought he should stay the course. McNamara later became disillusioned and resigned to become president of the World Bank. But Rusk was a bitter-ender.

Johnson was one president who gave us some insight into the highs and lows of the Oval Office. It was not unusual for him to invite the press to lunch in the family quarters or have us tag along for the ride in the presidential limousine. Once he even put me in "Lady Bird's seat" on the helicopter. I had been getting a little wind-tossed standing near the rotating blades of the chopper before it took off and when I was seated, LBJ took one look at my disheveled hair, pronounced me a "mess" and handed me a comb.

He gave reporters the closest look they have ever had into the home life of a president. We toured his ranch and went on boat rides on the man-made lake, one of the many federal projects he brought to his beloved Texas. We dined with him, were guests at his famous barbecues and listened to his fascinating stem-winders about his relatives and the politicians he knew in the Texas hill country where he was born and grew up.

Having been in the LBJ doghouse on several occasions, usually for a story I had written about his daughters, I could sympathize with his staff, who worked long days and longer nights and would be subject to the famous LBJ wrath if he called at any time and they weren't available.

With reporters, this was the most extreme love-hate relationship I've ever seen in the White House. He was always complaining to us, "Y'all have the First Amendment," as if the Constitution had left presidents bereft.

When the indomitable Liz Carpenter, Mrs. Johnson's press secretary, had to handle the clamor for details about Luci's wedding to Pat Nugent and Lynda Bird's marriage to Charles Robb, Johnson said she ran "the hell department."

When he took office, he told Doug Cornell and me that he was going to have an open administration and told us that we could see "anything on my desk."

Our skepticism was totally justified. For as open as he seemed to be, Johnson could not stand for anyone to know what he was going to do next. He would be furious if it was reported he was going to make an appointment before he had a chance to make the announcement himself.

In 1965, he persuaded Supreme Court Justice Arthur Goldberg to step down from the bench and become U.S. ambassador to the United Nations. In an impromptu session, reporters asked him who he was considering for a replacement—perhaps Abe Fortas, his longtime adviser. Johnson looked at the group squarely and said he had not started to think about a nominee. About a day later, the White House announced Johnson would nominate Fortas to the high court.

Nor could he tolerate anyone writing that he had changed his policy. But then no president ever wanted to admit he had changed policy—or changed his mind—even when it was obvious.

As a former member of the House and as the former Senate majority leader, Johnson was masterful in handling Congress and getting what he wanted, which was plenty. If sweet-talking members of Congress did not do the trick, he always knew where the bodies were buried or what the price would be.

When Senator Frank Church of Idaho began voicing more antiwar views, Johnson went up to him at a White House party and asked him, "Where do you get your ideas?"

"From Walter Lippmann," Church replied.

"Well, the next time you need a dam in Idaho, just ask Walter Lippmann," Johnson told him.

He was the same way with labor and management. When a rail strike threatened to cripple the country, he locked the leaders in a room in the Executive Office Building, sent in coffee and sandwiches and did not let them out until they had reached an agreement.

When one of them told Johnson that he was "just a country boy," Johnson said, "That's when I reached for my back pocket to see if my wallet was still there."

Johnson was very conscious of the impact a presidential illness would have on the economy. After he underwent gallbladder surgery, the first thing Bill Moyers, his press secretary, said to him, was "Mr. President, the stock market opened steady."

While he was recovering at the LBJ ranch, I asked his cousin Oriole how he looked. She told me he did not look good, but "Lyndon told me not to say that because I would start a depression."

Johnson was ridiculed for showing his scar to reporters and photographers at Bethesda Naval Hospital. But as he later explained, he wanted to show the world that he was operated on in exactly the right place for his gallbladder to reassure Americans that he did not have cancer. He later told Smitty, "Thousands, maybe millions of Americans were beginning to gossip that their president has cancer. The scar was right where it should have been for a gallbladder. And don't forget this, people with cancer don't go around bragging about it."[2]

As his presidency was coming to an end, Johnson agreed to sit for his official portrait by artist Peter Hurd. When it was finished, LBJ took one look at it and called it "the ugliest thing I ever saw." He then gave the task to Elizabeth Shoumatoff, who had been painting FDR at Warm Springs, Georgia, when he suffered a massive stroke and died.

Johnson liked her painting so much, he ended up asking her to paint several portraits of him in different outfits, including his ranch attire. When Johnson departed the room, a distressed Shoumatoff summoned curator James Ketchum and quite indignantly told him that Johnson "thinks I'm a Xerox machine."

A favorite story of mine occurred when the Johnsons celebrated an Abraham Lincoln anniversary with a White House luncheon for a number of scholars and other noted guests, including the poet Carl Sandburg.

After lunch, Lady Bird asked several of the guests if they would like to see the Lincoln Bedroom, which has a framed copy of the Emancipation Proclamation on the wall. They all readily accepted, got up and followed her, leaving LBJ sitting forlornly at the table. He turned to another group of guests and said, "Would you like to see my bedroom?" and they all dutifully got up and followed him out of the room.

Wauhillau LaHay, a wonderful, witty newswoman, was in LBJ's group and as they entered his quarters, he said to her slyly, "Bet you've never been in a president's bedroom before."

"No," she answered, "not since Millard Fillmore."

After he made his electrifying announcement in March 1968 that he would not seek another presidential term, I never quite believed that he had no interest in being drafted for the job. I thought he might be harboring some hope that when the Democrats gathered in Chicago in 1968, there would be such a movement. But Lady Bird explained later that LBJ felt he no longer had it in him to give eighteen hours a day for four more years. "It's just like climbing a mountain every day," she said, "and it haunted him and it certainly haunted me."

There is considerable evidence that as much as Johnson liked and admired Humphrey, it was difficult to tell just which candidate Johnson actually supported to replace him. I still wonder at LBJ's insistence that Humphrey was not allowed to go to Winston Churchill's funeral as the president's emissary when LBJ's doctors ruled he could not go because of a chest cold.

Asked at a news conference later why he did not send Humphrey to the funeral in London, Johnson just said: "When I was vice president I didn't go to everyone's funeral."

Humphrey and his advisers knew that they could not win if they stayed too close to Johnson's Vietnam policy, and in his campaign he tried to separate himself from it. On September 10, I traveled with Johnson to New Orleans where he addressed the American Legion convention and gave a strong defense of his actions in Vietnam, and said no one could predict when the war would end. An aide later told him that everyone interpreted the speech as a "real blast at Humphrey."[3]

On September 12, Humphrey announced his intention to start bringing troops home in 1969, and in speeches a few weeks later declared, "Come January, it's a new ball game. Then I will make peace." He added that if he were elected, "I would stop the bombing of North Vietnam as an acceptable risk for peace."[4]

In the meantime, indications were popping up all over the place that Nixon had sent an emissary to tell South Vietnam's president Nguyen Van Thieu not to go along with Johnson's bombing halt in preparation for the Paris peace talks.

The back-channel machinations that went on eventually boiled down to Humphrey losing the election by less than .01 percent of the popular vote, although he lost the electoral college 301–191. His aides had pressed him to publicize the story of Nixon's betrayal and Johnson's silence, but Humphrey, a big man, decided against it.

He later attributed his defeat to the loss of "some of my personal identity and forcefulness . . . It would have been better that I stood my ground and remembered that I was fighting for the highest office in the land. I ought not to have let a man who was going to be a former president dictate my future."[5]

I do believe that Humphrey might have won the White House if Johnson had exposed the opposition and given Humphrey the freedom he needed.

After Nixon became president, he threw two birthday parties for LBJ in two years and Johnson amused the guests at one gathering, saying he hoped Nixon would make the birthday celebration a routine. Then, in mock rueful tones, he said that in his retirement, he had been "doing some ranchin' and writing and I already have seven unfavorable reviews on a book that hasn't been written."

Reporters used to make jokes on how they pitied the LBJ Ranch foreman when Johnson retired. They knew he would never know a moment's peace—LBJ would be barking orders or taunting him about jobs undone.

When he left office, LBJ remained active building his library in Austin, lecturing at the Lyndon Baines Johnson School of Public Affairs at the University of Texas and writing his memoirs. But he was not a happy man. His multipack-a-day smoking habit began again even though he suffered from angina.

On January 22, 1973, he collapsed at his ranch and two of his Secret Service agents carried him onto his plane to fly him to a hospital in San Antonio. The doctor on board pronounced him dead before removing the body from the plane.

He lay in state at his library in Austin on January 23 through the next morning and then at the Capitol Rotunda January 24 and 25. After an aide reported a comment from Lady Bird, that "the thing Lyndon hated most was to be by himself," a group of his friends kept watch at the casket all night.[6]

But my favorite story came from Harry Middleton, the executive director of LBJ's library, when he assigned someone to keep count of how many people paid their respects to LBJ in Austin. The total was in the neighborhood of 32,000. Someone asked Middleton why he wanted that information and he replied, "Because I know that somewhere, sometime, President Johnson is going to ask me."[7]

Richard Nixon

> I have been accused of megalomania. Actually, I suffer from paranoia and the good thing about working in government instead of the academic world is that I can have real enemies.
>
> —Henry Kissinger, in a note to Attorney General John Mitchell, who accused Kissinger of being an egomaniac

And their boss lived by the credo: Never give up.

When I think about the Nixon White House I'm still astounded by that incredible confluence of men and events that foisted such trauma on the American political system: a kaleidoscope from hell.

Richard Nixon often liked to quote Teddy Roosevelt's speech about the "man in the arena" who finds the strength to pick himself up and fight another day. Life for him was a battlefield, and he was an energetic and calculating warrior. He told AP's Saul Pett in 1973, "I believe in the battle, whether it's the battle of the campaign or the battle of this office, which is a continuous battle. It's always there wherever you go. I, perhaps, carry it more than others because that's my way."[1]

But it seemed like he always had two battle plans and had a bad habit of choosing the wrong one. Either that, or he had one of the most off-kilter moral compasses that ever guided the Oval Office.

For myself, the man was like a roller coaster of contradictions that I am still trying to sort out. In the twenty-four years since he left office, every now and then I feel a twinge of pity. Then another Watergate tape gets released and I get ticked off all over again.

He used to extol the "firsts" he achieved in his presidency, especially the breakthough trip to China. But he had been part of the China lobby that blocked any rapprochement for twenty years. His best-known personal "first" was an ignominious one: the first to be forced to resign the presidency for the abuse of power and lying. And even on that score, while acknowledging the break-in of Democratic National headquarters as a "mistake," in an interview on CBS on April 8, 1984, ten years after his resignation, he told his former speechwriter Frank Gannon, "There's no way you could apologize that is more eloquent, more decisive, more finite, or to say that you're sorry, which would exceed resigning the presidency of the United States. That said it all and I don't intend to say any more."

He also said that if he thought the Oval Office tapes "revealed criminal activities, I would have been out of my mind not to destroy them."

I wonder whether he or his staff ever came to terms with the truth. I also wonder whether he ever came to terms with himself.

Nixon served in the Navy in World War II, and his political career began in 1946 when California Republicans handpicked him to run for Congress, and he found the limelight early as the junior congressman who rode the crest of the anticommunism wave in the United States with his role in the Alger Hiss case. He spiraled up to the Senate and then made the great leap forward as Eisenhower's running mate in 1952. That dream almost got derailed when it was revealed that a private slush fund had been established by supporters for Nixon. He gained back the high ground with his famous "Checkers" speech and Ike, who had considered dropping Nixon from the ticket, read the sympathetic polls and declared, "He's my boy."

As vice president, Nixon traveled the world and steeped himself in foreign policy, something that would be the hallmark of his eventual presidency.

Equally early on in his political life he was convinced the media was against him because "I'm a conservative and they're liberals." He never gave up on that view either.

After his defeat by Kennedy in 1960, he ran for governor of California in 1962 and was beaten by the incumbent, Edmund Brown. That race is remembered for Nixon's news conference and his final blast at the media, telling them, "You won't have Dick Nixon to kick around anymore. This is my last press conference."

But after his wounds healed and he developed a calmer, more confident image, he was back at the old stand. He didn't give up.

Between 1962 and 1968, he practiced law, traveled and eventually made up his mind to seek the presidency. In his campaign he kept saying he had a "plan for peace" in Vietnam, a plan that included keeping the press well fed but in the dark, especially about the details.

Actually, his plan was one that had been suggested in the Johnson administration. "Vietnamization" was supposed to prepare South Vietnam to face its enemy from the North as U.S. troops were gradually withdrawn. The public bought it along with Nixon's appeal to the "silent majority." Whatever the policy, it didn't work. Less than a year after he took office, America woke up to the fact that Nixon's road map was leading to an expanded war. His 1968 campaign made much of pointing up the differences between the "old Nixon" and the "new Nixon." When he moved into the White House in 1969, I think the "new Nixon" lasted about fifteen minutes.

I will never forget when, in the fall of 1969, a half-million antiwar protesters staged a peaceful demonstration on the Ellipse. A few members of the press pool were allowed inside the Oval Office for a picture-taking session and Nixon told his group of visitors, "I'm going to watch football this afternoon."

And when he decided to invade Cambodia in May 1970, I don't think he had a clue as to how that decision would tear the country apart. Antiwar protests escalated and he seemed to become more isolated. By the time the bombing of Hanoi took place over Christmas 1972, he made no public appearances for nearly three weeks.

Before the end of 1972, however, he made diplomatic history with his trip to China, still considered a master stroke of foreign policy. Working in tandem with National Security Adviser Henry Kissinger, that visit also opened another door to the peace talks that led to the end of the Vietnam War.

As I've said, secrecy is endemic in the White House, but in the Nixon administration it was epidemic: from the secret bombing of Cambodia to stonewalling about Watergate, from the creation of the "plumbers' unit" to the "enemies list," to Kissinger turning over to the FBI a list of his top aides whom he suspected of leaking information to reporters.

As far as my impressions of the man, all I can do is count up the contradictions: He could mix a mean martini, he loved movies and he liked to take his family out to dinner. He wasn't great with small talk but he was a great host at White House functions. He was awkward in small groups but could confidently address crowds numbering in the thousands. He could call campus protesters "bums" and accompany Pearl Bailey on the piano at a state dinner. He could hate the press but he could still walk into the pressroom, as he did on April 30, 1973, after announcing the resignations of H. R. Haldeman and John Erlichman—whom he described as "two of the finest public servants it has been my privilege to know"—and say to us, "When I'm wrong, keep giving me hell. I want to be worthy of your trust."[2]

He was a president who claimed executive privilege to hold back the Oval Office tapes detailing Watergate and a president who introduced Sunday worship services in the East Room. He was a president who would invite about four hundred people to share spiritual sustenance and a president who would insist the guest list be kept secret.

One weekend, when we were assigned to the presidential "body watch" in the duck blind at Camp David, Doug and I got to talking to a young Marine sergeant we had come to know from our previous trips. He told us he would like to attend one of the White House worship services; the next day, Doug called the White House social office to see if arrangements could be made for him to attend. The answer was no; the young man was transferred and we never saw him at Camp David again.[3]

He was a president who allowed the press to cover the services and I always did, but I was also always getting Ron Ziegler's dander up when I asked the guests questions. Nixon later discontinued the Sunday services.

He was a president whose vice president, Spiro Agnew, resigned after pleading nolo contendere to charges of tax evasion. He was a president whose attorney general, John Mitchell, the nation's top cop, went to jail.

He was a political realist on August 8, 1974, when he told the nation he would step down from the presidency. The night before, he gathered with his family in the solarium in the family quarters and the tears flowed freely as Pat and his daughters urged him to fight on.

There are many stories about the days leading up to his resignation and Nixon's state of mind. Ten days before he resigned, word of possible emotional instability reached the Pentagon and precautions were taken that any orders coming in from the commander in chief would be carefully screened.

I will admit, I felt great sadness in those days.

True to his "never give up" philosophy, Nixon spent some time in exile in San Clemente, California, but he was not about to be counted out. In a few years, he was delivering speeches and getting standing ovations. He wrote his memoirs and other books and he quietly stayed in touch with his successors, who often privately sought his political advice.

Still, I sometimes wonder and marvel at the depth of compassion this nation bestows on its shamed officials. In April 1995, the U.S. Postal Service issued a commemorative stamp of Nixon and his portrait has hung in the White House like all the others.

In 1985, there was a small ceremony at the Justice Department where John Mitchell and his daughter, Marty, watched as Mitchell's portrait was unveiled and hung in the Great Hall along with the portraits of other attorneys general. It was painted by Oklahoma artist Gloria Schumann, who had done a portrait of Mitchell in 1969—the one Martha got rid of after her husband moved out of their New York apartment. In an interview, Schumann said, "I feel John Mitchell is a man of courage, strength and patience. He is very considerate of the other fellow. He knows how to keep his mouth shut. He also has a great sense of humor. These are the things I tried to portray." The $15,000 she was paid for the portrait, she said, was less than her usual fee because she was doing the job for the government and "felt patriotic."[4] The portrait was hung on the second floor, where the department's criminal division is located, but in 1989, it was relegated to the seventh floor in a corridor outside the appellate branch of the civil division, an area rarely visited by tourists.

And in 1995, Agnew returned to Washington to watch as an Italian marble bust of himself was placed in the Capitol along with those of vice presidents past. "I am not blind or deaf to the critics who say this should not take place," he said at the ceremony. "This has less to do with Spiro Agnew than the office I held. It's not so much about me as the office." Still, a few of the city's pundits couldn't resist suggesting things like perhaps the sculptor should have been paid his $40,000 fee in cash in an unmarked envelope, much the same way Agnew accepted payments from Maryland contractors when he served in three elected offices: Baltimore County executive, governor of Maryland and vice president. And a few suggested the bust would have been more artistically accurate if some dollar signs had been carved into it.[5]

I guess in the contest of tradition versus political reality, we'd rather honor tradition—or maybe just forgive and forget. I've often said I don't waste my sympathy on presidents. They're responsible for their actions, and when they screw up, they have to be held accountable.

But back to that evening of April 30, 1973: I was running down West Executive Avenue to get to the pressroom and stopped short. There was Richard Nixon, coming out of a side entrance and heading for his office in the Executive Office Building. His shoulders were hunched; his face was gray.

"Good evening, Mr. President," I said, "and good luck."

He grabbed my hand gratefully and said, "I know we don't have the same religion. But will you say a prayer for me?"

"I will, Mr. President," I said, feeling deeply moved by the tragedy of it all. I did say a prayer for him. I also said one for the country.

In 1974, with the Nixon presidency in free fall, I went to Chambersburg, Pennsylvania, to make a speech for the local paper, which was celebrating its one hundredth anniversary.

After my speech there was a question-and-answer session and a man asked me, "When did you first know Nixon was lying?"

Without a flicker of an eyelash, I promptly replied:

"In nineteen forty-six"

But there are days when I still ponder the contradictions.

Gerald Ford

Is there ever a right time?

—Gerald R. Ford, responding to aides' questions on the timing of his pardon of

Richard Nixon

Within an hour's time on August 9, 1974, I witnessed a fallen president depart in disgrace and a successor sworn in with the blessing of a nation and its high hopes. I couldn't get that phrase out of my mind: "The king is dead, long live the king."

The transition was easier than we thought it would be. On that day I recalled President Nixon sitting at his desk in the Oval Office and saying to a friend, "Can you imagine Jerry Ford sitting in this chair?"

Gerald R. Ford, who had served some three decades in Congress and had aspired to be Speaker of the House, did fit comfortably in the Oval Office. He was indeed the man of the hour, one able to stabilize the country in the aftermath of the national trauma of the Watergate scandal.

A year earlier, Ford was selected with the wholehearted support of the Democratic-controlled Congress to fulfill the unfinished term of Vice President Spiro Agnew after he resigned.

As Betty Ford held the Bible, a nervous Gerald Ford was sworn in as the thirty-eighth president. His close aide and speechwriter Robert Hartmann came up with the right words and the eloquence, but Ford supplied the sincerity that lent poignancy to the moment, saying: "Our long national nightmare is over. Our Constitution works. Our great Republic is a government of laws, not of men. Here the people rule." Hartmann reported that Ford at first balked at the "long nightmare" line, but was persuaded to say it. It was the most memorable of his address. He acknowledged that "I assume the presidency under extraordinary circumstances. This is an hour of history that troubles our minds and hurts our hearts.

"Truth is the only glue that holds government together," he added. His promise to the press was "straight talk" and to Congress a seeking of "conciliation, compromise and cooperation."

A fiscal conservative, Ford's idea of government was pre–New Deal, based on the theory that the least government is the best government. He often used his newfound power via the veto, but he also was overridden by a Congress that was not totally hostile, just more sympathetic to domestic social issues.

His mother had taught him early to control his temper and he often boasted that he had no enemies, only adversaries. I think that was true. He was recognized as a decent man, well-liked, easygoing and stubborn but well-meaning. He grew up in Grand Rapids, Michigan, attended the University of Michigan, earned a law degree at Yale and served in the Navy in World War II.

I think he made a fatal mistake in announcing early on that he would have no new programs and would basically follow Nixon's domestic and foreign policies. Stasis is not the American style, and presidents who do not move forward are left behind. Ford had a one-dimensional approach to decision-making and usually stood firm once he'd made up his mind.

One might argue that Ford's biggest mistake was to pardon Nixon, an act that probably contributed to his defeat when he ran for a full term as president in 1976. But costly as it may have been to his career, he has always defended the pardon on grounds that the country had to put that dark episode behind it. He also felt that his own tenure would be paralyzed by the impeachment process that would have gone on for months.

In his book *Time and Chance: Gerald Ford's Appointment with History,* James Cannon wrote that Nixon's chief of staff Alexander Haig went to see Ford on August 1 on Nixon's behalf and proposed that Ford agree to pardon Nixon if he resigned. The offer was tempting and Ford heard him out. Hours passed while he wrestled with the decision. But Ford finally grasped the enormity of the swap and what the public would have thought if he had attained the presidency through a bargain—and he walked away from it.

On August 3, he made a speech proclaiming Nixon's innocence. He later said he did not want to undermine his predecessor, although he knew it was all over. But one month after he took office, Ford pardoned Nixon. Cannon quoted Ford as saying he knew there were some people "who want to believe that a deal was made" but he had a clear conscience.

"I'm certain there was no deal arranged between Haig and me, and Nixon or me, or anybody else," Ford said, and long after he left office, he maintained, "My feelings are even stronger than they were at the time. It was the right thing to do."[1]

Ford held his first presidential news conference a couple of weeks after he was sworn in. On the first question, I asked him whether he would pardon Nixon or let the legal process continue. He was ambiguous but seemed to imply he would allow events to unfold. During this period, Nixon's daughters and sons-in-law were calling Betty Ford and White House staffers, pleading for a pardon for the distraught Nixon. However, I should have kept my ears a little more open. Ten days after he became president, I traveled with Ford to Chicago where he announced to a gathering of the Veterans of Foreign Wars a limited amnesty for those who had avoided the draft during the Vietnam War.

Louis Foy, a correspondent for Agence France-Presse, was following a text of the speech and said to me, "He's talking about amnesty for Nixon."

I didn't ask Ford on the trip back whether a pardon was indeed in the works and I could still kick myself for not doing so, but he probably wouldn't have told me anyway.

Ford also paid a price with the pardon by losing a wonderful press secretary, Jerry ter Horst, who had worked as a reporter for the *Detroit News* and had covered Ford in Congress. The press corps respected him but ter Horst resigned in short order after a couple of reporters got wind of the fact that a pardon was in the works and ter Horst, misled by the White House counsel's office, told them it was not true.

On Sunday, September 8, 1974, AP's Gaylord Shaw and I walked across Lafayette Park to do the "body watch" on Ford as he attended services at St. John's Episcopal Church. When Ford emerged I had my routine question: What would he be doing for the rest of the day?

Ford paused for a moment and then said tersely, "There will be an announcement shortly."

Shaw and I raced back to the White House pressroom, only to find other reporters and photographers also racing in from all over town.

"Oh, my God, he's going to pardon Nixon," I murmured as we stood together waiting for the announcement. But I still wasn't 100 percent certain until the press aide began passing out the text of the announcement that Ford had granted Nixon a "full, free and absolute pardon."

A short time later, we were ushered into the Oval Office and ordered to stand behind a velvet rope. Ford walked in, looking grim. He had banned any picture-taking or television cameras, an extraordinary move for a statement of that magnitude. He took no questions.

It was clear that his intent was to make the event as low-key as possible—making such a statement on a Sunday morning was hardly the way to alert the nation. But not long afterward, angry groups of people gathered in Lafayette Park and drivers going past the White House honked their horns.

Ford's popularity in the polls dropped 16 points shortly after the announcement. Throughout his vice presidency, he maintained that Nixon had not committed an impeachable act, but at his second news conference, I asked him if he believed that acceptance of a pardon implied Nixon's "admission of guilt" and Ford replied that it could be construed as such, adding that Nixon had resigned in "shame and disgrace."

Following ter Horst in the press secretary's office was Ron Nessen, who made a point of telling us he would never lie but who also accused us of cynicism and mistrust, and he considered our stories on the presidency some kind of personal attack on him, especially those noting Ford's less than graceful stumbles at times.

But overall, Ford enjoyed a good rapport with the press and the traditional "honeymoon period" lasted longer than most. He had been a familiar face at the White House when he was in Congress. When he and Senate Republican leader Hugh Scott would meet with Nixon to review the legislative agenda, they would both come into the pressroom afterward and answer our questions.

At the outset of his administration, Ford kept on many Nixon cabinet members, most notably Secretary of State Henry Kissinger (this reportedly was done at Nixon's request). When asked if Kissinger was indispensable Ford replied he was "indispensable to the country."

Still, the Ford team wasn't too happy when Kissinger told us that he was responsible for 90 percent of the nation's foreign policy decisions. His two-hat trick—secretary of state and national security adviser—came to an end when General Brent Scowcroft was named head of the National Security Council.

Also left behind in the Watergate rubble were several Nixon staffers who thought their tenure might continue with the new Republican president. One of Nixon's speechwriters was John McLaughlin, famous these days for his weekly "McLaughlin Report" television show of raucous, braying political commentary. I asked him one day about his future plans and he responded that he was going to stay on at the White House.

Then, as I was still taking notes with my head lowered, he said, "You really don't think so, do you?"

"No," I said quietly, having heard rumors of a housecleaning.

Ford chose former New York governor Nelson Rockefeller as his vice president. Rockefeller, known for his liberal stances on some issues, took it in good grace when Ford selected Bob Dole as his running mate in 1976, knowing the expediency of politics all too well.

Some presidents evoke extremist feelings no matter how much they may embody the middle ground. It is still inconceivable to me that Ford would be the target of not one but two assassination attempts—both in California, both by women, occurring about two weeks apart in 1975.

In Sacramento on September 5, 1975, Ford had just left the Senator Hotel and was walking to the State Capitol building, taking a shortcut through the park. Lynette "Squeaky" Fromme, dressed in a red cape, suddenly stepped out from the crowd and aimed a .45-caliber pistol point-blank at the president. Secret Service agent Larry Buendorf, within arm's length of her, grabbed the gun and put his hand between the gun's hammer and the firing pin. The gun was loaded but there was no round in the firing chamber.

After she was subdued, she kept repeating, "I can't believe it didn't go off."

Fromme, a follower of convicted mass murderer Charles Manson, was the first woman in history convicted of attempted assassination of a president. But history didn't stop there.

Seventeen days later, in San Francisco, I was in a press pool van in front of the St. Francis Hotel when we heard shots fired from across the street. There was a mad scramble and Secret Service agents shoved Ford into his armored limousine and sped away, with the other vehicles in the motorcade trying to keep up.

Meanwhile, onlookers had wrestled Sara Jane Moore to the ground.

I got in touch with UPI's San Francisco bureau—they were on top of the details while I had been confined to the van. It was a wild night. Later we learned that Ford, lying on the floor of the car, had asked the agents to turn on the air-conditioning.

No one was hurt but I am sure Ford had some trepidation whenever he went out in public after those two incidents. Truth be told, we all did.

In 1976, on the campaign trail, I saw him blanch when, as he was working a rope line shaking hands, a flashbulb in a photographer's camera exploded. It sounded just like a gunshot.

Fromme and Moore both ended up at a women's facility in Alderson, West Virginia, to serve their life sentences. Moore escaped from the prison in 1979 but was recaptured twenty-four hours later. Fromme escaped in 1987 and was recaptured two days later about two miles from the prison.

When John W. Hinckley, convicted in the 1981 assassination attempt on Ronald Reagan, tried to obtain a pass to spend a day off-campus from St. Elizabeth's Hospital where he is serving a life term, officials found letters he had written to Fromme.

And in 1992, when Deborah Butler came close to firing on George Bush, she later told authorities she considered Moore her "role model."

In terms of Ford's presidency, I found it hard to reconcile some paradoxes. Here was a nice guy who could oppose federal aid to education and school lunch programs in the name of fiscal responsibility. Once, Ford traveled to Detroit to make a speech, when the city had been tagged the "murder capital" of the United States due to the extremely high rate of homicides. After the speech, I asked Ford if he might be a little more amenable to gun control after visiting the city and was sorely disappointed when he said no.

He also was reluctant to support civil rights legislation, and yet when he and his son Steve were guests on "Larry King Live" a few years ago, Ford told the story of the year he was selected Most Valuable Player by his teammates on the University of Michigan's football team. On the team was Willis Ward, a black, who was one of Ford's closest friends.

Ford said that southern colleges were "very, very reluctant" to play against a team that had black members and Georgia Tech had told Michigan that unless Ward was kept off the field, they would cancel the game. Ford said he wrote to his father and asked him whether he should quit the team.

Ward went to the coach and withdrew so the game could be played, even though his teammates told him to stand fast. Michigan won the contest 9–7, its only victory that season, and Steve noted his father had been willing to take a stand on racial discrimination as far back as 1934.

In foreign policy, he presided over the end of the Vietnam War, but when asked what were its lessons, he said a bigger defense budget was needed.

He also went to Finland to negotiate the Helsinki accords with Soviet leader Leonid Brezhnev. The accords reduced restrictions to travel in Eastern Europe and expressed a deep concern for human rights.

Ford did a lot of traveling in his short time as president, sometimes making more headlines for the gaffes than the policy. On a visit to Japan, he wore formal attire of striped pants and cutaway coat for his meeting with Emperor Hirohito, but the pants stopped somewhere around his ankles.

In the several interviews I had with him, he was always cordial and frank. One of those interviews, done in tandem with AP's Frank Cormier, was held inside the presidential retreat at Camp David, which had always been off-limits to reporters. I also spoke with the family when they spent their Christmas vacations in Vail, Colorado, but only intermittently. While I take some physical risks for my job, I was not about to don a pair of skis and follow him to the top of a mountain so I could ask a few questions. I would wait for him at the bottom of the hill and when he got there, I'd shout out a few queries.

Ford once said that, as a reporter, I practiced a "fine blend of journalism and acupuncture."

On September 18, 1974, in the first days of his administration, Ford attended the inaugural of Ronald Sarro of the *Washington Star-News* as the new president of the National Press Club. In his remarks, Ford directed some of his banter at me:

> Anybody in public life is well aware of how important the judgments of the press are. I'm firmly convinced that if the good Lord had made the world today, he would have spent six days creating the heavens and earth and all the living creatures upon it. But on the seventh day, he would not have rested. He would have had to justify it to Helen Thomas.

We were told by ter Horst within a week or so after Ford became what was known as the "accidental president" that he had every intention of seeking the presidency on his own.

By the time the 1976 campaign rolled around, however, Ford had some unexpected opposition from Governor Ronald Reagan of California and his strong conservative constituency. At the convention in Kansas City, in search of conservative delegates, Ford had replaced Rockefeller as his running mate with Kansas senator Bob Dole, whose later ballistic outbursts in his debate with vice presidential nominee Senator Walter Mondale of Minnesota made headlines as he blamed the Democrats for everything, including two world wars.

I was in the motorcade when Ford went to pay a courtesy call on Reagan after Ford clinched the Republican presidential nomination. Reagan, as I recall, bitterly rebuffed him.

And we were a little amused when we traveled to Russell, Kansas, where Ford went to pay a call on Dole's mother before the rally. Mrs. Dole, as it turned out, was not at home.

His campaign suffered a bad setback in the debate with Jimmy Carter in Philadelphia when Ford responded to a question by *New York Times* reporter Max Frankel, saying Poland was not under Soviet domination. Frankel gave him a second chance with a follow-up question and Ford unfortunately repeated the gaffe.

Rising inflation and the deleterious effects on the economy also hampered Ford's administration and subsequent presidential campaign, and his "Whip Inflation Now" initiative was a fiasco.

But it was clear he wanted to win the presidency in his own right and he campaigned tirelessly and vigorously against Carter. The morning after the election, it fell to Betty to read her husband's concession statement as Ford was suffering with laryngitis. It read:

Dear Jimmy: It is apparent that you have won our long and intense struggle for the presidency. . . . I congratulate you in your victory. As one who has been honored to serve the people of this great land—both in Congress and as president—I believe that we must now put the divisions of the campaign behind us. . . .

Although there will continue to be disagreements over the best means to us in pursuing our goals, I want to assure you that you will have my complete and wholehearted support as you take the oath of office this January.

I also pledge to you that I and all members of my administration will do all that we can to insure that you begin your term as smoothly and effectively as possible.

May God bless you and your family as you undertake your new responsibilities.

Sincerely, Jerry Ford

On inauguration day, Carter noted Ford's efforts in a difficult time in American history. In his address, he paid tribute to Ford by saying, "For myself and our nation, I want to thank my predecessor for all he has done to heal our land."

Jimmy Carter

From the moment he left the White House on January 20, 1980, Jimmy Carter never looked back. He has since become a most admired ex-president, but his administration was another story.

I always thought that Carter, son of a peanut farmer and former governor of Georgia, saw a higher mission in life for himself, and the presidency was a stepping-stone along the way. His deep convictions about peaceful resolutions and his diplomatic above-the-fray demeanor led to his later career as a mediator and conciliator of conflicts around the world.

The first man from the Deep South elected to the presidency in the twentieth century, he came to Washington in 1976 as an outsider on a campaign billed as "running against the elite establishment." And he left as an outsider. It was a case of never the twain shall meet.

I was sent to the tiny hamlet of Plains in southwest Georgia in 1976 to cover Carter during his presidential campaign. The press stayed at a Best Western Hotel in Americus, hardly the five-star accommodation we had known in other eras with other candidates. Nevertheless, I liked the ambience. The people of Plains were friendly and everybody we ran into was either a friend or a relative who knew Carter and his family from childhood. It all helped me to get a fix on the southern politician who hoped to depose President Ford and to move into the White House.

We conducted the obligatory stakeout across the street from the Carter home. We never knew what he would be up to next, but getting acquainted with his team was fairly easy. The Georgia Mafia he eventually brought to Washington were a group of hotshots planning campaign stops, strategizing and counting delegates.

Carter was busy building a no-nonsense image. But he gave everyone pause when he revealed in an interview in *Playboy* magazine that he had lusted in his heart for other women. In view of what has happened subsequently in American politics, this small sign of human frailty was titillating, certainly not politically fatal—though it did show some naïveté.

During his campaign and after he was elected, Carter had a ritual that gave us the kind of close-up access that we had not had since LBJ. Casually attired, he would walk down Main Street and we would follow or walk beside him, watching him stop every few feet to converse with people and visit the storekeepers. We did not have to look far for colorful future stories, depicting the man from Plains who was destined to become the thirty-ninth president. His walks also gave us an opportunity to ask him questions on the issues of the day, and we often wound up those strolls with "hard news" to call in to our offices.

Another stakeout site where a good story was usually to be found was the all-white Plains Baptist Church. One Sunday, I asked Carter why there were no blacks in the church, and he replied, "I don't know." At some point in his presidency, he began attending a different church, one where blacks and whites worshiped together.

Carter was in his element when he taught Sunday school, which he did often in Plains and in Washington. In Plains, I tried to observe him as he taught an all-male class but was asked to leave. After a loud protest I was allowed to stay. It was fascinating to listen to him discuss his favorite passages of the Bible. For the sake of research and to keep up with the deeply religious candidate, I confess many of us in the press corps liberated a few Gideon Bibles from our hotel, but we did return them eventually.

Another regular stop where I could pick up the local gossip was a service station owned by Carter's brother, Billy. Billy was a favorite of mine. Ask him a question and he would give you an honest answer—maybe too honest for his brother's taste, but refreshing. Billy once told me that he would sleep under the seven-foot bed in the Lincoln Bedroom at the White House because he did not want to ruin his redneck image.

He was easygoing and kind. When he visited the White House he would drop into the pressroom and pay me a visit in the UPI booth, and we would greet each other like long-lost friends.

My other all-time family favorite was "Miz Lillian," a truly remarkable woman who joined the Peace Corps at the age of sixty-eight—her son was making his first bid for governor of Georgia when she saw a television commercial in 1966 that told her "age is no barrier." Her husband had died years earlier and she said she was bored going fishing with her daughter Gloria and playing bridge. She volunteered and asked to go to India where she was able to use her nurse's training at the clinic of a manufacturing company. She also worked in the field, caring for victims of leprosy. When she returned in 1968, she said her time there "meant more to me than any other one thing in my life."

She was a woman who called them as she saw them, which did not endear her to many of the more conservative folks on Main Street. She once sent a birthday cake to Martin Luther King, Jr., when he was arrested and jailed in Americus during a civil rights march.

When her son won the 1976 Democratic presidential nomination, she advised him to "quit that stuff about never telling a lie and being a Christian and how he loves his wife more than the day he met her" and furthermore, pick a "good-looking" running mate.[1]

She lived in what was called the Pond House in Plains that her children had built for her while she was in India, but she held court in her rocking chair at the old campaign headquarters on Main Street, very much the grande dame, signing autographs and posing for hundreds of tourists. There came a time when the pain of the arthritis in her hands prevented her from shaking hands or signing autographs, and her solution was to wrap one arm in a sling. Once I saw a man come up to her and when she drew her hand away, he asked, "May I kiss you?"

"Hell no," Miss Lillian replied.

She once invited me to lunch in the White House mess, the first time I had ever been allowed inside that sacrosanct cafeteria, which was off-limits to all members of the press corps.

In a profile in 1977, *Time* magazine wrote that Miss Lillian asked her son Jimmy, "What you gonna do after you are through being governor?" and he told her, "I'm going to run for president."

"President of what?" she asked.

"Mama, I'm going to run for president of the United States and I'm going to win."

After he won, he quickly set about establishing a new informality. At his swearing-in on January 20, 1977, he wore a business suit instead of formal dress and took the oath of office as "Jimmy Carter" rather than as James Earl Carter, Jr. He and his wife, Rosalynn, disdained the limousine and walked down Pennsylvania Avenue hand in hand from the Capitol to the White House with their nine-year-old daughter, Amy.

We knew then and there that this was going to be a new kind of president who would set a new style, one that involved eliminating several of the trappings of power.

He sold the *Sequoia*, the Navy yacht that had been used by first families for cruises on the Potomac. He stopped the Marine Band from playing "Hail to the Chief" and substituted Irving Berlin's "I'll Be Loving You Always." When he traveled he carried his own bags. He eliminated hard liquor at White House parties and receptions. For female guests who were invited to sit in the presidential box at the Kennedy Center the rule was "no see-through blouses."

He wanted to deimperialize the presidency, and in so doing stripped the office of some of the qualities that give it that sense of awe so many of us are still moved by. He was a micromanager, notorious for making such minor decisions as who would use the White House tennis court.

Carter always seemed to be a man in search of an image. When he moved into the Oval Office, he emulated FDR's "fireside chats" in a televised appearance and he imported for his desk Harry Truman's plaque reading, "The Buck Stops Here." Later into his first term, I noticed he moved the plaque to a side table.

About a thousand days into his tenure, Carter, who had been groping with the energy crisis, put a gloomy assessment on the atmosphere of the country. His pollster, Patrick Caddell, used the phrase *national malaise* at a press briefing and it became the tagline everyone used. To solve the problem, Carter held a "domestic summit" at Camp David that lasted for nearly two weeks during which he summoned academics, outside experts and others to help him to reorganize his administration. They gave him lots of advice, not all of which he took, and he certainly kept his corps of Georgia advisers intact. He did not broaden his base as much as he was advised to do.

But he did make some major changes, including firing several cabinet members, among them Defense Secretary James Schlesinger, whom Carter's advisers had written off as arrogant.

His close friend budget director Bert Lance used to say that Carter "runs liberally and governs conservatively." Lance ran into deep trouble when some of his previous banking dealings came under investigation, and in a painful press conference after many months of trying to deal with the situation, Carter announced Lance's resignation.

Carter was a loner and reclusive—not exactly great attributes for a politician. His efforts to get acquainted with the federal bureaucracy he led had a few strange moments. He would drop in on various cabinet departments to greet the workers and to promote family values, telling government employees, "If you are living in sin, get married, and if you are separated from your spouse, get back together again." Indeed, he was a preacher at heart.

He was compassionate by nature, but often failed to say so much as "good morning" to the uniformed Secret Service agents who worked in the West Wing. (Don't think they didn't notice.) His hero was Admiral Hyman Rickover, and Carter chose the title for one of his books—*Why Not the Best?*—from a comment Rickover had made to him. Around the pressroom we used to call that book "zero-based humility."

Carter had his goals as president, but early on it became evident they ran counter to the Democratic agenda. House Speaker Thomas "Tip" O'Neill and Senate majority leader Robert Byrd tried to coach him in the ways of becoming an insider on Capitol Hill, but he kept marching to his own drummer and there was a disconnect with his lieutenants in Congress. He used to tell the legislators that they were "good instructors" and that he was learning a lot. But I think he resented the "to get along, you go along" attitude. Not surprisingly, while Gerald Ford spent time vetoing bills passed by

Congress, Carter spent a lot of time seeing his legislation get overridden by Congress.

Relations between the two branches only got worse when Carter unexpectedly announced he was rescinding a $50 tax rebate he had proposed for all taxpayers. It did not sit well with congressional Democrats who, against their better judgment, had agreed to support his plan.

High inflation, high unemployment and an energy crisis also plagued his administration, and again, it seemed he lacked a focus. U.S. reliance on foreign oil had climbed to more than 50 percent of total demand. Carter went to work on an energy program that combined conservation and developing more resources at home. Unfortunately, the program, produced in secret, was complex and confusing—and Congress was having none of it.

As far as press relations, there was Carter, chief of staff Hamilton Jordan and press secretary Jody Powell—one White House insider who quickly learned the ways of Washington and put reporters in their place. He was brilliant, glib and many times employed his facile wit as a weapon. "I never have to tell Jody what to say," Carter once remarked, so confident was he of Powell's dexterity and so close was the relationship between the two. One reporter, comparing the White House press operation with previous administrations, said, "Well, they still lie, but they return your phone calls."

Despite the heavy southern atmosphere, Vice President Walter "Fritz" Mondale had no problem fitting into the inner circle. As Carter once described their relationship, "I don't feel threatened by him and he doesn't feel threatened by me."

One of the key women in the Carter White House was Midge Costanza, who was in charge of liaison with women's and other groups. Midge was a ball of fire and popular around the White House. I best remember her comment about her boss, "I don't mind Carter being born again. But did he have to come back as himself?"

He liked to remind us that "I do not intend to lose. . . . I do not intend to make a mistake." Well, mistakes he made—as they all do—but he also had his triumphs.

His greatest contribution was to make human rights the centerpiece of his foreign policy. The lives of many political dissidents in Latin America were saved because of his policies and U.S. intervention.

The Camp David accords stand out as a landmark agreement that opened the way to peace in the Middle East. It was Carter's tolerance and incredible patience that brought Israeli prime minister Menachem Begin and Egypt's Anwar Sadat to the negotiations at the presidential retreat in western Maryland, and compelled them not to leave empty-handed.

Our pressroom was in the VFW Hall in Thurmont, Maryland, and we complained that the Israeli press were getting better and more accurate information than Powell was passing on to us. In fact, the White House put a news blackout on the negotiations while they were under way and we had a very difficult time getting any information on the talks.

Carter's determination also led to the signing of the Panama Canal treaty, which had very strong opposition in Congress. He was able to negotiate the SALT II nuclear arms limitation treaty and even to sign it at a ceremony with Soviet premier Leonid Brezhnev in Vienna. Brezhnev was a very sick man at the time, but I remember his words vividly: "Mankind will never forgive us" if the superpowers did not forge ahead to limit their destructive nuclear arsenals. But the treaty was never ratified and was quickly shelved by the Senate when the Soviet Union invaded Afghanistan.

But even those foreign policy initiatives couldn't help Carter on November 4, 1979—one year before the next presidential election—when Iranians seized the U.S. embassy in Tehran and held 53 Americans hostage. Over 444 days, newspapers and television focused on the crisis and it became the blight of the Carter presidency.

There were sleepless nights and tense days at the White House and Carter became a virtual prisoner in the Oval Office as he made repeated attempts to negotiate the hostages' release.

In 1980, he gave the green light for the ill-fated military rescue mission that turned into a nightmare. The operation had to be aborted because several helicopters broke down and worse, one of them collided with a transport plane and eight crew members were killed. Carter took full responsibility.

It was not a question of helplessness. Carter was a man of peace and he did not want to jeopardize the lives of the hostages when he felt there was still a chance to avoid bloodshed and to bring them back alive. After all the tears, they were released at nearly the same time Ronald Reagan was sworn in as the fortieth president.

I was with Carter on the West Coast when he made his last few campaign stops in November 1980, and it was clear to all that he would not be reelected to a second term. It was one of the gloomiest atmospheres I've ever witnessed aboard Air Force One.

In fact, gloom seemed to dominate the entire 1980 campaign with Carter enduring Reagan's "there you go again" in the presidential debates, to the ridicule when he recounted, in discussing the nuclear threat, that his daughter had come home from school one day and asked, "Daddy, what's a megaton?"

He also had to contend with a breakaway Democratic faction that was supporting Senator Edward Kennedy for the presidency. Carter portrayed himself as a man for the 1980s who favored belt-tightening, lowered expectations and aspirations, and he kept expounding that there were no magic answers to the problems the nation faced. In the end, Carter prevailed and won the nomination at the Democratic National Convention in New York. But I will never forget that sad and humiliating moment on the big stage when Carter went over to shake Kennedy's hand and Kennedy turned away from him.

In an interview at the White House with a few reporters, Carter told us, "I want to be close to you." The words were nice, but practicing them was another thing. I remember how he would give us the slip when we were on "body watch" at Camp David and head for a favorite fishing spot in Pennsylvania.

Furthermore, he did not live up to his word of holding regular news conferences when the going got tough, but that is par for the course. I do believe that Carter's religion served him in good stead and helped him through some of the crises that inevitably fall on presidential shoulders. As one reporter put it, "Politics doesn't affect Carter's religion. Religion affects his politics."

I interviewed him a few months after he left office. He was philosophical about his defeat with no trace of bitterness and, at that time, kept most of his feelings about Reagan to himself. He was ready to move on to new projects, new challenges and new achievements. What he has accomplished as an ex-president has been impressive: from author to carpenter to diplomat-without-portfolio. Retirement doesn't seem to be a word in his vocabulary.

In February 1990, he persuaded Daniel Ortega, leader of the Sandinista National Liberation Front, to concede to Violetta Chamorro in the Nicaraguan presidential elections that Carter had monitored.

In 1993, the United States and North Korea were at a tense standoff over North Korea's repeated refusal to allow inspectors into its nuclear facilities. Korean President Kim Il Sung declared that proposed sanctions to thwart his country's nuclear program would be considered an act of war. Consequently, the Senate voted to beef up U.S. forces in South Korea as a backup to possible sanctions.

Carter traveled to North Korea, sat down with Kim Il Sung and persuaded him to modify the nuclear program.

In December 1994, he went to war-torn Bosnia and patched together an initial truce that got Serbs and Muslims communicating. In September 1994, he arrived in Haiti with former Joint Chiefs chairman Colin Powell and Senator Sam Nunn of Georgia to meet with Lt. General Raoul Cedras, who had overthrown the civilian government in 1991. The U.S. team forged an agreement with Cedras to end military control of the government and managed to avert an imminent U.S. military invasion of the island nation.

His Atlanta-based Carter Center works on conflict resolution in the world's trouble spots, initiates public health programs, coordinates immunization efforts for children all over the world and runs agricultural education programs. Among its achievements was a significant reduction of river blindness in third-world countries and the near-elimination of Guinea worm disease, which once infected millions of people in India and Africa.

He and Rosalynn are the best-known volunteers for Habit for Humanity, a volunteer organization that builds homes for the needy, the dispossessed and victims of natural disasters. One house he helped build in 1994 was for seventy-seven-year-old Annie Mae Rhodes of Albany, Georgia, who lost her home to flooding in the region. She had worked as a nanny for the Carter family in 1933.

He has had other mountains to climb, including some real ones. He climbed Mount Kilamanjaro in 1986 and Mount Fuji in 1994.

In April 1998, the Navy named its newest submarine the U.S.S. *Jimmy Carter* in honor of his military service.

He has written eight books, including a volume of poetry, and has joked now and then that one can always find them in the remainder bin of any bookstore. Some have sniped that he failed to follow the life of quiet retirement that has long been customary for many presidents, but as he explained in a 1995 interview with the *Los Angeles Times,* he is simply continuing the life he had in the White House. "A lot of people distrusted my motivations and thought my expressions were not sincere," he said. "Others thought that someone who talks about peace, human rights and environmental quality is weak; that it's better to be macho and send in troops. . . . I have no regrets about who I am or what I did."[2]

Ronald Reagan

> No, no. Jimmy Stewart for president. Ronald Reagan for best friend.
> —Warner Bros. studio chief Jack Warner

Of all the presidents I've covered, for Ronald Reagan it was the role of a lifetime. The former actor who became the nation's fortieth president had a singular mission in his administration: to turn the country to the right.

Indeed, there was a Reagan Revolution and it brought to power a conservative movement that has pervaded American politics since he left office.

Reagan, who hailed from rural Illinois, grew up in the pre-Depression years and after graduating from Eureka College followed his star to a radio station in Des Moines, Iowa. From that point on he was always at home in front of a microphone and later a camera. It was here that he learned to become "the great communicator."

Wending his way to Hollywood he became a movie star. In that period he served six times as head of the Screen Actors Guild. In that liberal setting, he was pro-union, pro-labor and an activist Democrat. But as his film career waned and he found the movie offers more B- than A-list, he turned to television and became the host of the popular "General Electric Theater." He made a number of speeches at GE conventions and trade shows, and along the way began to embrace conservative politics. In the 1950s, he changed political parties. He also reached the ideological conclusion that government was too big, too intrusive and cost too much—something he learned in his high-paying actor days. That philosophy stayed with him through the rest of his life.

He came to the attention of GOP power brokers with a speech at the Republican National Convention in San Francisco in 1964, when Senator Barry Goldwater won the presidential nomination. That appearance also catapulted him into politics, and in 1966, he ran for governor of California and won two terms of office.

He launched presidential campaigns in 1968 and 1976. As it turned out, the unelected incumbent Gerald Ford had to fend off Reagan in the primaries all the way to the convention.

In 1980, he had made short work of all his rivals—Bob Dole and George Bush among them—in the primaries and had sewn up the nomination long before the delegates convened in Detroit in July. There was just one problem: He hadn't named a running mate.

In one of the quirkier notes of political history, he approached Gerald Ford about joining the ticket. Discussions revolved around Ford seeking assurances that he be given a much more expanded role, but there was another concern in play: Both men were California residents and the Constitution would have prohibited members of the electoral college from California from voting for both men. For Ford, there was another, more important concern: the public perception of such a move. In the end, Ford declined the offer and Reagan said later, "His instinct told him it was not the right thing to do." His former primary rival George Bush got the nod.

In the debates with Jimmy Carter, Reagan scored points with his broadbrush approach, his easy, relaxed manner, his arguments about the "window of vulnerability" in the nation's security and the growing Soviet threat. He also had the advantage in those debates since he had a copy of the briefing book Carter used to prepare for their encounter. The book apparently had been delivered by a still-unidentified "mole" who had access to the Carter White House.

His campaign agenda was simple: Reduce the federal bureaucracy to the point of obliteration, deregulate wherever possible and destroy the "Evil Empire." As he often said, "Government is the problem, not the solution." He was so stalwart in his stance against government intrusion that he refused to check the $1 box on his income tax form as a political contribution. His aides used to explain he was against the checkoff "on principle." But he still accepted $26 million in federal campaign funds in his runs for the White House.

As a candidate, he was as insulated from the press as Richard Nixon was in 1968. His managers, strategists and handlers did their jobs extremely well—push the message and keep him away from the media.

At the start of his first administration, he put in charge of every agency men and women whose goals hardly matched that agency's mandate. Secretary of Interior James Watt was a prime advocate of turning the nation's finite resources over to private interests. Anne Gorsuch Burford, head of the Environmental Protection Agency, had voted against every environmental bill when she was a member of the Colorado legislature.

Some officials didn't exactly follow the leader. Education Secretary Terrell Bell found himself at odds with the Reagan White House, as one of his boss's campaign promises was to abolish the department. Bell had served there during the Nixon administration and had helped initiate a number of federal aid programs. He tried to resign his post but Reagan refused the resignation. Bell then went on to have the department publish the landmark study "A Nation at Risk," outlining the declining state of American education. The report drew considerable public response and instead of dismantling the agency, Bell found himself in the spotlight. He still resigned, in 1985, when larger cuts in the department's budget were proposed.

The primary issue and the predominant news story during the Reagan years was the federal budget deficit. It more than doubled in the 1980s, from less than 3 percent of the gross domestic product in 1980 to 6.3 percent in 1983. The United States ceased being the world's creditor nation and became the world's largest debtor nation. Between 1981 and 1983, unemployment rose to 10.8 percent; more than 11.5 million people lost their jobs and a new, unnerving social condition began hitting the nation: homelessness.

To address all that, it was "Reaganomics" to the rescue, the president's policy that included supply-side, free-market, deregulatory action. We all got a 1 percent tax cut and he got to increase defense spending by 9 percent.

By the end of 1988, the country was $1.5 trillion deeper in debt than the day he took office.

During his first year in office, a leaked story in the *Washington Post* said that Reagan was prepared to secretly spend $1 trillion on a new weapons program over the coming five years. The administration responded to the leaked information by ordering the twenty-five officials who had attended the secret meeting to take lie detector tests. Five years later, it was disclosed that Reagan had spent $1.5 trillion on the modern weapons program, many of the designs still on the drawing board when the Cold War ended.

Reagan's polls dropped considerably as the recession ground on; at his lowest point in early 1983 they were at 35 percent. But by the campaign season of 1984, the employment picture brightened, the inflation rate dropped dramatically and his popularity went up, contributing to his landslide victory in 1984.

Through all of this, we reporters marveled—and chafed—at the state-of-the-art management and manipulation of the news that the Reagan staffers brought with them. His deputy chief of staff—and chief image-maker—Michael Deaver would decide what was the "story of the day" or the "picture of the day" and we were at his mercy. Aiding him were two of what came to be known as the Reagan troika, chief of staff James Baker and Edwin Meese, who held the title counselor to the president. They scripted their boss every day, every inch of the way. I always thought Reagan was more than adept at handling himself in any situation, including dealing with us, but we hardly ever got the chance to find out.

He had his own methods of avoiding our questions that didn't require a script. He developed a habit of cupping his ear to let us know he couldn't hear us when he headed for the presidential helicopter or he'd point to his watch. Often, Rex, the reigning White House dog—a King Charles spaniel given to him by columnist William F. Buckley—would run interference to distract us.

I remember a campaign stop in 1980 when we went to the rubble-ridden Bronx. Standing in an open lot, surrounded by decaying buildings in the blighted neighborhood, Reagan, standing alone in a Deaver-managed cameo appearance, told us "We're going to change all this." He never did.

The audacity and arrogance of his staff was something to behold and it was beyond me how they not only helped their boss run the country but also took care of business without telling him. Meese attained a certain amount of notoriety when Reagan was in California on August 19, 1981, and U.S. Navy jets shot down two Libyan fighter jets in the Gulf of Sidra. He decided not to wake the president and inform him of what had happened.

The most amazing thing to me occurred at the end of Reagan's first term, when Baker switched jobs with Treasury Secretary Donald Regan. Not that there's anything unusual about what they did, but they apparently decided to put the plan in motion and then consult the boss—or so went the buzz around the pressroom. I think any other president would have been apoplectic over such presumption and the usurpation of his authority, but Reagan later wrote he thought it was a fine idea.

Baker had been looking for a way out of his chief of staff job and had asked Reagan to consider him for the top job at the National Security Council after Bill Clark notified the president he'd like to step down. Baker proposed that Mike Deaver take over as chief of staff, but Meese, Clark, CIA director William Casey and Defense Secretary Casper Weinberger were opposed and were able to block it with Reagan.

Two weeks before he was inaugurated the second time, Reagan wrote, Regan and Baker "came to me separately in the Oval Office with a proposal. It was Regan's idea. . . . They told me they wanted to swap jobs. After I thought it over I approved the switch, thinking the enthusiasm both would bring to their new jobs would be good for the administration." [1]

Nevertheless, Reagan's team worked well for him. The problem was that they didn't always work well with each other. There were continual turf wars between Meese, the voice for the conservatives in the White House, and Baker, one of the more pragmatic Republicans, who was protective of the political interests of Vice President George Bush, his friend and fellow Texan.

Over at State, Alexander Haig always seemed to be out of sync with the Reagan team and was often undercut. Of course, he attracted some bad publicity with his "I am in control here" after the assassination attempt on Reagan in 1981. He resigned in 1982, frustrated in his tenure and a victim of the palace guard. His successor, George Shultz, fared better and served Reagan until he left office in 1989. Many believe Shultz was a steadying, stabilizing influence on the administration's foreign policy, until Iran-Contra broke and Shultz was not a team player.

Reagan was known to all as "Mr. Nice Guy" and he did convey his campaign theme of "morning in America" to the country in every way imaginable.

But it was hard to reconcile "Mr. Nice Guy" with someone who said the homeless sleep on grates "because they want to," or headed an administration that said ketchup was a vegetable for school lunch programs or, as I heard Ed Meese tell me and two other wire service reporters, that there were no hungry children in America and people went to soup kitchens because the food was free.

Still, "Mr. Nice Guy," with his engaging style, his charm and his correct, albeit 1940s attire seemed to be what most Americans were looking for in a president. He was at home in the Oval Office and when it came to his work habits, he joked easily about "burning the midday oil" and putting a sign on his chair that said, "Ronald Reagan slept here."

His management style was strictly chairman of the board and he described it in his book *An American Life*:

> I don't believe a chief executive should supervise every detail of what goes on in his organization. The chief executive should set broad policy and general ground rules, tell people what he or she wants them to do, then let them do it; he should make himself (or herself) available, so that members of his team can come to him if there is a problem. If there is, you can work on it and if necessary, fine-tune the policies. But I don't think a chief executive should peer constantly over the shoulders of the people who are in charge of a project and tell them every few minutes what to do.[2]

Reagan had confidence, strong convictions and his views seemed to be set in concrete, yet he could compromise if necessary. As the plaque on his desk said, "There is no limit to how far you can go or what you can do if you don't care who gets the credit."

He may have seemed simplistic at times, but when it came to talking to people, there was no one who could compare to him. His stable of speechwriters came up with the draft, but Reagan came up with the delivery. He would rewrite a speech in a way that connected with every American, and practiced every pause and the cadence until he had it down with his own perfect timing.

That timing showed in August 1981 when, during a photo opportunity in the Oval Office, I asked him if he would have something to say about the air traffic controllers' strike. His staff went ballistic that I'd had the audacity to ask a question, but fifteen minutes later he came out into the Rose Garden and signed an executive order firing the thirteen thousand striking controllers. The action was viewed as a signal to business that there would be no concessions to organized labor.

The irony was not lost on many when, in 1998, the Republican-dominated Congress renamed Washington's National Airport the Ronald Reagan Washington National Airport.

In that same year, another ironic honor came to the ex-president. Long known for his crusade against big government and federal spending, an $816 million, 3.1-million-square-foot building was dedicated as the Ronald Reagan Building and International Trade Center. By the way, it's second in size only to the Pentagon. And one of its tenants is the Environmental Protection Agency, which Reagan tried so mightily to diminish.

Reagan held the first of his prime-time news conferences in the East Room in January 1981 and made no pretense about his lack of regard for the Soviets. Responding to a question by ABC's Sam Donaldson, he said they "reserve unto themselves the right to commit any crime, to lie, to cheat."

In 1983, the Russians shot down a Korean airliner that had strayed into Soviet airspace, killing all 269 people aboard. An irate Reagan said, "We can stop fooling ourselves" and relations between the two superpowers devolved into an angry exchange between Reagan and Soviet leader Yuri Andropov in speeches and public announcements. The incident fueled the hostile fires, and while the Soviet Union got a black eye for its handling of the event, the Reagan administration appeared to be the voice of reason.

As usual, I got the first or second question at those news conferences and I remember that Reagan would always nod at me and say "Helen . . ." a little hesitantly. I threw him the best I had, but most times he was able to deflect the substance of most of our questions. Once, though, I had him at a loss for words.

In 1982, as the congressional session was ending, it appeared that the MX missile program was going to be killed. Reagan summoned the leaders of both parties to the Oval Office to see if a compromise could be worked out. After the meeting, he came into the pressroom and announced rather triumphantly that a compromise had been worked out to continue funding for the missile program. Reagan began his remarks by praising the leaders for their patriotism and their ability to work out a deal. He went on and on and finally I asked him, "Mr. President, what *is* the compromise?"

He stopped cold, then turned to Senator John Tower of Texas and asked if he would be so kind as to explain the details of the compromise. Tower stepped up to the platform and Reagan disappeared from the room. As I said, he never wanted to be bothered with the details. But he was always gracious and never seemed to take offense at being put on the spot.

I was on my way to Rhode Island to address a UPI press gathering when John Hinckley, Jr., shot at Reagan on March 30, 1981, outside the Washington Hilton Hotel. As soon as my plane had landed in Providence, I heard the PA system paging me, got to a telephone, and then got on the next plane back to Washington.

One bullet had struck Reagan in the chest, but more critically wounded was his press secretary James Brady, who was shot in the head and suffered permanent paralysis on his right side. The president was rushed to George Washington Hospital, where the trauma unit was already on alert and Reagan immediately went into surgery.

The spin doctors went on alert as well, quick to set the stage and control the information so that the country never knew until months later how critically Reagan was injured. During his recovery, I interviewed Dr. Daniel Ruge, the White House physician, and he said that Reagan could have bled to death if they had not gotten him to the hospital quickly and the trauma unit had not been on hand.

Reagan was lucky. The administration had signaled that in the coming weeks they planned to cut federal funding for such emergency services around the country.

Reagan's longtime political strategist Lyn Nofziger, a former press officer, took over the briefings at GW Hospital. Deaver supplied the color and the lighter touches to demonstrate that all was well. We could write that the president was on the road to recovery. He passed the word that Reagan took one look at his doctors who were ready to operate and quipped, "I hope you're all Republicans" and that when he first saw his wife, Nancy, after the shooting, he said, "Honey, I forgot to duck."

Jim Gerstenzang, then with Associated Press, and I were among the first to be granted an interview with Reagan when he returned to the White House. He described for us the "sharp" pain that he first felt after he was shoved into his limousine and Jerry Parr, the chief of his Secret Service detail, fell on him as the motorcade sped to the hospital. He also said he felt the "hand of God" was on his shoulder and that his mission in life was still to be accomplished.

I remember asking Reagan if now he would be in favor of gun control, given the assassination attempt. He replied he could not support such legislation, but that he favored tough sentences for anyone using a gun in a crime. Ten years later, he expressed his support for the Brady gun control bill, which requires a five-day waiting period to purchase a handgun.

In July 1985, Reagan underwent surgery for colon cancer and spokesman Larry Speakes, who was told how much he could and could not tell the press, withheld the details for as long as he could after the operation. He also refused to read on camera Reagan's letter to Bush turning over the powers of the presidency to him while he was under anesthesia.

Copies of the letter had been passed out and the television correspondents began broadcasting the crucial news from their seats, disrupting Speakes' briefing. I told him it behooved him to read the letter aloud, since he was on camera anyway.

Murphy's Law prevailed throughout Reagan's stay at Bethesda Naval Hospital. Nancy got upset when a battery of Reagan's surgeons came into the briefing room to discuss the president's operation. Their many medical terms puzzled us and when we asked for clarification, Dr. Stephen Rosenberg, the head of the National Cancer Institute, stepped forward and said simply: "The president has cancer."

That was quite the bombshell and the consequent fallout was considerable. It would have been a lot easier if the White House had just told the truth rather than gone into its usual spin. In fact, sometime later when I interviewed Reagan with another AP correspondent, Reagan just said simply, "I *had* cancer" and he was confident that he had conquered the disease.

The spinners finally got with it, however, and Reagan's recuperation was dubbed as "spectacular" with the president eager to get back on his horse and ride the range. We were told the president was in good spirits and wanted to get back to the job of running the country.

We've all become used to listening to a president's Saturday morning radio address but may not remember that it was Reagan who instituted the practice. He was a pro when it came to speaking on the radio and he used the medium well—except once. During a warmup one morning for his speech, he was unaware the mike was open and said, "My fellow Americans, I am pleased to announce I have just signed legislation which outlaws Russia forever. The bombing begins in five minutes."

When he ordered the invasion of Grenada, he appeared in the pressroom with Prime Minister Eugenie Charles of Dominica to inform us that American troops had landed on the island.

"What right do we have to invade a foreign country?" I asked him.

He paused for a moment, looking a bit bewildered at the question, and Charles jumped in, declaring that it was not an invasion; it was simply a move to protect Americans on the island.

There was a press blackout and reporters and photographers were barred from the Caribbean island for several days. When Reagan made a triumphal appearance in Grenada, we went along with him. At a press reception later, Reagan extolled Thomas Jefferson and the First Amendment. When he came down the line to shake our hands, Sam Donaldson and I peppered him with questions on why the press had been barred from covering the operation while at the same time he was praising Thomas Jefferson. "Thomas Jefferson would have lost the war," he told us.

When American troops were sent to Beirut as peacekeepers, I remember *Washington Times* reporter Jerry O'Leary, a former military man, asking Reagan at a news conference why they were not on the high ground. Reagan said it was because the airport was flat. When a truck bomb exploded near the barracks, killing 241 Marines in October 1983, Reagan came out on the South Lawn, made a brief statement in which he took full responsibility, then headed for the helicopter that was taking him on a trip. That was his only public statement of the tragedy.

In 1984, when it became clear that American forces in Beirut were in danger, Reagan quietly decided to pull them out. He traveled to California to spend a few days at his ranch near the Santa Ynez Mountains. At the airport, Speakes handed out a brief statement announcing that the American troops in Lebanon were being redeployed. Most of the press corps was still in Albuquerque, New Mexico, filing their stories and the White House knew there were few Saturday papers, so the late announcement would not get much play. By the time the weekend was over, there was only a sense of relief on the part of Americans who began to feel that it was a no-win situation for Marines to be posted in Lebanon.

The centerpiece of Reagan's foreign policy was, like most of his agenda, a simple one, nurtured by his antipathy over the years: to break the back of communism in Europe. One method to achieve that was to push the arms race with Moscow and to spend the Soviets into bankruptcy. From that view came the idea for the Strategic Defense Initiative—"Star Wars." The program, if it worked, would give the United States a distinct advantage over the Soviets. The only problem was that no one knew if SDI would really work— or if the technology even existed. But Reagan's commitment to the plan worried the Soviets. Whether it was actually feasible or just an ace up Reagan's sleeve in arms negotiations didn't matter. Soviet leader Mikhail Gorbachev made it the focus of his discussions with Reagan, seeking assurances the United States would forgo its development and accusing Reagan of seeking first-strike capability.

But prodded by his wife and overtures for some rapprochement from Gorbachev, who was beginning to open the Kremlin's windows a bit, Reagan softened his view somewhat and began serious discussions on nuclear arms reduction. The Strategic Arms Limitation Treaty, which had been shelved after the Soviets invaded Afghanistan, gave way to a new administration proposal, START, or strategic arms reduction treaty, which was signed in 1982.

Reagan and Gorbachev met in Geneva in 1985 and Gorbachev accepted Reagan's invitation to visit the United States in 1986. Earlier that year, the Soviets had offered a proposal that both sides withdraw their intermediate nuclear missiles from Europe over the next several years, what was known as the Zero-Zero option. At their summit in Reykjavík, Iceland, in October 1986, Reagan reaffirmed the Zero-Zero option and added the removal of shorter-range missiles. Gorbachev, however, stubbornly linked the deal to Reagan's assurance that the United States would not move forward on SDI. Reagan, just as stubbornly, insisted on developing SDI and softened the line by saying that once the system was operational, the Soviets could share in the technology. Gorbachev then offered to cut strategic weapons by 50 percent if Reagan would back off SDI, but he continued to resist.

I had been staked out a few yards from the house with other members of the press corps for several hours in the biting cold. We literally froze, and were not amused to see some of Reagan's top aides looking out the window of the warm house, holding cups of tea. Our only realization that the Iceland summit was a flop was when we saw Reagan and Gorbachev bidding each other good-bye and stepping into their limousines. Their expressions told the whole story. They had failed, and they had only a few courteous words as they parted company. For several months, the arms control issue stayed at a stalemate, until Gorbachev in April offered to dismantle all shorter-range missiles from Europe. In 1987, negotiators finally nailed down a pact to remove 2,500 U.S. and Soviet missiles from Europe, and that December, the two leaders signed the Intermediate Nuclear Forces Treaty, which provided for on-site inspections by both sides, or, as Reagan had put it, "trust but verify."

In June 1987, after the economic summit in Venice, Reagan traveled to West Berlin and spoke at an outdoor gathering at the Brandenburg Gate. He later wrote he considered the Berlin Wall "as stark a symbol as anyone could ever expect to see of the contrast between two different political systems,"[3] and he delivered one of his most memorable addresses of his administration: "General Secretary Gorbachev, if you seek peace, if you seek prosperity for the Soviet Union and Eastern Europe, if you seek liberalization: Come here to this gate! Mr. Gorbachev, open this gate! Mr. Gorbachev, tear down this wall!"

The wall finally came down in 1989 after Reagan left office. Many consider him the driving force behind its removal and the point man for a shift in U.S.-Soviet relations. A six-thousand-pound chunk of the dismantled wall was sent for display at Reagan's presidential library.

On Memorial Day weekend in 1988, Reagan held his fourth and final summit with Gorbachev in Moscow. For him, the Evil Empire no longer existed and he was welcomed with open arms. When we returned to Washington, I said to him, "Mr. President do you think that if you had gone to Moscow ten years ago, twenty years ago, you might have found out that the Russians laugh, they cry and they're human?"

"No," he replied. "They've changed." And so had he.

The relentless hawk had come full circle and decided that the United States could do business with the Soviet Union. And while he clung to a military buildup through his two terms, one of his biggest successes was the arms reduction accord, which in turn triggered a global sigh of relief.

Reagan's biggest foreign policy crisis in his second term was the Iran-Contra scandal, which got so bad there were calls for his impeachment. Both he and Secretary of State George Shultz had pounded the podium repeatedly for months, declaring that they would never deal with Iran, a terrorist nation. But Reagan did deal, motivated by compassion for the American hostages in Beirut and the promise that Iran could influence the Hezbollah to release the American captives.

As a result, under a clandestine arrangement implemented by national security adviser Robert McFarlane; his deputy, John Poindexter; and Marine Lt. Colonel Oliver North, arrangements were made for shipments of arms to Iran through Israel to promote the freedom of the hostages.

A Lebanese magazine, *Al Shirra*, disclosed the secret operation, and when first asked about it, Reagan dismissed it as a report from a Middle Eastern "rag." But as the revelations continued and the scandal grew, Reagan went underground. The distraught first lady began calling the Washington insiders, including Robert Strauss, for advice.

Attorney General Edwin Meese first revealed the details of the operation in which arms were sold to the Iranians and the funds from the sales were placed in Swiss bank accounts to be funneled to the Contra rebels who were seeking to overthrow the Sandinista government in Nicaragua—all in direct violation of the Boland Amendments.

The House passed the first Boland Amendment in 1983. Massachusetts Democrat Edward Boland, the chairman of the House Select Committee on Intelligence, sponsored it. It forbade any U.S. covert action to overthrow the Sandinistas and limited CIA financial aid to the Contras to $24 million, with the condition that the money not be used to try to topple the Sandinista government. In late 1984, a second Boland Amendment was passed, which cut all funding for the Contras and specifically forbade any U.S. agency, including the CIA, to aid the Contras in any way.

No evidence has ever shown that Reagan himself broke any laws, but many of his staff did, and the conflicting testimony has been abundant as to whether he understood the illegality of the operation and whether he authorized it. Documents were shredded, White House officials lied to congressional investigating committees and the full truth will likely never be known. On November 13, Reagan tried to portray the arms-for-hostages deal as an effort to reopen relations with Iran's moderates, much in the way Richard Nixon had opened China, and he accused the media of being "sharks in the water" on the story.

In the summer of 1987, Congress convened a special committee to investigate the affair. As the tales of secret deals, cover-ups and back-channel sleight of hand filled the nation's airwaves and newspapers, it was undoubtedly Reagan's darkest hour. The joint committee concluded that the White

House aides had knowingly engaged in deception and had broken the law. Independent counsel Lawrence Walsh, in his report issued in 1994, stated that even though "no reliable evidence" existed that Reagan himself had done so, he had "set the stage" for illegal activities by encouraging continued support for the Contras after Congress had passed the Boland Amendments.

As with the Watergate scandal, the question raised repeatedly was "What did the president know and when did he know it?" He kept saying that he was trying to find out what happened, and I kept saying to Larry Speakes and the other press aides, "Why doesn't he ask Poindexter and North?" Apparently it wasn't that simple, or maybe nobody really wanted to know.

At a news conference and in a televised speech on August 12, 1987, Reagan came as close as he ever had to acknowledging some personal responsibility. "I let my preoccupation with the hostages intrude into areas where it didn't belong," he said. "I have thought long and often about how to explain to you what I intended to accomplish, but I respect you too much to make excuses. The fact of the matter is that there is nothing I can say that will make the situation right. I was stubborn in my pursuit of a policy that went astray."

The scandal had left the administration in shambles; Reagan's credibility with the American public was in question and in an effort to clean up the mess, he brought in former senator Howard Baker of Tennessee as his chief of staff. He won back his popularity and finished his term as one of the most popular presidents in modern history.

So much for the chairman of the board who allowed a second government to be set up in the basement of the White House to carry on covert projects.

Iran-Contra wasn't the only scandal in Reagan's presidency. Over at the Department of Housing and Urban Development, political appointees who knew little about HUD and its programs—not unlike its chief, Samuel Pierce—approved budget cuts that cost the department many of its career civil servants. Several former HUD officials became consultants for construction companies seeking federal funding. A congressional investigation in 1989 later revealed that Pierce and some of his aides used billions of dollars of HUD money for some private transactions that netted contracts for friends and associates.

Some officials implicated in the HUD abuses were former interior secretary James Watt, Pierce himself and former attorney general John Mitchell, who had already served prison time for the Watergate scandal.

Wedtech was another embarrassment, involving fraud and influence buying. In 1981, the company, based in the South Bronx, was foundering. A manufacturer of small engines, it had status as a minority-owned business and had secured a couple of government contracts but had lost out on a five-year contract to build small engines for the Army. That year, the company hired E. Bob Wallach, a close friend of Meese.

In 1982, Lyn Nofziger quit his White House job to open a public relations office and signed Wedtech as a client. After much back and forth, including a meeting at the White House, Wedtech signed a $27.7 million contract with the Army to build gasoline engines and won a $3 million grant from the Small Business Administration. Nofziger and Wallach had shares in the company and things started to unravel in the wake of a stock deal. Several Wedtech officers and consultants sold their shares for something in the neighborhood of $10 million, which got the Securities and Exchange Commission curious. The SBA later revoked Wedtech's minority status. Wallach and another consultant were indicted for racketeering, fraud and conspiracy. Meese also came under investigation. Wallach and Nofizger were convicted as a result of the scandal but Nofziger had his conviction overturned on appeal. Meese was not indicted but several Justice Department aides resigned in protest. Wedtech went out of business.

It was another blow when a report in the *Wall Street Journal* turned out to be in some part a government-inspired disinformation campaign. The newspaper reported on August 25, 1986, citing unidentified intelligence officials, that Libya was plotting new terrorist attacks and noted the United States and Libya were on a "collision course" with each other. The problem was reporters were having a hard time verifying the credibility of the evidence and, more to the point, many government and military officials couldn't confirm it either.

The confusion stemmed from an order Reagan had given to "get two messages across to Libya: that the administration was seeing signs of Libyan involvement in terrorist activity and that it remained ready to punish Libya with military force if that action continued."[4] What Reagan apparently hadn't specified was how to get those jobs done.

According to accounts, it turned out that one or maybe several officials of the National Security Council staff took it upon themselves to provide information for a news article. The *Washington Post* reported on October 2 that the *Journal* had published "false information" provided by the administration. Later, the *Journal* issued a statement that if the government had conducted a "domestic disinformation campaign, we were among its many victims."[5]

It was reminiscent of previous administrations I'd covered where at some time with some policy, the central question was: Does a government have the right to lie? I think not. Apparently, neither did State Department spokesman Bernard Kalb, who quit. In an interview, Kalb, who had spent years covering diplomatic news for CBS and NBC, said he had been "agonizing about this thing. I knew nothing about it. I was concerned. I was concerned with the impact of any such program on the credibility of the United States and the word of America and what the word of America means."[6]

But Shultz defended the idea in principle and when a reporter called the report of such a plan "a serious charge," Shultz countered: "Why is it a charge? If I were a private citizen reading about it, and I read that my government was trying to confuse somebody who was conducting terrorist acts and murdering Americans, I would say 'Gee, I hope it is true.' I don't see why you think this is a charge."[7]

The media thought otherwise and I think Eugene Roberts, then executive editor of the *Philadelphia Inquirer,* put it best. He called the reported campaign "deplorable" but noted it was not the first, nor would it be the last, time the press was deceived "in a systematic way. When critics of the press say the press is too skeptical, this and other similar episodes should be kept in mind. There is good reason for the press to be diligent and unrelenting in its questions."[8]

For all the pointed questions I lobbed at Reagan in his eight years in office, he never seemed to take any personal umbrage, and I think that was true of his attitude toward all the reporters. He even sent me the following letter when I received the National Press Club's Fourth Estate Award in 1984:

Dear Helen:

   I'm delighted to join your colleagues and many friends in congratulating you on being chosen to receive the National Press Club's Fourth Estate Award.

   This award is a well-deserved tribute to your exemplary professionalism as a journalist. You have a worldwide reputation for being the best—always first, always accurate, always fair. Millions of citizens are enlightened through your work and you are [an] inspiration to all who seek to be good reporters. Hardly a day goes by when I don't ask the staff, "what is Helen writing?" For your experience and wisdom have become a barometer on the issues of the day.

   You are not only a fine and respected professional; you have also become an important part of the American Presidency. I am proud to salute you tonight.

Sincerely,
Ronald Reagan

Of course, he held only three press conferences in his first eight months in office (he held a total of forty-four in eight years), rarely gave interviews and preferred to make pronouncements rather than allow a follow-up. And no matter what the scandal du jour of his administration, Democratic congresswoman Pat Schroeder's term *Teflon president* was never truer than with Reagan. No matter how he was treated by the media, he stayed popular.

The consummate politician even when he wasn't seeking office, Reagan campaigned for Vice President George Bush like no other president for a selected successor. He traveled back and forth across the country, made at least two appearances a week and would announce triumphantly, "We are the change." He skewered Democrats with what became known as the dreaded "L-word," and branded Democratic presidential candidate Michael Dukakis as "liberal, liberal, liberal," making it a term of opprobrium.

He always would conclude his remarks at a rally to win one last one "for the Gipper," a reference to one of his favorite film roles as football star George Gipp in *Knute Rockne, All American.*

On Bush's inauguration day, January 20, 1989, the presidential helicopter made one final circle of the White House for the Reagans before they headed to Andrews Air Force Base and home to California.

The Reagans moved into their new elegant home in Bel Air and he followed the agenda of most past presidents, to build their libraries and to write their memoirs. They also made a brief visit to Japan in 1989. They flew in a specially equipped Boeing 747 with a retinue of 20 staffers, a dozen Secret Service agents and 229 U.S. military dependents invited to visit their relatives stationed in Japan. Reagan was interviewed on Japanese television, made two speeches and came home $2 million richer. It was one time his adoring public was not amused and his popularity dropped for a time.

There was only one other time I can think of when Reagan drew outrage and disappointment from his fellow Americans, and that was his visit to the Bitburg cemetery in 1985. West German chancellor Helmut Kohl had invited Reagan to make a state visit following the economic summit in Bonn. The two decided to make the visit a celebration of the fortieth anniversary of the end of World War II, and Kohl invited Reagan to visit the military cemetery at Bitburg. Buried at the cemetery were soldiers of Hitler's army and forty-eight members of the Waffen SS, the agency that had direct responsibility for carrying out the Holocaust.

Public opinion polls showed that most Americans opposed Reagan visiting the site and even the first lady weighed in against it. But Reagan was determined not to embarrass Kohl, and the chancellor tried to alleviate some of the pressure by inviting Reagan to visit the concentration camp at Dachau as well. Reagan ended up visiting both Bitburg and the concentration camp at Bergen-Belsen, where he delivered an address in honor of the Holocaust victims. Chief of staff Donald Regan later wrote that the visit to Bitburg was "an almost inconceivable blunder."

In February 1994, Reagan spoke to 2,500 people at a celebration of his eighty-third birthday in Washington. Before the dinner he chatted with a number of people, including British prime minister Margaret Thatcher, but he seemed to have difficulty recognizing others. In September 1994, while recording speeches in support of several Republican congressional candidates, he had trouble reading from the TelePrompTer and later said, "You know, I am not remembering things well."

On November 5, 1994, he released a handwritten letter in which he told that he had been diagnosed with Alzheimer's disease. "I now begin the journey," he wrote, "that will lead me into the sunset of my life. I know that for America there will always be a bright dawn ahead."

George Bush

HT: Did the prime minister bring a check along? And have you solved the rice problem? And do you think there's a growing anti-Japan sentiment in this country?

GB: I can handle this one. Before I answer the question may I say that I predicted with 100 percent accuracy who would ask the first question and what it would be.

—George Bush responding to Helen Thomas, Kennebunkport, July 11, 1991

George Bush's political career was grounded in statesmanship and he carried that background into his presidency. He was a chief executive who evinced great personal courage and humanity, but he always seemed to be at odds with the public's perception of his leadership.

He was a well-born son from a privileged background who loved pork rinds, country music and zipping around in his speedboat. He had a patrician air about him but he took the ideas of duty and public service seriously. He took pains to project an image of self-control but he had one of the worst poker faces I've ever seen. He could focus with pinpoint accuracy when it came to dealing with global problems and global leaders but he seemed to have trouble with "the vision thing." The word around the White House when he took office was now it was time for an administration guided by noblesse oblige, but like a kid on Christmas morning, he seemed to take a unique delight in being president and he never got over how special it was to hold the highest office in the land.

Sarah McClendon, who covered him during his days as a Texas congressman, said his nickname at the CIA was "Ice Pick"—and yet just before his election as president, the term *wimp* got pinned on him and he spent four years trying to yank it off.

He guided the nation through an air and land war with Iraq, he ousted corrupt Panamanian leader Manuel Noriega, but he took a lot of heat for what many considered a lack of action toward China after Tiananmen Square. He worked with Soviet leaders Mikhail Gorbachev and Boris Yeltsin to improve relations and witnessed communism's collapse. On the day the Berlin Wall fell, a subdued Bush told a group of us in the Oval Office, "I'm very pleased," but he was not about to "beat my chest and dance on the wall." We had expected to see an exuberant Bush and were shocked at his restraint. He later said he did not want to gloat over what was considered a defeat for Gorbachev.

Oh, yes: He loved his dog Ranger and he hated broccoli.

The son of Connecticut's senator Prescott Bush, he began his political career as a representative in Congress in the Texas delegation. In the Nixon administration, he served as U.S. ambassador to the United Nations and as chief of the Republican National Committee. President Ford sent him to China as head of the U.S. Mission in Beijing in 1974 and he returned in 1976 to become CIA director.

He landed on the national political stage when he launched a presidential run in 1980 and gained headlines when he called Ronald Reagan's fiscal policies "voodoo economics." When Reagan had a lock on the presidential nomination and nabbed 1,939 out of 1,994 delegate votes at the convention in Detroit, his choice of running mate was still a mystery. There had been talks with Gerald Ford that didn't lead anywhere. Reagan later called Bush and told him, "It seems to me that the fellow who came closest and got the next most votes for president ought to be the logical choice for vice president. Will you take it?"[1]

As vice president, Bush was the soul of discretion, and the model of a team player. He made sure he did not step on any toes of the men in Reagan's inner circle or give them any cause to believe he had an agenda of his own.

On March 30, 1981, Bush was traveling in Texas with House majority leader Jim Wright and Republican congressmen Jim Collins and Bill Archer. The plane he was flying in, designated Air Force Two, was the Boeing 727 that had brought Lyndon Johnson to Texas for John F. Kennedy's visit to the state on November 21, 1963. Bush had attended a ceremony at the Hyatt Hotel in Fort Worth. The building was formerly known as the Old Texas Hotel and it was where JFK spent his last night.

When word reached them in Austin that Reagan had been shot, the plane refueled and returned to Washington. Arriving at Andrews, Bush chose to go to the vice president's residence and then by car to the White House, telling an aide, "Only the president lands on the South Lawn." Walking into the White House Situation Room, he was informed of Reagan's condition and told those assembled he would meet with the congressional leadership and the cabinet the next day. "The more normal things are, the better," he said. "If reports about the president's condition are encouraging, we want to make the government function as normally as possible. Everybody has to do his job."[2]

He was, in the words of chief of staff James Baker, a "model vice president" for eight years.

He launched his candidacy for the party's presidential nomination on October 13, 1987, in Houston, promising "steady and experienced leadership," but early on, he found himself tarred by the Iran-Contra brush. In the Iowa caucuses he finished third, behind Bob Dole and Pat Robertson. He bounced back in New Hampshire, coming in nine points ahead of Dole. On the following "Super Tuesday," he took 57 percent of all votes cast. A strong victory in Pennsylvania put him over the top with 1,139 delegates.

On Iran-Contra, he told a reporter for the *Washington Post* that he was "not in the loop," drawing a distinction between initiating and implementing policy. His opponents sought to portray his position as a contradiction since he had attended meetings where the policy, already approved by Reagan, was discussed. Later on he amended his statements to say his role was "not operational," although he had received national security briefings on the subject and did not oppose it.

In his acceptance speech at the Republican National Convention, he called for a "kinder, gentler nation" to be achieved through volunteerism, and warned that citizens must not sit and wait for Washington to set the rules—and he urged America's cultural diversity to create "a new harmony, like stars, like a thousand points of light in a broad and peaceful sky."

For the record, the Thousand Points of Light Foundation that grew out of his venture to encourage Americans to volunteer is now housed on two floors of a building where UPI's Washington headquarters used to be.

While he was pushing his "kinder, gentler" message, his campaign team, headed by Lee Atwater and Roger Ailes, composed the now-infamous attack ads against the Democratic nominee, Governor Michael Dukakis of Massachusetts. None was more notorious than the Willie Horton campaign.

Horton had served a three-year term in South Carolina for assault with intent to kill, and had been convicted in Massachusetts for the murder of a gas station attendant. Sentenced to a life term, he was one of four prisoners given a weekend furlough when Dukakis was governor. He made his way to Oxon Hill, Maryland, where he held a twenty-eight-year-old man captive, beating and stabbing him, and when the victim's fiancée returned home, Horton assaulted and raped her.

Using focus groups, the campaign team tested Dukakis's record and Atwater later said he was intent on making "Willie Horton his running mate." The "Revolving Door" ad that was eventually filmed showed a silent procession of men in prison garb moving out through a gate and into society. A narrator spelled out Dukakis's record of vetoing the death penalty and issuing furloughs to violent criminals.

In speeches around the country, Bush denounced Dukakis in much the way Reagan had made short work of his opponents, using the "L-word" and referring to his opponent as a "card-carrying member of the ACLU."

His selection of Indiana senator Dan Quayle as his running mate had the support of Atwater and Ailes but came as a shock to both the pols and conservatives. There had been other names on the list—Bob Dole, Jack Kemp, Alan Simpson among them. Quayle had appeared on "This Week with David Brinkley" with Dole and Kemp and asserted that "the themes, the issues, the articulation on the campaign will be George Bush's."[3]

Anything but a routine choice, the surprise had reporters scrambling for biographical information on Quayle. And Quayle was unprepared for the blitz of media attention and the negative questions: Why had he joined the Indiana National Guard instead of serving in Vietnam? One particular bombshell story put him at a party with several lobbyists at a Florida resort in 1980 along with a young woman who had posed nude for *Playboy* magazine.

Bush stood by his designated running mate, expressing confidence and loyalty in him. In his diary, however, he later wrote about the firestorm that followed his announcement, "It was my decision and I blew it, but I'm not about to say that I blew it."[4]

For someone who gave the impression of having less than populist views, Bush opened the gates to the White House on his first day in office and 4,500 people who had waited through the night, strolled into and around the grounds of the "people's house." When he was inaugurated, he paid a small tribute to Martin Van Buren, the last sitting vice president who had been elected to the presidency.

Also on his first day in the Oval Office, he found a note from Reagan, written on stationery with the phrase "Don't Let the Turkeys Get You Down."

"Dear George," Reagan wrote. "You'll have moments when you want to use this particular stationery. Well, go to it, George. I treasure the moments we shared and wish you all the very best. You'll be in my prayers. God bless you and Barbara. I'll miss our Thursday lunches. Ron."

His one campaign promise that came back to haunt him was his pledge not to raise taxes. "The Congress will push me to raise taxes, and I'll say no," he told the crowd in Atlanta. "And they'll push, and I'll say no. And they'll push again, and I'll say to them 'read my lips: no new taxes.'"

He did manage to hold the line through most of 1990. His State of the Union address noted real economic growth at nearly 3 percent, the creation of almost 2 million new jobs and the first revision of the Clean Air Act in a decade. He also had signed the Americans with Disabilities Act, something he had supported before becoming president and his most singular push to a "kinder and gentler" society.

But by June of that year there was a budget impasse with Congress, mandatory spending cuts under the Gramm-Rudman-Hollings deficit reduction act, the savings and loan bailout situation and the Federal Reserve was unwilling to lower interest rates.

I was in the pressroom the day the press office issued a one-paragraph statement from Bush: "It is clear to me that both the size of the deficit problem and the need for a package that can be enacted require all of the following: entitlement and mandatory program reform, tax revenue increases, growth incentives, discretionary spending reductions, orderly reductions in defense expenditures, and budget process reform to assure that any bipartisan agreement is enforceable and that the deficit problem is brought under responsible control. The bipartisan leadership agree with me on these points."

It took all of us a little time to read between the lines since the words "income" and "tax" weren't mentioned consecutively, but we all figured it out. A key campaign pledge had been broken. That issue haunted him during the 1992 election.

If the number of news conferences a president holds is interpreted as an index of the openness of his administration, his should be considered one of the most open of modern times, statistically speaking. While his predecessor held forty-four news conferences in eight years, Bush held close to two hundred in four, according to his press secretary Marlin Fitzwater. But he still tried to lay down the law when he first entered the White House: no questions in the Oval Office, especially when he was meeting with a visiting head of state and we would be present for only a picture-taking. As expected, I didn't obey his orders.

The signal moment of his presidency was the forty-three-day war with

Iraq. When Saddam Hussein's troops moved over the border into Kuwait he deployed U.S. troops to take up defensive positions in Saudi Arabia as part of Operation Desert Shield.

On August 8, 1990, after troops had been dispatched to Saudi Arabia, I asked him, "Mr. President, are we in a war?"

"We're not in a war," he replied. "We have sent troops to defend Saudi Arabia. Other nations—I will have announcements about other nations that will be participating with the Saudis. I believe Margaret Thatcher, after talking to King Fahd, has announced the forces will be going in. And then I think you'll see other such actions. But I'd prefer to leave that to Saudi Arabia . . . indeed, it's their country." Thatcher, who had been pushing intervention, was said to have chided Bush, "Now don't go wobbly on me."

Meanwhile, the United States won several votes at the U.N. Security Council condemning Iraq and putting economic sanctions in place. Bush set to work, masterfully pulling together twenty-eight nations into a coalition, including Russia, which had sent envoys several times to Baghdad to urge a retreat.

On August 14, 1990, I asked Bush, "After successfully internationalizing opposition to the Iraqi aggression through the U.N., why did you jump the gun and unilaterally order a blockade, upsetting other members? And is the U.S. policy against the annexation of captured lands in the Middle East an across-the-board policy with the United States?"

He denied upsetting other members and said that the country was acting within its legal rights. As for opposition to annexation of conquered lands, he said he did not know if there were any exceptions, but that the invasion of Kuwait would not stand.

By Thanksgiving 1990, I was traveling with him and the first lady aboard Air Force One for a visit with the troops stationed in Saudi Arabia.

General Norman H. Schwarzkopf, who commanded the Desert Storm troops, was on the flight and came back to hand us gas masks and to show us how to put them on. He was in good spirits, ebullient about the military readiness and brimming with confidence.

We found the same esprit de corps and high morale when we talked to the troops in the hot Saudi desert. I chatted with several of the young soldiers and one in particular got teary-eyed as he told me he was anxious to get home for Christmas.

At a dinner several years later, Sarah McClendon reminded me that she'd asked a young radio reporter to keep an eye on me, given the heat of the desert and our frantic-paced trip, which also included Czechoslovakia, France, Germany, Egypt and an unplanned stop in Geneva. Sarah wanted to make sure I got back in one piece, I guess. When we returned to Washington, she asked the young man how the trip went.

"It was pretty rough," he told her. "I couldn't keep up with Helen."

As the threat of war with Iraq was beginning to turn into reality, Bush continued to try to do his best with business-as-usual in the White House. He met one day with a group of education advisers and told the group of assembled reporters, "Hey, listen, life goes on."

"You look grim," I interjected.

"Come on, Helen, lighten up," he responded.

However, the night before he gave the order for the missile attack on Iraq, he called noted evangelist Billy Graham, who spent the night at the White House, much the same way Lyndon Johnson used to summon Graham when he needed, as he put it, some "good tall praying." The day the Gulf War began, he took a large contingent of his entire cabinet with him to an early morning church service.

By January 16, 1991, Congress passed a resolution by 98–0 expressing its support for Bush's policy in the Gulf and ordering troops to the Middle East. As Senate minority leader Bob Dole of Kansas stated, while war was being waged, "all other considerations come to an end, and we join united, not as Republicans or Democrats, but as Americans, behind our president."

It may seem laughable now, but at every news conference leading up to the U.S. involvement, I would ask Bush if we were going to war. One day before the start of a National Security Council meeting, I asked him about military options and he said, "I'm not contemplating any such action, and I again would not discuss it if I were."

On January 17, all my previous "war" questions got answered. Bush came into the pressroom and as Louise Sweeney of the *Christian Science Monitor* wrote, "Helen Thomas . . . piped up and wrote the lead for everyone's story with her next question: 'Are you saying the war is going to start today?' "[5]

The air strikes on Baghdad had begun.

From the time of the Iraqi invasion, to appear undistracted by it all, Bush took his traditional vacation at Kennebunkport that year and had his crisis meetings with national security adviser Brent Scowcroft sometimes aboard his cigarette boat *Fidelity*, proving the point that no matter where the president is, that is where the White House is. Of course, I never believed crisis affairs could be conducted away from Washington, where all the lines of communication are secure and officials are on standby.

Desert Storm ended in 42 days, with only 4 days of ground fighting. The United States suffered 137 casualties while thousands died in Iraq. A much weakened, but apparently not chastened, Saddam remained in power to oppress the Kurdish population and execute his enemies, including his two sons-in-law after promising them a safe return from Jordan.

It's almost unbelievable to me that seven years later, Saddam is still in power and has caused no small amount of tension with his treatment of U.N. weapons inspectors, to the point where President Clinton launched a number of air strikes against Iraq in hopes of deposing Saddam.

At home, Bush had two other signal moments: his nominations of John Tower to be secretary of defense and Clarence Thomas to the Supreme Court.

The Tower nomination marred the "honeymoon period" of his first one hundred days in office. Some had warned Bush not to send Tower's name to the Senate for confirmation. Rumors of Tower's drinking and womanizing began to surface, along with FBI files of an affair with a Russian ballerina. Tower had assured Bush of his loyalty, promising to be "the best secretary of defense we ever had" and Bush continued to support his nominee, but the vote in the Senate Armed Services Committee was 11–9 along party lines and the nomination was turned back.

In the summer of 1991, Bush nominated Clarence Thomas to the Supreme Court to replace the retiring Justice Thurgood Marshall. He described Thomas as "the best-qualified man in the country for the job," and the nomination seemed a sure thing. Then Anita Hill, a law professor from Oklahoma, who had worked for Thomas at the Department of Education and the Equal Employment Opportunity Commission, accused him of sexual harassment.

This resulted in a sensational set of televised hearings in October. Few can forget Senator Alan Simpson of Wyoming talking about faxes and letters to his office alleging Hill was crazy, or Utah's Orrin Hatch holding up a copy of *The Exorcist,* or of watching the chairman Joseph Biden get sandbagged at nearly every turn while Senator Ted Kennedy seemed a little too quiet. Few can forget Senator Arlen Specter's prosecutorial line of questioning of Hill—and the consequent backlash he encountered.

And very few will forget Thomas describing to the committee his sense of being a victim of a "high-tech lynching for uppity blacks who deign to think for themselves." The Senate approved the confirmation 58–42. When Thomas was sworn in at the White House, I noticed no one talked to Specter and he seemed to be the loneliest man at the South Lawn ceremony.

At the end of the Gulf War, Bush's popularity rating was 90 percent and he seemed unbeatable. Unfortunately, what should have been a by-the-book reelection campaign turned into a disorganized mess. In short, it was a disaster, and it was on a collision course with the well-oiled campaign machine of Bill Clinton and the third-party candidacy of Ross Perot. Having broken his "no new taxes" pledge and with a sluggish economy plaguing him, Bush's popularity ratings plummeted. Moreover, his health became an issue when millions of TV viewers saw him collapse and throw up in the lap of the Japanese prime minister when he was in Tokyo.

Despite all the assurances that he was healthy and his own assertion that he was primed for the campaign, many thought he seemed tired, if not ill.

The race seemed to boil down to the three presidential debates in October with the second a "town meeting" forum in Richmond, Virginia, where a young woman asked Bush how the national debt affected him personally. He looked a little puzzled until he realized she had been speaking about the recession and his response sounded disjointed. Then, when Perot was holding forth, the camera caught Bush glancing at his wristwatch. He was checking to see if Perot had exceeded the time limit for responses but the image was one of a man bored and uninterested.

At the debate on October 19, I reminded him of the "no new taxes" pledge and asked him, "Mr. President, why have you dropped so dramatically in the leadership polls from the high eighties to the low forties? And you have said that you will do anything to get reelected. What can you do in two weeks to win reelection?"

"Well, I think the answer to why the drop, I think, has been the economy is in the doldrums," he began. "And then, Helen, I really believe we— people are going to ask this question about trust because I do think there's a pattern by Governor Clinton of saying one thing to please one group and then trying to please another group. It doesn't work that way when you're president. Truman is right, the buck stops here. And you have to make decisions even when it's against your own interests. And I've done that. It was against my political interests to say go ahead and go along with the tax increase, but I did what I thought was right at the time."

There were a few moments of levity during that debate and my favorite was when Perot made his case for taking issues to the people and said: "I just love the fact that everybody, particularly in the media, goes bonkers over the town hall. I guess it's because you will lose your right to tell them what to think." Despite what everyone perceived to be a lackluster performance, Bush shot back quickly: "Let me say, I would like the record to show to the panelists that Ross Perot took the first shot at the press. My favorite bumper sticker, though, is 'Annoy the media. Re-elect President Bush.' And I just had to work that in." Then he looked at me and said, "Sorry, Helen . . . I'm going to pay for this later on."

Up until about a week before the election the polls showed Bush and

Clinton near even. Then the Friday before the election, the specter of Iran-Contra again clouded the White House. Independent counsel Lawrence Walsh entered a one-count indictment against former defense secretary Caspar Weinberger. While Bush had maintained his arm's-length involvement with Iran-Contra, the indictment included evidence of Bush's presence at a meeting in the secretary's office and his tacit agreement in the arms-for-hostages swap.

Another poll shortly before the election seemed to seal it. The Clinton team had seized on the slogan "It's the economy, stupid" and had hammered Bush for not delineating an economic recovery program. Actually, the economy had slowly but surely been ticking upward, showing a 3.5 percent growth rate. However, the survey showed that most Americans believed the economy was in bad shape. And Clinton had promised change.

Election Day 1992, Houston: I'd had the feeling for some time that Bush would have preferred to be at home with his family, play with his grandchildren, race his boat and relax, but he still wanted to win. After we made the requisite trip to the polls to watch him vote, the motorcade made a stop at a shopping mall where he bought some fishing tackle and some country music CDs.

I later saw him in the hotel dining room and he called me over for a brief chat. I thought he seemed in low spirits—resigned but still hopeful. By early afternoon, the exit polls were not looking good. I believe it was excruciating for him and Barbara to go before their supporters, because he was and is a man who thinks of public service as a duty and an honor.

The final electoral count was Clinton 357, Bush 168, and zero for Perot.

The weekend after the election Colin Powell and his wife, Alma, joined the Bushes at Camp David and the two men went for a walk. "It hurts," Bush told him. "It really hurts to be rejected."[6]

But he was graceful in defeat. When we returned to the White House from Texas, a number of loyalists turned out to cheer him and he said, "Let's finish this job in style. I can think of nothing other to say except let's finish this job with style. Let's get the job done, cooperate fully with the new administration. The government goes on as well it should. . . . We will support the new president and give him every chance to lead this country into greater heights."

He went on to say that he was grateful for the "wonderful four years . . . and nobody can take that away from any of us. It's been good and it's been strong. And I think we've really contributed something to the country and maybe history will record it that way."

Before his term ended, however, he dealt with another foreign crisis.

Tribal warfare and crime lords were creating chaos in Somalia, disrupting
U.N. efforts to distribute food and relief to the famine-ravaged country. On
November 24, U.N. Secretary-General Boutros Boutros-Ghali visited Bush
and delivered a letter pleading for help.

With Congress's approval, he sent in twenty-eight thousand U.S. troops
in what was dubbed Operation Restore Hope. In early January, he traveled
to Somalia to check out the situation, just as he had done in Panama and
Saudi Arabia.

In December, his gloom at being defeated seemed to have abated a bit. He
invited the comedian Dana Carvey—who had been doing dead-on impressions of Bush on "Saturday Night Live"—to spend the night at the White
House. Upon meeting Cito Gaston, the manager for the Toronto Blue Jays,
he recalled his days as captain of the Yale baseball team and told Gaston he
was "a rookie ballplayer who needs a job."

And on December 23, he told a group of reporters gathered on the South
Lawn that "amnesty has been granted to Helen Thomas and all the rest of
you guys."

He also gave six participants in the Iran-Contra mess a Christmas present
by granting them pardons and citing the need "for the country to move on."

He has stayed busy since but I do wonder at some of his activities. In February 1997, he spoke at the International Parachute Symposium in Houston
and was presented with a silk parachute, the same kind that he had used in
1944 when, as a nineteen-year-old Navy flier, he bailed out of his burning
plane. At the symposium he vowed that he would jump again.

On March 25, accompanied by two members of the Army's Golden
Knights parachute team, he bailed out of a plane and made a perfect
landing.

Let me say for the record I am extremely glad he decided to do this *after*
he left office. Standing on the ground watching the president of the United
States in free fall for 4,500 feet and wondering if he'd pull the rip cord in
time would have been a bit much for this reporter.

In July 1998, I traveled to Chicago to participate in a panel discussion and
Bush was the keynote speaker. He greeted me warmly, gave me a big bear
hug and treated me like an old friend. Somehow most ex-presidents I run
into manage to forgive me for all those hard-hitting questions after they're
out of the White House.

He jokes these days that he's referred to as "Barbara Bush's husband" or
"George W. Bush's father," but I think the best description came from him in
1997 when his library was dedicated in Texas. Quoting Lou Gehrig, he said,
"Today, I consider myself the luckiest man on the face of the earth."

I think he still might.

Bill Clinton

It is not in my hands, it is in the hands of Congress and the people of this country, ultimately, in the hands of God. Personally, I am—I am fine. I have surrendered to this.

—President Clinton, October 8, 1998, two hours after the House of Representatives
voted to begin an impeachment inquiry

Back when I was beginning to work on this book, I got a call from the reporters for the *Washington Post*'s "Reliable Source" column. They had heard this was in the works and asked me what I planned to write about. I remember joking with the reporter and telling her, "Well, I wonder if anyone will want to buy it. There won't be any sex in it."

So much for that.

William Jefferson Clinton made several statements and a few apologies after a seven-month grand jury investigation turned over eighteen boxes of documents to Congress citing eleven possible impeachable offenses stemming from his affair with Monica Lewinsky.

But he left many questions unanswered, especially my all-time favorite: Why? And my second all-time favorite: How? How could he compartmentalize—as he often said was his method of dealing with the various issues of his presidency—to this degree? How could he stand the headlines and the furor? And how could he think he could get away with it?

Why did he take such chances getting involved with a White House intern? Why would he continue to take such a risk beginning in 1995 when he was already facing the sexual harassment lawsuit from Paula Jones? Why did he behave in such a reckless manner knowing the independent counsel, Kenneth Starr, was engaged in his zealous pursuit? Why did he lie to his wife, his daughter, his staff, his cabinet, his attorneys, his friends, his ministers? Did he also lie to himself?

On January 26, 1998, I stood with the rest of the press pool in the Roosevelt Room and watched Clinton, with Hillary at his side and a congressional delegation in attendance, wag his finger at our questions and insist, "I want to say one thing to the American people. I want you to listen to me. I'm going to say this again: I did not have sexual relations with that woman, Miss Lewinsky."

Fast-forward to August 17: "I did have a relationship with Miss Lewinsky that was not appropriate. In fact, it was wrong."

Was it farce or Greek tragedy? Was it biblical or just human? Was it a constitutional crisis or just a seamy sexual indiscretion?

When you put all that against what he accomplished, there are just too many baffling questions. He was the first Democratic president to be elected to a second term in sixty years, the first president in seventeen years to submit a balanced budget to Congress. During his tenure, the country enjoyed its lowest rate of inflation since the early 1960s and in 1998 the nation's budget posted its first surplus in thirty years, while unemployment dropped significantly.

He told Lewinsky there was a "void" in his life.

After his reelection, maybe there was some truth to that. For someone who was nothing less than an *über*-political animal, there would be no more campaigns, no more center stage, no more presidency. I remember Richard Nixon saying he felt let down after he won his second term. Was it the arrogance of power expressed by a consummate politician who loved living on the edge? Was it hubris?

We sat down for an interview on October 27, 1998, days before the surprising midterm elections that netted a Democratic gain in Congress and as a result had the pundits recasting their earlier impeachment predictions.

I started out by asking him "What's it like to be president?"—a simple enough question—and he noted right off that the "simplest questions are always the hardest."

And despite the flood of events that had engulfed him for the past year, he said being president "is an incredible honor. And it's something I think about every day."

He went on to say that "It's the opportunity of a lifetime to do things that are important, that change people's lives for the better, that strengthen the country, that prepare us—particularly right now, because we're moving into not just a new century and a new millennium, but really a whole new way of living and working and relating to the world. It's an incredible opportunity. . . . And it also, as you know, can be immensely enjoyable and occasionally painful. But the most important things I think about are honor and opportunity—and I have loved every day of it."

Then he laughed and said, "It's a good thing we've got the Twenty-second Amendment, or I'd run again."

On January 20, 1997, Clinton took his second oath of office with an eye to his place in history. "Each and every one of us, in our own way, must assume personal responsibility, not only for ourselves and our families, but for our neighbors and our nation," he said. He also chose a biblical passage from Isaiah, which stated: "Thou shalt raise up the foundation of many generations; and thou shalt be called the repairer of the breach, the restorer of paths to dwell in."

There is no doubt he loved being president. The presidency may not have loved him in his first term, but if there was ever someone who was more single-mindedly focused on the idea of being president, I haven't met him—or her—yet.

By the beginning of his second term, though, despite comments about presidential lassitude—as former campaign strategist Dick Morris said, "I thought he might go left, I thought he might go right but I didn't think he'd go to sleep"—his legacy seemed assured, given the burgeoning economy, his growth as a leader in foreign policy and his domestic agenda of small but important steps.

There was just one test he failed: the test of self-discipline. I believe he had the potential to be one of the nation's best presidents, with a clear vision of where the country should be headed, and he has been one of the hardest-working presidents I've ever seen. But the scandals both public and private gravely wounded his presidency and the legacy he hoped to leave behind. I think it's safe to say that his face won't be appearing on Mount Rushmore.

Toward the end of his reelection campaign, an editorial in the *New York Times* on October 27, 1996, praised his rapid education in leadership and said: "The presidency he once dreamed is still within his reach if he brings the requisite integrity to the next four years. By adding self-discipline to vision, he can build on the achievements he has already made and make a fair bid to leave Washington in 2001 as one of the notable presidents of the 20th century."

Indeed, the star he followed during the 1996 campaign and afterward was to be the president who would "build a bridge to the twenty-first century," having preached the need for the country to be prepared to maintain its leadership.

There was something else about him that baffled me. For all his popularity, I could never get a bead on exactly why people who didn't like him just "didn't like him," they hated him. When I would make a speech, invariably someone would come up to me and unleash a dose of vitriol about Clinton. It always surprised me. Not even Nixon generated that kind of hostility at his worst times.

Once when I was in the Oval Office, I said to him, "Do you know that a lot of people hate you, and I ask them, 'Why? What exactly is it about this man that you can't stand?'"

He laughed and said, "What do they say?"

I told him that they had no answer, just that the reaction was visceral and vitriolic.

I also think he never understood that in the high-wire act of the presidency, one does not take unnecessary risks—the necessary risks are quite enough—but some of those he took in office resulted in more investigations than of any president I've covered. From the day he moved into the White House, there was one probe after another: the Whitewater land venture, the firing of the White House travel office staff, the mishandling of FBI files on

Reagan and Bush appointees, Paula Jones's sexual harassment suit, the months-long grand jury investigation of his affair with Monica Lewinsky. Through all of it, he continued to confound his friends and mislead his most ardent staff and supporters. From my reporter's slot here, I can only say he bought himself a lifetime of remorse, repentance and regret, or as he told the grand jury, "I would give anything not to have to admit what I have to admit today."

None of his apologies were contrite enough to suit his detractors in Congress. They wanted him to grovel and ask for mercy.

He's had some company when it comes to special prosecutors. Besides himself and his wife, five cabinet officials at one time or another were or are the subjects of independent counsel investigations: former commerce secretary Ron Brown, former agriculture secretary Mike Espy, former HUD secretary Henry Cisneros, Interior Secretary Bruce Babbitt and Labor Secretary Alexis Herman.

In his first term, the usual "honeymoon" period with the press never materialized, partly because of the White House staff's attitude and partly because of the series of events that began the Whitewater investigation. It also was a presidency marked by tragedy when deputy White House counsel Vincent Foster, who had worked with Hillary Rodham Clinton at the Rose Law Firm in Arkansas, committed suicide.

It was a jarring beginning to an administration rocked with constant turmoil and a sharp contrast to the image of the young man who visited the White House in 1963 as a member of Boys Nation and shook President Kennedy's hand.

Funny thing, I was in the Rose Garden that day too, and I even have a picture of it: Clinton shaking hands with Kennedy and me off to the side, looking skeptical as usual. Little did I know at the time that there was a future president among the wide-eyed group in the presence of Kennedy, who, of course, urged them all to think about a career in public service. (I shook Kennedy's hand too and I never expected to be president. Must have been a lack of "the vision thing.")

In our interview, he said that when he was sixteen "I don't know that I thought I would be president but I did decide when I was sixteen—I remember making a very conscious decision—that I would like to go into public life and be an elected official. And I did it, I think, because first I was moved by the importance of public life because of the challenges the country was facing, especially the civil rights challenge. More than any other issue it affected my early life."

He was born in Hope, Arkansas, a village whose name resonated for him all his life. He never knew his father, who died in an automobile accident before he was born. He was close with his vivacious, caring mother, Virginia Kelley, who married three times—twice to the same man. Her last husband was Dick Kelley, who remained close to Clinton after his mother died in January 1994.

In observance of Mother's Day in 1996, Clinton took over his wife's weekly newspaper column and wrote about his mother: "I miss her every day."

He recalled that when he was a small child, he watched her from a railway platform when she left to study nursing and young Bill stayed in Arkansas with his grandparents. She was "sobbing and waving good-bye to me and my grandmother. As the train pulled away she sank to her knees." It was a difficult time, he recalled, but she was determined "to get the skills she needed to provide for both of us." And he said that the image of her at the train station "has stayed with me throughout my life, a powerful memory of her constant love."

"Mother taught me about family, hard work, sacrifice and putting her children first, and about always being positive for them even on the bad days," he wrote. And when he decided on a career in politics, she threw herself into that fray "to help me through victory and defeat, and encouraged my brother in his career while never giving up her unshakable belief that he would recover from his drug problem."

"No matter what adversity she faced," he wrote, "she always tried to enjoy herself and she loved seeing other people lap up life, too. She never begrudged other people their success and happiness. She just wanted the same for herself and her children."

He studied at Georgetown University, won a Rhodes scholarship to Oxford and attended Yale Law School, where he met his future wife, Hillary Rodham.

In 1992, the heavy hitters in the Democratic Party, including House majority leader Richard Gephardt, took a pass rather than run against President Bush, whose approval polls had hit 90 percent after the successful conclusion of the Gulf War. Clinton was the leader of a crop of Democratic politicians who personified what he called "the new center" on domestic issues and who, heeding the success of the Reagan and Bush campaigns that used the "L-word" like a weapon, read the mood of the country and helped create a new breed called a "New Democrat."

Despite his many negatives, such as dodging the Vietnam draft, smoking marijuana but denying he inhaled and the surfacing of Gennifer Flowers, who claimed to have had a twelve-year relationship with Clinton, his campaign manager James Carville found the key that hit a home run with the voters: "It's the economy, stupid." Any of the accusations during that campaign would have forced out a lesser presidential candidate, but Clinton rode out the storm and the self-designated "Comeback Kid" seemed unstoppable.

Clinton's campaign reflected the energy and enthusiasm the public always looks for in a candidate, not to mention that indispensable "charisma" that enhances all successful politicians.

During his first presidential campaign I was one of the three panelists at the third and last debate between Bush, Clinton and Texas tycoon Ross Perot. It was held at Michigan State University in East Lansing—the alma mater of many of my nieces. PBS newsman Jim Lehrer was the moderator and when my turn rolled around I asked:

"Governor Clinton, your credibility has come into question because of your different responses on the Vietnam draft. If you had it to do over again, would you put on the nation's uniform, and if elected, could you in good conscience send someone to war?" Clinton replied:

> If I had it to do over again, I might answer the questions a little better. You know, I've been in public life a long time and no one had ever questioned my role, and so I was asked a lot of questions about things that happened a long time ago. I don't think I answered them as well as I could have.
>
> Going back twenty-three years, I don't know, Helen. I was opposed to the war. I couldn't help that. I felt very strongly about it and I didn't want to go at the time. It's easy to say in retrospect I would have done something differently. President Lincoln opposed the war and there were people who said maybe he shouldn't be president. But I think he made a pretty good president in wartime. We got a lot of other presidents who didn't wear their country's uniform and had to order our young soldiers to the battle, including President Wilson and President Roosevelt. So the answer is I could do that. I wouldn't relish doing it, but I wouldn't shrink from it. I think that the president has to be prepared to use the power of the nation when our vital interests are threatened. When our treaty commitments are at stake. When we know that something has to be done that is in the national interest and that is a part of being president. Could I do it? Yes, I could.

When he won the election, he seemed to understand the political forces at play and where the American people stood on most issues, but he missed the boat in so many ways during his first two years in office. One of his biggest mistakes was to bring on board his young, enthusiastic but naïve campaign workers, who had no problem running a campaign but had some big problems understanding how Washington, the government and the Congress worked. What they lacked in experience, however, they more than made up in arrogance. The situation had all the makings of a disaster.

At a roast for former press secretary Marlin Fitzwater, I told the group how Marlin had offered to show the new members of the White House press staff around and give them the benefit of his experience. His offer was rebuffed, I told the crowd, and he was told, "We'd rather make our own mistakes." "They did," I said, "in spades."

Arrogance pervaded, and as I've said, the decision was made to do as many end runs as possible around the White House press. Another area, though I'm not quite sure if this was due to arrogance or just plain ineptitude, was what we came to call "Clinton Standard Time." In the White House, there is a full-time employee whose job it is to keep all the clocks running, whether they need winding or batteries replaced. While I'm sure this person does his job well, I just wonder whether anyone on staff looked at a clock the first six months Clinton was in office. Time seemed to be a fairly fluid concept, as we would wait and wait and wait for the president to appear. Ten minutes, twenty minutes, a half hour—we would cool our heels in the Rose Garden, on the South Lawn, at Andrews Air Force Base, you name it. It almost became a joke when the PA system would announce the president's departure to somewhere—our cue to line up outside the press office and board the vans, and invariably wait for the next announcement: "He's running a few minutes late."

When David Gergen came aboard in 1993, he did what none of us thought was possible: He got his boss to show up on time, and as one presidential aide remarked, "If that is all David Gergen does for this White House, he will help us."[1]

It all seemed so strange, especially since things didn't start out that way. On their first day in the White House, the Clintons wanted to express their gratitude to their supporters and those who had traveled a distance to attend the inauguration. Tickets had been handed out for them to visit the residence and to shake hands with the Clintons. But a glitch developed in the welcoming ceremony and many of them were not admitted to the White House grounds. The first lady was overheard on an open microphone bemoaning that hundreds of people who had come to shake their hands would be left out in the cold because of poor scheduling. "We've just screwed a lot of people," she said. They made their amends by opening the place and standing for hours as thousands of people filed through to shake their hands and wish them well.

And shortly after they moved in, the first couple invited about forty members of the press and some members of Congress for a black-tie dinner in the family quarters. I was one of the reporters invited and I brought my colleague Tom Ferraro as my guest. At this small gathering, Clinton was affable, genial and bursting with enthusiasm about his new surroundings. Tom later commented that he was like a man showing off his new home—and he was. He took some of us on a tour of the family quarters, and seemed particularly enchanted with the Lincoln Bedroom, showing us the framed Emancipation Proclamation in that room that Lincoln had signed. (By the start of 1997, more than nine hundred "friends" of the Clintons had spent a night in the Lincoln Bedroom.)

It is rare for reporters to see the White House family quarters, and I was most impressed with these new young residents, as was Tom, who later remarked about the first lady, "Can you imagine, she thanked *me* for taking the time to join them."

I thought they were in awe of where they were and what their new home meant to the nation. But sadly, despite that grand evening, I have to say the Clintons seemed to lack a reverence for the historic mansion and seemed to resent the lack of privacy it afforded.

One of my first complaints about Clinton was that he was an early-morning jogger. We would accompany him riding in the motorcade, usually along the Potomac River, jump out, toss out questions and jump back into the van. I used to say he could run but he couldn't hide. Well, maybe he could.

Any way you look at it, Clinton's first two years in office were a fiasco, amateur hour. Not only were many of the staffers out of their league, but Clinton did not seem to have a clue about what he was going to do about a number of looming foreign crises. Gone was his boyhood friend Thomas "Mack" McLarty as chief of staff, in was former budget director and former congressman Leon Panetta of California. Gone was Dee Dee Myers as press secretary, in was Mike McCurry. Gone was a lot of hostility to the press corps, in was a more orderly operation—one much more adept at navigating the political shoals so unique to the nation's capital.

To his credit, Clinton did try to appoint a cabinet that had the "look of America" as he promised, putting women in high places, including Attorney General Janet Reno, Health and Human Services Secretary Donna Shalala and Madeleine Albright, who served first as U.S. ambassador to the United Nations and then was named secretary of state in Clinton's second term. But he had colossal problems as well.

In an interview we had early in his presidency, he told me that "even the bad days are good." But what bad days they were:

Two days after he was inaugurated for his first term, his nominee for attorney general, Zoe Baird, withdrew her name after it was disclosed she had hired illegal aliens, and his second nominee, Kimba Wood, likewise bowed in and bowed out. In April, he nominated Lani Guinier to be assistant attorney general for civil rights and withdrew her nomination on June 3, after news reports called her "one of Clinton's quota queens" and a barrage of attacks appeared about her academic writings, which conservatives pegged as antithetical to the American electoral system. Some presidents I've seen would have basically told Congress to go to the devil, stood fast behind a nominee and let the Senate Judiciary Committee make its decision. The process smacked of backing off before the process had a chance to play out and only added fuel to the accusations of Clinton's constant caving in tough situations.

Nine days after taking office, he ordered the Pentagon to stop asking military recruits about sexual orientation—the "don't ask, don't tell" policy—setting off a firestorm of controversy that is still being debated today. Two months later, eighty-six Branch Davidians died in Waco, Texas, following a fifty-one-day standoff with federal agents. In May, the White House travel office staff was fired. In July, Vincent Foster committed suicide. In September, Clinton unveiled his health care reform package. In October, he ordered additional ground troops to Somalia after eighteen American soldiers were killed. In December, he nominated Bobby Ray Inman to replace Les Aspin as secretary of defense. It became apparent that Inman didn't want the job. He staged a press conference in which his rambling, disjointed discourse left everyone shaking their heads. It was a masterpiece of obfuscation—but Clinton got the message.

On December 19, a story appeared quoting two Arkansas state troopers as saying they helped facilitate Clinton's extramarital affairs when he was governor. Four days later, Clinton ordered papers concerning the Whitewater land deal turned over to the Justice Department.

During the first half of his first term, Clinton focused almost entirely on domestic policy. He deigned to meet Secretary of State Warren Christopher only once a week despite the turmoil in several parts of the world. But inevitably, he was drawn into the problems in Bosnia, Somalia, Rwanda, Haiti, Iraq, Ireland and the perennial problem between Israel and the Palestinians.

He ordered an attack against the Iraqi intelligence headquarters in Baghdad in June 1993, after receiving "compelling evidence" that a plot was in the works to assassinate George Bush on his planned visit to Kuwait. Under Clinton's leadership, the United States also ousted the military dictatorship in Haiti and restored President Jean Bertrand Aristide to the presidency. After prolonged negotiations with the Haitian military junta, Clinton forged ahead over the opposition of the Republicans in Congress and ordered five thousand U.S. troops into Haiti on September 19, 1994, to pave the way for Aristide's return.

Similarly, after much waffling and hesitation, Clinton decided to move aggressively to hammer out a cease-fire and end the four years of genocide that decimated the former Yugoslavia. He laid the groundwork for the opposing parties in Bosnia and Herzegovina to negotiate the Peace Accords at Dayton, Ohio. He ordered U.S. troops into Bosnia to carry out the accords in 1995, and announced that they would stay for one year. In extending the U.S. mission beyond the one-year deadline, he traveled to Tuzla and told the American soldiers, "I believe it is worthwhile and I hope you believe it is worthwhile." They remained through 1998, working to maintain a fragile peace amid calls by Congress for a unilateral withdrawal.

After the election in 1992, President Bush, in the last days of his presidency, dispatched American armed forces to Somalia to help distribute food to millions in that African nation who were facing starvation. Somalia turned out to be a foreign policy hot potato for Clinton with disastrous results. With the bodies of U.S. troops being dragged through the streets and no clear end in sight, the mission was terminated.

No president worked as hard to achieve peace in Northern Ireland as Clinton. His persistence paid off and he was able to get the longtime belligerents to talk to each other after decades of enmity. With the assistance of former senator George Mitchell acting as a patient and fair mediator, the Sinn Fein and the Protestants agreed to sit down together. One place where Clinton will always be welcome is Ireland for his well-known devotion to that country.

One of the most exciting moments of the Clinton foreign policy agenda took place on September 13, 1993, on the White House grounds, as we witnessed the signing of the Israeli-Palestinian peace accord. Attending the ceremony were Jimmy Carter and George Bush, both of whom had worked so hard for peace in the region. It was a beautiful fall day and there was a remarkable spirit of joy in the air with everyone hoping that the day would lead to a new era of reconciliation in the Middle East.

I recall that unforgettable handshake between Israeli prime minister Yitzak Rabin and Palestinian leader Yasser Arafat and Rabin telling the audience, "Ladies and gentlemen, the time for peace has come"—even though I thought I saw Rabin gulp a couple of times before the handshake. Speaking in Arabic, Arafat told Clinton the Palestinian people stand with the American people and share their "values of freedom, justice and human rights for which my people have been striving."

But tragedy struck later and the reconciliation came to a standstill with Rabin's assassination in 1995.

The year 1994 began with another tragedy, the death of Clinton's mother, Virginia Kelley, on January 6. Six days later, he agreed to the appointment of a special counsel to investigate the transactions surrounding the Whitewater land venture.

In the fall of that year, Clinton remained optimistic about the future, although the Republicans were predicting a big victory in the November elections. I told him that the pundits were beginning to count him out for 1996 and asked him how he accounted "for this very dark picture, political picture, and what are you going to do about it?"

"In the end, this is a decision for the people to make in ninety-four and ninety-six," he said. "When I showed up here, I knew there was always a great deal of enthusiasm for change in the beginning, but the process of change is difficult, exacting, and it requires discipline and confidence and you have to stay at it. There are always dark times. There has never been a time when the organized forces of the status quo haven't been able to drive down the popularity of a president who really fought for change. I'm not worried about that. I am not at issue here. The real issue is what is the future the American people wish for themselves? I am looking forward to having a chance to go out and say what I think the direction should be and then let the people make their decision."

Well, voters did make their decision, and things came crashing down when the Republicans swept both houses of Congress for the first time in forty years. And the bottom dropped out of his grand plan for universal health care for all Americans. In our interview, he cited that as one of his regrets.

"I think that the fact that the number of working people without health insurance is increasing is a terrible tragedy. But since there are no easy answers to hard problems, it's easier to stop something from happening than to make something happen," he said. "That's why the only significant thing I pledged to do as president in ninety-two in all that long, long laundry list of things I said I'd do—the one thing I haven't been able to achieve is to provide access to affordable health insurance for all Americans."

The 1994 election defeat devastated Clinton, who began to seek out behavioral experts and motivational gurus, meeting them at Camp David to hash out what went wrong, particularly since he was intent on seeking a second term. His friends and biographers compared the situation to his defeat for reelection as governor of Arkansas in 1980.

And in December 1994, he fired his controversial surgeon general, Joycelyn Elders, after she made a few provocative statements about sexuality at a U.N. event commemorating World AIDS Day.

After more retrenching, regrouping and reexamination, he declared in his 1995 State of the Union address that the "era of big government is over," and started subsuming some of the longtime agenda items Republicans had been touting for years: a balanced budget, the line-item veto and an integrated global economy.

That year he announced his support for reaching a balanced budget in ten years. Many Democrats were furious at the decision but his political payoff came in November when the battle lines were drawn over the budget. The Republican leadership was pushing ahead to balance the budget but calling for substantial reductions in Medicare and other entitlement spending. Clinton vetoed the budget, which led to a partial shutdown of the government.

Using the same pen Lyndon Johnson used in 1965 to sign the legislation that created Medicare and Medicaid, Clinton said, "Today I am vetoing the biggest Medicare and Medicaid cuts in history, deep cuts in education, a rollback in environmental protection and a tax increase on working families."

He called the Republican effort to balance the budget a case of "misplaced priorities. Now it's up to all of us to go back to work together to show we can balance the budget and be true to our values and our economic interests."

There was a second government shutdown as the fiscal battle raged but Clinton's polls rose as most Americans blamed the Republicans for the impasse.

Around that same time, Clinton visited the chief of staff's office for a birthday party. Also attending was Monica Lewinsky. He invited her to his private study. If most Americans consider the White House hallowed ground, the Oval Office has always been its revered, respected, powerful center, where decisions that affect the nation and the world have been made for the better part of two hundred years.

I suppose you could say 1995 was a turning point in the administration on a number of levels.

But the political momentum had started and with an eye to the 1996 election, Hillary Rodham Clinton summoned Dick Morris, who had helped Clinton to recover the governorship in Arkansas, to help them prepare for the campaign.

Morris, aka "The Triangulator," who had engineered Clinton's move to the center, took charge. One of the first changes he made was in Hillary's public profile.

Enter a kinder, gentler Hillary. Enter the big push for big campaign money. Morris told Clinton that he needed lots of it to keep all the Democratic contenders out of the primary races. The funds were needed for costly television ads, but in retrospect, both Clinton and Vice President Al Gore paid a bigger price for all that fund-raising. Gore was accused of using his office phone to call potential donors. I'm sure that must have come as a huge surprise to all the senators and congressmen who apparently never would have thought of such a thing. In the end, the attorney general found no grounds to appoint a special prosecutor.

Clinton himself seemed to have no moral compass when it came to fund-raising improprieties. It seemed that he bought every idea to raise the ante for Democratic Party donors, even putting the Lincoln Bedroom up for sleep overs at $250,000 a crack. When I heard that the Lincoln suite was on the campaign auction block, I was especially dismayed because I recalled that black-tie dinner when the Clintons first moved into the White House and they had seemed properly dazzled over the prospect of living in the historic mansion.

After the election, Clinton turned the Lincoln Bedroom story into a story of his own and I was part of it. At the 1997 White House Correspondents dinner he delivered the traditional end-of-evening speech and commented on the opening of the Freedom Forum's Newseum. "And then there is a whole wing dedicated to historic scoops," he said. "For example, did you know that Helen Thomas broke the story about the Lincoln Bedroom— while Lincoln was sleeping in it?"

Granted, George Bush and Ronald Reagan had receptions for high-rolling donors as well, but in 1996, it was the overwhelming excess of it all— not to mention the stories that emerged later about money being accepted from noncitizens and possible cash infusions funneled from the Chinese military.

Also during the election year, on April 5, Monica Lewinsky was removed from her White House job and transferred to the public affairs office at the Pentagon.

Then there were those "coffees," where deep-pocket donors got to meet with administration officials in the White House Map Room, where Franklin D. Roosevelt kept track of the military action in World War II—the same room in which Clinton eventually appeared via videotape before a federal grand jury and answered questions posed by independent counsel Kenneth Starr.

It appeared that during those driven fund-raising days, nothing was sacred. In an op-ed piece in the *New York Times,* Charles Lewis, executive director of the Center of Public Integrity, a nonpartison organization, wrote a strong indictment of Clinton's decision "to raise huge sums of campaign cash for aggressive media advertising" a year before the election. He quoted the president as saying, "We got strict advice, legal advice, about what the rules were and everyone knew what the rules were."

Whatever the "rules were," the campaign went full-speed ahead against the Republican nominee, former Senate majority leader Bob Dole, and blazed to victory.

The 1996 campaign was not without its pitfalls. On the very day Clinton was to be nominated for the presidency at the Democratic National Convention in Chicago, reports surfaced that Dick Morris had been trysting with a prostitute in Washington and had allowed her to listen in on telephone conversations with Clinton when political strategy was being discussed.

But the president emerged victorious and began what he hoped would be his place in history. Then, on May 27, 1997, the Supreme Court unanimously rejected Clinton's claim that he should be immune from civil lawsuits, thereby allowing Paula Jones's case to proceed.

In August of that year I celebrated another birthday, and that year, as he had in the past, Clinton staged a celebration—and he was always courtly enough that he never asked me my age. I was in the Cabinet Room with the rest of the press pool for a picture-taking session and on the table was a birthday cake. When I had trouble blowing out the candles, I asked the president to help me, saying, "This is painful," meaning the attention. He complied with my request but noted, "It's painful for me too." He had interrupted the start of his meeting with about twenty corporate executives to celebrate my birthday, all of whom seem to be getting a charge out of my embarrassment.

When it was time to leave, Clinton said, "Now you can have your cake and eat it," and I shot back, "That will be the first time."

I always thought President Clinton's heart was in the right place as far as wanting the best for America. Of all the presidents I covered, he was the most racially color blind. His gift for spellbinding oratory would be at its peak when he spoke in black churches and he wasted no time in marshaling all the law enforcement agencies at his command when many of those churches were burned to the ground. He also was a persistent voice warning against terrorism and spoke eloquently for an outraged nation when the federal building in Oklahoma City was bombed, leaving 168 people dead.

In our interview in October 1998, he recalled his grandparents' influence on matters of race, noting that they had "just a different feel about these issues. They very much both felt that the schools should be integrated, that the children should be given equal opportunity, and they had a real impact on me."

As president, he said he felt the race problem was "America's great tragedy . . . the continuing rebuke to the promise of the Declaration of Independence. And now we're in a position where, as we become more diverse and way beyond the black-white issue, it has become sort of our gateway to the twenty-first century. If we could figure out how to handle all this diversity, it enables us not only to capitalize economically on what is going on but to be a greater force for peace and reconciliation, because in the aftermath of the Cold War, so much of what is consuming the world, from the Middle East to Bosnia to Africa to Ireland, is this whole unfinished legacy of racial and religious and ethnic [issues]."

In March 1998, at the Gridiron dinner, Clinton managed the required self-deprecating humor to comment on all that had been reported so far about the Lewinsky situation. "So . . . how was your week?" he began, and proceeded to tell the crowd to "please withhold the subpoenas until all the jokes have been told. I offer my remarks with this caveat: They were a whole lot funnier before the lawyers got hold of them."

Gridiron members were concerned that it would be difficult for Clinton to make fun of himself that night in view of the plethora of problems that faced him, but he left them laughing. Painful as it must have been, he also attended the annual White House Correspondents dinner in 1998, an event that had its own surreal note with the attendance of Paula Jones.

But by April, U.S. District Judge Susan Webber Wright dismissed Paula Jones's suit, and even with the grand jury still hearing testimony and Starr issuing subpoenas, the economy was humming along with low inflation and low unemployment. There was a balanced budget with a surplus to boot. There had been productive trips to Africa and China. And then it all fell apart.

By July, Monica Lewinsky was granted immunity and testified before the grand jury, telling her detail-laden story of her affair with the president, and Clinton was asked for a blood sample for DNA testing and comparison to a stain on Lewinsky's dress.

On August 17, Clinton testified before the grand jury, acknowledging "inappropriate intimate contact" but insisting that the deposition he gave in the Jones case was legally accurate. In a televised appearance that night, Clinton told the nation that his relationship with Lewinsky "constituted a critical lapse in judgment and a personal failure on my part" but also noted that "It is time to stop the pursuit of personal destruction and the prying into private lives and get on with our national life. Our country has been distracted by this matter for too long, and I take responsibility for my part in all of this. Now it is time—in fact, it is past time—to move on."

Starr turned in his report to Congress on September 9, 1998, saying that it contained "substantial and credible information" that could constitute grounds for impeachment. Clinton made a televised appearance that night; the House Judiciary Committee released the Starr report on the Internet.

Members of his cabinet who had defended him long and loudly were shocked, hurt, angry and disappointed. When a contrite Clinton summoned them to a meeting to apologize, Health and Human Services Secretary Donna Shalala questioned his moral authority. An upset Clinton responded that if such questions had been put to John F. Kennedy in 1960, Richard Nixon would have won the presidency.

On September 11, the apology that everyone wanted to hear came when Clinton appeared at the White House's annual prayer breakfast. Teary-eyed and contrite he said, "I don't think there is a fancy way to say that I have sinned. If my repentance is genuine and sustained, and if I can maintain both a broken spirit and a strong heart, then good can come of this for our country as well as for me and my family. The children of this country can learn in a profound way that integrity is important and selfishness is wrong, but God can change us and make us strong at the broken places."

The videotape of his grand jury testimony was later aired on television and contrary to reports that he was a poor witness, defiant and angry, he held his ground and said firmly, "I'm trying to be truthful but not helpful."

Confounding the pollsters, his popularity took a few dips but, on average, most Americans thought he was doing a good job as president.

One of his ministers, J. Philip Wogaman of United Foundry Methodist Church, said that Clinton had made "serious mistakes" but that he was "resilient" and "repentant."

Clinton has always been able to stay focused at least publicly even in times of great crisis. But I think instead of biting his lip, he should have bitten the bullet and told the truth early and often. It would have taken courage and a certain nobility. In the end, he hurt his presidency and his legacy. Worst of all, he disappointed the American people who were his true believers. But they were willing to forgive and forget.

Once his secret was out, Clinton confided that he felt a tremendous sense of relief, a burden had been lifted from his shoulders.

When we spoke, he said one concern that had grown out of the entire situation was the effect it would have on people considering a life in public service. "I think the larger question that we need to face as a society is whether we really want to get into a position where basically if someone has some problem in their private life, that that should be used to, in effect, disqualify them from public service, or to distract their public service."

He went on to tell me that "maybe the voters will have to ratify it somehow. They'll have to decide; in the end the citizens have to decide. But we ought to have good people in public life. We'll have very few who are perfect.

And it is important, I think, not to overreact and for people who are in public life to basically, ultimately, trust the citizens to get it right. But the level of personal pain can just become unbearable for some people. . . ."

People in public service, he added, "shouldn't feel that the politics of personal destruction is the dominant force in American life. One of the things that I hope I can do is to right that balance, just by going out and trying to do my best."

Like so many others, as the months ground on and it appeared he was headed for impeachment, I felt a profound sadness, and was reminded of some favorite lines by John Greenleaf Whittier: "Of all the sad words of tongue or pen, the saddest of all are it might have been."

When I asked Clinton what advice he would have for his successor, his answer was focused, unsparing and illuminating:

> What I would tell my successor is no matter what happens, never forget it's an honor; never forget it's an opportunity. On worst days you can always do something to make America a better place. And do not waste a lot of time worrying about your present condition if you get in a tight situation. And don't worry about the image instead of the substance. That the American people are very smart; they always get it when they're given enough time.
>
> And I would say, decide what you want to do, what you believe is right for the country, and then just work at it. That I think sometimes we lose—because politics is so much about public image and about press and about coverage, we lose the perspective that it is still a job and that all you can really control is what you do with your time, what your administration does with its time. And then how you communicate that to the American people. And so I would say—my number one advice is decide what you believe is right for America and then just work like crazy and try to enjoy it.

He noted that he didn't consider the presidency a lonely job. "It's only lonely if people allow themselves to be overcome by it. It's a wonderful thing. You don't have to become victimized by the difficulties of the office. You just don't. You've just got to fight that. You can't be defined by the dilemmas of the moment. . . . In the worst days here in the last year, there is always a child whose letter you can sign, there is always an executive order you can sign. There is always something you can do that makes the country a better place."

When he leaves the White House, he said, he hopes to continue working on a number of twenty-first-century issues and that "I hope I can be productive. You know, President Carter has been very productive. He's probably been the most successful former president we've ever had. . . . So I'll try to stay healthy and do something useful."

I thought later about the year Clinton arrived at the White House. It was the year I served as president of the Gridiron Club and at the annual dinner, I reminded him that "you are the eighth president I have covered, so I hope you won't think it presumptuous of me to give you a bit of friendly advice." The advice stemmed from the mistakes of the past presidents:

> Ask not what you can do for the country; ask what the country can do for you.
>
> Forget about the buck stopping here; after all, what are vice presidents for?
>
> Don't jog and chew gum at the same time.
>
> It gets lonely in the White House but don't talk to the portraits.
>
> Be sure to burn the tapes.
>
> Better still, don't tape anything.
>
> For goodness sakes, don't pray with Henry Kissinger.
>
> When a young sailor comes up to you and tells you, "Sir, your helicopter is waiting," you just tell him, "Son, they're *all* mine."
>
> When mistakes are made, all you have to say is you were out of the loop.
>
> Don't fall asleep when you meet the pope.
>
> Don't show any of your scars, interesting as they may be.
>
> Don't pick up Socks by his ears.
>
> If you're attacked by a killer rabbit, best to keep it to yourself.
>
> And don't worry about your future. You can always give a lecture in Japan for a million bucks.

It was all lighthearted and tongue-in-cheek and he laughed with the audience. Lately, though, I wish I had had the chance to give him the two most important words of advice that any president should take to heart: Never lie.

In 1982, I received an award from Danny Thomas in connection with the organization that supports St. Jude's Children's Hospital in Memphis, Tennessee.

I found a copy of the remarks I made at the event and I believe they still hold true today:

> I have always thought a president should know right from wrong. When a president deals in less than the truth, the country is the victim.

Too often in my years at the White House there has been a lack of candor and misjudgment of the character of the people in a democratic society. Secrecy in matters of public interest can be destructive.

At the White House, I see instant history and watch the man who has push-button power over our lives. For that reason, I hope that only the most highly principled persons will occupy the Oval Office. It has not always been so. I do believe that our democracy can endure and prevail only if the American people are informed. The people decide, and therein lies the transcending greatness of the land we love.

There is no doubt Clinton was traumatized when he realized all his deceptions were being revealed. I saw the familiar signs of a beleaguered presidency when Chelsea rushed back from California and his brother Roger arrived from Texas to spend a painful weekend at Camp David.

He avoided the press when he could, allowing only still photographers in the Oval Office and answering questions only at news conferences with heads of state. But gradually he recouped and plunged back into statesmanship with his Middle East peace efforts and even surfacing at high-profile events around the White House.

As he put it, he kept busy doing the work "the American people elected me to do."

His September 11 remarks at the prayer breakfast probably were the closest he would ever come to baring his soul and admitting "a mistake," like some of his predecessors. But we can still ask "why"—why the mindless risk-taking, why jeopardize a presidency at the altar of a tawdry affair?

He did, however, say something to me that gave me an inkling that perhaps he had come to terms with the depth of his folly and how history would record his presidency when he said, "You know, I think that for every president, what happens in your personal life and your family life, probably when you come to the end of your life and you look back, you have to admit that that's the most important thing. And if it didn't work out very well, then it would be a source of great disappointment. But it's different from using those things, in effect, to make life intolerable for people who choose public service. I don't think that's good for the country."

On December 19, 1998, with Representative Henry Hyde of Illinois, Chairman of the Judiciary Committee, at the helm, the House Judiciary Committee succeeded in winning two counts of impeachment against Clinton for perjury and obstruction of justice. The lame-duck Republican House voted strictly on party lines, thus making Clinton the second chief executive in American history to be impeached.

Clinton spent some time in the Oval Office with Tony Campolo, one of his spiritual mentors, before the vote. Afterward, the Democratic leaders and other party members rushed to the White House in a show of support.

Three weeks later, the Senate trial ensued with 100 senators sitting silent as "impartial jurors." Although they were mute while in session, as soon as it broke up, there was a mad rush to the cameras and microphones.

Try as they did for vindication of their impeachment vote, the House so-called managers or prosecutors failed to muster the necessary sixty-seven Senate votes to remove Clinton from office.

Throughout the ordeal, Clinton was depicted publicly by his aides as detached and aloof, simply focused on the job he was elected to do. They said he did not read the Starr report, nor did he watch the videotape of Lewinsky's deposition during its public airing in the Senate.

Except for rumors and the president's puffy eyes, it was difficult to envision his human side in the crisis of his life. He held no news conferences during the crucial period of the trial and the months before. He did manage to score points in a seventy-seven-minute State of the Union address and in other appearances, but there was a surreal quality about it all, as though it was happening to someone else.

The only personal touch during the trial was supplied by fellow Arkansan and former senator Dale Bumpers, who delivered a boffo oration in Clinton's defense that was marked by humor and southern grace. It was Bumpers who ridiculed those who said the Clinton trial was about lies. He assured everyone it was about "sex."

Addressing the Senate, Bumpers said the Clintons have been "about as decimated as a family can get." He explained that the relationship between the president and his wife and daughter was "incredibly strained if not destroyed."

As the scandal unfolded day by day leading up to the trial, the president was denounced as despicable, a cad, a scoundrel—his actions decried as reprehensible. He endured the drumbeat of twenty-four-hour repetitious cable news reports and scathing ridicule showered on him by the late-night comedians, all for laughs.

But much to the bafflement and discomfort of his detractors, his popularity polls remained high, despite the humiliating revelations.

Somehow, the president managed to ride out the immediate storm, but the fallout has yet to be assessed.

On the face of it, he dishonored the presidency, shattered its moral aura, tarnished his legacy and by his misdeeds hurt his family and so many who had stuck their necks out to defend him. Starr's scorched-earth policy in hauling witness after witness before the federal grand jury put the Secret Service on notice that they are no longer sacrosanct and may be called on to testify against those they protect. Politicians and potential candidates may also find themselves with no privacy zone and no questions off-limits.

The legislators who declared that the voters' opinions did not count during the impeachment process may face a day of reckoning when the millennium elections roll around.

And as for President Clinton, I think deep down he may ponder for the rest of his life how he could have jeopardized an honorable place in American history.

FOURTEEN

Short Takes
on Long Views

Helen Thomas is not just the longest-serving correspondent in the White House, which is why she got this award. She's still the hardest-working, I dare say. By my calculations she's had about ten thousand mornings, been through thousands of notebooks, thousands of ballpoint pens, thousands of cups of coffee—some of them brought to her by White House staff—but it never has compromised her yet. For all of us in the White House she is a rock, the embodiment of fearless integrity for her insistence on holding government accountable.

—President Clinton, April 25, 1998, White House Correspondents Association dinner

In 1997, I was honored to be the first "Journalist of the Day" at the dedication of the Newseum in Arlington, Virginia. It's quite a place; operated by Gannett Corp.'s Freedom Forum, it has room after room depicting the history of journalism in society, illustrating through pictures, documents, videos and other media the importance of a free press.

I told the assembled crowd that while I was thrilled to see my picture on the wall, my friends have always said they thought my image would end up somewhere else: in Madame Tussaud's wax museum with a little sign that read: "The Torturer of Presidents." Maybe "press secretaries" would be added as a footnote.

I'm sure they have all felt that way at one time or another. But I didn't get into this business to be loved; I'd rather be respected for being fair. I wanted to break down that wall of secrecy we see so much in government. Without a doubt, the perpetrators and guardians of that secrecy are the presidents themselves.

Too often those in government have lied to reporters, and in so doing, they have lied to the American people. In the Kennedy era, Pentagon press officer Arthur Sylvester, a former newsman, said the government has the right to lie in times of nuclear danger. The same thesis has been argued by some of his successors. We saw it in the Vietnam War, the invasion of Grenada and the Persian Gulf War. I believe the lie dishonors those who fight in those wars. There may be times when all cannot be told. Then, I say, silence is better than deliberate lies.

I once spent an extremely long day a number of years ago—about twelve hours or so—covering a "president" for about two minutes. I was making a brief appearance in the movie *Dave* starring Kevin Kline and Sigourney Weaver. In the scene I appeared in—the familiar pressroom with Kevin Kline at the familiar podium—the "president" is making a grand announcement about a bold, new program for America.

The camera then pans over to me, just in time to catch me rolling my eyes.

After the movie was released, UPI's executive editor at the time, Steve Geimann, asked me, "Did anyone tell you to roll your eyes?"

"No, it was pretty much a natural reaction," I said. "I've heard those promises so many times before, in real life." Was I being too cynical? Not really. As Samuel Johnson said, "We live from hope to hope."

In terms of recognition, though, I got more mileage out of one line in a movie than a host of bylines over the years.

In the early years, reporters on the national scene were relatively unknown to the public at large. But when they became the mainstay of so many television programs, their faces became as familiar to the world as any movie star's, sometimes more so. Television has become the big identifier. In years gone by, our bylines were known to our family, friends and colleagues. In the television age we lost anonymity. We became prominent and hated as arrogant, pontifical and part of the elite corps. Oftentimes, the real loss was one of our most precious assets, objectivity.

As National Public Radio's Daniel Schorr said in an address to the State Bar of California in 1978, and I think it still applies:

> Once a reporter was perceived as a relentless and unusually impecunious pursuer of the truth. Today the report is often as not perceived as the well-heeled and arrogant offspring of a giant amusement industry.
>
> We have come a long way from Peter Zenger, fighter for press freedom in colonial times, and Hildy Johnson of *The Front Page*.

"The press, once perceived as antiestablishment, is itself a huge establishment," he added.

Now we see newspapers owned by large faceless conglomerates, and major television networks by industrial giants or big entertainment corporations. The twenty-four-hour news cycle that used to be the sole province of the wire services is now standard operating procedure, with the explosion of all-news cable channels, the Internet and other innovations. There used to be a line between what is known as the "mainstream press" and the tabloids, but the line has become blurrier. A tabloid broke the Gennifer Flowers story and the first news about Monica Lewinsky was posted on a Web site. "The press" or "the media" is no longer just one organism; it is a collection of news outlets that pick up one another's stories and compete ever more ferociously to be first.

Once upon a time, the newspaper and television pioneers were devoted to free, unfettered news gathering to bring what Justice William Douglas called "fulfillment of the public's right to know."

One goal hasn't changed in all that time, however. Reporters have an unending mission to seek the truth and find it and report it. That is the ideal to which we aspire. Or, as the renowned Martha Gellhorn, who covered wars from the Spanish Civil War to Vietnam, said in an interview at the Freedom Forum on February 18, 1998: "Proof of the power of the press is the fear of the press by government."

Our profession still tries to maintain its ethical standards, but I see the task becoming more and more difficult in view of the changes in mass communications. There is nothing wrong with high ratings or huge profits or healthy circulation. But economic performance is one thing, journalistic integrity is another. In some ways, we could take heed of the Hippocratic oath: "First, do no harm." For in our hands lies the ability to ruin reputations and lives. I do not take that responsibility lightly.

I do not have all the answers, but I do know that our report cards are available every day, be it on a front page, a news broadcast or a Web site. Just as the president can do nothing once he loses his credibility, neither can we.

I know how difficult it is in these days to get the full story, the full meaning and the full context, and most times we do fall short. But we must keep trying.

And even on days when I get the "full story," there is a battery of editors who will question it—and rightfully so. In the presidential campaign of 1984, I got a tip that Walter Mondale was considering a woman for the vice presidential slot. I followed up on the tip and got a name—Geraldine Ferraro. While I considered the story "solid," my editors did not and spiked it pending further confirmation. I lost a huge exclusive and a twenty-four-hour "beat" on the competition. Upset? Yes. Angry? A little. But I look at what has happened with some of the major news events of the day in the recent past—with rumor passing as fact and innuendo masquerading as research—and it seems that perhaps the "spike" should be reinstated a little more forcefully.

I salute with all my heart United Press International, which in its heyday, like the Associated Press, made objectivity the keystone of our profession. "Just the facts, ma'am" is what I was taught to deliver to the reading and listening public.

In my years at UPI, I have been incredibly fortunate to work with some great editors and reporters. Accuracy, thoroughness and speed were stressed, but they also cared. My, did they ever care. And they still do, even those who went on to more lucrative positions by necessity or choice. So many of them still look back longingly on the days when they struggled in UPI bureaus all over the world, working eighteen hours a day, and sometimes putting their lives at risk in war. They were dedicated to the proposition that the story was the thing and they loved every moment of it. We had an esprit de corps. One refrain I hear from ex-UPI people no matter how long they've been away or how successful they have become in other pursuits is, "Yeah, the pay was lousy, the hours were long—but the most fun job I ever had is when I worked for UPI."

Ex-Unipressers are constantly in touch and when they pass on, we mourn them and recall their wonderful journalistic coups and exploits. Our camaraderie never ends. Few companies can boast such loyalty, especially in the current climate when it seems to be every man for himself.

There has never been an election or a major news break in recent years when a former Unipresser has not called in to offer his or her help, even to take dictation—help that has always been welcome.

One of my favorite stories about one of my favorite reporters, the late Steve Gerstel, occurred when he celebrated his thirtieth anniversary as a member of the Senate and House press galleries. Senate Democratic leader George Mitchell invited him to stand in front of the leader's desk and told Steve that for once, he would ask the first question.

"You've been covering the Senate for thirty years," Mitchell said. "Do you figure you wasted your life?"

"Absolutely," quipped Steve, "and you'll feel the same way in twenty-two years."

But long after he retired from UPI, Steve would give the bureau a call around election time and ask if we needed any "help." His talent and expertise and ability to reach into that filing cabinet of a brain and pick out the right detail at the right time made him invaluable on those incredibly busy nights. We were in awe of his flawless writing.

Yes, UPI has had a long and colorful history. From the day I started working there, it was supposed to be going out of business.

E. W. Scripps, who founded United Press in 1907, said the wire service was his "greatest contribution to journalism." In the late 1950s, United Press merged with Hearst-owned International News Service and became UPI.

True, UPI lost millions and became expendable to the heirs and the accountants who abetted its demise. But I'll always believe it could have remained the shining star in the Scripps-Howard newspaper galaxy and it would have been true to the remarkable legacy of Mr. Scripps.

UPI has come on hard times, too many hard times to relate. There were some who did not believe in it and others who did not understand its validity in a profession that thrives on competition. But enough of this lecture. The saddest words of all are "It might have been." But I still look to the future.

When I look back at the journalists who worked for UPI and went on to greater fame—Walter Cronkite, Harrison Salisbury, William Shirer to name a few—I can't help but be proud of what this wire service has contributed to our country—often the first draft of history, as Ben Bradlee called news stories.

We Unipressers can never get together without recalling our great colleagues of the past and the stories that sent them to far-flung and sometimes impossible places.

At the risk of sounding overly impressionable, I am in awe of all the reporters I worked with or against. Of course, not all the great reporters worked for UPI. ABC's Sam Donaldson is one of the finest correspondents I have ever met. He lights up the pressroom and fires up reporters when he is at the White House. He was missed—by me, at least—when he left in 1990 and I welcomed him back with open arms in 1998. He credits—or should I say blames—me for his hard-driving approach to newsmakers, especially presidents. When his book *Hold On, Mr. President* came out, his wrote the following inscription in my copy: "To Helen Thomas: All the bad habits I have in covering presidents, you taught me. And I am grateful!" While it seems his modus operandi is to take no prisoners, he has a big and sympathetic heart.

Sarah McClendon is an icon in the White House pressroom. Her questions have made presidents squirm and I'm sure she's also made their blood boil—but they always answer her. Furthermore, she puts them to shame and makes them act.

In 1973, she found out that veterans who were attending school under the GI Bill were not receiving their checks for tuition, books and living expenses. She kept asking the White House what it was doing about the problem and, finally, at a news conference she confronted President Nixon and informed him that some of his civil servants "aren't giving you the right information ... Many a young man in this country is being disillusioned totally by his government these days because of the hardships being put upon him."

Nixon told her that VA director Donald Johnson had assured him that the late checks were a minor problem and Sarah retorted that Johnson "is the very man I am talking about who is not giving you the correct information. He stood up there at the White House the other day and gave us false information. He has no real system for getting at the statistics of this problem."

While Sarah took some heat in the media for her vehemence, Nixon took action and not only cleared up that situation but implemented a number of reforms at the VA, including a new director.

There are so many others, but I especially want to single out that special group of talented women I saw put in fifteen-hour days at the White House: Judy Woodruff, Andrea Mitchell, Anne Compton, Lesley Stahl and Rita Braver.

There is one group you may not think of as reporters, but they are some of the best journalists on the Washington scene, and they have helped me through the years to see things as they really are, the photographers: Frank Cancellare, Maurice Johnson, Stan Stearns, Joe Marquette, David Hume Kennerly, Larry Downing, Daryl Heikis, Ricardo Watson, Tim Clary, Ron Bennett, Frank Johnston, Percy Arrington and so many others, including some top-notch folks at AP, Scott Applewhite and Ron Edmonds. Edmonds, who started at UPI, Kennerly and Applewhite all won Pulitzer prizes. Television cameramen and technicians Leroy Johnson and Hank Brown are aces.

President Bush affectionately called them the "photo dogs." President Truman loved the photographers—many of whom were his poker pals, so it was easy enough for Truman to comply when they said, "Just one more hand."

Through the years, I have learned that photographers are always welcome and reporters hardly ever at the White House, especially in the Oval Office. Photographers don't ask questions, but their images certainly tell a story.

Many photographers gave their lives in World War II, the Korean War and Vietnam. They take risks and their bravery is legendary. They work under impossible conditions. The still photographers move as a pack, carrying their many cameras, their ladders, their cell phones and their laptops to send to their bureaus their photographs within minutes after they are taken. The same is true for the TV cameramen, who have to spring into action at a moment's notice with their cameras and cables, ready to capture presidents in their moments of triumph and despair.

Who can forget that photograph by the late George Thames of the *New York Times* of President Kennedy, his back to the camera, standing and looking out a window of the Oval Office? Of course there is the memorable photograph of LBJ showing his scar after his gallbladder surgery, which became a classic in White House photographic lore.

As former UPI and Reuters correspondent Gene Gibbons recalled in the *White House News Photographers Association Magazine,* Michael Dukakis might have had a fighting chance against George Bush in the 1989 election if he had not donned a helmet and played tank commander. That devastating picture was all over the country.

So many times, the photographers, with their impeccable eye for composition, have alerted me to some small detail, some tiny feature I might have missed. ABC's Douglas Allmond spotted not one but two hearing aids worn by President Reagan, which we ended up reporting. Allmond also spotted the three-year-old son of one of President Carter's guests playing under Carter's desk in the Oval Office and picking up the "red phone," the direct line to Moscow. Carter laughed and told the child, "Tell Brezhnev to get out of Afghanistan."

No one can do justice to the courage of the photographers all over the world. President Johnson had said, when Vietnam was raging, that "If I've lost Cronkite, I've lost the country," but he also told Walter in his first interview after he left the White House that it was the images that played every night in the "living room war" that mortally wounded his presidency.

The unofficial archivist for the White House photographers is Kenneth L. Blaylock of ABC, who has chronicled the historic photographs of the White House occupants for so many years.

On the writing side, of course I learned a lot of Journalism 101 at the feet of the master—Merriman Smith—and in the heat of the battle to get to a phone to get the story out, I often emulated him and barked at my colleagues. I hereby apologize. Over a few days on the UPI Downhold e-mail system, my former colleagues took the time to get revenge and to recall some of those days. But blame it on Smitty. He always told me to "write everything":

"It was [Jon] Frandsen's first or second day on the WA [Washington] dictation bank . . . and Helen began dictating rapid-fire from the Kennedy Center, where she was with Carter. Frandsen, who concedes he could barely type, struggled dutifully, and Helen generously slowed down somewhat, as was her wont.

"But to show that even Helen's patience had a breaking point, she could control herself no longer, and barked, 'Have you got a computer or are you taking this stuff longhand?' This to the son of her ex-boss, Julius Frandsen."

Ron Cohen

". . . I was the world's worst typist and always dreaded the slot editor standing over me . . . to grab copy out of the typewriter when it was finished . . . Helen was dictating a story about David Eisenhower and she wanted to be sure I got the punctuation right. She said 'David possessive grandmother.' And I dutifully typed out not 'David's grandmother' but 'David's possessive grandmother.'"

David Rosso

"As second person on the [late-night shift] on the WA desk in the early 1980s, I often had to take dictation from Helen when the lone dictationist was busy. It was always an experience and Helen was unfailingly polite, if crisp. Today, I am often asked how I learned to type so fast. 'Taking dictation from Helen Thomas,' I inevitably reply."

Elaine Povich

"This would have to have been prior to the mid-1980s when I transferred from DX [Denver] to DA [Dallas]: Helen was following the president around the Central Division, filing from each city. When the tour switched to KP [Kansas City] DA bugged the bureau for a lead, to which KP replied: 'Thomas dictating. Will file lead or publish in paperback asap.'"

Paul Harral

My close friend and former colleague Maggie Kilgore jokingly called UPI "an incestuous wire service," but she also noted that it was "closer than any fraternity." Maggie should know. She covered Capitol Hill for years and decided the trench warfare up there was too tame. She volunteered to go to Vietnam as a war correspondent. No armchair reporter, she.

Maggie also reminded me that we were in anything but our armchairs at the Democratic National Convention in 1968.

Late one evening I suggested to Maggie that it might be a good time for an updated feature on Muriel Humphrey as her husband was about to take the presidential nomination.

That convention, as most recall, was marred by riots, police violence against the antiwar protesters in Grant Park. We knew security would be tight at Humphrey headquarters on the twenty-fifth floor of the Hilton Hotel, across from the park.

To circumvent security, we decided to walk up the twenty-five flights of the indoor fire escape and search for Mrs. Humphrey, figuring no one would be mean enough to throw us out if we made it all the way up the stairs at midnight.

We started climbing, laughing at how out of shape we were and teetering on our high heels. The air in the stairwell was acrid with the smell of tear gas that had wafted in from outside and our eyes began to burn. But we kept huffing and puffing our way up the stairs and finally reached the twenty-fifth floor—only to be greeted by a giant security guard standing in front of the fire exit door with his arms crossed in front of him. He wore a black suit and had a very big grin on his face and told us he'd been watching us scale this Matterhorn of a stairwell the entire time.

We gasped out that we knew Mrs. Humphrey—I think the words "best friends" got interjected somewhere—but he told us she and her husband had gone to bed and he was paid to keep reporters out of the suite. We asked if we could at least ride the elevator down to the lobby but he told us to go back the same way we'd come in.

The next morning, Maggie was covering Mrs. Humphrey at some event and Mrs. Humphrey noticed Maggie was limping. When she asked her what was wrong, Maggie recounted the story of our nocturnal raid on the Hilton. Mrs. Humphrey said, "Oh, that's too bad. Why didn't you and Helen simply call me on the telephone? You know I would have talked to you."

Maggie mumbled yes, we should have taken that less strenuous route and then Mrs. Humphrey added, "By the way, the children and I are hiding out at the *Astor Towers*."

In 1984, most of the Washington staff was down in Houston covering the Republican National Convention when a message came through for all of us: Don't cash your paycheck—it'll bounce. UPI had gone into its first Chapter 11 bankruptcy. I won't repeat the cursing, the swearing, the carrying on that swept through that newsroom. But I will say that everyone calmed down, saw the job that had to be done and went back to work. That was the way we were.

I can't help but feel gratitude for being able to have this front-row seat to some of the more historic events of the past forty years:

The assassination of a president. Men walking on the moon. A wrong war that began in a small Southeast Asian nation tearing the United States apart for years before it finally ended nearly a decade after it began. Civil rights marches.

Women's rights. A breakthrough trip to China. The resignation of a president. The Camp David accords. U.S. citizens taken hostage for more than a year in Iran. A president accused of trading arms for those hostages. Four assassination attempts on three presidents. America celebrating its two hundredth birthday. Communism starting to disintegrate. The Berlin Wall coming down. The invasion of Panama. The Gulf War. A deadly bombing in Oklahoma City. A president called to testify before a grand jury. A president describing to the nation his "inappropriate relationship" with a former intern.

As far as my future, I'd like to go on reporting. Let me recount one of my favorite stories in a wonderful book, *Robert T. Smith, Revisited*, a compilation of columns Smith wrote when he was a correspondent for the *Minneapolis Star-Tribune*. In one column, he told of a funeral for another reporter, Paul Presbey, who would leave no fact unturned when he was covering a story. In his will, Presbey had left instructions for a party when he passed on and it was held at a lovely mansion where his friends drank, ate, swapped stories and celebrated Presbey's life as a consummate reporter. As Smith was about to leave, he overheard another reporter say of Presbey: "You know, if there's life after death, we'll soon know."

And when Larry McQuillan, the president of the White House Correspondents Association, presented me with the first Helen Thomas Lifetime Achievement Award in April 1998, he was quick to clarify my plans to the audience:

"I don't want any confusion," Larry said. "Helen is not retiring. She's not leaving the beat. As a matter of fact, she's not going anywhere. I used to work for UPI and I worked at the White House with Helen. I served notice to take another job and the bureau chief said I was being really foolish because I was next in line . . . and that was in the early 1980s. The bureau chief has long since retired."

So I'm still here, still arriving at the White House in the wee hours of the morning, reading the papers and checking the wire, still waiting for the morning briefing, still sitting down to write the first story of the day and still waiting to ask the tough questions.

Soon enough there will be another president, another first lady, another press secretary and a whole new administration to discover. I'm looking forward to it—although I'm sure whoever ends up in the Oval Office in a new century may not be so thrilled about the prospect. I can only leave that new president with the following story about one of his predecessors:

In 1980, I traveled to Georgia for a postelection interview with Jimmy Carter. He already was getting busy on a number of projects, including writing his memoirs, and he couldn't wait to show me his new computer, pointing out all of its functions and capabilities.

Then he sat down, typed my name on the screen, looked at me and grinned. "Now watch," he said, "I can even delete you." He pressed a key and letter by letter "Helen Thomas" disappeared.

But not for long.

NOTES

CHAPTER 1 BEGINNINGS

1. Letter from Virginia Nicoll, private collection.
2. *Congressional Record*, July 30, 1986, p. 1.

CHAPTER 2 WASHINGTON: THE EARLY YEARS

1. Letter from Betty Lersch, private collection.
2. Stephen E. Ambrose, *D-Day, June 6, 1944: The Climactic Battle of World War II* (New York: Touchstone), p. 504.

CHAPTER 3 A LITTLE REBELLION NOW AND THEN

1. Speech delivered to National Press Club luncheon, April 1996.
2. *The Evening Star*, May 16, 1960, p. B-6.
3. H. R. Haldeman, *The Haldeman Diaries: Inside the Nixon White House* (New York: G.P. Putnam, 1995), p. 347.

CHAPTER 4 NEW FRONTIERS

1. Gerry Van der Heuvel, "Newswomen Who Cover the New Frontier," *Editor and Publisher*, August 5, 1961, p. 15.
2. Ibid.

CHAPTER 5 WHERE EVERYBODY KNOWS MY NAME

1. Sally Quinn, "Mama's Place: 'Closest Thing to Casablanca,'" *Washington Post*, January 5, 1970, p. D-2.
2. Ibid.
3. Merriman Smith, *Thank You, Mr. President* (New York: Macmilllan, 1946), p. 26.
4. Gregory Gordon and Ronald E. Cohen, *Down to the Wire: UPI's Fight for Survival* (New York: McGraw-Hill, 1990), pp. 21–22.

CHAPTER 6 ACCESS DENIED

1. White House logs, various entries, Lyndon B. Johnson Library and Museum, Austin, Texas, Boxes 3, 15, 16.
2. Michael Beschloss, *Taking Charge: The Johnson White House Tapes* (New York: Simon & Schuster, 1997), p. 330.
3. Ibid., p. 332.
4. Tim Smith, ed., *Merriman Smith's Book of Presidents: A White House Memoir* (New York: W. W. Norton, 1972), p. 45.
5. Letter from Lyndon B. Johnson, May 15, 1963, private collection.
6. James Deakin, *Straight Stuff: The Reporters, the White House and the Truth* (New York: William Morrow, 1984), p. 114.

CHAPTER 7 "...AND I'D LIKE A FOLLOW-UP"

1. Transcript of White House news conference as printed in the *Washington Post,* April 30, 1971, p. A-12.
2. Note from Tom Brokaw, November 6, 1995, private collection.

CHAPTER 8 NOT EXACTLY NINE TO FIVE

1. Haldeman, *The Haldeman Diaries,* pp. 227–28.
Pierre, George, Marlin, Mike—and All the Rest
1. Pierre Salinger, *With Kennedy* (New York: Doubleday, 1966).
2. George Christian, "The Night Lyndon Quit," *Texas Monthly,* April 1988, p. 109.
3. Ibid., p. 168.
4. Ibid.
5. Ibid.
6. Ibid.
7. White House briefing, transcript, April 1973.
8. Deakin, *Straight Stuff,* p. 304.
9. White House briefing, transcript, March 1976.
10. Mollie Dickenson, *Thumbs Up: The Life and Courageous Comeback of White House Press Secretary Jim Brady* (New York: William Morrow, 1987), p. 42.
11. Ibid., pp. 448–49.
12. Marlin Fitzwater, *Call the Briefing!* (New York: Times Books/Random House, 1995), p. 66.
13. Ibid., p. 3.
14. Ibid., p. 59.
15. Ibid., p. 232; White House briefing May 16, 1989.
16. Fitzwater, *Call the Briefing!,* p. 234.
17. Maureen Dowd, "Washington at Work: In Bush's White House, the Press Secretary Is the One with the White Hat," *New York Times,* January 17, 1990, A-20.
18. Fitzwater, *Call the Briefing!,* p. 332.
19. Michael Kranish and Michael Putzel, "Clinton Taps Ex-GOP Aide in White House Shakeup," *Boston Globe,* May 30, 1993.
20. David Gergen, *U.S. News & World Report,* May 10, 1993.
21. White House briefing, December 22, 1994.
22. Peter Baker and Howard Kurtz, "McCurry Exit: A White House Wit's End," *Washington Post,* July 24, 1998, p. A-22.
23. James Bennet, "Clinton's Spokesman Will Leave in the Fall," *New York Times,* July 24, 1998, A-18.
24. Melinda Henneberger, "Speaking for the President, With Knowing Humor," *New York Times,* October 5, 1998, p. A-13.
25. Ibid.

CHAPTER 9 ON THE ROAD

1. J. F. ter Horst and Col. Ralph Albertazzie, *The Flying White House* (New York: Coward, McCann & Geoghegan, 1979), p. 127.
2. Interview aboard Air Force One, April 1, 1968.
3. Ter Horst and Albertazzie, *Flying White House,* p. 249.
4. Bill Gully with Mary Ellen Reese, *Breaking Cover* (New York: Simon & Schuster, 1980), p. 32.

5. Ter Horst and Albertazzie, *Flying White House,* p. 250.
6. Ibid., p. 256.
7. Ibid., p. 257.
8. According to the White House counsel's office, hotel, air travel, ground transportation and per diem costs for government employees in the president's official delegation, including members of Congress, are covered by the State Department. Hotel, air travel and ground transportation expenses for private citizens traveling as members of delegations are paid for by the individual or his or her employer.
9. Ter Horst and Albertazzie, *Flying White House,* p. 244.
10. Ibid., p. 224.
11. Smith, *White House Memoir,* pp. 210–11.
12. Robert F. Boyd, "The Response of the Chinese People," *The President's Trip to China* (New York: Bantam, 1972), p. 135.
13. Helen Thomas, "With the First Lady," *The President's Trip to China,* p. 29.
14. Joint communiqué, February 28, 1972.
15. Helen Thomas, "With the First Lady," p. 31.
16. Ter Horst and Albertazzie, *Flying White House,* p. 55.
17. Dan Rather, *The Camera Never Blinks* (New York: William Morrow, 1977), p. 218.

CHAPTER 10   "SHE TOLD THE TRUTH"

1. Helen Thomas, *Dateline: White House* (New York: Macmillan, 1975), p. 227.
2. Susanna McBee, "Who Needs Martha Mitchell?," *McCall's,* January 1971, p. 104.
3. Helen Thomas, story notes, date unknown.
4. Ibid.
5. Isabelle Hall, UPI wire story, September 18, 1971.
6. Ibid.
7. Ibid.
8. "CBS Morning News," November 21, 1969.
9. Rob Zaleski, "Watergate, Martha Mitchell Behind Him Now," *Capital Times,* November 21, 1986.
10. Haldeman, *Haldeman Diaries,* p. 475.
11. Stanley I. Kutler, *Abuse of Power: The New Nixon Tapes* (New York: The Free Press/Simon & Schuster, 1997), p. 614.
12. Excerpt from Tape 297, "Abuse of Power," National Archives.
13. Clare Crawford, "Up Front," *People,* March 11, 1974, p. 2.
14. Helen Thomas, interview with Dr. Meyer, taken from story notes, date unknown.
15. Ibid.
16. Ibid.
17. Telephone interview, T. Gordon Young, taken from story notes, date unknown.
18. Telephone interview, Clifford Kunz, taken from story notes, date unknown.
19. Telephone interview, Ray West, taken from story notes, date unknown.
20. Compilation of unpublished story notes, notes from telephone interviews, May–June 1976.
21. *Congressional Record,* June 3, 1976.

CHAPTER 11   DOUG

1. Smith, *Thank You, Mr. President,* p. 47.
2. Private files, date unknown.

3. Private files.

4. Connecticut Walker, "Reporter Helen Thomas: When a Woman Covers the White House," *Parade*, February 24, 1974, p. 6.

CHAPTER 12   THE SMALLEST SORORITY

Lady Bird Johnson

1. Jacqueline Kennedy Onassis, oral history, Lyndon B. Johnson Library and Museum, Austin, Texas.

2. Ibid.

3. Carl Sferazza Anthony, *As We Remember Her: Jacqueline Kennedy Onassis in the Words of Her Friends and Family* (New York: Harper Collins, 1997), p. 345.

Pat Nixon

1. Nixon's farewell address to White House staff, August 9, 1974.

2. Christopher Matthews, *Kennedy and Nixon* (New York: Simon & Schuster, 1996), p. 294.

3. Julie Nixon Eisenhower, *Pat Nixon* (New York: Simon & Schuster, 1986), p. 333.

4. Carl Sferazza Anthony, *First Ladies, Volume 2: The Saga of the Presidents' Wives and Their Power* (New York, William Morrow, 1991), p. 218.

Betty Ford

1. Paul F. Boller, *Presidential Wives* (New York: Oxford University Press, 1988), p. 421.

2. Betty Ford, *The Times of My Life* (New York: Harper & Row, 1978), p. 67.

Rosalynn Carter

1. "The New Women: Tough and Gracious," *Christian Century 100*, May 11, 1983, p. 443.

2. Ralph G. Martin, "When Jimmy Carter Married Her, He Married Magic," *Ladies' Home Journal*, March 1979, p. 101.

3. Rosalynn Carter, *First Lady from Plains* (Boston: Houghton Mifflin Co., 1984), p. 279.

4. Boller, *Presidential Wives*, p. 443.

5. R. Carter, *First Lady from Plains*, p. 323.

Nancy Reagan

1. Frank Lombardi, "Nancy Takes the Pulpit," *New York Daily News*, May 5, 1987, p. 3.

Barbara Bush

1. Barbara Bush, *Barbara Bush: A Memoir* (New York: St. Martin's Press [paperback edition], 1995), p. 160.

2. Ibid., p. 50.

3. Ibid., p. 208.

4. Ibid., p. 302.

5. Ibid., p. 293.

6. Ibid., p. 163.

7. Ibid., p. 526.

Hillary Clinton

1. Donnie Radcliffe, *Hillary Rodham Clinton: A First Lady for Our Time* (New York: Warner Books, 1993), p. 118.

2. Ibid., p. 119.

3. Ibid., p. 131.

4. Evelyn Bielenson and Ann Tenenbaum, eds., *The Wit and Wisdom of Famous American Women* (New York: Peter Pauper Press, 1995), p. 31.

CHAPTER 13 "A SPLENDID MISERY"

John Kennedy

1. Norm Clarke, "Talk of the Town," *Rocky Mountain News,* June 15, 1997, 6-A.

Lyndon Johnson

1. Thomas, *Dateline,* p. 43.
2. Ibid., p. 76.
3. Robert Dallek, *Flawed Giant: Lyndon Johnson and His Times* (New York: Oxford University Press, 1998), p. 577.
4. Ibid., p. 579.
5. Carl Solberg, *Hubert Humphrey: A Biography* (New York: Norton, 1984), p. 407.
6. Dallek, *Flawed Giant,* p. 623.
7. Ibid.

Richard Nixon

1. Thomas, *Dateline,* p. 145.
2. Ibid., p. 195.
3. Ibid., p. 158.
4. David Lawsky, "Mitchell's Portrait Hung in Justice Department," UPI, January 9, 1985.
5. Editorial, *Baltimore Sun,* June 5, 1995.

Gerald Ford

1. James Cannon, *Time and Chance: Gerald Ford's Appointment in History* (New York: Harper Collins, 1994), p. xv.

Jimmy Carter

1. "Lillian Carter Is Dead at 85: Mother of the 39th President," *New York Times,* October 31, 1983, p. 1.
2. Bettijane Levine, "President, Peacemaker, Poet," *Los Angeles Times,* February 10, 1995, p. 1-E.

Ronald Reagan

1. Ronald Reagan, *Ronald Reagan: An American Life* (New York: Simon & Schuster, 1990), p. 488.
2. Ibid., p. 161.
3. Ibid., p. 680.
4. Alex S. Jones, "Initial Reports on Libyan Plots Stirred Skepticism," *New York Times,* October 3, 1986, p. A-7.
5. Ibid.
6. Bernard Weinraub, "The Ex-Spokesman," *New York Times,* October 9, 1986, p. A-14.
7. "Kalb Resigns as State Department Spokesman Over Deception Issue," *New York Times,* October 9, 1986, A-14.
8. Robert D. McFadden, "News Executives Express Outrage," *New York Times,* October 3, 1986, p. A-7.

George Bush

1. Herbert S. Parmet, *George Bush, The Life of a Lone Star Yankee* (New York: Scribner/A Lisa Drew Book, 1997), p. 245.
2. Alexander Haig, *Caveat,* p. 162, quoted in ibid., p. 271.
3. Parmet, *George Bush,* p. 345.
4. Ibid., p. 349, from Bush diaries, August 21, 1988.
5. Louise Sweeney, "War in the Briefing Room," *Christian Science Monitor,* January 24, 1991, p. 12.

6. Parmet, *George Bush,* p. 508.

Bill Clinton

1. Thomas B. Rosenstiel, "The Spin Doctor's Prognosis," *Los Angeles Times,* July 14, 1993, p. A-1.

Index